THE JEFFERSONIAN AND HAMILTONIAN TRADITIONS IN AMERICAN POLITICS

ALBERT FRIED was born in Brooklyn, New York, in 1930 and attended Brooklyn College and Columbia University. He has taught history at Upsala College in East Orange, New Jersey, and at Brooklyn and Queens Colleges in New York. He is the editor of *The Essential Jefferson* and *Day of Dedication: The Political Writings of Woodrow Wilson*, coeditor of *The Essential Lincoln*, *Charles Booth's London* and *Socialist Thought*, and the author of a number of articles.

The
Jeffersonian and Hamiltonian
Traditions in American Politics

A DOCUMENTARY HISTORY

EDITED BY ALBERT FRIED

ANCHOR BOOKS
DOUBLEDAY & COMPANY, INC.
GARDEN CITY, NEW YORK
1968

The Anchor Books edition is the first publication of *The Jeffersonian and Hamiltonian Traditions in American Politics.*

Anchor Books edition: 1968

For Edith

CONTENTS

Jeffersonian and Hamiltonian political ideas are not merely theories dwelling in the human mind, remote from facts of American political behavior. They are expressions of chosen phases and factors among those facts, but they are also something more: namely, forces which have shaped those facts and which are still contending to shape them in the future this way and that.

John Dewey, *The Public and Its Problems*

THE JEFFERSONIAN AND HAMILTONIAN
TRADITIONS IN AMERICAN POLITICS

CHAPTER I. GENERAL INTRODUCTION

When George Washington was sworn in as President on April 30, 1789, no one knew what to expect of the new government and in particular of the executive branch. The Constitution left the presidential authority undefined except in the most general terms. Washington had no policy, no staff, no precedent, no body of laws. His first task was to build the rudiments of an administration, and in August and September he established the departments of State, Treasury, War and Justice to handle the essential business of government. Of these the most important were State, which was responsible for conducting the nation's foreign affairs, and Treasury, which was responsible for collecting revenue and managing the country's fiscal and credit system. Accordingly, Washington appointed the two best men he could find to head these departments: Thomas Jefferson of Virginia as Secretary of State and Alexander Hamilton of New York as Secretary of the Treasury.

Having worked with both men in the past, Washington knew their capacities well. He had been especially close to Hamilton, who, at the age of twenty-three, had served with typical brilliance as his aide-de-camp and secretary during the Revolution. Later, he and Hamilton, along with other men prominent in public life, had been instrumental in organizing the Constitutional Convention and seeing it through to a successful conclusion. Washington was immensely impressed by Hamilton's general intelligence, by his broad national outlook and by his mastery of political economy. No man, in Washington's estimation, was better qualified to run the Treasury.

Washington's association with Jefferson, though less intimate, was older. It went back to the time the two squires, who were among the largest landowners in Virginia, had sat in the colonial House of Burgesses as leading members of the Patriot party. As the author of the Declaration of Independence, among other notable state papers, Jefferson, too, had served the Revolution with great distinction. During the years that Washington and Hamilton were working to form a stronger national government, Jefferson was abroad, having taken Benjamin Franklin's place as American minister to France. Jefferson's breadth of learning, knowledge of European affairs and languages, and popularity with Virginians made him Washington's first choice to head the State Department.

Hamilton and Jefferson hardly knew each other before Washington brought them together, though they may have known something of each other's political views. They certainly were unaware of just how deeply antithetical were their conceptions of America's destiny. They had thrown in their lot with the Revolution for very different reasons. Hamilton, bred up in the bustling environment of the New York City countinghouses and commercial establishments, fought for American independence in the belief that an indigenous Whig class would come into its own, a class not of landowners, as in Britain or the South, but of bankers, manufacturers and merchants. It was because Britain had placed numerous obstacles in the path of American entrepreneurs—fostering local monopolies, imposing numerous trade and banking restrictions, etc.—that he joined the revolutionary movement. For Hamilton it was a matter of getting rid of one set of rulers in order to make way for another.

While the Revolution was in progress Hamilton was busy with his next task: to define the basis under which the entrepreneurial class would assume control in America. His model was the political arrangement that had prevailed in Britain since the great settlement of 1688. That settlement had brought about an identity of interests between the propertied classes and the government. With the ouster of the Stuarts it had become the chief functions of Crown and Parliament to protect property rights and the freedom of contracts, guarantee credit and private capital (through such institutions as the Bank of England, set up in 1694), and, at the same time, prevent the disenfranchised classes from rising up and claiming *their* rights, as they had done in the

Civil War. The Glorious Revolution had exorcised the twin evils of despotism and democracy and had written the sacred doctrine of life, liberty and property into the law of the land.

Hamilton would have wanted the American Revolution to be as glorious as Britain's. Conditions in America, however, made it difficult to achieve a comparable settlement in behalf of the propertied classes. The main difficulty, of course, was that America lacked a central government worthy of the name. Sovereignty rested with the thirteen states, more particularly with the countless little communities dispersed across the continent from Canada to New Spain. This decentralization of power was a tremendous impediment to business, which depended upon the separate states or localities to enforce contract obligations and secure credit. Many of the state legislatures were notoriously obedient to democratic majorities, which, to Hamilton's mind, were made up exclusively of confiscatory debtors, unruly mobs and self-serving politicians. An American settlement, it followed, required the creation of a strong national government that would simultaneously advance the interests of the entrepreneurial class and suppress factious democracy.

Hamilton's Federalist collaborators in the early 1780s—Washington, James Madison, John Jay, among others—also thought that the Revolution would be incomplete until a government was formed that could restrain the states and localities and protect property-owning minorities. But they advocated the establishment of an "extensive republic" only as a negative or countervailing instrument of power, as a check against anti-republican or democratic movements that might surge up from below. Hamilton, however, entertained more grandiose hopes. He envisaged the central government acting as a positive force in its own right, using its authority as the representative of the whole people to help the business elite attain the privileged status it must have if the nation was to prosper and grow. He assumed that the engine of economic progress, thus set in motion, would transform America from an agricultural and rural and democratic society to an industrial and urban and oligarchic one.

Jefferson saw the purpose of the Revolution in the opposite

terms. He could conceive of hardly a worse fate for America than to model herself, even in part, upon Great Britain. He was convinced that America would become the teacher and exemplar of mankind, provided she remained true to the passion of 1776. America, he hoped, would prove to the world that people could live under republican rule, free of political inequalities, free of distinctions based on class, hereditary rights and ecclesiastical privileges. For Jefferson the Declaration of Independence expressed both the ideal and the fact of the American experience.

While Hamilton accurately reflected the rising commercial and creditor interests of the North, Jefferson, the leading apostle of American egalitarianism, was an aristocrat, a descendant of one of the best Virginia families, the owner of a huge estate and a multitude of slaves. Later, his opponents were to explain this anomaly by asserting that he was really a clever poseur and demagogue who aroused the ignorant masses with propaganda about the rights of man only in order to secure his own economic and political prerogatives. But Jefferson's whole public career, which lasted over forty years, his thousands of private letters, all that we know about him, contradict this claim. If anything, he acted against his own interest. He proposed, for example, that the Virginia legislature eliminate slavery in the state. Logically, his defense of majority rights was scarcely the best way of serving himself and the squirearchy. And when in power he was furthest from being a demagogue.

Jefferson belonged to an extraordinary group of Virginia landholders, among them Richard Henry Lee, George Mason, George Wythe and John Taylor of Caroline, who held the most advanced ideas of the times. In morals and politics no major Enlightenment philosopher of the eighteenth century—neither Montesquieu, nor Bolingbroke, nor Voltaire, nor even Rousseau—raised the oriflamme of liberty so high as they. The Virginia liberals assumed that natural law, grasped by the common sense and reason of ordinary men, led straight to republicanism, a social system in which every person was master of his own life, in which force and domination were absent or minimal, and in which the principle of equal rights regulated all laws.

Jefferson took up an even more radical position than his friends. He maintained that equality must not only regulate laws, it must be present in the everyday lives of men; it must be a habit as well as an abstract and remote ideal. And he located the place where equality had become a habit: among the majority of Americans, the class of small, self-sufficient, self-governing farmers who answered their modest needs by their own toil. Jefferson was confident that republicanism in America was safe so long as this class remained the overwhelming majority, so long, in other words, as wealth and power continued to be widely dispersed and nearly equal. He envisioned a nation of small farmers filling up the endless tracts of land beyond the Appalachians, thereby reinforcing in every generation America's revolutionary commitment to freedom, virtue and happiness.

Hamiltonianism and Jeffersonianism, then, can be said to have existed before Hamilton and Jefferson themselves met as members of the same cabinet. It was shortly after their first encounter that they became conscious of the magnitude of their ideological differences. When Jefferson arrived in the capitol in March 1790 Hamilton had already launched his great program to "improve the public credit." He proposed, as the first step in his plan to advance the cause of the business class, that the federal government gather up all the debts incurred by the Confederation and by the thirteen states during the Revolution, a considerable sum at the time. Congress passed these proposals much as Hamilton had prescribed. His next step, which came a year later, was to recommend, first, the establishment of a federally supported bank (called the Bank of the United States) to stabilize credit and divert capital from the agricultural sector of the economy to the industrial and mercantile sectors, and, second, the imposition of an excise tax on farmers. By the time these recommendations were enacted into laws in 1791, Hamilton and Jefferson were avowed political enemies and were beginning to organize the nucleus of opposing factions.

Hamilton came to dominate the Washington administration long before Jefferson resigned from office late in 1793. Thereafter, and for the remainder of the decade, the conflict between them widened and intensified. The country was riven by the administration's increasingly hostile attitude toward the French Revolution, by its suppression of farmers who refused to pay a tax on whisky, by its sponsorship of Jay's Treaty, which appeared to be a sellout to Britain, and finally by its break with France, which prompted the passage of the Alien and Sedition acts, the mobilization of the armed forces, and the introduction of new taxes. By then, full-blown Hamiltonian and Jeffersonian movements had arisen, along with corresponding Federalist and Republican parties. The Federalists accused the Republicans of inciting mob violence, of promoting native Jacobin societies, of seeking to tear down the Constitution and the federal government, thereby restoring the old anarchic order. The Republicans denounced the Federalists, Hamilton especially, for attempting to enrich speculators, bankers and other privileged interests, corrupt the morals of the people with endless drafts of paper money, destroy local government, extirpate civil liberties, and, in a word, re-establish the British system that had been overthrown in 1776.

The party battles, the bitter charges and countercharges, arose because momentous questions of federal policy were at stake and had to be settled one way or the other. Would the nation in the crucial formative years of its history favor the entrepreneurial elite or the agrarian class? Would it promote the claims of a privileged minority or those of the majority—the concentration or the distribution of wealth and power? Would it, in other words, follow a Hamiltonian or Jeffersonian course? By the early 1800s the answers were no longer in doubt. Jefferson had been elected President; both Houses of Congress were solidly Republican; and no Federalist-held office, not even in the most conservative redoubts of New England, was safe. And what made the Republican victory so thoroughgoing, so permanent, so frustrating to the Federalists was the fact that the new Western states were certain to be staunchly Republican; this had already been demonstrated by Kentucky and Tennessee. The direction of federal policy was definitively set in 1803 when Jefferson agreed to purchase the Louisiana Territory. No one could calculate the number of states that would eventually be carved out of it. Jefferson had good reason to feel confi-

dent about the future. Hamiltonianism would be cast out;
America would remain an agrarian civilization, just as he had
prophesied long ago. And he could take special pride in being the instrument of his own prophecy.

But America did not remain an agrarian civilization, and
the Hamiltonian cause did not die; it flourished, in fact, under Jefferson's very nose. And Jeffersonianism continued to
live after America had ceased to be a nation of small farmers.
The point is that both ideologies have been relevant throughout American history, even though the specific circumstances
that shaped them and first brought them into opposition disappeared. In the broadest sense Hamiltonianism and Jeffersonianism have presented the country with alternative ends,
and the country has always had to choose between them. It
has had to choose between federal policies seeking to provide
either opportunities for limitless personal enrichment or
guarantees of equality for all, to advance property rights
or human rights. The conflict between Hamiltonian and
Jeffersonian traditions has been the central theme of American life. It has maintained the line of continuity between
the generations, emerging anew in every epoch.

We must distinguish between means and ends. Too often
historians have confused them. The quintessential difference between Hamiltonianism and Jeffersonianism has not
turned on legal and constitutional formalities: on the precise
scope of federal authority or the precise relation between the
federal government and the states. It is true that Jefferson
narrowly construed the Constitution in the years when he
led the opposition to Hamilton's policies. But in office Jefferson and his party were no less nationalistic, no less broad in
the application of federal power than Hamilton and his party
had been in the 1790s. For their part the Federalists, executing a spectacular about-face, became the arch proponents of
states' rights. Their ends, however, had remained constant.
Jeffersonians and Hamiltonians had simply adopted each
other's means.

So it has been throughout American history. In the twentieth century the Jeffersonian movements, representing at various times workers, small farmers and businessmen, Negroes
and other ethnic groups, have called for the greatest degree

of federal intervention. For only the federal government has commanded the power and resources to redress the increasing imbalance in wealth brought about by private control of modern technology and markets. Since the Civil War and the rise of industrialism the direction of the economy has been Hamiltonian, with the result that methods that were originally Hamiltonian have been necessary to achieve Jeffersonian purposes. Meanwhile the spokesmen for the large entrepreneurial and agricultural interests have freely employed Jeffersonian rhetoric to argue that the federal government, with its elephantine bureaucracy, threatens to obliterate local government, personal initiative and fiscal responsibility. The Hamiltonian and Jeffersonian traditions have concealed themselves behind veils of irony.

They have easily taken on each other's characteristics because they have had so much in common. No major party professing in the Jeffersonian manner to champion equal rights has eschewed the pursuit of economic advantage, sought to level down the country's wealth, or denounced property as an institution. Rather, the great Jeffersonian movements from the 1790s to the mid-twentieth century have fought monopolies and special privileges in the hope of extending economic opportunities to the majority and so widening the field of property ownership. And except for the ante-bellum Southern Democratic party no major American party has been reactionary in the Old World sense of the term; no significant group of oligarchs has conspired to invalidate the will of the majority. The Hamiltonian and Jeffersonian traditions have both reflected the dominant middle-class ethic and thus have rarely gone very far off center. Ideological distinctions in America have been drawn in shades of gray.

But the importance of these distinctions should not be minimized. Every society has its own forms of conflict and its own ways of resolving them. The tensions between the Hamiltonian and Jeffersonian traditions have maintained the delicate equilibrium of American politics. The egalitarian principles that underlay the nation's public life have made it possible for sizable numbers of Americans to succeed in business and the professions on the strength of their talents.

But success inevitably has led to privilege and privilege to conservatism. Just as inevitably, however, new egalitarian movements have sprung up to assault the bastions of privilege, the ossified special interests, and have opened up once again fresh possibilities for men of enterprise and ambition.

Third parties have registered the first signs of change in the public mood. They have acted as the harbingers of a new phase in the Hamiltonian-Jeffersonian cycle. It has been their function to dwell exclusively on the issues, usually in the name of equal rights and the principles of the Declaration of Independence. If the issues have persisted these parties have triumphed, but only at the price of their own martyrdom. The death of third parties has followed the assimilation of their programs by one or both of the major parties. In this way American history has gone forward, passing through regular cycles of retrenchment and reform, through successive Hamiltonian and Jeffersonian phases, each varying in duration and intensity.

These phases have marked the transitional moments in American politics. Jeffersonianism has customarily sounded the arrival of a new era and the knell of the old. It has done so through new coalitions of groups and interests determined to acquire their just share of power. Jefferson's Republican party took office representing the country's agrarian majority. Jackson's Democratic party spoke for small farmers and businessmen and urban mechanics. The Republican party of the 1850s and '60s consisted of Northern free-soilers, workers and entrepreneurs, German-Americans and other recent immigrants. The progressive movement that permeated both parties before World War I drew its main strength from the small towns and rural communities of the South and West. The New Deal rested on the votes primarily of workers, Negroes and other minority groups who tenanted the big cities. In every instance the particular reform administration—Jefferson's, Jackson's, Lincoln's, Wilson's, Franklin D. Roosevelt's—has accomplished its task in only a few years. There has followed a protracted period of quiescence and stability, during which time the victorious coalition, content with the fruits of its hard-won struggle, has entered the Hamiltonian phase. But by then a new Jeffersonian coalition has crystallized, and with it the prospect of a new conflict, a new transition, a new era in American history.

Such, at any rate, has been the pattern of change, or "progress," down to the Second World War. Conditions since then, however, have cast a shadow over the Jeffersonian tradition. In the past Jeffersonianism was distinguished by its appeal to the majority and by its opposition to the privileged few whose concentrated power appeared to threaten the country as a whole. But since the war most Americans have been satisfied with the status quo. With production and income rising steadily, with various welfare programs providing a modicum of security, they have not been overly concerned about the recent manifestations of neo-Hamiltonianism: about the relentless consolidation of industry in fewer and fewer mammoth corporations; about the close interdependence between these corporations, most of which engage in defense and space work, and the federal government; and about the increasing reliance by the major bureaucratic establishments—namely business, labor and government—upon an oligarchy of experts and technicians.

The civil rights movement that surged up in the mid-1950s has offered the one example of a sustained affirmation of Jeffersonian principles since the war. But Negroes, who constitute a little more than 10 per cent of the population, have been unable to enlist a majority coalition willing to advance their specific aims beyond very narrow limits. Increasingly, in fact, they have found themselves an isolated minority. The very success of the civil rights movement in its early stages has conspired to bring this about. Most whites who live outside the South have been sympathetic, or at least unopposed, to the political and legal rights that Negroes have obtained thanks to a host of Supreme Court decisions and to the sweeping civil rights acts of 1964 and 1965. But these rights have failed to touch the lives of the millions of Negroes who inhabit the slum ghettos of the nation. Attempts to integrate neighborhoods, schools and jobs, even on the most token scale, have met ferocious white resistance. De facto segregation is as pronounced and as deeply rooted in the North as in the South.

And so, oppressed by brutal and unyielding economic inequalities and faced with the prospect of being permanently condemned to big-city slums—at a time, moreover, when they have been led to expect an imminent birth of freedom—many Negroes have rebelled. Cataclysms of violence, burning and looting have broken loose in a number of Northern ghettos, notably in Los Angeles, Newark and Detroit. So far as the Jeffersonian ideal of equal rights is concerned, the situation has grown alarming. On the one hand, more and more Negroes have totally rejected American values, which they have come to think are empty and hypocritical, and wishing to separate from, not integrate with, white communities, have turned to one or another species of black nationalism. On the other hand, the white majority, feeling increasingly threatened, has prepared to impose extreme repressive measures upon Negroes in general, whatever the cost to civil liberties. Carried to its logical terminus, white repression would enclose the ghetto behind a band of steel, thereby dividing America into two nations, two armed camps.

Not since the conflict over slavery in the 1840s and '50s has America confronted such a serious long-term threat to her existence as a liberal democracy. The choice has become clearer as the crisis has worsened. If America succumbs to race warfare she will write the epitaph to the Jeffersonian tradition—and perhaps to the Hamiltonian as well. But if Negroes acquire the full measure of their freedom, and so come to enjoy social and economic as well as political equality, America will write the noblest chapter in her history.

CHAPTER II. HAMILTON AND THE FEDERALISTS

The overthrow of British colonial rule released opposing forces in American life. On the one hand, the Revolution called forth deep feelings of nationalism, an unprecedented sense of solidarity, and a commitment to a common struggle and a common set of principles. On the other, it severed the one bond, established over the centuries by King and Parliament, that had kept America from breaking into pieces and becoming a new Holy Roman Empire. After 1776 the locus of authority rested not with the caretakers of national unity—the Continental Congress and the Continental Army—but with the thirteen states, each of which was, in effect, a separate and independent republic, answerable to none and allied to the Confederation primarily out of convenience and self-interest. The state legislatures enjoyed unchallenged supremacy, and this, in turn, meant that the localities, the counties and towns, were the ultimate repositories of power in America.

Soon after the war with Britain ended in 1783, a number of men who had gained prominence in the Revolution—chief among them George Washington—concluded that the process of disintegration had gone too far. They formed a movement to strengthen the central government, reasoning that only a federal system could save republican liberty from its own "excesses"—too much power in the hands of local communities. Disparate groups lent their support to the Federalist cause: merchants, who suffered because each state imposed its own tariffs and determined its own conditions of trade; creditors, who were at the mercy of legislatures that passed laws in behalf of debt-ridden farmers; the upper classes in general, who sought protection against the leveling tendencies of the people; and, not least, men who advanced no particular interest but who feared that the country, surrounded by potential enemies and lacking a strong government, was in great jeopardy. But whatever their motives, the Federalists agreed that a crisis confronted the American people and that unless it was resolved at once the work of the Revolution would be undone.

They agreed, too, that democracy, or rule by popular majorities, was at the root of the crisis. For democracy, in their view, was the form of government characteristic of American localities and, therefore, of the state legislatures. The Federalists believed democratic republicanism was founded on the illusion that all men were innately good and hence entitled to equal rights as citizens, regardless of their station in life or whether they owned property. In truth, the Federalists maintained, men were innately selfish and predaceous, the more so if they were poor; equality was an *ignis fatuus*, a utopian fantasy. This being so, democracy bred the most intense, the most virulent factional conflicts, with demagogues leading the poor against the rich, debtors against creditors, majorities against minorities. The destruction of the propertied class was the destruction of liberty, property being the best guarantor of republican sobriety and moderation. If democracy were allowed to run its course it would produce in America factional disorder, internecine war and, in the end, tyranny, as it had in ancient Greece and Rome and in the city-states of medieval Europe.

The Federalists' objective was merely to restrain the conflicts engendered by local democracies, not end them. To attempt to end conflict once and for all was to run the risk of imposing tyranny—an evil still greater than factious democracy. The Federalists assumed that a national government, sovereign in its sphere, with its authority derived from the "people" as a whole, would make it immensely more difficult for local majorities to obtain absolute power. For, as specified by the Constitution, such a government would be twice removed, and in the case of the federal courts, altogether removed, from the popular will. The Federalists, in short, conceived of the Constitution as a neutralizing force, a negative instrument of power. The function of the federal government was to regulate the passions of the community, to set down and administer the rules of conflict without itself becoming involved in factional disputes. Scrupulous impartiality—*vox judiciae, vox dei*—was to be the defining principle of the federal government.

But there was an obvious flaw in the Federalist logic, a flaw typical of the eighteenth-century conception of man and society. Man was held to be ineluctably driven by the desire for wealth and power and by the need to form rival parties. Yet he was deemed capable of exercising self-restraint through the use of higher reason. The Federalists' belief in the impartiality of the Constitution manifestly contradicted their premises. Why should the federal government be less factious than states and localities? How could it avoid the partisanship and class struggles inherent in human nature?

That the federal government could not in fact avoid them became apparent very soon after its establishment in 1789. The policies introduced by Secretary of the Treasury Alexander Hamilton split the inner councils of the government —both the congressional and executive branches—into opposing factions, and then divided the country at large into antagonistic parties. The original Federalist belief that the Constitution would create an Archimedean point of reason and justice was shattered by the time Washington left the Presidency in 1797.

Hamilton himself had never quite shared that belief. During the 1780s, as one of the leading exponents of Federalism, he consistently maintained that a central government must be coercive, that it must do far more than act as a limit on states and localities. Federal coercion, he argued, was both necessary and right—necessary because all governments, by definition, relied on force to accomplish their ends; and right because the prosperity of the nation, its *summum bonum*, depended on the submission of the people to a single, sovereign authority. For Hamilton, these twin ideals of national unity and prosperity were bound up with the fortunes of the nascent class of bankers, merchants and manufacturers. These entrepreneurs, he thought, carried the future in their hands. With amazing prescience, he foresaw the time when industry, aided by government, would drive the dispersed agricultural population off the land and into factories and cities. The rise of industry, he believed, would thus destroy the economic base of American democracy and create a centralized, hierarchical society in which power, resting on the weight of concentrated wealth, would be exercised responsibly—a society in which statesmen could frame farsighted national policies without fear of obstruction from the ignorant and fickle multitude.

Hamilton had no faith in abstractions or sentiments, and his writings were always directed toward some concrete purpose. He realized that if government and business were to become partners they must be united by some mutually advantageous interest. He found precisely such an interest in the national debt, which the Confederation had incurred during the War of Independence but could not pay because it lacked the power to tax the people directly. Far from being a curse, the debt, in Hamilton's view, was a potential blessing. For in taking up the debt, a strong central government must tax the people; it must use coercion. The money collected would flow from the pockets of consumers, nearly all of them farmers, to the banking and commercial centers, and creditors, knowing that the state had the power to enforce obligations, would invest their increasing capital in productive industries. The center of gravity would therefore shift from agriculture to manufacturing. To insure the protection of creditors, Hamilton proposed to influential officials as early as 1780 that the government, in co-operation with private citizens, set up a central bank on the British model with authority to regulate the country's finances. A national debt, a system of direct taxation and a bank—these, Hamilton felt, would radically transform American life and at the same time forge the links of solidarity between property and power.

Hamilton, then, had already excogitated a policy of reform when he was appointed Secretary of the Treasury in 1789. Moreover, he was in a position to carry it out. He presided over the largest department in the new government, and furthermore, since no clear line of demarcation separated one department from another at this formative period, he tended to usurp many of the functions and responsibilities of the other three secretaries. Washington trusted him implicitly—their friendship went back to the early years of the

Revolution when he had served as Washington's aide-de-camp—and he became, in effect, the prime minister of the cabinet.

As such, Hamilton performed wonders. His state papers were models of eloquence and cogent reasoning. He was a master strategist, trimming his sails when necessary, using all his charm and powers of persuasion, but never losing sight of his objectives. Within a year and a half after he took office Congress had enacted his entire program for improving the public credit: debts totaling seventy million dollars, contracted by both the Confederation and the thirteen states, had been nationalized—a considerable amount of money at that time for a nation of four million self-sufficient farmers; a bank, created according to Hamilton's specifications, had been chartered, establishing close relations between the federal government, which owned a fifth of the shares, and the banking community; and taxes had been levied directly upon the people.

It was not so much the enlargement of the government's powers as it was the ends to which they were directed that gave rise to controversy. James Madison, who had been one of the prime movers of the Federalist cause, and who perhaps more than any other single man was responsible for getting the Constitution drawn up and ratified, broke with Hamilton only a few months after the government was organized. Madison, the leader of the Virginia delegation to the House of Representatives, objected to Hamilton's plan for funding the debt, on the grounds that it aided speculators. The breech widened over the scheme to assume state debts—Madison arguing that it was unfair to those states like Virginia which had been meeting their obligations faithfully —and finally developed into full-scale conflict over the banking and revenue bills. By then Jefferson, the Secretary of State, had become the tacit leader of the anti-Hamilton forces.

Before long, the conflict spread beyond the precincts of the federal government. By 1792 the Hamiltonians and anti-Hamiltonians were conducting open warfare, accusing each other of undermining the country's welfare and violating the intent of the Constitution. Hamilton complained, chiefly to

Washington, that Jefferson and Madison were organizing a Gracchian conspiracy against him. The two Virginians, for their part, regarded Hamilton as an enemy of republicanism who was determined, through his mystifying revenue and credit policies, to reimpose "monocratic" government. Underlying these differences between them was the clash of economic and sectional interests. While Hamilton consolidated the alliance between the government and the northern business community, farmers and planters were beginning to form the nucleus of an insurgent faction.

The French Revolution exacerbated the differences, turning factional conflicts into ideological ones. The anti-Hamiltonians rejoiced in the Revolution as it progressed from constitutional monarchy to republicanism. Many of them embraced the principles of Jacobin democracy in all its phases, including the Terror, though Jefferson himself did not go quite that far in supporting the Revolution, at least not publicly. Hamilton and his friends considered the Revolution a disaster in every respect, especially after war broke out between France and Britain in 1793. They detested democracy more than ever now that it had shown its teeth. At every opportunity they sided with Britain, even though the United States and France technically were still allies; for Hamilton not only admired the British political system, his own hopes for America rested on the increasingly close ties between the two countries. British trade and credit, he contended, must furnish the nutriment for America's economic growth. Without it his whole domestic program might collapse.

After Jefferson resigned at the end of 1793, the Washington administration gravitated steadily to the right in both foreign and domestic affairs. Washington held the French Revolution responsible for arousing radical passions in America and for bringing on the blatant disrespect for authority that the people were beginning to manifest. He therefore welcomed the chance to reassert that authority, and in 1794 forcibly suppressed the rebellion of the yeomen farmers of western Pennsylvania against paying the federal tax on whisky, which they traditionally used in place of currency. Hamilton resigned from the government in 1795 for personal reasons, but he remained the dominant power behind the scenes; his friends were safely installed in the cabinet, and Washington continued to rely on him for advice.

The dispute over Jay's Treaty marked a turning point in the political history of the era. As a consequence of the war with France, Britain had been seizing American ships and impressing American seamen into her navy. Partly to assuage public opinion, which was starting to clamor for war, and partly to settle the numerous differences between the two countries, most of them going back to the Revolution, the government sent Chief Justice John Jay to Britain in 1794. But the treaty that Jay brought back a year later hardly assuaged the public: it made no mention of impressment; it conceded to British ships the exclusive right to carry such major staple commodities as cotton, sugar and molasses from American ports to the West Indies; and while it set up a commission to handle pre-Revolutionary debts, it failed to compensate planters for the slaves the British army had taken. Britain's only important concession was to withdraw her troops from the northwest posts. Opponents of the federal government, led by Southern planters, protested that the treaty was a sellout. To them it was irrefutable proof that the government wished to keep America in a state of permanent servitude to Britain.

Nor were all supporters of the government satisfied with the treaty—the New England shippers, for example, who were denied a large segment of the carrying trade. Washington himself had strong reservations about it. But in the face of the assault from radicals, small farmers and planters, conservative opinion rallied to the defense of the administration. Hamilton proved to be the Jay treaty's most effective advocate. Writing from New York, he issued one broadside after another in the progovernment press, arguing that America's concessions were a small price to pay in return for friendship with Britain. Thanks largely to his efforts, the treaty passed Congress after a yearlong struggle. Hamilton had again demonstrated that he was by far the best polemicist of the day.

The struggle over the treaty had the effect of dividing the country on an issue about which no one could be neutral—

America's relations with Britain. Political differences, hitherto amorphous, rapidly crystallized. Rudimentary national party organizations suddenly formed. The terms Federalist and Republican, representing pro- and anti-government parties, took on precise meaning for the first time. Paradoxically, the Republicans adopted the position that the Federalists had assumed in the 1780s: that the government must be neutral and free of factional commitment, and the Constitution never construed as an instrument of power, serving particular groups or interests. A number of old Federalists, who otherwise had no sympathy for agrarianism or radical ideologies of any sort, agreed that the government had become intolerably partisan. John Dickinson of Delaware, one of the earliest and most prominent of the Federalists and always a conservative, was repelled by Jay's Treaty, as he was by Hamilton's policies in general, and he threw his support to the Republicans. They revealed the measure of their strength in the 1796 election, when Jefferson, their presidential candidate, received only three fewer electoral votes than John Adams, the incumbent Vice-President.

With Washington gone, the Federalists split into factions of their own. Adams was President, but Hamilton still ran the party. The two men disliked each other for both personal and ideological reasons. Adams never quite went along with Hamilton's fiscal schemes. Furthermore, being an old-fashioned Federalist, he distrusted ambition and power, whatever the ends, and so he distrusted Hamilton. Hamilton, for his part, regarded Adams as a pompous and vain old man, hidebound by abstract principles and incapable of leading or following. Each had arrived at a fairly accurate estimation of the other.

The crisis with France, which began when that nation, retaliating against Jay's Treaty, seized American ships trading with the British West Indies, brought the latent hostility between the two leading Federalists into the open. Adams sent to France a special commission of three—two Federalists and a Republican—to work out a treaty; but the XYZ affair, foreign minister Talleyrand's attempt to obtain a bribe from the United States—a common practice at the time—shattered the negotiations. When Adams released the secret XYZ documents early in 1798, the American public rose up in fury against France.

Hamilton and his followers, riding the crest of popular sentiment, pressed for war. These extreme Federalists, who dominated Adams's cabinet, were as pugnacious toward France as they had been conciliatory, or servile, toward Britain. They believed that war with France would unify the country under their leadership and would, once and for all, extirpate the threat of radical Republicanism. The events of 1798 justified their hopes. Between March and July Congress passed a plethora of war legislation: it rescinded the alliance with France, laid the foundation of a national navy and army (with Hamilton as its second-in-command), levied new taxes on farmers and planters, and enacted a series of extremely repressive laws, in direct contravention of the Bill of Rights, against alleged French sympathizers and critics of the government.

Adams, however, suddenly destroyed the hopes of the Hamiltonians. Responding to peace feelers, he appointed a minister to France in February 1799. A commission followed close after, and in 1800 the two countries signed a treaty. By then the war fever had subsided, and popular revulsion against the emergency measures passed by the Federalist Congress had sharply risen. The Hamiltonians did not forgive Adams for his perfidy, and they opposed him for a second term. Adams replied by firing his Hamiltonian secretaries of State and War. The schism in the Federalist ranks was thus complete. Jefferson's election in 1801 brought to an end the era of the Federalist party, which dwindled into a sect and then disappeared altogether.

Hamilton towered over the Federalist era. Under his direction the federal government came to exert great influence in American life, giving coherence and focus to the nation as a whole, and providing a concrete symbol of unity. At the same time, however, the federal government became the arena of the most acerbic party conflicts. Hamilton antagonized not only the radicals, who had opposed him from the start, but the broad center of public opinion as well—the moderates and even conservatives, such as Dickinson and Adams. His policies aligned the government too closely with privileged interests at home and with the fortunes of Great Britain abroad, and, in fact, his belief that only a tight little oligarchy deserved to rule was more Tory than republican. In assuming that the majority of voters would passively accept such a government, he failed to gauge the temper of the people and, even worse for a strategist of his acumen, their capacity to resist. This failure was his undoing, and it was the undoing of the Federalist cause.

Alexander Hamilton to Robert Morris
April 15, 1781

[Hamilton was only twenty-four and Washington's aide-de-camp in the Continental Army when he wrote this letter to the country's superintendent of finance. It indicates how early in his life Hamilton's ideas on the relation of credit to state policy had matured.]

. . . To surmount these obstacles, and give individuals ability and inclination to lend in any proportion to the wants of government, a plan must be devised which, by incorporating their means together and uniting them with those of the public, will, on the foundation of that incorporation and union, erect a mass of credit that will supply the defect of moneyed capital, and answer all the purposes of cash; a plan which will offer adventurers immediate advantages analogous to those they receive by employing their money in trade, and eventually greater advantages, a plan which will give them the greatest security the nature of the case will admit for what they lend: and which will not only advance their own interest and secure the independence of their country, but, in its progress, have the most beneficial influence upon its future commerce, and be a source of national strength and wealth.

I mean the institution of a NATIONAL BANK. This I regard, in some shape or other, as an expedient essential to our safety and success; unless, by a happy turn of European affairs, the war should speedily terminate in a manner upon which it would be unwise to reckon. There is no other that can give to government that extensive and systematic credit which the defect of our revenues makes indispensably necessary to its operations.

The longer it is delayed the more difficult it becomes. Our affairs grow every day more relaxed and more involved; public credit hastens to a more irretrievable catastrophe; the means for executing the plan are exhausted in partial and temporary efforts. The loan now making in Massachusetts would have gone a great way in establishing the funds on which the bank must stand.

I am aware of all the objections that have been made to public banks; and that they are not without enlightened and respectable opponents. But all that has been said against them only tends to prove that, like all other good things, they are subject to abuse, and, when abused, become pernicious. The precious metals, by similar arguments, may be proven to be injurious. It is certain that the mines of South America have had great influence in banishing industry from Spain, and sinking it in real wealth and importance. Great power, commerce, and riches, or, in other words, great national prosperity, may, in like manner, be denominated evils; for they lead to insolence, an inordinate ambition, a vicious luxury, licentiousness of morals, and all those vices which corrupt government, enslave the people, and precipitate the ruin of a nation. But no wise statesman will reject the good from an apprehension of the ill. The truth is, in human affairs there is no good, pure and unmixed; every advantage has two sides; and wisdom consists in availing themselves of the good, and guarding as much as possible against the bad.

The tendency of a national bank is to increase public and private credit. The former gives power to the state, for the protection of its rights and interests: and the latter facilitates and extends the operations of commerce among individuals. Industry is increased, commodities are multiplied, agriculture and manufactures flourish: and herein consists the true wealth and prosperity of a state.

Most commercial nations have found it necessary to institute banks; and they have proved to be the happiest engines that ever were invented for advancing trade. Venice,

Genoa, Hamburg, Holland, and England are examples of their utility. They owe their riches, commerce, and the figure they have made at different periods, in a great degree to this source. Great Britain is indebted for the immense efforts she has been able to make, in so many illustrious and successful wars, essentially to that vast fabric of credit raised on this foundation. 'T is by this alone she now menaces our independence. . . .

A national debt, if it is not excessive, will be to us a national blessing. It will be a powerful cement of our Union. It will also create a necessity for keeping up taxation to a degree which, without being oppressive, will be a spur to industry, remote as we are from Europe, and shall be from danger. It were otherwise to be feared our popular maxims would incline us to too great parsimony and indulgence. We labor less now than any civilized nation of Europe; and a habit of labor in the people is as essential to the health and vigor of their minds and bodies, as it is conducive to the welfare of the state. We ought not to suffer our self-love to deceive us in a comparison upon these points. . . .

George Washington to John Jay
August 1, 1786

[In this letter Washington explains why he supports the movement to establish a stronger central government as a check on democracy. The Constitutional Convention took place less than a year later.]

Your sentiments, that our affairs are drawing rapidly to a crisis, accord with my own. What the event will be, is also beyond the reach of my foresight. We have errors to correct. We have probably had too good an opinion of human nature in forming our confederation. Experience has taught us, that men will not adopt and carry into execution measures the best calculated for their own good, without the intervention of a coercive power. I do not conceive we can exist long as a nation without having lodged some where a power, which will pervade the whole Union in as energetic a manner as the authority of the State governments extends over the several States.

To be fearful of investing Congress, constituted as that body is, with ample authorities for national purposes, appears to me the very climax of popular absurdity and madness. Could Congress exert them for the detriment of the public, without injuring themselves in an equal or greater proportion? Are not their interests inseparably connected with those of their constituents? By the rotation of appointment, must they not mingle frequently with the mass of citizens? Is it not rather to be apprehended, if they were possessed of the powers before described, that the individual members would be induced to use them, on many occasions, very timidly and inefficaciously for fear of losing their popularity and future election? We must take human nature as we find it. Perfection falls not to the share of mortals. Many are of opinion, that Congress have too frequently made use of the suppliant, humble tone of requisition in applications to the States, when they had a right to assert their imperial dignity and command obedience. Be that as it may, requisitions are a perfect nullity where thirteen sovereign, independent, disunited States are in the habit of discussing and refusing compliance with them at their option. Requisitions are actually little better than a jest and a by-word throughout the land. If you tell the legislatures they have violated the treaty of peace, and invaded the prerogatives of the confederacy, they will laugh in your face. What then is to be done? Things cannot go on in the same train for ever. It is much to be feared, as you observe, that the better kind of people, being disgusted with the circumstances, will have their minds prepared for any revolution whatever. We are apt to run from one extreme into another. To anticipate and prevent disastrous contingencies would be the part of wisdom and patriotism.

What astonishing changes a few years are capable of producing. I am told that even respectable characters speak of a monarchical form of government without horror. From thinking proceeds speaking; thence to acting is often but a single step. But how irrevocable and tremendous! What a triumph for our enemies to verify their predictions! What a triumph for the advocates of despotism to find, that we are incapable of governing ourselves, and that systems founded on the basis of equal liberty are merely ideal and fallacious! Would to God, that wise measures may be taken in time to avert the consequences we have but too much reason to apprehend. . . .

James Madison, Federalist Number 51
February 8, 1788

[The Federalist papers were written by Hamilton, Madison and John Jay in late 1787–early 1788, in the hope of persuading the voters of New York State to ratify the Constitution. They provided the best statement of the moderate Federalist position. Madison wrote most of the papers, including the one below.]

To the People of the State of New York:
To what expedient, then, shall we finally resort, for maintaining in practice the necessary partition of power among the several departments, as laid down in the Constitution? The only answer that can be given is, that as all these exterior provisions are found to be inadequate, the defect must be supplied, by so contriving the interior structure of the government as that its several constituent parts may, by their mutual relations, be the means of keeping each other in their proper places. Without presuming to undertake a full development of this important idea, I will hazard a few general observations, which may perhaps place it in a clearer light, and enable us to form a more correct judgment of the principles and structure of the government planned by the convention.

In order to lay a due foundation for that separate and distinct exercise of the different powers of government, which to a certain extent is admitted on all hands to be essential to the preservation of liberty, it is evident that each department should have a will of its own; and consequently should be so constituted that the members of each should have as little agency as possible in the appointment of the members of the others. Were this principle rigorously adhered to, it would require that all the appointments for the supreme executive, legislative, and judiciary magistracies should be drawn from the same fountain of authority, the people, through channels having no communication whatever with one another. Perhaps such a plan of constructing the several departments would be less difficult in practice than it may in contemplation appear. Some difficulties, however, and some additional expense would attend the execution of it. Some deviations, therefore, from the principle must be admitted. In the constitution of the judiciary department in particular, it might be inexpedient to insist rigorously on the principle: first, because peculiar qualifications being essential in the members, the primary consideration ought to be to select that mode of choice which best secures these qualifications; secondly, because the permanent tenure by which the appointments are held in that department, must soon destroy all sense of dependence on the authority conferring them.

It is equally evident, that the members of each department should be as little dependent as possible on those of the others, for the emoluments annexed to their offices. Were the executive magistrate, or the judges, not independent of the legislature in this particular, their independence in every other would be merely nominal.

But the great security against a gradual concentration of the several powers in the same department, consists in giving to those who administer each department the necessary constitutional means and personal motives to resist encroachments of the others. The provision for defence must in this, as in all other cases, be made commensurate to the danger of attack. Ambition must be made to counteract ambition. The interest of the man must be connected with the constitutional rights of the place. It may be a reflection on human nature, that such devices should be necessary to control the abuses of government. But what is government itself, but the greatest of all reflections on human nature? If men were angels, no government would be necessary. If angels were to govern men, neither external nor internal controls on government would be necessary. In framing a government which is to be administered by men over men, the great difficulty lies in this: you must first enable the government to control the governed; and in the next place oblige it to control itself. A dependence on the people is, no doubt, the primary control on the government; but experience has taught mankind the necessity of auxiliary precautions.

This policy of supplying, by opposite and rival interests, the defect of better motives, might be traced through the whole system of human affairs, private as well as public. We see it particularly displayed in all the subordinate distributions of power, where the constant aim is to divide and arrange the several offices in such a manner as that each may be a check on the other—that the private interest of every individual may be a sentinel over the public rights. These inventions of prudence cannot be less requisite in the distribution of the supreme powers of the State.

But it is not possible to give to each department an equal power of self-defence. In republican government, the legislative authority necessarily predominates. The remedy for this inconveniency is to divide the legislature into different branches; and to render them, by different modes of election and different principles of action, as little connected with each other as the nature of their common functions and their common dependence on the society will admit. It may even be necessary to guard against dangerous encroachments by still further precautions. As the weight of the legislative authority requires that it should be thus divided, the weakness of the executive may require, on the other hand, that it should be fortified. An absolute negative on the legislature appears, at first view, to be the natural defence with which the executive magistrate should be armed. But perhaps it would be neither altogether safe nor alone sufficient. On ordinary occasions it might not be exerted with the requisite firmness, and on extraordinary occasions it might be perfidiously abused. May not this defect of an absolute negative be supplied by some qualified connection between this weaker department and the weaker branch of the stronger department, by which the latter may be led to support the constitutional rights of the former, without being too much detached from the rights of its own department?

If the principles on which these observations are founded be just, as I persuade myself they are, and they be applied as a criterion to the several State constitutions, and to the federal Constitution, it will be found that if the latter does not perfectly correspond with them, the former are infinitely less able to bear such a test.

There are, moreover, two considerations particularly applicable to the federal system of America, which place that system in a very interesting point of view.

First. In a single republic, all the power surrendered by the people is submitted to the administration of a single government; and the usurpations are guarded against by a division of the government into distinct and separate departments. In the compound republic of America, the power surrendered by the people is first divided between two distinct governments, and then the portion allotted to each subdivided among distinct and separate departments. Hence a double security arises to the rights of the people. The different governments will control each other, at the same time that each will be controlled by itself.

Second. It is of great importance in a republic not only to guard the society against the oppression of its rulers, but to guard one part of the society against the injustice of the other part. Different interests necessarily exist in different classes of citizens. If a majority be united by a common interest, the rights of the minority will be insecure. There are but two methods of providing against this evil: the one by creating a will in the community independent of the majority—that is, of the society itself; the other, by comprehending in the society so many separate descriptions of citizens as will render an unjust combination of a majority of the whole very improbable, if not impracticable. The first method prevails in all governments possessing an hereditary or self-appointed authority. This, at best, is but a precarious security; because a power independent of the society may as well espouse the unjust views of the major, as the rightful interests of the minor party, and may possibly be turned against both parties. The second method will be exemplified in the federal republic of the United States. Whilst all authority in it will be derived from and dependent on the society, the society itself will be broken into so many parts, interests, and classes of citizens, that the rights of individuals, or of the minority, will be in little danger from interested combinations of the majority. In a free government the security for civil rights must be the same as that for religious rights. It consists in the one case in the multiplicity of interests, and in the other in the multiplicity of sects. The degree of security in both cases will depend on the number of interests and sects; and this may be presumed to depend on the extent of country and number of people comprehended under the same government. This view of the subject must particularly recommend a proper federal system to all the sincere and considerate friends of republican government, since it shows that in exact proportion as the territory of the Union may be formed into more circumscribed Confederacies, or States, oppressive combinations of a majority will be facilitated; the best security, under the republican forms, for the rights of every class of citizens, will be diminished; and consequently the stability and independence of some member of the government, the only other security, must be proportionally increased. Justice is the end of government. It is the end of civil society. It ever has been and ever will be pursued until it be obtained, or until liberty be lost in the pursuit. In a society under the forms of which the stronger faction can readily unite and oppress the weaker, anarchy may as truly be said to reign as in a state of nature, where the weaker individual is not secured against the violence of the stronger; and as, in the latter state, even the stronger individuals are prompted, by the uncertainty of their condition, to submit to a government which may protect the weak as well as themselves; so, in the former state, will the more powerful factions or parties be gradually induced, by a like motive, to wish for a government which will protect all parties, the weaker as well as the more powerful. It can be little doubted that if the State of Rhode Island was separated from the Confederacy and left to itself, the insecurity of rights under the popular form of government within such narrow limits would be displayed by such reiterated oppressions of factious majorities that some power altogether independent of the people would soon be called for by the voice of the very factions whose misrule had proved the necessity of it. In the extended republic of the United States, and among the great variety of interests, parties, and sects which it embraces, a coalition of a majority of the whole society could seldom take place on any other principles than those of justice and the general good; whilst there being thus less danger to a minor from the will of a major party, there must be less pretext, also, to provide for the security of the former, by introducing into the government a will not dependent on the latter, or, in other words, a will independent of the society itself. It is no less certain than it is important, notwithstanding the contrary opinions which have been entertained, that the larger the society, provided it lie within a practical sphere, the more duly capable it will be of self-government. And happily for the *republican cause*, the practicable sphere may be carried to a very great extent, by a judicious modification and mixture of the *federal principle*.   PUBLIUS

John Adams to Samuel Adams
October 15, 1790

[John Adams was one of the leading moderate Federalists and would no doubt have played an important part in the Constitutional Convention had he not been abroad on a diplomatic mission in the summer of 1787. Here he succinctly sets forth his conservative political philosophy to his radical second cousin Samuel.]

. . . I am very willing to agree with you in fancying that in the greatest improvements of society, government will be in the republican form. It is a fixed principle with me that all good government is and must be republican. But, at the same time, your candor will agree with me that there is not in lexicography a more fraudulent word. Whenever I use the word *republic* with approbation, I mean a government in which the people have collectively, or by representation, an essential share in the sovereignty. The republican forms of Poland and Venice are much worse, and those of Holland and Bern very little better, than the monarchical form in France before the late revolution. By the republican form, I know you do not mean the plan of Milton, Nedham, or Turgot. For, after a fair trial of its miseries, the simple monarchical form will ever be, as it has ever been, preferred to it by mankind. Are we not, my friend, in danger of rendering the word *republican* unpopular in this country by an indiscreet, indeterminate, and equivocal use of it? The people of England have been obliged to wean themselves from the use of it, by making it unpopular and unfashionable, because they found it was artfully used by some, and simply understood by others, to mean the government of their interregnum parliament. They found they could not wean themselves from that destructive form of government so entirely as that a mischievous party would not still remain in favor of it, by any other means than by making the words *republic* and *republican* unpopular. They have succeeded to such a degree that, with a vast majority of that nation, a republican is as unamiable as a witch, a blasphemer, a rebel, or a tyrant. If, in this country, the word *republic* should be generally understood, as it is by some, to mean a form of government inconsistent with a mixture of three powers, forming a mutual balance, we may depend upon it that such mischievous effects will be produced by the use of it as will compel the people of America to renounce, detest, and execrate it as the English do. With these explanations, restrictions, and limitations, I agree with you in your love of republican governments, but in no other sense.

With you, I have also the honor most perfectly to harmonize in your sentiments of the humanity and wisdom of promoting education in knowledge, virtue, and benevolence. But I think that these will confirm mankind in the opinion of the necessity of preserving and strengthening the dikes against the ocean, its tides and storms. Human appetites, passions, prejudices, and self-love will never be conquered by benevolence and knowledge alone, introduced by human means. The millennium itself neither supposes nor implies it. All civil government is then to cease, and the Messiah is to reign. That happy and holy state is therefore wholly out of this question. You and I agree in the utility of universal education; but will nations agree in it as fully and extensively as we do, and be at the expense of it? We know, with as much certainty as attends any human knowledge, that they will not. We cannot, therefore, advise the people to depend for their safety, liberty, and security upon hopes and blessings which we know will not fall to their lot. If we do our duty then to the people, we shall not deceive them, but advise them to depend upon what is in their power and will relieve them. . . .

We have human nature, society, and universal history to observe and study, and from these we may draw all the real principles which ought to be regarded. Disciples will follow their masters, and interested partisans their chieftains; let us like it or not, we cannot help it. But if the true principles can be discovered, and fairly, fully, and impartially laid before the people, the more light increases, the more the reason of them will be seen, and the more disciples they will have. Prejudice, passion, and private interest, which will always mingle inhuman inquiries, one would think might be enlisted on the side of truth, at least in the greatest number; for certainly the majority are interested in the truth, if they could see to the end of all its consequences. "Kings have been deposed by aspiring nobles." True, and never by any other. "These" (the nobles, I suppose) "have waged everlasting war against the common rights of men." True, when they have been possessed of the *summa imperii* in one body, without a check. So have the plebeians; so have the people; so have kings; so has human nature, in every shape and combination, and so it ever will. But, on the other hand, the nobles have been essential parties in the preservation of liberty, whenever and wherever it has existed. In Europe, they alone have preserved it against kings and people, wherever it has been preserved; or, at least, with very little assistance from the people. One hideous despotism, as horrid as that of Turkey, would have been the lot of every nation of Europe if the nobles had not made stands. By nobles, I mean not peculiarly an hereditary nobility, or any particular modification, but the natural and actual aristocracy among mankind.

The existence of this you will not deny. You and I have seen four noble families rise up in Boston—the CRAFTS, GORES, DAWES, and AUSTINS. These are as really a nobility in our town as the Howards, Somersets, Berties, &c., in England. Blind, undistinguishing reproaches against the aristocratical part of mankind, a division which nature has made, and we cannot abolish, are neither pious nor benevolent. They are as pernicious as they are false. They serve only to foment prejudice, jealousy, envy, animosity, and malevolence. They serve no ends but those of sophistry, fraud, and the spirit of party. It would not be true, but it would not be more egregiously false, to say that the people have waged everlasting war against the rights of men.

"The love of liberty," you say, "is interwoven in the soul of man." So it is, according to La Fontaine, in that of a wolf; and I doubt whether it be much more rational, generous, or social in one than in the other, until in man it is enlightened by experience, reflection, education, and civil and political institutions, which are at first produced and constantly supported and improved by a few; that is, by the nobility. The wolf, in the fable, who preferred running in the forest, lean and hungry, to the sleek, plump, and round sides of the dog, because he found the latter was sometimes restrained, had more love of liberty than most men. The numbers of men in all ages have preferred ease, slumber, and good cheer to liberty, when they have been in competition. We must not, then, depend alone upon the love of liberty in the soul of man for its preservation. Some political institutions must be prepared, to assist this love against its enemies. Without these, the struggle will ever end only in a change of impostors. When the people who have no property feel the power in their own hands to determine all questions by a majority, they ever attack those who have property, till the injured men of property lose all patience, and recur to finesse, trick, and stratagem to outwit those who have too much strength, because they have too many hands to be resisted any other way. Let us be impartial, then, and speak the whole truth. Till we do, we shall never discover all the true principles that are necessary. The multitude, therefore, as well as the nobles, must have a check.

Popularity, that has great fortune to dazzle; splendid largesses, to excite warm gratitude; sublime, beautiful, and uncommon genius or talents, to produce deep admiration; or anything to support high hopes and strong fears, will be proud; and its power will be employed to mortify enemies, gratify friends, procure votes, emoluments, and power. Such family popularity ever did and ever will govern in every nation, in every climate, hot and cold, wet and dry, among civilized and savage people, Christians and Mahometans, Jews and heathens. Declamation against family pride is a pretty, juvenile exercise, but unworthy of statesmen. They know the evil and danger is too serious to be sported with. The only way, God knows, is to put these families into a hole by themselves, and set two watches upon them; a superior to them all on one side, and the people on the other. . . .

Let us be impartial. There is not more of family pride on one side than of vulgar malignity and popular envy on the other. Popularity in one family raises envy in others. But the popularity of the least deserving will triumph over envy and malignity; while that which is acquired by real merit will very often be overborne and oppressed by it.

Let us do justice to the people and to the nobles; for nobles there are, as I have before proved, in Boston as well as in Madrid. But to do justice to both, you must establish an arbitrator between them. This is another principle.

It is time that you and I should have some sweet communion together. I do not believe that we, who have preserved for more than thirty years an uninterrupted friendship, and have so long thought and acted harmoniously together in the worst of times, are now so far asunder in sentiment as some people pretend; in full confidence of which, I have used this freedom, being ever your warm friend. . . .

Alexander Hamilton to Edward Carrington
May 26, 1792

[By 1792 pro- and anti-Hamiltonian factions had begun to form in the states. Below, Hamilton gives his version of the dispute over his policies to one of his allies in Virginia.]

. . . When I accepted the office I now hold, it was under full persuasion, that from similarity of thinking, conspiring with personal good-will, I should have the firm support of Mr. Madison, in the general course of my administration. Aware of the intrinsic difficulties of the situation, and of the powers of Mr. Madison, I do not believe I should have accepted under a different supposition. I have mentioned the similarity of thinking between that gentleman and myself. This was relative, not merely to the general principles of national policy and government, but to the leading points, which were likely to constitute questions in the administration of the finances. I mean, first, the expediency of funding the debt; second, the inexpediency of discrimination between original and present holders; third, the expediency of assuming the State debts. . . .

[A]fterwards repeated intimations were given to me that Mr. Madison, from a spirit of rivalship, or some other cause, had become personally unfriendly to me; and one gentleman in particular, whose honor I have no reason to doubt, assured me that Mr. Madison, in a conversation with him, had made a pretty direct attempt to insinuate unfavorable impressions of me. Still I suspended my opinion on the subject. I knew the malevolent officiousness of mankind too well to yield a very ready acquiescence to the suggestions which were made, and resolved to wait till time and more experience should afford a solution. It was not till the last session that I became unequivocally convinced of the following truth: "that Mr. Madison, cooperating with Mr. Jefferson, is at the head of a faction decidedly hostile to me and my administration; and actuated by views, in my judgment, subversive of the principles of good government and dangerous to the Union, peace, and happiness of the country." . . .

Mr. Jefferson, with very little reserve, manifests his dislike of the funding system generally, calling in question the expediency of funding a debt at all. Some expressions, which he has dropped in my presence (sometimes without sufficient attention to delicacy), will not permit me to doubt on this point representations which I have had from various respectable quarters. I do not mean that he advocates directly the undoing of what has been done, but he censures the whole, on principles which, if they should become general, could not but end in the subversion of the system. In various conversations, with foreigners as well as citizens, he has thrown censure on my principles of government and on my measures of administration. He has predicted that the people would not long tolerate my proceedings, and that I should not long maintain my ground. Some of those whom he immediately and notoriously moves have even whispered suspicions of the rectitude of my motives and conduct. In the question concerning the bank he not only delivered an opinion in writing against its constitutionality and expediency, but he did it in a style and manner which I felt as partaking of asperity and ill humor toward me. As one of the trustees of the sinking fund, I have experienced in almost every leading question opposition from him. When any turn of things in the community has threatened either odium or embarrassment to me, he has not been able to suppress the satisfaction which it gave him. A part of this is, of course, information, and might be misrepresentation, but it comes through so many channels, and so well accords with what falls under my own observation, that I can entertain no doubt. . . .

Whatever were the original merits of the funding system, after having been so solemnly adopted, and after so great a transfer of property under it, what would become of the government should it be reversed? What of the national reputation? Upon what system of morality can so atrocious a doctrine be maintained? In me, I confess it excited indignation and horror!

What are we to think of those maxims of government by which the power of a Legislature is denied to bind the nation, by a contract in the affair of property for twenty-four years? For this is precisely the case of the debt. What are to become of all the legal rights of property, of all charters to corporations, nay, of all grants to a man, his heirs and assigns, for ever, if this doctrine be true? What is the term for which a government is in capacity to contract? Questions might be multiplied without end, to demonstrate the perniciousness and absurdity of such a doctrine.

In almost all the questions, great and small, which have arisen since the first session of Congress, Mr. Jefferson and Mr. Madison have been found among those who are disposed to narrow the federal authority. The question of a national bank is one example. The question of bounties to the fisheries is another. Mr. Madison resisted it on the ground of constitutionality, till it was evident, by the intermediate questions taken, that the bill would pass; and he then, under the wretched subterfuge of a change of a single word, "bounty" for "allowance," went over to the majority, and voted for the bill. On the militia bill, and in a variety of minor cases, he has leaned to abridging the exercise of federal authority, and leaving as much as possible to the States; and he lost no opportunity of sounding the alarm, with great affected solemnity, at encroachments, meditated on the rights of the States, and of holding up the bugbear of a faction in the government having designs unfriendly to liberty.

This kind of conduct has appeared to me the more extraordinary on the part of Mr. Madison, as I know for a certainty, it was a primary article in his creed, that the real danger in our system was the subversion of the national authority by the preponderancy of the State governments. All his measures have proceeded on an opposite supposition. I recur again to the instance of Freneau's paper. In matters of this kind one cannot have direct proof of men's latent views; they must be inferred from circumstances. As coadjutor of Mr. Jefferson in the establishment of this paper, I include Mr. Madison in the consequences imputable to it. In respect to foreign politics, the views of these gentlemen are, in my judgment, equally unsound and dangerous. They have a womanish attachment to France and a womanish resentment against Great Britain. They would draw us into the closest embrace of the former, and involve us in all the consequences of her politics; and they would risk the peace of the country in their endeavors to keep us at the greatest possible distance from the latter. This disposition goes to a length, particularly in Mr. Jefferson, of which, till lately, I had no adequate idea. Various circumstances prove to me that if these gentlemen were left to pursue their own course, there would be, in less than six months, an open war between the United States and Great Britain. I trust I have a due sense of the conduct of France towards this country in the late revolution; and that I shall always be among the foremost in making her every suitable return; but there is a wide difference between this and implicating ourselves in all her politics; between bearing good-will to her and hating and wrangling with all those whom she hates. The neutral and the pacific policy appears to me to mark the true path to the United States.

Having delineated to you what I conceive to be the true complexion of the politics of these gentlemen, I will not attempt a solution of these strange appearances. Mr. Jefferson, it is known, did not in the first instance cordially acquiesce in the new Constitution for the United States; he had many doubts and reserves. He left this country before we had experienced the imbecilities of the former.

In France, he saw government only on the side of its abuses. He drank freely of the French philosophy, in religion, in science, in politics. He came from France in the moment of a fermentation, which he had a share in exciting, and in the passions and feelings of which he shared both from temperament and situation. He came here probably with a too partial idea of his own powers; and with the expectation of a greater share in the direction of our councils than he has in reality enjoyed. I am not sure that he had not peculiarly marked out for himself the department of the finances.

He came, electrified with attachment to France, and with the project of knitting together the two countries in the closest political bands.

Mr. Madison had always entertained an exalted opinion of the talents, knowledge, and virtues of Mr. Jefferson. The sentiment was probably reciprocal. A close correspondence subsisted between them during the time of Mr. Jefferson's absence from the country. A close intimacy arose upon his return. . . .

A word on another point. I am told that serious apprehensions are disseminated in your State as to the existence of a monarchical party meditating the destruction of State and republican government. If it is possible that so absurd an idea can gain ground, it is necessary that it should be combated. I assure you, on my private faith and honor as a man, that there is not, in my judgment, a shadow of foundation for it. A very small number of men indeed may entertain theories less republican than Mr. Jefferson and Mr. Madison, but I am persuaded there is not a man among them who would not regard as both criminal and visionary any attempt to subvert the republican system of the country. Most of these men rather fear that it may not justify itself by its fruits, than feel a predilection for a different form; and their fears are not diminished by the factious and fanatical politics which they find prevailing among a certain set of gentlemen and threatening to disturb the tranquillity and order of the government.

As to the destruction of State governments, the great and real anxiety is to be able to preserve the national from the too potent and counteracting influence of those governments. As to my own political creed, I give it to you with the utmost sincerity. I am affectionately attached to the republican theory. I desire above all things to see the equality of political rights, exclusive of all hereditary distinction, firmly established by a practical demonstration of its being consistent with the order and happiness of society. As to State governments, the prevailing bias of my judgment is that if they can be circumscribed within bounds, consistent with the preservation of the national government, they will prove useful and salutary. If the States were all of the size of Connecticut, Maryland, or New Jersey, I should decidedly regard the local governments as both safe and useful. As the thing now is, however, I acknowledge the most serious apprehensions, that the government of the United States will not be able to maintain itself against their influence. I see that influence already penetrating into the national councils and preventing their direction. Hence, a disposition on my part towards a liberal construction of the powers of the national government, and to erect every fence, to guard it from depredations which is, in my opinion, consistent with constitutional propriety. As to any combination to prostrate the State governments, I disavow and deny it. From an apprehension lest the judiciary should not work efficiently or harmoniously, I have been desirous of seeing some national scheme of connection adopted as an amendment to the Constitution, otherwise I am for maintaining things as they are; though I doubt much the possibility of it, from a tendency in the nature of things towards the preponderancy of the State governments.

I said that I was affectionately attached to the republican theory. This is the real language of my heart, which I open to you in the sincerity of friendship; and I add that I have strong hopes of the success of that theory; but, in candor, I ought also to add that I am far from being without doubts. I consider its success as yet a problem. It is yet to be determined by experience whether it be consistent with that stability and order in government which are essential to public strength and private security and happiness.

On the whole, the only enemy which Republicanism has to fear in this country is in the spirit of faction and anarchy. If this will not permit the ends of government to be attained under it, if it engenders disorders in the community, all regular and orderly minds will wish for a change, and the demagogues who have produced the disorder will make it for their own aggrandizement. This is the old story. If I were disposed to promote monarchy and overthrow State governments, I would mount the hobby-horse of popularity; I would cry out "usurpation," "danger to liberty," etc., etc.; I would endeavor to prostrate the national government, raise a ferment, and then "ride in the whirlwind, and direct the storm." That there are men acting with Jefferson and Madison who have this in view, I verily believe; I could lay my finger on some of them. That Madison does not mean it, I also verily believe; and I rather believe the same of Jefferson, but I read him upon the whole thus: "A man of profound ambition and violent passions." . . .

Alexander Hamilton, Camillus, Number 18
1795

[In a series of articles under the name of Camillus, Hamilton defended Jay's Treaty. The following article takes up one of the most unpopular features of the Treaty—that dealing with America's debts to Great Britain. Many Americans did not understand why such debts had to be paid while Britain was seizing American ships and impressing American seamen.]

It is provided by the tenth article of the treaty that "neither debts due from individuals of one nation to individuals of the other, nor shares, nor moneys, which they may have in the public funds, or in the public or private banks, shall ever in any event of war, or national difference, be sequestered or confiscated; it being unjust and impolitic, that debts and engagements contracted and made by individuals, having confidence in each other, and in their respective governments, should ever be destroyed or impaired by national authority on account of national differences and discontents."

The virulence with which this article has been attacked cannot fail to excite very painful sensations in every mind duly impressed with the sanctity of public faith, and with the importance of national credit and character; at the same time that it furnishes the most cogent reasons to desire that the preservation of peace may obviate the pretext and the temptation to sully the honor and wound the interests of the country by a measure which the truly enlightened of every nation would condemn.

I acknowledge, without reserve, that in proportion to the vehemence of the opposition against this part of the treaty, is the satisfaction I derive from its existence, as an obstacle the more to the perpetration of a thing, which, in my opinion, besides deeply injuring our real and permanent interest, would cover us with ignominy. No powers of language at my command can express the abhorrence I feel at the idea of violating the property of individuals, which, in an authorized intercourse, in time of peace, has been confided to the faith of our Government and laws, on account of controversies between nation and nation. In my view, every moral and every political sentiment unite to consign it to execration.

Neither will I dissemble, that the dread of the effects of the spirit which patronizes that idea, has ever been with me one of the most persuasive arguments for a pacific policy on the part of the United States. Serious as the evil of war has appeared, at the present stage of our affairs, the manner in which it was to be apprehended it might be carried on, was still more formidable, in my eyes, than the thing itself. It was to be feared, that in the fermentation of certain wild opinions, those wise, just, and temperate maxims, which will for ever constitute the true security and felicity of a state, would be overruled; and that a war upon credit, eventually upon property, and upon the general principles of public order, might aggravate and embitter the ordinary calamities of foreign war. The confiscation of debts due to the enemy, might have been the first step of this destructive process. From one violation of justice to another, the passage is easy. Invasions of right, still more fatal to credit, might have followed; and this, by extinguishing the resources which that could have afforded, might have paved the way to more comprehensive and more enormous depredations for a substitute. Terrible examples were before us; and there were too many not sufficiently remote from a disposition to admire and imitate them.

The earnest and extensive clamors against the part of the treaty under consideration, confirm that anticipation; and while they enhance the merit of the provision, they also inspire a wish, that some more effectual barrier had been erected against the possibility of a contrary practice being ever, at any ill-fated moment, obtruded upon our public councils. It would have been an inestimable gem in our national Constitution, had it contained a positive prohibition against such a practice, except, perhaps, by way of reprisal for the identical injury on the part of another nation. . . .

It is at once curious and instructive to mark the inconsistencies of the disorganizing sect. Is the question, to discard a spirit of accommodation, and rush into war with Great

Britain? Columns are filled with the most absurd exaggerations, to prove that we are able to meet her, not only on equal, but superior terms. Is the question, whether a stipulation against the confiscation or sequestration of private debts ought to have been admitted into the treaty? Then are we a people destitute of the means of war, with neither arms, nor fleets, nor magazines—then is our best, if not our only, weapon of defence, the power of confiscating or sequestrating the debts which are due to the subjects of Great Britain; in other words, the power of committing fraud, of violating the public faith, of sacrificing the principles of commerce, of prostrating credit. Is the question, whether free ships shall make free goods, whether naval stores shall or shall not be deemed contraband? Then is the appeal to what is called the *modern* law of nations; then is the cry, that recent usage has changed and mitigated the rigor of ancient maxims. But is the question, whether private debts can be rightfully confiscated or sequestered? Then ought the utmost rigor of the ancient doctrine to govern, and modern usage and opinion to be discarded. The old rule or the new is to be adopted or rejected, just as may suit their convenience. . . .

Away with these absurd and incongruous sophisms! Blush, ye apostles of temerity, of meanness, and of deception! Cease to beckon us to war, and at the same time to freeze our courage by the cowardly declaration that we have no resource but in fraud! Cease to attempt to persuade us that peace may be obtained by means which are unequivocal acts of war. Cease to tell us that war is preferable to dishonor, and yet, as our first step, to urge us into irretrievable dishonor. A magnanimous, a sensible people cannot listen to your crude conceptions. Why will ye persevere in accumulating ridicule and contempt upon your own heads?

In the further observations which I shall offer on this article, I hope to satisfy, not the determined leaders or instruments of faction, but all discerning men, all good citizens, that, instead of being a blemish, it is an ornament to the instrument in which it is contained; that it is as consistent with true policy as with substantial justice; that it is, in substance, not without precedent in our other treaties, and that the objections to it are futile.

Timothy Dwight, *Duty of Americans at the Present Crisis*
1798

[Dwight, president of Yale College, was a militant Federalist who hated the Enlightenment and liberalism. In this widely circulated tract the Calvinist divine alerts his fellow New Englanders to the threat of advancing Jeffersonianism.]

Without religion we may possibly retain the freedom of savages, bears, and wolves; but not the freedom of New-England. If our religion were gone, our state of society would perish with it; and nothing would be left, which would be worth defending. Our children of course, if not ourselves, would be prepared, as the ox for the slaughter, to become the victims of conquest, tyranny, and atheism. . . .

The sins of these enemies of Christ, and Christians, are of numbers and degrees, which mock account and descriptions. All that the malice and atheism of the Dragon, the cruelty and rapacity of the Beast, and the fraud and deceit of the false Prophet, can generate, or accomplish, swell the list. No personal, or national, interest of man has been uninvaded; no impious sentiment, or action, against God has been spared; no malignant hostility against Christ, and his religion, has been unattempted. Justice, truth, kindness, piety, and moral obligation universally, have been, not merely trodden under foot; this might have resulted from vehemence and passion; but ridiculed, spurned, and insulted, as the childish bugbears of drivelling idiocy. Chastity and decency have been alike turned out of doors; and shame and pollution called out of their dens to the hall of distinction, and the chair of state. Nor has any art, violence, or means, been unemployed to accomplish these evils.

For what end shall we be connected with men, of whom this is the character and conduct? Is it that we may assume the same character, and pursue the same conduct? Is it, that our churches may become temples of reason, our Sabbath a decade, and our psalms of praise Marseillais hymns? Is it, that we may change our holy worship into a dance of Jacobin phrenzy, and that we may behold a strumpet personating a Goddess on the altars of Jehovah? Is it that we may see the Bible cast into a bonfire, the vessels of the sacramental supper borne by an ass in public procession, and our children, either wheedled or terrified, uniting in the mob, chanting mockeries against God, and hailing in the sounds of Ça ira the ruin of their religion, and the loss of their souls? Is it, that we may see our wives and daughters the victims of legal prostitution; soberly dishonoured; speciously polluted; the outcasts of delicacy and virtue, and the loathing of God and man? Is it, that we may see, in our public papers, a solemn comparison drawn by an American Mother club between the Lord Jesus Christ and a new Marat; and the fiend of malice and fraud exalted above the glorious Redeemer?

Shall we, my brethren, become partakers of these sins? Shall we introduce them into our government, our schools, our families? Shall our sons become the disciples of Voltaire, and the dragoons of Marat; or our daughters the concubines of the Illuminati? . . .

Alexander Hamilton's Attack on John Adams
October 1800

[As the presidential election drew near, Hamilton showed his close friends a long, bitter indictment he had written of Adams. He did so in the course of drumming up support for a rival Federalist candidate. The attack on Adams soon became known to the public and made the schism in Federalist ranks irreparable.]

. . . On other topics, my sensations are far less neutral. If, as I have been assured from respectable authorities, Mr. Adams has repeatedly indulged himself in virulent and indecent abuse of me; if he has denominated me a man destitute of every moral principle; if he has stigmatized me as the leader of a British faction; then, certainly, I have a right to think that I have been most cruelly and wickedly traduced; then have I a right to appeal to all those who have been spectators of my public actions; to all who are acquainted with my private character in its various relations, whether such treatment of me by Mr. Adams is of a nature to weaken or strengthen his claim to the approbation of wise and good men; then will I so far yield to the consciousness of what I am, as to declare, that in the cardinal points of public and private rectitude, above all, in pure and disinterested zeal for the interests and service of this country, I shrink not from a comparison with any arrogant pretender to superior and exclusive merit.

Having been repeatedly informed that Mr. Adams had delineated me as the leader of a British faction, and having understood that his partisans, to counteract the influence of my opinion, were pressing the same charge against me, I wrote him a letter on the subject, dated the first of August last. No reply having been given by him to this letter, I, on the first of the present month, wrote him another; of both which letters I send you copies.

Of the purity of my public conduct in this, as in other particulars, I may defy the severest investigation. . . .

Let any fair man pronounce, whether the circumstances which have been disclosed bespeak the partisan of Great Britain, or the man exclusively devoted to the interests of this country. Let any delicate man decide, whether it must not be shocking to an ingenuous mind, to have to combat a slander so vile, after having sacrificed the interests of his family, and devoted the best part of his life to the service of that country, in counsel and in the field.

It is time to conclude. This statement, which has been made, shows that Mr. Adams has committed some positive and serious errors of administration; that in addition to these, he has certain fixed points of character which tend naturally to the detriment of any cause of which he is the chief, of any administration of which he is the head; that by his ill humors and jealousies he has already divided and distracted the supporters of the government; that he has furnished deadly weapons to its enemies by unfounded accusations, and has weakened the force of its friends by decrying some of the most influential of them to the utmost of his power; and let it be added, as the necessary effect of such conduct, that he has made great progress in undermining the ground which was gained for the government by his predecessor, and that there is real cause to apprehend it might totter, if not fall, under his future auspices. A new government, constructed on free principles, is always weak, and must stand in need of the props of a firm and good administration, till time shall have rendered its authority venerable, and fortified it by habits of obedience.

Yet with this opinion of Mr. Adams, I have finally resolved not to advise the withholding from him a single vote. The body of Federalists, for want of sufficient knowledge of facts, are not convinced of the expediency of relinquishing him. It is even apparent, that a large proportion still retain the attachment which was once a common sentiment. Those of them, therefore, who are dissatisfied, as far as my information goes, are, generally speaking, willing to forbear opposition, and to acquiesce in the equal support of Mr. Adams with Mr. Pinckney; whom they prefer. Have they not a claim to equal deference from those who continue attached to the former? Ought not these, in candor, to admit the possibility that the friends who differ from them act not only from pure motives, but from cogent reasons? Ought they not, by a co-operation in General Pinckney, to give a chance for what will be a *safe* issue, supposing that they are right in their preference, and the best issue, should they happen to be mistaken? Especially, since by doing this they will increase the probability of excluding a third candidate, of whose unfitness all sincere Federalists are convinced. If they do not pursue this course, they will certainly incur an immense responsibility to their friends and to the government.

To promote this co-operation, to defend my own character, to vindicate those friends, who with myself have been unkindly aspersed, are the inducements for writing this letter. Accordingly, it will be my endeavor to regulate the communication of it in such a manner as will not be likely to deprive Mr. Adams of a single vote. Indeed, it is much my wish that its circulation could forever be confined within narrow limits. I am sensible of the inconveniences of giving publicity to a similar development of the character of the Chief Magistrate of our country; and I lament the necessity of taking a step which will involve that result. Yet to suppress truths, the disclosure of which is so interesting to the public welfare as well as to the vindication of my friends and myself, did not appear to me justifiable. . . .

Alexander Hamilton to James A. Bayard
January 16, 1801

[The 1800 presidential election had ended in a tie between the two Republican candidates, Jefferson and Aaron Burr. The election thus went to the House of Representatives, where Federalists held the balance of votes and so determined who the winner would be. Hamilton advised the Federalists, among them James A. Bayard of Maryland, to support Jefferson.]

I was glad to find, my dear sir, by your letter that you had not yet determined to go with the current of the federal party in the support of Mr. Burr, and that you were resolved to hold yourself disengaged till the moment of final decision. Your resolution to separate yourself in this instance from the federal party, if your conviction shall be strong of the unfitness of Mr. Burr, is certainly laudable. So much does it coincide with my ideas, that if the party shall, by supporting Mr. Burr as President, adopt him for their official chief, I shall be obliged to consider myself as an *isolated* man. It will be impossible for me to reconcile with my notions of *honor* or policy the continuing to be of a party which, according to my apprehension, will have degraded itself and the country.

I am sure, nevertheless, that the motives of many will be good, and I shall never cease to esteem the individuals, though I shall deplore a step which, I fear, experience will show to be a very fatal one. Among the letters which I receive assigning the reasons *pro* and *con* for preferring Burr to J., I observe no small exaggeration to the prejudice of the latter, and some things taken for granted as to the former, which are at least questionable. Perhaps myself the first, at some expense of popularity, to unfold the true character of Jefferson, it is too late for me to become his apologist; nor can I have any disposition to do it.

I admit that his politics are tinctured with fanaticism; that he is too much in earnest in his democracy; that he has been a mischievous enemy to the principal measures of our past administration; that he is crafty and persevering in his objects; that he is not scrupulous about the means of success, nor very mindful of truth, and that he is a contemptible hypocrite. But it is not true, as is alleged, that he is an enemy to the power of the Executive, or that he is for confounding all the powers in the House of Representatives. It is a fact which I have frequently mentioned, that, while we were in the administration together, he was generally for a large construction of the Executive authority and not backward to act upon it in cases which coincided with his views. Let it be added that in his theoretic ideas he has considered as improper the participations of the Senate in the Executive authority. I have more than once made the reflection that, viewing himself as the reversioner, he was solicitous to come into the possession of a good estate. Nor is it true that Jefferson is zealot enough to do any thing in pursuance of his principles which will contravene his popularity or his interest. He is as likely as any man I know to temporize—to calculate what will be likely to promote his own reputation and advantage; and the probable result of such a temper is the preservation of systems, though originally opposed, which, being once established, could not be overturned without danger to the person who did it. To my mind a true estimate of Mr. Jefferson's character warrants the expectation of a temporizing rather than a violent system. That Jefferson has manifested a culpable predilection for France is certainly true; but I think it a question whether it did not proceed quite as much from her *popularity* among us as from sentiment, and, in proportion as that popularity is diminished, his zeal will cool. Add to this that there is no fair reason to suppose him capable of being corrupted, which is a security that he will not go beyond certain limits. It is not at all improbable that under the change of circumstances Jefferson's Gallicism has considerably abated. . . .

John Adams to Benjamin Stoddard
March 31, 1801

[Disappointed and embittered, Adams explains why the Federalists lost.]

. . . We federalists are much in the situation of the party of Bolingbroke and Harley, after the treaty of Utrecht, completely and totally routed and defeated. We are not yet attainted by act of Congress, and, I hope, shall not fly out into rebellion. No party, that ever existed, knew itself so little, or so vainly overrated its own influence and popularity, as ours. None ever understood so ill the causes of its own power, or so wantonly destroyed them. If we had been blessed with common sense, we should not have been overthrown by Philip Freneau, Duane, Callender, Cooper, and Lyon, or their great patron and protector. A group of foreign liars, encouraged by a few ambitious native gentlemen, have discomfited the education, the talents, the virtues, and the property of the country. The reason is, we have no Americans in America. The federalists have been no more Americans than the anties. . . .

CHAPTER III. JEFFERSON AND AGRARIAN NATIONALISM

When Jefferson became Secretary of State in 1790 at the age of forty-seven, he already had a long and distinguished career in politics behind him. He rose to prominence in the late 1760s as a radical defender of American rights against the mother country. His first important state paper, written in 1774, affirmed the equality of the colonies and Parliament and proposed the establishment of an American dominion subject only nominally to the authority of the Crown. He then went on to draft the Virginia constitution, the Declaration of Independence, and a few years later, a thoroughgoing revision of the Virginia laws, proposing, among other reforms, the manumission of slaves, the creation of a system of public education, and the separation of church and state. In 1779 he was chosen governor of Virginia and served two one-year terms, during which time he learned how powerless was his office in the teeth of legislative supremacy.

In 1784 he returned to national affairs as a Virginia delegate to the Confederation Congress, and again he drew up important bills and recommendations for reform, most notably the ordinance for the Northwest Territory, which was later incorporated into the law of the land. The following year, Congress appointed him Commissioner to Paris, and soon after, Minister to France, a post he held for three years. No other period in his life was more eventful and satisfying to him. He counted among his friends some of the leading scientists and philosophers of Paris, and he traveled extensively through western Europe, carefully noting down his impressions at every stop. Above all, he was privileged to witness firsthand the opening phase of the French Revolution, which he described at length in letters to his friends. He left France just before the momentous "October Days" of 1789 to take up his duties as Secretary of State in the new government.

In his public career, Jefferson at once epitomized and transcended the liberal Virginia school that had emerged in the 1750s and '60s. Like his fellow patricians—Wythe, Mason, Pendleton, Richard Henry Lee, and others—he assumed that all men had the inalienable right to self-government, that liberty had been conferred upon men by the same natural law that moved and ordered the universe, and that any authority, secular or religious, that restricted men's liberty violated the very nature of things and therefore deserved to be overthrown without compunction. To be sure, these sentiments were interpreted by some as simple rationalizations, for the interests of the Virginia aristocracy dictated resistance to the London creditors, to whom its estates were mortgaged, and to Parliament for encroaching upon its prerogatives after 1763. But the ideals of these liberals—the belief in the rights of man, in the possibility of happiness, in the force of reason and rationality, and in the inevitability of progress—went far beyond the motives of self-interest that prompted them and acquired a character and meaning of their own. Many other Virginia aristocrats, responding to similar motives of self-interest, became Tories during the revolutionary crisis.

But the philosophy of Virginia liberalism—like so much of the philosophy thrown up by the Enlightenment—dealt in abstractions, in empty universalities: liberty and equality embraced men in general, not any particular group of men. This enabled the liberal exponents of the social contract theory to distinguish between natural rights, which belonged to all, and civic rights, which belonged to only a few. Jefferson attempted to close this gap by identifying the cause of freedom and humanity with the cause of the American yeomen farmers, that is, with the majority of American people. It was in this respect that he went beyond even the most radical of his patrician contemporaries.

Jefferson was above all a moralist, and in the self-sufficient farmer whose simple needs could be met by his own labor he saw the embodiment of all the classic virtues that had so far eluded mankind. Jefferson often contrasted the happiness and wholesome well-being of the American farmer with the

wretchedness of the rest of the world, including the privileged classes, who, as he pictured them, were sunk in de-
bauchery, decadence and lassitude. In America's forests and
fields he found the fulfillment of Locke's primal state of nature, in which every man, living by his own labor and secure
in his own freehold, owed to others neither more nor less
than he received from them, and in which, therefore, social
equality could not be separated from natural equality. In the
whole of political literature no man has written more en-
thusiastically nor more eloquently in praise of the yeoman
life than Jefferson.

His agrarian ideals underlay his work as a revolutionist and
reformer. He regarded that government as best which was
closest to the people: simple, uncoercive and entirely responsible to the constituency it served. Conversely, as governments
grew more distant from the people, he held, so the number
of public officials and retainers increased, with a consequent
increase in taxes to support them. In this way governments
became repressive and society hierarchical, class-ridden, idola-
trous and morally profligate. Only the maintenance of strict
agrarian virtue prevented this descent into empire and
despotism.

Though Jefferson believed that each small community
should be politically sovereign, his outlook was national in
scope. He envisioned the planting of agrarian communities
across the American continent, including territories still occupied or under foreign rule. America was to be a unique
polity, at once republican in its form of government and its
concern for individual happiness and freedom, and continental, or rather imperial, in its vastness and the possibilities
it offered to common men. Jefferson, then, was primarily
an agrarian nationalist and not an apostle of local and states'
rights. He was as intensely nationalist as the Federalists.

He joined Washington's cabinet in the belief that the government would encourage agrarian nationalism, or at least
place no obstacle in the path of its development. But by
1791, within a year after taking office, he had concluded that,
with Hamilton bent on encouraging trade, manufacturing and
the propagation of paper money, an opposing idea of nationalism was directing the policies of the government.

He interpreted Hamilton's "system," or "machine," as a deliberate assault on virtue, an attempt to destroy the independence of the small farmer and of the agricultural class in general. Instead of promoting the diffusion of wealth and population, the federal government was promoting their concentration. These events, coupled with the government's growing dependence on Britain and its estrangement from revolutionary France, led Jefferson to assume that America was returning to the "monocratic" principle overthrown in 1776.

Within a year after he took office Jefferson defined the strategy that the Republican party was to pursue throughout the 1790s. In February 1791 he advised Washington to veto Hamilton's plan to establish the Bank of the United States; the federal government could do only what the Constitution gave it explicit and unequivocal permission to do, he maintained, and the Constitution said nothing about banks or publicly sponsored monopolies. Jefferson's argument here laid the ideological groundwork of the Republican party during its period of insurgency, when it grew from a small faction of anti-Hamiltonians centered in Virginia and New York to a large national movement of small farmers, planters and mechanics that controlled the presidency, Congress and nearly every state house in the Union. Thus the Republicans assumed, as had the early Federalists, that the federal government was a mere component in the system of checks and balances and, as such, exercised only negative and judicatory functions. In the most extreme version of this doctrine, propounded in his Kentucky Resolutions of 1798, Jefferson went so far as to affirm the states' right to nullify federal law for which there was no Constitutional warrant.

The party conflicts of the period have given rise to the belief, or rather myth, that Republicans in general and Jefferson in particular were not only anti-Hamiltonian and anti-Federalist, but also anti-nationalist, pro-states' rights, and even in favor of returning to the anarchy of the pre-Constitutional period. But if this were so it would be hard to understand why there was a Republican party to begin with, and why Jefferson, between 1790 and 1800, spent seven years in the federal government. Moreover, if the political context of Jefferson's actions at this time were examined more closely it would be seen that his principal concern was to advance the interests of the yeoman class. He opposed the Bank of the United States because it was to be an *anti-agrarian* monopoly. And he wrote the Kentucky Resolutions because he feared, rightly as it turned out, that with the passage of the Alien and Sedition Acts in 1798 the government was about to begin a purge of Republican leaders.

The central conflict before 1800, it should be emphasized again, was concerned less with the degree than with the direction and ends of federal power and the social groups that this power should serve. Simply stated, Jefferson and Hamilton represented opposing conceptions of the national good and of the responsibilities the government should undertake to advance it.

The measure of Jefferson's attachment to the Union may be gauged from a remarkable letter written on June 1, 1798, only weeks before the Alien and Sedition Acts were passed, to his friend John Taylor, who had proposed that some of the Southern states secede from the Union.

Be this as it may, [Jefferson wrote] in every free and deliberating society, there must, from the nature of man, be opposite parties, and violent dissentions and discords; and one of these, for the most part, must prevail over the other for a longer or shorter time. Perhaps this party division is necessary to induce each to watch and relate to the people the proceedings of the other. But if on a temporary superiority of the one party, the other is to resort to a scission of the Union, no federal government can ever exist. If to rid ourselves of the present rule of Massachusetts and Connecticut, we break the Union, will the evil stop there? Suppose the New England States alone cut off, will our nature be changed? Are we not men still to the south of that, and with all the passions of men? Immediately, we shall see a Pennsylvania and a Virginia party arise in the residuary confederacy, and the public mind will be distracted with the same party spirit. What a game too will the one party have in their hands, by eternally threatening the other

that unless they do so and so, they will join their northern neighbors. If we reduce our Union to Virginia and
North Carolina, immediately the conflict will be established between the representatives of these two States,
and they will end by breaking into their simple units.
Seeing, therefore, that an association of men who will
not quarrel with one another is a thing which never yet
existed, from the greatest confederacy of nations down
to a town meeting or a vestry; seeing that we must have
somebody to quarrel with, I had rather keep our New
England associates for that purpose, than to see our
bickerings transferred to others. . . . A little patience,
and we shall see the reign of witches pass over, their
spells dissolved, and the people recovering their true
sight, restoring their government to its true principles.

As President, Jefferson acted in accordance with his commitment to agrarianism and to his ideal of a yeoman civilization rising beyond the Appalachians. In doing so, he was as
pragmatic, as free in construing federal authority, as he
thought it necessary to be. Hamilton had long before seen
this possibility. "It is a fact, which I have frequently mentioned," Hamilton wrote in 1800, "that while we were in the
administration together, he was generally for a large construction of Executive authority." To be sure, Jefferson was true
to his promises of the 1790s: he reduced the national debt,
removed all internal taxes, drastically cut down the size of
the armed forces and allowed the Alien and Sedition Acts
to expire. But he kept his policy of retrenchment and
frugality in government, and his solicitude for states' rights,
within the limits defined by his larger objectives.

The most important deed of his administration, the Louisiana Purchase, is a case in point. The Louisiana Territory,
which comprised a land area nearly as large as the United
States, had been by turns a French and a Spanish possession before Napoleon took it back in 1802 as the first step
in his grand design to add the New World to his empire. When
it appeared that Napoleon might send an army to New Orleans, Jefferson was prepared to "marry" the United States "to
the British fleet and nation," a step that Hamilton had never

proposed taking. When Napoleon suddenly offered to sell Louisiana in April 1803—his plan of conquest having run aground in Haiti—Jefferson unhesitatingly accepted, even though the Constitution failed to give the federal government express permission to acquire new territories. Likewise, when Napoleon asked nearly fifteen million dollars for it, Jefferson promptly paid the sum, thereby significantly increasing the national debt. Given his long-range hopes, Jefferson really had no choice but to strike as soon as the iron was on the anvil. His justification might have been uttered by any militant Federalist in the 1790s. "I know," he asserted in his Second Inaugural Address, "that the acquisition of Louisiana has been disapproved by some, from a candid apprehension that the enlargement of our territory would endanger its Union. But who can limit the extent to which the federative principle may operate effectively? The larger our association, the less it will be shaken by local passions. . . ."

With the purchase of Louisiana, the government took on an immensely increased responsibility. The country was now almost a continent; Jefferson worried about how it could be drawn closer together into an integral, self-sufficient community. The main preoccupation of his second term was to devise a national plan, with the consent of the states and by means of a constitutional amendment, for using surplus federal revenue to subsidize "public education, roads, rivers, canals and other such objects of public improvement," as he put it in his message to Congress in 1806. "By these operations new channels of communications will be open between the States; the lines of separation will disappear, their interests will be identified, and their union cemented by new and indissoluble ties." Among his more daring suggestions along these lines was a "national establishment for education." He maintained that "a public institution can alone supply those sciences which, though rarely called for, are yet necessary to complete the circle, all the parts of which contribute to the improvement of the country, and some of them to its preservation." With these proposals, which were not to be enacted on any appreciable scale until the twentieth century, Jefferson went beyond anything the Federalists had ever suggested.

By the time Jefferson retired in 1809 the frontier had bred a new type of Republican, who was at once more expansionist, more nationalist and more federalist than his Eastern counterpart. The particular needs of Western settlers forced them to rely on paternalistic government to secure cheap land, free access to the sea, internal improvements and easy credit. Their appetite for new territories was insatiable, and war against the colonial powers of the New World, Britain and Spain, held no terrors for them. In their more visionary moments they saw America extending from sea to sea, from pole to pole. They raised Jefferson's modest ideal of agrarian nationalism into a vaulting, aggressive ideology. The acquisition of West Florida in 1810 resulted directly, and the War of 1812 indirectly, from the political power that these Republican "war hawks" had come to wield in national affairs.

The settlement of the West coincided with the sudden rise of industry in the North and that of cotton production in the South. Gone, then, was the pristine Jeffersonian ideal of a homogeneously agrarian civilization. Under the administrations of Jefferson's hand-picked successors, Madison and Monroe, the Republican party evolved into a grand coalition of sectional and economic interests, with the federal government acting as their broker and seeing to it that they maintained a proper equilibrium. A neo-Hamiltonian system had emerged. A Second Bank of the United States was chartered in 1816, and in the same year the government for the first time imposed a protective tariff—in effect a subsidy to American producers—on a variety of manufactured goods. Both these flagrantly Hamiltonian measures were passed by a Republican Congress and signed by Madison, Jefferson's closest collaborator.

What became of the Federalist party during this time? Its history provides an instructive commentary on the age of Jeffersonian Republicanism. Jefferson's "atheism" and "anarchism" troubled Federalists less than the long-term effects of his expansionist policies; they knew that every state coming into the Union, being militantly agrarian, diminished that much more their chances of ever taking power again.

They fought against the Louisiana Purchase by invoking Jefferson's constitutional arguments. When this did not avail, the extreme Federalists of New England hatched a wild scheme to establish a seven-state Northern confederation. How badly they had calculated the temper of the people even in their own section may be judged by the fact that in the 1804 election every one of the New England states except Connecticut went for Jefferson. The Federalists thereafter shrank to a small, embittered opposition.

The party's fortunes rose, however, during the period of Republican diplomatic troubles between 1807 and 1815, and its appeal to states' rights sentiment found a correspondingly wider appeal. With the resumption of war in Europe, American shipping was caught between Napoleon's restrictions and Britain's. Jefferson's fixed policy was to preserve the peace at all costs, and at the same time to protect American interests and dignity. Driven to extremities, he decided late in 1807 to embargo practically all trade with foreign countries. But despite a series of enforcement acts that gave federal inspectors extraordinary powers of search and confiscation, the embargo was violated with impunity, especially in New England and New York. Moreover, none of the belligerents suffered from its effects as much as America did. With the laws thus flouted and public opinion turning against him, Jefferson lifted the embargo just before retiring from the presidency.

Northern opposition to Republican diplomacy mounted as every attempt by Madison to force the belligerents to modify their violations of American neutrality failed; this succession of failures culminated in the declaration of war on Britain in 1812. Federalists vehemently turned against the government, and in 1814 representatives from the New England states convened at Hartford to register their "interposition" against federal authority. This was to be the first step toward reforming the Union. But the Federalists succeeded only in adding irony to farce. The offspring of Hamilton had become the advocates of nullification and state sovereignty. The Hartford Convention, which ended just before news of the peace treaty arrived, finished the Federalist party in fact, though it did put up a candidate in the 1816 presidential election. The economic interests that had always supported the Federalist cause, however, had no reason to grieve over the demise of their party, for they had already found a secure place for themselves within the Republican camp.

Federalists could also rejoice in the fact that the Supreme Court successfully held out against the Republican tide. In his remarkable thirty-five-year tenure as Chief Justice, John Marshall maintained, even enlarged, the prerogatives that the Constitutional Fathers had assigned the Court. They had envisioned the Court as a decisive check on the states to ensure that contracts, or property rights, remained safe from the fickle will of majorities. True to that vision in an age of advancing democracy, Marshall, in one precedent-setting decision after another, struck down state laws that attempted to modify or void contracts, some of which had been signed many decades before and had become monopolies in restraint of trade. To Marshall, as to conservatives in general, a contract once made was binding and irreversible; it was the only security that creditors and men of property had against the enfranchised lower classes. Marshall also struck down state laws that in any way infringed on federal authority or prevented its broadest possible application, under the implied powers of the Constitution, to society as a whole.

Marshall followed the early Federalists in one further respect. Just as the federal government was sovereign over all other jurisdictions, so, he argued, the Supreme Court was sovereign over the other branches of the federal government. This was the burden of his first great decision, *Marbury* v. *Madison* (1803), in which he affirmed the doctrine of judicial review. It was for the Court, he declared, to pass final judgment on the constitutionality of any congressional or presidential act. But Marshall shrewdly avoided carrying the doctrine to the point of open conflict; he was content to pronounce it as an obiter dictum, and on one occasion only. He knew that he could not impose judicial review on a deeply hostile Republican Congress and President. Judicial review, in fact, was used sparingly until the late nineteenth century, when the Court, invoking the spirit of Marshall—as Marshall had invoked that of Hamilton—again became the main bulwark of property rights in America.

Thomas Jefferson, *Notes on Virginia*
1781

[Jefferson wrote the *Notes* in response to a request from a French diplomat who was interested in the customs, laws and natural conditions of the American states. Of the book's twenty-three chapters, each an answer to a particular query, numbers XVIII and XIX best reveal Jefferson's radical agrarian philosophy. His strictures against slavery were notable in view of the fact that he was one of the largest slaveowners in the country.]

QUERY XVIII

The particular customs and manners that may happen to be received in that State?

It is difficult to determine on the standard by which the manners of a nation may be tried, whether *catholic* or *particular*. It is more difficult for a native to bring to that standard the manners of his own nation, familiarized to him by habit. There must doubtless be an unhappy influence on the manners of our people produced by the existence of slavery among us. The whole commerce between master and slave is a perpetual exercise of the most boisterous passions, the most unremitting despotism on the one part, and degrading submissions on the other. Our children see this, and learn to imitate it; for man is an imitative animal. This quality is the germ of all education in him. From his cradle to his grave he is learning to do what he sees others do. If a parent could find no motive either in his philanthropy or his self-love, for restraining the intemperance of passion towards his slave, it should always be a sufficient one that his child is present. But generally it is not sufficient. The parent storms, the child looks on, catches the lineaments of wrath, puts on the same airs in the circle of smaller slaves, gives a loose to the worst of passions, and thus nursed, educated, and daily exercised in tyranny, cannot but be stamped by it with odious peculiarities.

The man must be a prodigy who can retain his manners and morals undepraved by such circumstances. And with what execration should the statesman be loaded, who, permitting one half the citizens thus to trample on the rights of the other, transforms those into despots, and these into enemies, destroys the morals of the one part, and the *amor patriae* of the other. For if a slave can have a country in this world, it must be any other in preference to that in which he is born to live and labor for another; in which he must lock up the faculties of his nature, contribute as far as depends on his individual endeavors to the evanishment of the human race, or entail his own miserable condition on the endless generations proceeding from him. With the morals of the people, their industry also is destroyed. For in a warm climate, no man will labor for himself who can make another labor for him. This is so true, that of the proprietors of slaves a very small proportion indeed are ever seen to labor. And can the liberties of a nation be thought secure when we have removed their only firm basis, a conviction in the minds of the people that these liberties are of the gift of God? That they are not to be violated but with His wrath? Indeed I tremble for my country when I reflect that God is just; that his justice cannot sleep forever; that considering numbers, nature and natural means only, a revolution of the wheel of fortune, an exchange of situation is among possible events; that it may become probably by supernatural interference! The Almighty has no attribute which can take side with us in such a contest. But it is impossible to be temperate and to pursue this subject through the various considerations of policy, of morals, of history natural and civil. We must be contented to hope they will force their way into every one's mind. I think a change already perceptible, since the origin of the present revolution. The spirit of the master is abating, that of the slave rising from the dust, his condition mollifying, the way I hope preparing, under the auspices of heaven, for a total emancipation, and that this is disposed, in the order of events, to be with the consent of the masters, rather than by their extirpation.

QUERY XIX

The present state of manufactures, commerce, interior and exterior trade?

We never had an interior trade of any importance. Our exterior commerce has suffered very much from the beginning of the present contest. During this time we have manufactured within our families the most necessary articles of clothing. Those of cotton will bear some comparison with the same kinds of manufacture in Europe; but those of wool, flax and hemp are very coarse, unsightly, and unpleasant; and such is our attachment to agriculture, and such our preference for foreign manufactures, that be it wise or unwise, our people will certainly return as soon as they can, to the raising raw materials, and exchanging them for finer manufactures than they are able to execute themselves.

The political economists of Europe have established it as a principle, that every State should endeavor to manufacture for itself; and this principle, like many others, we transfer to America, without calculating the difference of circumstance which should often produce a difference of result. In Europe the lands are either cultivated, or locked up against the cultivator. Manufacture must therefore be resorted to of necessity not of choice, to support the surplus of their people. But we have an immensity of land courting the industry of the husbandman. Is it best then that all our citizens should be employed in its improvement, or that one half should be called off from that to exercise manufactures and handicraft arts for the other? Those who labor in the earth are the chosen people of God, if ever He had a chosen people, whose breasts He has made His peculiar deposit for substantial and genuine virtue. It is the focus in which he keeps alive that sacred fire, which otherwise might escape from the face of the earth. Corruption of morals in the mass of cultivators is a phenomenon of which no age nor nation has furnished an example. It is the mark set on those, who, not looking up to heaven, to their own soil and industry, as does the husbandman, for their subsistence, depend for it on casualties and caprice of customers.

Dependence begets subservience and venality, suffocates the germ of virtue, and prepares fit tools for the designs of ambition. This, the natural progress and consequence of the arts, has sometimes perhaps been retarded by accidental circumstances; but, generally speaking, the proportion which the aggregate of the other classes of citizens bears in any State to that of its husbandmen, is the proportion of its unsound to its healthy parts, and is a good enough barometer whereby to measure its degree of corruption. While we have land to labor then, let us never wish to see our citizens occupied at a workbench, or twirling a distaff. Carpenters, masons, smiths, are wanting in husbandry; but, for the general operations of manufacture, let our workshops remain in Europe. It is better to carry provisions and materials to workmen there, than bring them to the provisions and materials, and with them their manners and principles. The loss by the transportation of commodities across the Atlantic will be made up in happiness and permanence of government. The mobs of great cities add just so much to the support of pure government, as sores do to the strength of the human body. It is the manners and spirit of a people which preserve a republic in vigor. A degeneracy in these is a canker which soon eats to the heart of its laws and constitution. . . .

Richard Henry Lee, *Letters of a Federal Farmer*
1787

[Lee had been a leading Virginia radical since the Stamp Act more than twenty years before. It was he who formally introduced in the Continental Congress the resolution proposing that America declare itself independent of Great Britain. The Constitution brought him into the lists again. His series of letters, published when the states were debating ratification of the Constitution, was the best critique of Federalism before the party battles of the 1790s. Following is the first letter.]

Dear Sir,

My letters to you last winter, on the subject of a well-balanced national government for the United States, were the result of free enquiry; when I passed from that subject to enquiries relative to our commerce, revenues, past administration, etc. I anticipated the anxieties I feel, on carefully examining the plan of government proposed by the convention. It appears to be a plan retaining some federal features; but to be the first important step, and to aim strongly at one consolidated government of the United States. It leaves the powers of government, and the representation of the people, so unnaturally divided between the general and state governments, that the operations of our system must be very uncertain. My uniform federal attachments, and the interest I have in the protection of property, and a steady execution of the laws, will convince you, that, if I am under any bias at all, it is in favor of any general system which shall promise those advantages. The instability of our laws increases my wishes for firm and steady government; but then, I can consent to no government, which, in my opinion, is not calculated equally to preserve the rights of all orders of men in the community. My object has been to join with those who have endeavored to supply the defects in the forms of our governments by a steady and proper administration of them. Though I have long apprehended that fraudulent debtors, and embarrassed men, on the one hand, and men, on the other, unfriendly to republican equality, would produce an uneasiness among the people, and prepare the way, not for cool and deliberate reforms in the governments, but for changes calculated to promote the interests of particular orders of men. . . .

The present moment discovers a new face in our affairs. Our object has been all along, to reform our federal systems, and to strengthen our governments—to establish peace, order and justice in the community—but a new object now presents. The plan of government now proposed is evidently calculated totally to change, in time, our condition as a people. Instead of being thirteen republics, under a federal head, it is clearly designed to make us one consolidated government. Of this, I think, I shall fully convince you, in my following letters on this subject. This consolidation of the states has been the object of several men in this country for some time past. Whether such a change can ever be effected in any manner; whether it can be effected without convulsions and civil wars; whether such a change will not totally destroy the liberties of this country—time only can determine.

To have a just idea of the government before us, and to show that a consolidated one is the object in view, it is necessary not only to examine the plan, but also its history, and the politics of its particular friends.

The confederation was formed when great confidence was placed in the voluntary exertions of individuals, and of the respective states; and the framers of it, to guard against usurpation, so limited and checked the powers, that, in many respects, they are inadequate to the exigencies of the union. We find, therefore, members of congress urging alterations in the federal system almost as soon as it was adopted. It was early proposed to vest congress with powers to levy an impost, to regulate trade, etc. but such was known to be the caution of the states in parting with power, that the vestment, even of these, was proposed to be under several checks and limitations. During the war, the general confusion, and the introduction of paper money, infused in the minds of people vague ideas respecting government and credit. We expected too much from the return of peace, and of course we have been disappointed. Our government has been new and unsettled; and several legislatures, by making tender, suspension, and paper money laws, have given just cause of uneasiness to creditors. By these and other causes, several orders of men in the community have been prepared, by degrees, for a change of government; and this very abuse of power in the legislatures, which, in some cases, has been charged upon the democratic part of the community, has furnished aristocratical men with those very weapons, and those very means, with which, in great measure, they are rapidly effecting their favorite object. And should an oppressive government be the consequence of the proposed change, posterity may reproach not only a few overbearing unprincipled men, but those parties in the states which have misused their powers.

The conduct of several legislatures, touching paper money,

and tender laws, has prepared many honest men for changes in government, which otherwise they would not have thought of—when by the evils, on the one hand, and by the secret instigations of artful men, on the other, the minds of men became sufficiently uneasy, a bold step was taken, which is usually followed by a revolution, or a civil war. A general convention for mere commercial purposes was moved for—the authors of this measure saw that the people's attention was turned solely to the amendment of the federal system; and that, had the idea of a total change been started, probably no state would have appointed members to the convention. The idea of destroying, ultimately, the state government, and forming one consolidated system, could not have been admitted—a convention, therefore, merely for vesting in congress power to regulate trade was proposed. This was pleasing to the commercial towns: and the landed people had little or no concern about it. September, 1786, a few men from the middle states met at Annapolis, and hastily proposed a convention to be held in May, 1787, for the purpose, generally, of amending the confederation—this was done before the delegates of Massachusetts, and of the other states arrived—still not a word was said about destroying the old constitution, and making a new one—The states still unsuspecting, and not aware that they were passing the Rubicon, appointed members to the new convention, for the sole and express purpose of revising and amending the confederation —and, probably, not one man in ten thousand in the United States, till within these ten or twelve days, had an idea that the old ship was to be destroyed, and he put to the alternative of embarking in the new ship presented, or of being left in danger of sinking—The States, I believe, universally supposed the convention would report alterations in the confederation, which would pass an examination in congress, and after being agreed to there, would be confirmed by all the legislatures, or be rejected. Virginia made a very respectable appointment, and placed at the head of it the first man in America: In this appointment there was a mixture of political characters; but Pennsylvania appointed principally those men who are esteemed aristocratical. Here the favorite moment for changing the government was evidently discerned by a few men, who seized it with address. Ten other states appointed, and tho' they chose men principally connected with commerce and the judicial department yet they appointed many good republican characters—had they all attended we should now see, I am persuaded a better system presented. The non-attendance of eight or nine men, who were appointed members of the convention, I shall ever consider as a very unfortunate event to the United States.—Had they attended I am pretty clear that the result of the convention would not have had that strong tendency to aristocracy now discernible in every part of the plan. There would not have been so great an accumulation of powers, especially as to the internal police of the country, in a few hands, as the constitution reported proposes to vest in them—the young visionary men, and the consolidating aristocracy, would have been more restrained than they have been. Eleven states met in the convention, and after four months close attention presented the new constitution, to be adopted or rejected by the people. The uneasy and fickle part of the community may be prepared to receive any form of government; but, I presume, the enlightened and substantial part will give any constitution presented for their adoption a candid and thorough examination; and silence those designing or empty men, who weakly and rashly attempt to precipitate the adoption of a system of so much importance—We shall view the convention with proper respect—and, at the same time, that we reflect there were men of abilities and integrity in it, we must recollect how disproportionably the democratic and aristocratic parts of the community were represented.—Perhaps the judicious friends and opposers of the new constitution will agree, that it is best to let it rest solely on its own merits, or be condemned for its own defects. . . .

Thomas Jefferson to George Washington
September 9, 1792

[By mid-1792 Jefferson and Hamilton were conducting open warfare within the cabinet. The President, hoping to bring about their reconciliation, wanted to know why they objected to each other. Here Jefferson tells what he thinks of Hamilton and the Hamiltonian "system."]

. . . When I embarked in the government, it was with a determination to intermeddle not at all with the Legislature, and as little as possible with my co-departments. The first and only instance of variance from the former part of my resolution, I was duped into by the Secretary of the Treasury, and made a tool for forwarding his schemes, not then sufficiently understood by me; and of all the errors of my political life, this has occasioned me the deepest regret. It has ever been my purpose to explain this to you, when, from being actors on the scene, we shall have become uninterested spectators only. The second part of my resolution has been religiously observed with the War Department; and as to that of the Treasury, has never been further swerved from than by the mere enunciation of my sentiments in conversation, and chiefly among those who, expressing the same sentiments, drew mine from me. If it has been supposed that I have ever intrigued among the members of the Legislature to defeat the plans of the Secretary of the Treasury, it is contrary to all truth. As I never had the desire to influence the members, so neither had I any other means than my friendships, which I valued too highly to risk by usurpation on their freedom of judgment, and the conscientious pursuit of their own sense of duty. That I have utterly, in my private conversations, disapproved of the system of the Secretary of the Treasury, I acknowledge and avow; and this was not merely a speculative difference. His system flowed from principles adverse to liberty, and was calculated to undermine and demolish the Republic, by creating an influence of his department over the members of the Legislature. I saw this influence actually produced, and its first fruits to be the establishment of the great outlines of his project by the votes of the very persons who, having swallowed his bait, were laying themselves out to profit by his plans; and that had these persons withdrawn, as those interested in a question ever should, the vote of the disinterested majority was clearly the reverse of what they made it. These were no longer the votes then of the representatives of the people, but of deserters from the rights and interests of the people; and it was impossible to consider their decisions, which had nothing in view but to enrich themselves, as the measures of the fair majority, which ought always to be respected. If, what was actually doing, begat uneasiness in those who wished for virtuous government, what was further proposed was not less threatening to the friends of the Constitution. For, in a report on the subject of manufactures (still to be acted on), it was expressly assumed that the General Government has a right to exercise all powers which may be for the *general welfare*, that is to say, all the legitimate powers of government; since no government has a legitimate right to do what is not for the welfare of the governed. There was, indeed, a sham limitation of the universality of this power *to cases where money is to be employed*. But about what is it that money cannot be employed? Thus the object of these plans, taken together, is to draw all the powers of government into the hands of the general Legislature, to establish means for corrupting a sufficient corps in that Legislature to divide the honest votes, and preponderate, by their own, the scale which suited, and to have the corps under the command of the Secretary of the Treasury, for the purpose of subverting, step by step, the principles of the Constitution which he has so often declared to be a thing of nothing, which must be changed. Such views might have justified something more than mere expressions of dissent, beyond which, nevertheless, I never went. Has abstinence from the department, committed to me, been equally observed by him? To say nothing of other interferences equally known, in the case of the two nations, with which we have the most intimate connections, France and England, my system was to give some satisfactory distinctions to the former, of little cost to us, in return for the solid advantages yielded us by them; and to have met the English with some restrictions which might induce them to abate their severities against our commerce. I have always supposed this coincided with your sentiments. Yet the Secretary of the Treasury, by his cabals with members of the Legislature, and by high-toned declamations on other occasions, has forced down his own system, which was exactly the reverse. He undertook, of his own authority, the conferences with the ministers of those two nations, and was, on every consultation, provided with some report of a conversation with the one or the other of them, adapted to his views. These views, thus made to prevail, their execution fell, of course, to me; and I can safely appeal to you, who have seen all my letters and proceedings, whether I have not carried them into execution as sincerely as if they had been my own, though I ever considered them as inconsistent with the honor and interest of our country. That they have been inconsistent with our interest is but too fatally proved by the stab to our navigation given by the French. So that if the question be by whose fault is it that Colonel Hamilton and myself have not drawn together? the answer will depend on that to two other questions, whose principles of administration best justify, by their purity, conscientious adherence? and which of us has, notwithstanding, stepped farthest into the control of the department of the other? . . .

Thomas Jefferson, Notes on Christoph D. Ebeling's Letter of July 20, 1795

[Ebeling, a German writing on the United States, had asked Jefferson for information about American politics, among other subjects. Jefferson drew up his reply—of which the following are the rough notes—while Jay's Treaty was being debated.]

The inconveniences of an inefficient government, driving the people as is usual, into the opposite extreme, the elections to the first Congress ran very much in favor of those who were known to favor a very strong government. Hence the anti-republicans appeared a considerable majority in both houses of Congress. They pressed forward the plan therefore of strengthening all the features of the government which gave it resemblance to an English constitution, of adopting the English forms and principles of administration, and of forming like them a monied interest, by means of a funding system, not calculated to pay the public debt, but to render it perpetual, and to make it an engine in the hands of the executive branch of government which, added to the great patronage it possessed in the disposal of public offices, might enable it to assume by degrees a kingly authority. The biennial period of Congress being too short to betray to the people, spread over this great continent, this train of things during the first Congress, little change was made in the members to the second. But in the mean time two very distinct parties had formed in Congress; and before the third election, the people in general became apprised of the game which was playing for drawing over them a kind of government which they never had in contemplation. At the 3d election therefore a decided majority of Republicans were sent to the lower house of Congress; and as information spread still farther among the people after the 4th election the anti-republicans have become a weak minority. But the members of the Senate being changed but once in 6 years, the completion of that body will be much slower in its assimilation to that of the people. This will account for the differences which may appear in the proceedings and spirit of the two houses. Still however it is inevitable that the Senate will at length be formed to the republican model of the people, and the two houses of the legislature, once brought to act on the true principles of the Constitution, backed by the people, will be able to defeat the plan of sliding us into monarchy, and to keep the Executive within republican bounds, notwithstanding the immense patronage it possesses in the disposal of public offices, notwithstanding it has been able to draw into this vortex the judiciary branch of the government and by their expectancy of sharing the other offices in the Executive gift to make them auxiliary to the Executive in all its views instead of forming a balance between that and the legislature as it was originally intended and notwithstanding the funding phalanx which a respect for public faith must protect, though it was engaged by false brethren. Two parties then do exist within the U.S. they embrace respectively the following descriptions of persons.

The Anti-republicans consist of

1. The old refugees and tories.

2. British merchants residing among us, and composing the main body of our merchants.

3. American merchants trading on British capital. Another great portion.

4. Speculators and holders in the banks and public funds.

5. Officers of the federal government with some exceptions.

6. Office-hunters, willing to give up principles for places. A numerous and noisy tribe.

7. Nervous persons, whose languid fibres have more analogy with a passive than active state of things.

The Republican part of our Union comprehends

1. The entire body of landholders throughout the United States.

2. The body of labourers, not being landholders, whether in husbanding or the arts.

The latter is to the aggregate of the former party probably as 500 to one; but their wealth is not as disproportionate, though it is also greatly superior, and is in truth the foundation of that of their antagonists. Trifling as are the numbers of the Anti-republican party, there are circumstances which give them an appearance of strength and numbers. They all live in cities, together, and can act in a body readily and at all times; they give chief employment to the newspapers, and therefore have most of them under their command. The Agricultural interest is dispersed over a great extent of country, have little means of intercommunication with each other, and feeling their own strength and will, are conscious that a single exertion of these will at any time crush the machinations against their government. As in the commerce of human life, there are commodities adapted to every demand, so there are newspapers adapted to the Anti-republican palate, and others to the republican. . . .

Thomas Jefferson to Elbridge Gerry
January 26, 1799

[Here Jefferson candidly defines his political principles in the course of answering the Federalist charge that he is pro-French. Gerry, a Massachusetts Republican, had just returned from France, where he had been on a diplomatic mission.]

. . . I do then, with sincere zeal, wish an inviolable pres-ervation of our present federal Constitution, according to the true sense in which it was adopted by the States, that in which it was advocated by its friends, and not that which its enemies apprehended, who therefore became its enemies; and I am opposed to the monarchising its features by the forms of its administration, with a view to conciliate a first transition to a President and Senate for life, and from that to an hereditary tenure of these offices, and thus to worm out the elective principle. I am for preserving to the States the powers not yielded by them to the Union, and to the legisla-ture of the Union its constitutional share in the division of powers; and I am not for transferring all the powers of the States to the General Government, and all those of that gov-ernment to the executive branch. I am for a government rigorously frugal and simple, applying all the possible savings of the public revenue to the discharge of the national debt; and not for a multiplication of officers and salaries merely to make partisans, and for increasing, by every device, the public debt, on the principle of its being a public blessing. I am for relying, for internal defence, on our militia solely, till actual invasion, and for such a naval force only as may pro-tect our coasts and harbors from such depredations as we have experienced; and not for a standing army in time of peace, which may overawe the public sentiment; nor for a navy, which, by its own expenses and the eternal wars in which it will implicate us, will grind us with public burthens, and sink us under them. I am for free commerce with all nations; political connection with none; and little or no diplomatic establishment. And I am not for linking ourselves by new treaties with the quarrels of Europe; entering that field of slaughter to preserve their balance, or joining in the confederacy of kings to war against the principles of liberty. I am for freedom of religion, and against all manœuvres to bring about a legal ascendancy of one sect over another: for freedom of the press, and against all violations of the Constitution to silence by force and not by reason the complaints or criticisms, just or unjust, of our citizens against the conduct of their agents. And I am for encouraging the progress of science in all its branches; and not for raising a hue and cry against the sacred name of philosophy; for awing the human mind by stories of raw-head and bloody bones to a distrust of its own vision, and to repose implicitly on that of others; to go backwards instead of forwards to look for improvement; to believe that government, religion, morality, and every other science were in the highest perfection in ages of the darkest ignorance, and that nothing can ever be devised more perfect than what was established by our forefathers. To these I will add, that I was a sincere well-wisher to the success of the French revolution, and still wish it may end in the establishment of a free and well-ordered republic; but I have not been insensible under the atrocious depredations they have committed on our commerce. The first object of my heart is my own country. In that is embarked my family, my fortune, and my own existence. I have not one farthing of interest, nor one fibre of attachment out of it, nor a single motive of preference of any one nation to another, but in proportion as they are more or less friendly to us. But though deeply feeling the injuries of France, I did not think war the surest means of redressing them. I did believe, that a mission sincerely disposed to preserve peace, would obtain for us a peaceable and honorable settlement and retribution; and I appeal to you to say, whether this might not have been obtained, if either of your colleagues had been of the same sentiment with yourself.

These, my friend, are my principles; they are unquestionably the principles of the great body of our fellow-citizens, and I know there is not one of them which is not yours also. In truth, we never differed but on one ground, the funding system; and as, from the moment of its being adopted by the constituted authorities, I became religiously principled in the sacred discharge of it to the uttermost farthing, we are united now even on that single ground of difference. . . .

Thomas Jefferson to Mazzei
December 30, 1801

[After ten months in office Jefferson was pleased with his progress in carrying out his Republican promises. In this letter to an old Italian friend he summarizes his accomplishments.]

. . . You cannot imagine what progress republican principles have made here. Business is conducted calmly, and with unanimous consent in both Chambers. The Tories are generally either converted or silenced by rational evidence or by prudence.

All the excess expenditures which were turning the ship of state toward monarchy are being rapidly abolished, and the fundamental principles of 1775 once more assert themselves vigorously. Briefly, there is every proof that people are enjoying life, although none have exclusive privileges, nor are there proscriptions for any except those guilty of infamous conduct.

Our country will be a haven for the oppressed, without fourteen years being necessary for qualification, and we have found a way of carrying on affairs without any need for an Act of Sedition. The appointments made by Mr. Adams to the District Courts, will, necessarily, have to be abandoned; the taxes on press and other things will be abolished; the '94 are suppressed; and, finally, all that is oppressive will be removed, and every encouragement will be given to naturalization, to commerce, to industry and to right conduct. You would really be surprised by the change which followed your departure. Those who wanted to burn the Jacobins now confess that the present government clearly shows a better knowledge of what is most salutary for this country than any which preceded it. . . .

Thomas Jefferson, Third Annual Message
October 17, 1803

[How broadly Jefferson construed his powers was amply demonstrated by his purchase of the Louisiana Territory. He wanted a constitutional amendment to give him express authority to take over the Territory, but there was not enough time; Napoleon might change his mind. And so the agreement with France was signed on April 30, 1803. It remained only for the Senate to approve it and the House to appropriate the money.]

To the Senate and House of Representatives of the United States,—

In calling you together, fellow citizens, at an earlier day than was contemplated by the act of the last session of Congress, I have not been insensible to the personal inconveniences necessarily resulting from an unexpected change in your arrangements. But matters of great public concernment have rendered this call necessary, and the interest you feel in these will supersede in your minds all private considerations.

Congress witnessed, at their last session, the extraordinary agitation produced in the public mind by the suspension of our right of deposit at the port of New Orleans, no assignment of another place having been made according to treaty. They were sensible that the continuance of that privation would be more injurious to our nation than any consequences which could flow from any mode of redress, but reposing just confidence in the good faith of the government whose officer had committed the wrong, friendly and reasonable representations were resorted to, and the right of deposit was restored.

Previous, however, to this period, we had not been unaware of the danger to which our peace would be perpetually exposed while so important a key to the commerce of the western country remained under foreign power. Difficulties, too, were presenting themselves as to the navigation of other streams, which, arising within our territories, pass through those adjacent. Propositions had, therefore, been authorized for obtaining, on fair conditions, the sovereignty of New Orleans, and of other possessions in that quarter interesting to our quiet, to such extent as was deemed practicable; and the provisional appropriation of two millions of dollars, to be applied and accounted for by the president of the United States, intended as part of the price, was considered as conveying the sanction of Congress to the acquisition proposed. The enlightened Government of France saw, with just discernment, the importance to both nations of such liberal arrangements as might best and permanently promote the peace, friendship, and interests of both; and the property and sovereignty of all Louisiana, which had been restored to them, have on certain conditions been transferred to the United States by instruments bearing date the 30th of April last. When these shall have received the constitutional sanction of the senate, they will without delay be communicated to the representatives also, for the exercise of their functions, as to those conditions which are within the powers vested by the constitution in Congress. While the property and sovereignty of the Mississippi and its waters secure an independent outlet for the produce of the western States, and an uncontrolled navigation through their whole course, free from collision with other powers and the dangers to our peace from that source, the fertility of the country, its climate and extent, promise in due season important aids to our treasury, an ample provision for our posterity, and a widespread field for the blessings of freedom and equal laws.

With the wisdom of Congress it will rest to take those ulterior measures which may be necessary for the immediate occupation and temporary government of the country; for its incorporation into our Union; for rendering the change of government a blessing to our newly-adopted brethren; for securing to them the rights of conscience and of property; for confirming to the Indian inhabitants their occupancy and self-government, establishing friendly and commercial relations with them, and for ascertaining the geography of the country acquired. Such materials for your information, relative to its affairs in general, as the short space of time has permitted me to collect, will be laid before you when the subject shall be in a state for your consideration. . . .

Thomas Jefferson, Second Inaugural Address
March 4, 1805

[Jefferson's federalism can be readily discerned in his Second Inaugural, in which he invokes Hamiltonian images in discussing the integrity of the Union and the leadership that the federal government should provide (through a constitutional amendment) to build up the country, encourage the arts, education, etc.]

Proceeding, fellow citizens, to that qualification which the constitution requires, before my entrance on the charge again conferred upon me, it is my duty to express the deep sense I entertain of this new proof of confidence from my fellow citizens at large, and the zeal with which it inspires me, so to conduct myself as may best satisfy their just expectations.

On taking this station on a former occasion, I declared the principles on which I believed it my duty to administer the affairs of our commonwealth. My conscience tells me that I have, on every occasion, acted up to that declaration, according to its obvious import, and to the understanding of every candid mind.

In the transaction of your foreign affairs, we have endeavored to cultivate the friendship of all nations, and especially of those with which we have the most important relations. We have done them justice on all occasions, favored where favor was lawful, and cherished mutual interests and intercourse on fair and equal terms. We are firmly convinced, and we act on that conviction, that with nations, as with individuals, our interests soundly calculated, will ever be found inseparable from our moral duties; and history bears witness to the fact, that a just nation is taken on its word, when recourse is had to armaments and wars to bridle others.

At home, fellow citizens, you best know whether we have done well or ill. The suppression of unnecessary offices, of useless establishments and expenses, enabled us to discontinue our internal taxes. These covering our land with officers, and opening our doors to their intrusions, had already begun that process of domiciliary vexation which, once entered, is scarcely to be restrained from reaching successively every article of produce and property. If among these taxes some minor ones fell which had not been inconvenient, it was because their amount would not have paid the officers who collected them, and because, if they had any merit, the state authorities might adopt them, instead of others less approved.

The remaining revenue on the consumption of foreign articles, is paid cheerfully by those who can afford to add foreign luxuries to domestic comforts, being collected on our seaboards and frontiers only, and incorporated with the transactions of our mercantile citizens, it may be the pleasure and pride of an American to ask, what farmer, what mechanic, what laborer, ever sees a tax-gatherer of the United States? These contributions enable us to support the current expenses of the government, to fulfil contracts with foreign nations, to extinguish the native right of soil within our limits, to extend those limits, and to apply such a surplus to our public debts, as places at a short day their final redemption, and that redemption once effected, the revenue thereby liberated may, by a just repartition among the states, and a corresponding amendment of the constitution, be applied, *in time of peace*, to rivers, canals, roads, arts, manufactures, education, and other great objects within each state. *In time of war*, if injustice, by ourselves or others, must sometimes produce war, increased as the same revenue will be increased by population and consumption, and aided by other resources reserved for that crisis, it may meet within the year all the expenses of the year, without encroaching on the rights of future generations, by burdening them with the debts of the past. War will then be but a suspension of useful works, and a return to a state of peace, a return to the progress of improvement.

I have said, fellow citizens, that the income reserved had enabled us to extend our limits; but that extension may possibly pay for itself before we are called on, and in the meantime, may keep down the accruing interest; in all events, it will repay the advances we have made. I know that the acquisition of Louisiana has been disapproved by some, from a candid apprehension that the enlargement of our territory would endanger its union. But who can limit the extent to which the federative principle may operate effectively? The larger our association, the less will it be shaken by local passions; and in any view, is it not better that the opposite bank of the Mississippi should be settled by our own brethren and children, than by strangers of another family? With which shall we be most likely to live in harmony and friendly intercourse? . . .

John Randolph, Speech in the House of Representatives March 13, 1806

[Vain, flamboyant John Randolph of Roanoke had for some time been Jefferson's chief lieutenant in the House. But Jefferson's strong executive leadership and nationalist policies, in particular his purchase of Louisiana, alienated Randolph, who remained an uncompromising advocate of states' rights. By 1806 Randolph had organized his own small group of extreme Republicans, sometimes called Quids, who challenged the administration. It was during a House debate over the administration's Non-Importation Bill, which threatened to ban goods from countries attacking American ships, that Randolph publicly announced his break with Jefferson.]

Mr. RANDOLPH. . . . I, who profess to yield a compliance not only to the laws of necessity, but of probabilities, and who consider politics as only a science of probabilities, can no longer find a medium between myself and those who disclaim all regard to the laws of necessity, and am obliged to confess that I am among the number of those who would negotiate with Great Britain.

I am perfectly aware of the tedious time the Committee

must have had in listening to my remarks—not more so, I assure you, to them than to myself. I am aware of the arguments offered directly out of doors, and indirectly in this House, against the course which I believe it is for the interest of this nation to pursue. One of the first causes of surprise which presented itself to me on coming to the seat of Government was, that, while the people of the United States thought all eyes were fixed on the shores of the Atlantic, all eyes were in fact fixed on the half-way house between this and Georgetown—that the question was not what we should do with France, or Spain, or England, but who should be the next President. And at this moment, every motion that is made—I do not mean, in the parliamentary sense of the word, at this place—is made with a view to the occupation of that House. And it is for this reason that certain men are to be put down, and certain men are to be put up. As I have said before, I have conceived it the greatest happiness attendant on the Government of this people, that all their political relations, the different parties and their connexions and bearings and effects, could be debated in the face of the nation. Now, we are told from good authority, that there is a certain party called the Federal party, and that there are other parties in the United States, called Republican parties. Well, sir; certain gentlemen have been held up as willing to court the attention and support of the Federal party—men by whom no villain has been spared, let him belong to what party he may—men by whom no villany has been spared, to whatever party it may have attached. So much for Federalism. There is another question relative to what is generally called *quiddism*. I am willing to meet gentlemen on that ground. If we belong to the third party, be it so. I am willing to meet them on other ground.

[There was here a loud call to order, in which Mr. THOMAS joined. The SPEAKER decided that Mr. RANDOLPH was in order. An appeal was taken to the House, who confirmed his decision.]

Mr. RANDOLPH proceeded. I am obliged to the gentleman for the respite he has given me, as I really felt much exhausted. I knew where the shoe pinched. I will take gentlemen on another principle—on the principle of Burrism, as it is called. Will gentlemen attack us on that ground? Will they say we are the rotten part of the Republican party—the go-between of any sects—the solicitors of any office—the tools of any faction? Now, sir, on the subject of Federalism—I mean no imputation to any man or party of men—are we the advocates of Federalism? Does the Administration, and especially the Department of the Navy, or does it not, administer the Government on the principle of Federalism? Has that Department ever been administered, or can it be administered on principles more Federal? There is another department—the Post Office Department—the sweetest engine ever put into the hands of an unprincipled man. Are we for administering the Government on principles of Burrism? This is a delicate subject—I speak with a full consciousness that it is. Now for the last *ism, Yazooism*. Are we Yazoo men? Have our enemies ever charged us with this? . . .

I am really sorry, Mr. Speaker, for the time I have occupied. When I came into the House yesterday, it appeared to me as if the proposition before us was to appoint a board of commissioners to settle the account current of every member with the House. We heard a great deal of palaver and blarney; but of that description which can never take me in. I abjure it. I raise my hand against it—I will never become its dupe. I am willing to allow that in the heat of debate, expressions improper for me to use, but not improper in their application to those to whom they referred, may have escaped me—the *verba ardentia* of an honest mind. I scorn to retract them. They were made in the presence of the nation, and in their presence I will defend them. I will never snivel, whatever may be the result. I have moved that the Committee rise, with a perfect knowledge of the existing circumstances. I knew the moment we adjourned over on Saturday, that the old story would be repeated, that gentlemen would seek the Lord—agree upon some given principle, that all might go together. And I have not been disappointed. But it is for you to say, whether at this moment, when you are watching your daily and nightly mails for news from Europe, when you are oscillating between Bonaparte and the coalition—you are prepared to decide ultimately on this subject. I feel for one that I am not. As to the accusation of being the apologist of Britain, it is the idlest charge that ever was made. When I first took a seat in this House I was denounced with being a French partisan, because I opposed those men who then held the reins of Government in their hands in their measures for carrying us into war with that nation; and now that I am for pursuing the same course towards Great Britain, which I was then in favor of pursuing towards France, I am charged with being the apologist of Britain. To this denunciation I am willing to submit, which all men must submit to who are not willing to risk the peace of their country.

Thomas Jefferson, Sixth Annual Message
December 2, 1806

[Here Jefferson sets forth his plan for a vast system of federally sponsored internal improvements to consolidate the Union.]

. . . The question, therefore, now comes forward,—to what other objects shall these surpluses be appropriated, and the whole surplus of impost, after the entire discharge of the public debt, and during those intervals when the purposes of war shall not call for them? Shall we suppress the impost and give that advantage to foreign over domestic manufactures? On a few articles of more general and necessary use, the suppression in due season will doubtless be right, but the great mass of the articles on which impost is paid is foreign luxuries, purchased by those only who are rich enough to afford themselves the use of them. Their patriotism would certainly prefer its continuance and application to the great purposes of the public education, roads, rivers, canals, and such other objects of public improvement as it may be thought proper to add to the constitutional enumeration of federal powers. By these operations new channels of communication will be opened between the States; the lines of separation will disappear, their interests will be identified, and their union cemented by new and indissoluble ties. Education is here placed among the articles of public care, not that it would be proposed to take its ordinary branches out of the hands of private enterprise, which manages so much better all the concerns to which it is equal; but a public institution can alone supply those sciences which, though rarely called for, are yet necessary to complete the circle, all the parts of which contribute to the improvement of the country, and some of them to its preservation. The subject is now proposed for the consideration of Congress, because, if approved by the time the State legislatures shall have deliberated on this extension of the federal trusts, and the laws shall be passed, and other arrangements made for their execution, the necessary funds will be on hand and without employment. I suppose an amendment to the constitution, by consent of the States, necessary, because the objects now recommended are not among those enumerated in the constitution, and to which it permits the public moneys to be applied.

The present consideration of a national establishment for education, particularly, is rendered proper by this circumstance also, that if Congress, approving the proposition, shall yet think it more eligible to found it on a donation of lands, they have it now in their power to endow it with those which will be among the earliest to produce the necessary income. This foundation would have the advantage of being independent on war, which may suspend other improvements by requiring for its own purposes the resources destined for them.

Albert Gallatin to William H. Crawford
January 20, 1811

[Gallatin, Secretary of the Treasury since 1801 and a close adviser of Jefferson, advocated retention of the Bank of the United States pretty much on Hamiltonian grounds. The bill to renew the Bank charter had to pass Congress by March 4, 1811, the date of the old charter's expiration. In this letter to the chairman of the Senate Finance Committee

Gallatin presents his reasons for favoring the Bank. But on February 20 the bill failed in the Senate by one vote—Vice-President George Clinton's—and the Bank died. Gallatin resigned from Madison's cabinet soon after.]

SIR:

Having already, in a report to the Senate, of 2d March, 1809, expressed my opinion in favor of a renewal of the charter of the Bank of the United States, an opinion which remains unchanged, I can only add a few explanatory remarks in answer to the inquiries of the committee, as stated in your letter of yesterday.

The banking system is now firmly established; and, in its ramifications, extends to every part of the United States. Under that system, the assistance of banks appears to me necessary for the punctual collection of the revenue, and for the safe keeping and transmission of public moneys. That the punctuality of payments is principally due to banks, is a fact generally acknowledged. It is, to a certain degree, enforced by the refusal of credit at the custom house, so long as a former revenue bond, actually due, remains unpaid. But I think, nevertheless, that, in order to ensure that precision in the collection, on which depends a corresponding discharge of the public engagements, it would, if no use was made of banks, be found necessary to abolish, altogether, the credit now given on the payment of duties—a measure which would affect the commercial capital, and fall heavily on the consumers. That the public moneys are safer by being weekly deposited in banks, instead of accumulating in the hands of collectors, is self-evident. And their transmission, whenever this may be wanted, for the purpose of making payments in other places than those of collection, cannot, with any convenience, be effected, on a large scale, in an extensive country, except through the medium of banks, or of persons acting as bankers.

The question, therefore, is, whether a bank, incorporated by the United States, or a number of banks, incorporated by the several States, be most convenient for those purposes. . . .

As it is not perceived, on the other hand, that a single advantage will accrue to the public from the change, no reason presents itself, on the ground of expediency, why an untried system should be substituted to one under which the treasury business has so long been conducted with perfect security to the United States, and great convenience not only to the officers, but also to all those who have had payments of a public nature to make or to receive.

It does not seem necessary to advert to the particular objections made against the present charter, as these may easily be obviated by proper alterations. What has been called a National Bank, or, in other words, a new Bank of the United States, instead of the existing one, may be obtained by such alterations. The capital may be extended, and more equally distributed; new stockholders may be substituted to the foreigners, as had been suggested in the report of 2d March, 1809; and any other modifications which may be thought expedient may be introduced, without interrupting the operations of the institution now in force, and without disturbing all the commercial concerns of the country.

If, indeed, the Bank of the United States could be removed without affecting either its numerous debtors, the other moneyed institutions, or the circulation of the country, the ordinary fiscal operations of Government would not be materially deranged, and might be carried on by means of another general bank, or of State banks. But the transition will be attended with much individual, and probably with no inconsiderable public injury. It is impossible that an institution which circulates thirteen millions of dollars, and to whom the merchants owe fourteen, should terminate its operations, particularly in the present unfavorable state of the American commerce, and after the great losses lately experienced abroad, without giving a serious shock to commercial, banking, and national credit. It is not intended to overrate the extent of an evil which there are no certain data to appreciate. And, without expatiating on the fatal and unavoidable effects on individuals; without dwelling on the inconvenience of repaying, at this time, to Europe, a capital of seven millions; and without adverting to other possible dangers, of a more general nature, it appears sufficient to state that the same body of men who owe fourteen millions of dollars to the bank, owe, also, ten or twelve to the United States, on which the receipts into the treasury, for this year, altogether depend; and that, exclusively of absolute failures, it is improbable that both debts can be punctually paid at the same time. Nor must it be forgotten that the approaching non-importation will considerably lessen the efficiency of the provision, by which subsequent credits are refused to importers who have not discharged former revenue bonds. Upon the whole, a perfect conviction is felt that, in the critical situation of the country, new evils ought not to be superadded, and a perilous experiment be attempted, unless required by an imperious necessity.

In these hasty remarks, I have not adverted to the question of constitutionality, which is not a subject of discussion for the Secretary of the Treasury. Permit me, however, for my own sake, simply to state, that the bank charter having, for a number of years, been acted upon, or acquiesced in, as if constitutional, by all the constituted authorities of the nation, and thinking, myself, the use of banks to be at present necessary for the exercise of the legitimate powers of the General Government, the continuation of a bank of the United States has not, in the view which I have been able to take of the subject, appeared to me to be unconstitutional.

Henry Clay, Statement on War with Great Britain
April 14, 1812

[Though Kentucky had only recently elected him to the House of Representatives, Clay, at thirty-five, had emerged as the leader of the agrarian nationalists. And, as Speaker of the House, he was in a strong position to impress his views on the administration and the Republican party. Like the other Westerners, Clay plumped for war with Britain on the grounds that Britain had prevented American expansion and had persistently humiliated America on the high seas. By the time he wrote the statement below in the form of an editorial for the *National Intelligencer* of Washington, war was imminent. A general embargo was on and troops were being called up. On June 18 Congress declared war on Britain.]

. . . [If] the reports which we now hear are true, that with England all hope of honorable accommodation is at an end, and that with France our negotiations are in a forwardness encouraging expectations of a favorable result, where is the motive for longer delay? The final step ought to be taken; and that step is WAR. By what course of measures we have reached the present crisis, is not now a question for freemen and patriots to discuss. It exists; and it is by open and manly war only that we can get through it with honor and advantage to the country. Our wrongs have been great; our cause is just; and if we are decided and firm, success is inevitable.

Let war therefore be forthwith proclaimed against England. With her there can be no motive for delay. Any further discussion, any new attempt at negotiation, would be as fruitless as it would be dishonorable. With France we shall still be at liberty to pursue the course which circumstances may require. The advance she has already made by the repeal of her decrees; the manner of its reception by our government; and the prospect which exists of an amicable accommodation, entitle her to this preference. If she acquits herself to the just claims of the U States, we shall have good cause to applaud our conduct in it, and if she fails we shall always be in time to place her on the ground of her adversary. And on that ground, in that event, it is hoped she will be placed.

But it is said that we are not prepared for war, and ought therefore not to declare it. This is an idle objection, which can have weight with the timid and pusillanimous only. The fact is otherwise. Our preparations are adequate to every essential object. Do we apprehend danger to ourselves? From what quarter will it assail us? From England, and by invasion? The idea is too absurd to merit a moment's consideration. Where are her troops? But lately, she dreaded an invasion of her own dominions, from her powerful and menacing neighbor. That danger, it is true, has diminished, but it has not entirely, and forever, disappeared. A gallant effort, which called forth the whole energies of the nation, has put it at a distance, but still it is one of those sparks which peer above the horizon, & excite alarm even in those least liable to it. The war in the peninsula, which lingers, requires strong armies to support it. She maintains an army in Sicily; another in India; and a strong force in Ireland, and along her own coast and in the West Indies. Can any one believe, that, under such circumstances, the British government could be so infatuated, or rather mad, as to send troops here for the purpose of invasion? The experience and the fortune of our revolution, when we were comparatively in an infant state, have doubtless taught her an useful lesson which cannot have been forgotten. Since that period our population has increased threefold, whilst her's has remained almost stationary. The condition of the civilized world, too, has changed. Although G. Britain has nothing to fear, as to her independence, and her military operations are extensive and distant, the contest is evidently maintained by her rather for safety than for conquest. Have we cause to dread an attack from her neighboring provinces? That apprehension is still more groundless. Seven or eight millions of people have nothing to dread from 300,000. From the moment that war is declared, the British colonies will be put on the defensive, and soon after we get in motion must sink under the pressure. Little predatory incursions on our frontier will not be encouraged by those who know that we can retort them tenfold, and pursue and punish the authors, retire where they may, if they remain in this hemisphere. Nor is any serious danger to be apprehended from their savage allies. Our frontiers may be easily protected against them. The colonial governments, aware of our superiority, and of the certainty of their subjugation in case of war, will feel their responsibility for the conduct of the Indian tribes, and keep them in order. But should the war lately terminated be renewed, the struggle will be short. Numberless expeditions from different quarters may be led forth against them. A single campaign would drive these unfortunate people into the most distant and desart wilds. . . .

The great question on which the United States have to decide, is, whether they will relinquish the ground which they now hold, or maintain it with the firmness and vigor becoming freemen. That the sense of the nation favors the latter course, is proved by a series of important and solemn facts, which speak a language not to be misunderstood. From the first attack by Great Britain on our neutral rights in 1805, to the present day, these facts have been multiplied, yearly, by the acts of Congress, by the proceedings of the state legislatures, and by the voice of the people. Let not the Representatives of the People, therefore, in either branch of the government, disappoint their reasonable wishes and just expectations.

The pretensions of Great Britain, so unjustly set up, and pertinaciously maintained, by her orders in council, not to enumerate other wrongs, particularly the impressment of our seamen, arrogate to her the complete dominion of the sea, and the exclusion of every flag from it, which does not sail under her license, and on the conditions which she imposes. These pretensions involve no local interest, nor are they of a transient nature. In their operation they violate the rights, and wound deeply the best interests, of the whole American people. If we yield to them, at this time, the cause may be considered as abandoned. There will be no rallying point hereafter. Future attempts to retaliate the wrongs of foreign powers & to vindicate our most sacred rights, will be in vain. The subject must be dismissed from the debates of Congress, and from our diplomatic discussions. An allusion to it will excite contempt abroad, and mortification and shame at home. Should any of our vessels be hereafter seized and condemned, however unjustly, and that all will be seized and condemned may be confidently expected, we must be silent, or be heard by foreign powers in the humble language of petition only.

Resolutions of the Hartford Convention
January 4, 1815

[The long-pent-up hatred that New England Federalists felt for the ruling Republican party exploded during the War of 1812. In late December 1814 delegates from Massachusetts, Connecticut, Rhode Island, Vermont and New Hampshire met in Hartford to see how they might best resist federal laws. By January 4 they had drawn up a list of grievances and resolutions, which they promptly dispatched to Washington. But by the time the resolutions arrived at the capital the battle of New Orleans had been fought and the peace treaty of Ghent signed.]

First.—A deliberate and extensive system for effecting a combination among certain states, by exciting local jealousies and ambition, so as to secure to popular leaders in one section of the Union, the controul of public affairs in perpetual succession. To which primary object most other characteristics of the system may be reconciled.

Secondly.—The political intolerance displayed and avowed in excluding from office men of unexceptionable merit, for want of adherence to the executive creed.

Thirdly.—The infraction of the judiciary authority and rights, by depriving judges of their offices in violation of the constitution.

Fourthly.—The abolition of existing taxes, requisite to prepare the country for those changes to which nations are always exposed, with a view to the acquisition of popular favour.

Fifthly.—The influence of patronage in the distribution of offices, which in these states has been almost invariably made among men the least entitled to such distinction, and who have sold themselves as ready instruments for distracting public opinion, and encouraging administration to hold in contempt the wishes and remonstrances of a people thus apparently divided.

Sixthly.—The admission of new states into the Union formed at pleasure in the western region, has destroyed the balance of power which existed among the original States, and deeply affected their interest.

Seventhly.—The easy admission of naturalized foreigners, to places of trust, honour or profit, operating as an inducement to the malcontent subjects of the old world to come to these States, in quest of executive patronage, and to repay it by an abject devotion to executive measures.

Eighthly.—Hostility to Great Britain, and partiality to the late government of France, adopted as coincident with popular prejudice, and subservient to the main object, party power. Connected with these must be ranked erroneous and distorted estimates of the power and resources of those nations, of the probable results of their controversies, and of our political relations to them respectively.

Lastly and principally.—A visionary and superficial theory in regard to commerce, accompanied by a real hatred but a feigned regard to its interests, and a ruinous perseverance in efforts to render it an instrument of coercion and war.

But it is not conceivable that the obliquity of any administration could, in so short a period, have so nearly consummated the work of national ruin, unless favoured by defects in the constitution. . . .

THEREFORE RESOLVED,

That it be and hereby is recommended to the legislatures of the several states represented in this Convention, to adopt all such measures as may be necessary effectually to protect the citizens of said states from the operation and effects of all acts which have been or may be passed by the Congress of the United States, which shall contain provisions, subjecting the militia or other citizens to forcible drafts, conscriptions, or impressments, not authorised by the constitution of the United States.

Resolved, That it be and hereby is recommended to the said Legislatures, to authorize an immediate and earnest application to be made to the government of the United States, requesting their consent to some arrangement, whereby the said states may, separately or in concert, be empowered to assume upon themselves the defence of their territory against the enemy; and a reasonable portion of the taxes, collected within said States, may be paid into the respective treasuries thereof, and appropriated to the payment of the balance due said states, and to the future defence of the same. The amount so paid into the said treasuries to be credited, and the disbursements made as aforesaid to be charged to the United States.

Resolved, That it be, and hereby is, recommended to the legislatures of the aforesaid states, to pass laws (where it has not already been done) authorizing the governors or commanders-in-chief of their militia to make detachments from the same, or to form voluntary corps, as shall be most convenient and conformable to their constitutions, and to cause the same to be well armed, equipped, and disciplined, and held in readiness for service; and upon the request of the governor of either of the other states to employ the whole of such detachment or corps, as well as the regular forces of the state, or such part thereof as may be required and can be spared consistently with the safety of the state, in assisting the state, making such request to repel any invasion thereof which shall be made or attempted by the public enemy.

Resolved, That the following amendments of the constitution of the United States be recommended to the states represented as aforesaid, to be proposed by them for adoption by the state legislatures, and in such cases as may be deemed expedient by a convention chosen by the people of each state.

And it is further recommended, that the said states shall persevere in their efforts to obtain such amendments, until the same shall be effected.

First. Representatives and direct taxes shall be apportioned among the several states which may be included within this Union, according to their respective numbers of free persons, including those bound to serve for a term of years, and excluding Indians not taxed, and all other persons.

Second. No new state shall be admitted into the Union by Congress, in virtue of the power granted by the constitution, without the concurrence of two thirds of both houses.

Third. Congress shall not have power to lay any embargo on the ships or vessels of the citizens of the United States, in the ports or harbours thereof, for more than sixty days.

Fourth. Congress shall not have power, without the concurrence of two thirds of both houses, to interdict the commercial intercourse between the United States and any foreign nation, or the dependencies thereof.

Fifth. Congress shall not make or declare war, or authorize acts of hostility against any foreign nation, without the concurrence of two thirds of both houses, except such acts of

hostility be in defence of the territories of the United States
when actually invaded.

Sixth. No person who shall hereafter be naturalized, shall
be eligible as a member of the senate or house of representatives of the United States, nor capable of holding any civil
office under the authority of the United States.

Seventh. The same person shall not be elected president
of the United States a second time; nor shall the president
be elected from the same state two terms in succession.

Resolved, That if the application of these states to the
government of the United States, recommended in a foregoing resolution, should be unsuccessful and peace should not
be concluded, and the defence of these states should be neglected, as it has since the commencement of the war, it will,
in the opinion of this convention, be expedient for the legislatures of the several states to appoint delegates to another
convention, to meet at Boston . . . with such powers and in-
structions as the exigency of a crisis so momentous may require.

John C. Calhoun, Speech on Internal Improvements
February 4, 1817

[There was no stauncher nationalist and war hawk in the
Republican ranks than Calhoun, who represented the western
part of South Carolina in the House of Representatives between 1811 and 1817. On February 4, 1817, he introduced a
measure in the House under which the federal government
would use its share of the profits from the Bank of the United
States to finance a huge internal improvements program.
Such a program would carry out Jefferson's hope of linking
the West to the East and the South to the North. Thanks
to overwhelming Western support the measure passed both
Houses, but President Madison vetoed it. Though he approved the idea, Madison thought that a constitutional
amendment was necessary to authorize it.]

. . . But on this subject of national power, what, said Mr.
C. can be more important than a perfect unity in every part,

in feelings and sentiments? And what can tend more powerfully to produce it, than overcoming the effects of distance?
No country, enjoying freedom, ever occupied any thing like
as great an extent of country as this Republic. One hundred
years ago, the most profound philosophers did not believe it
to be even possible. They did not suppose it possible that a
pure republic could exist on as great a scale even as the
Island of Great Britain. What then was considered as
chimerical, said Mr. C. we now have the felicity to enjoy;
and, what is most remarkable, such is the happy mould of
our government, so well are the state and the general powers
blended, that much of our political happiness draws its origin
from the extent of our Republic. It has exempted us from
the most of the causes which distracted the small republics of
antiquity. Let it not however be forgotten; let it, said he, be
forever kept in mind, that it exposes us to the greatest of all
calamities, next to the loss of liberty, and even to that in its
consequence—*disunion*. We are great, and rapidly, he was
about to say fearfully, growing. This, said he, is our pride and
danger—our weakness and our strength. Little, said Mr. C.
does he deserve to be entrusted with the liberties of this
people, who does not raise his mind to these truths. We are
under the most imperious obligation to counteract every tendency to disunion. The strongest of all cements is, undoubtedly, the wisdom, justice, and, above all, the moderation of
this House; yet the great subject on which we are now deliberating, in this respect, deserves the most serious consideration. Whatever, said Mr. C. impedes the intercourse of the
extremes with this, the center of the Republic, weakens the
union. The more enlarged the sphere of commercial circulation, the more extended that of social intercourse; the more
strongly are we bound together; the more inseparable are
our destinies. Those who understand the human heart best,
know how powerfully distance tends to break the sympathies
of our nature. Nothing, not even dissimilarity of language,
tends more to estrange man from man. Let us then, said Mr.
C. bind the Republic together with a perfect system of
roads and canals. Let us conquer space. It is thus the most
distant parts of the Republic will be brought within a few
days travel of the center; it is thus that a citizen of the

West will read the news of Boston still moist from the press. The mail and the press, said he, are the nerves of the body politic. By them, the slightest impression made on the most remote parts, is communicated to the whole system; and the more perfect the means of transportation, the more rapid and true the vibration. To aid us in this great work, to maintain the integrity of this Republic, we inhabit a country presenting the most admirable advantages. Belted around, as it is, by lakes and oceans, intersected in every direction by bays and rivers, the hand of industry and art is tempted to improvement. So situated, said he, blessed with a form of government at once combining liberty and strength, we may reasonably raise our eyes to a most splendid future, if we only act in a manner worthy of our advantages. If, however, neglecting them, we permit a low, sordid, selfish, and sectional spirit to take possession of this House, this happy scene will vanish. We will divide, and in its consequences will follow misery and despotism.

To legislate for our country, said Mr. C. requires not only the most enlarged views, but a species of self-devotion, not exacted in any other. In a country so extensive, and so various in its interests, what is necessary for the common good, may apparently be opposed to the interest of particular sections. It must be submitted to as the condition of our greatness. But were we a small republic; were we confined to the ten miles square, the selfish instincts of our nature might in most cases be relied on in the management of public affairs. . . .

If we are restricted in the use of our money to the enumerated powers, on what principle, said he, can the purchase of Louisiana be justified? To pass over many other instances, the identical power, which is now the subject of discussion, has in several instances been exercised. To look no further back, at the last session a considerable sum was granted to complete the Cumberland road. In reply to this uniform course of legislation, Mr. C. expected it would be said, that our Constitution was founded on positive and written principles, and not on precedents. He did not deny the position; but he introduced these instances to prove the uniform sense of Congress, and the country, (for they had not been objected to) as to our powers; and surely, said he, they furnish better evidence of the true interpretation of the Constitution than the most refined and subtle arguments.

Let it not be urged, that the construction for which he contended gave a dangerous extent to the powers of Congress. In this point of view, he conceived it to be more safe than the opposite. By giving a reasonable extent to the money power, it exempted from the necessity of giving a strained and forced construction to the other enumerated powers. For instance, he said, if the public money could be applied to the purchase of Louisiana, as he contended, then there was no constitutional difficulty in that purchase; but, if it could not, then were we compelled either to deny that we had the power to purchase, or to strain some of the enumerated powers, to prove our right. It had, for instance, been said, that we had the right to purchase, under the power to admit new states; a construction he would venture to say, far more forced than the one for which he contended. Such are my views, said he, on our right to pass this bill. . . .

Trustees of Dartmouth College v. Woodward
1819

[Chief Justice John Marshall was the last of the great Federalists to occupy a position of high importance in American life. His conservatism was especially manifest in this decision. In 1769 King George III had granted a charter to Dartmouth College. In 1816 the heavily Republican New Hampshire legislature liberalized the charter and formed a new board of trustees. The old board challenged the law, maintaining that the charter was a contract and so could not be impaired under the Constitution. Marshall's ruling, which upheld the trustees, threatened severely to restrict the power of local government, to subordinate democracy to the rights of corporations. During the Jacksonian era the Court took a somewhat different view of the matter.]

. . . It can require no argument to prove that the circumstances of this case constitute a contract. An application is made to the crown for a charter to incorporate a religious and literary institution. In the application it is stated that large contributions have been made for the object, which will be conferred on the corporation as soon as it shall be created. The charter is granted, and on its faith the property is conveyed. Surely in this transaction every ingredient of a complete and legitimate contract is to be found. The points for consideration are, 1. Is this contract protected by the constitution of the United States? 2. Is it impaired by the acts under which the defendant holds?

1. On the first point it has been argued that the word "contract," in its broadest sense, would comprehend the political relations between the government and its citizens, would extend to offices held within a state for state purposes, and to many of those laws concerning civil institutions, which must change with circumstances, and be modified by ordinary legislation; which deeply concern the public, and which, to preserve good government, the public judgment must control. That even marriage is a contract, and its obligations are affected by the laws respecting divorces. That the clause in the constitution, if construed in its greatest latitude, would prohibit these laws Taken in its broad, unlimited sense, the clause would be an unprofitable and vexatious interference with the internal concerns of a state, would unnecessarily and unwisely embarrass its legislation, and render immutable those civil institutions which are established for purposes of internal government, and which, to subserve those purposes, ought to vary with varying circumstances. That as the framers of the constitution could never have intended to insert in that instrument a provision so unnecessary, so mischievous, and so repugnant to its general spirit, the term "contract" must be understood in a more limited sense. That it must be understood as intended to guard against a power of at least doubtful utility, the abuse of which had been extensively felt, and to restrain the legislature in future from violating the right to property. That anterior to the formation of the constitution, a course of legislation had prevailed

in many, if not in all, of the states, which weakened the confidence of man in man, and embarrassed all transactions between individuals, by dispensing with a faithful performance of engagements. To correct this mischief, by restraining the power which produced it, the state legislatures were forbidden "to pass any law impairing the obligation of contracts," that is, of contracts respecting property, under which some . . . individual could claim a right to something beneficial to himself; and that, since the clause in the constitution must in construction receive some limitation, it may be confined, and ought to be confined, to cases of this description, to cases within the mischief it was intended to remedy.

The general correctness of these observations cannot be controverted. That the framers of the constitution did not intend to restrain the states in the regulation of their civil institutions, adopted for internal government, and that the instrument they have given us is not to be so construed, may be admitted. The provision of the constitution never has been understood to embrace other contracts than those which respect property or some object of value, and confer rights which may be asserted in a court of justice. It has never been understood to restrict the general right of the legislature to legislate on the subject of divorces. . . .

The parties in this case differ less on general principles, less on the true construction of the constitution in the abstract, than on the application of those principles to this case, and on the true construction of the charter of 1769. This is the point on which the cause essentially depends. If the act of incorporation be a grant of political power, if it create a civil institution to be employed in the administration of the government, or if the funds of the college be public property, or if the state of New Hampshire, as a government, be alone interested in its transactions, the subject is one in which the legislature of the state may act according to its own judgment, unrestrained by any limitation of its power imposed by the constitution of the United States.

But if this be a *private eleemosynary institution*, endowed with a capacity to take property for objects *unconnected with government*, whose funds are bestowed by individuals on the faith of the charter; if the donors have stipulated for the future disposition and management of those funds in the manner prescribed by themselves; there may be more difficulty in the case, although neither the persons who have made these stipulations, nor those for whose benefit they were made, should be parties to the cause. Those who are no longer interested in the property may yet retain such an interest in the preservation of their own arrangements as to have a right to insist that those arrangements shall be held sacred. Or, if they have themselves disappeared, it becomes a subject of serious and anxious inquiry whether those whom they have legally empowered to represent them forever may not assert all the rights which they possessed while in being; whether, if they be without personal representatives who may feel injured by a violation of the compact, the trustees be not so completely their representatives in the eye of the law as to stand in their place, not only as respects the government of the college, but also as respects the maintenance of the college charter. It becomes then the duty of the court most seriously to examine this charter, and to ascertain its true character. . . .

A corporation is an artificial being, invisible, intangible, and existing only in contemplation of law. Being the mere creature of law, it possesses only those properties which the charter of its creation confers upon it, either expressly or as incidental to its very existence. These are such as are supposed best calculated to effect the object for which it was created. Among the most important are immortality, and, if the expression may be allowed, individuality; properties, by which a perpetual succession of many persons are considered as the same, and may act as a single individual. They enable a corporation to manage its own affairs, and to hold property without the perplexing intricacies, the hazardous and endless necessity, of perpetual conveyances for the purpose of transmitting it from hand to hand. It is chiefly for the purpose of clothing bodies of men in succession with these qualities and capacities that corporations were invented and are in use. By these means, a perpetual succession of individuals are capable of acting for the promotion of the particular object, like one immortal being. . . .

According to the theory of the British constitution, their

Parliament is omnipotent. To annul corporate rights might give a shock to public opinion, which that government has chosen to avoid; but its power is not questioned. Had Parliament, immediately after the emanation of this charter and the execution of those conveyances which followed it, annulled the instrument, so that the living donors would have witnessed the disappointment of their hopes, the perfidy of the transaction would have been universally acknowledged. Yet then, as now, the donors would have had no interest in the property; then, as now, those who might be students would have had no rights to be violated; then, as now, it might be said that the trustees, in whom the rights of all were combined, possessed no private, individual, beneficial interest in the property confided to their protection. Yet the contract would at that time have been deemed sacred by all. What has since occurred to strip it of its inviolability? Circumstances have not changed it. In reason, in justice, and in law, it is now what it was in 1769. . . .

On what safe and intelligible ground can this exception stand? There is no expression in the constitution, no sentiment delivered by its contemporaneous expounders, which would justify us in making it. . . .

Almost all eleemosynary corporations, those which are created for the promotion of religion, of charity, or of education, are of the same character. The law of this case is the law of all. . . .

The opinion of the court, after mature deliberation, is, that this is a contract, the obligation of which cannot be impaired without violating the constitution of the United States. This opinion appears to us to be equally supported by reason and by the former decisions of this court. . . .

It results from this opinion, that the acts of the legislature of New Hampshire, which are stated in the special verdict found in this cause, are repugnant to the constitution of the United States; and that the judgment on this special verdict ought to have been for the plaintiffs. The judgment of the state court must, therefore, be reversed.

Thomas Jefferson to William Johnson
June 12, 1823

[Since the 1790s Jefferson had been quarreling with the federal judiciary for being anti-Republican. If anything, his dislike of the institution had grown since his retirement from public life in 1809. In recent years his old enemy, Marshall, had been handing down a succession of conservative and strongly nationalist opinions, some directed against Virginia. Jefferson here gives his views in a letter to a man he had appointed to the Court in 1804.]

. . . You request me confidentially, to examine the question, whether the Supreme Court has advanced beyond its constitutional limits, and trespassed on those of the State authorities? I do not undertake, my dear Sir, because I am unable. . . .

It may be impracticable to lay down any general formula of words which shall decide at once, and with precision, in every case, this limit of jurisdiction. But there are two canons which will guide us safely in most of the cases. 1st. The capital and leading object of the constitution was to leave with the States all authorities which respected their own citizens only, and to transfer to the United States those which respected citizens of foreign or other States: to make us several as to ourselves, but one as to all others. In the latter case, then, constructions should lean to the general jurisdiction, if the words will bear it; and in favor of the States in the former, if possible to be so construed. And indeed, between citizens and citizens of the same State, and under their own laws, I know but a single case in which a jurisdiction is given to the General Government. That is, where anything but gold or silver is made a lawful tender, or the obligation of contracts is any otherwise impaired. The separate legislatures had so often abused that power, that the citizens themselves chose to trust it to the general, rather than to their own special authorities. 2d. On every question of construction, carry ourselves back to the time when the constitution was adopted, recollect the spirit manifested in the debates, and instead of trying what meaning may be squeezed out of the text, or invented against it, conform to the probable one in which it was passed. . . .

. . . Can any good be effected by taking from the States the moral rule of their citizens, and subordinating it to the general authority, or to one of their corporations, which may justify forcing the meaning of words, hunting after possible constructions, and hanging inference on inference, from heaven to earth, like Jacob's ladder? Such an intention was impossible, and such a licentiousness of construction and inference, if exercised by both governments, as may be done with equal right, would equally authorize both to claim all power, general and particular, and break up the foundations of the Union. Laws are made for men of ordinary understanding, and should, therefore, be construed by the ordinary rules of common sense. Their meaning is not to be sought for in metaphysical subtleties, which may make anything mean everything or nothing, at pleasure. It should be left to the sophisms of advocates, whose trade it is, to prove that a defendant is a plaintiff, though dragged into court, *torto collo*, like Bonaparte's volunteers, into the field in chains, or that a power has been given, because it ought to have been given, *et alia talia*. The States supposed that by their tenth amendment, they had secured themselves against constructive powers. They were not lessoned yet by Cohen's case, nor aware of the slipperiness of the eels of the law. I ask for no straining of words against the General Government, nor yet against the States. I believe the States can best govern our home concerns, and the General Government our foreign ones. I wish, therefore, to see maintained that wholesome distribution of powers established by the constitution for the limitation of both; and never to see all offices transferred to Washington, where, further withdrawn from the eyes of the people, they may more secretly be bought and sold as at market.

But the Chief Justice says, "there must be an ultimate arbiter somewhere." True, there must; but does that prove it is either party? The ultimate arbiter is the people of the

Union, assembled by their deputies in convention, at the call of Congress, or of two-thirds of the States. Let them decide to which they mean to give an authority claimed by two of their organs. And it has been the peculiar wisdom and felicity of our constitution, to have provided this peaceable appeal, where that of other nations is at once to force. . . .

John Quincy Adams, First Annual Message
December 6, 1825

[Adams, the Federalist turned Republican, carried the Jeffersonian faith in science and education to an extreme. And like Jefferson, Adams, as President, proposed a federal plan to establish a scientific academy. But he never could implement the plan, which Congress ridiculed as paternalistic and apocryphal. The new era of democracy and individualism had already passed Adams by.]

. . . The great object of the institution of civil government is the improvement of the condition of those who are parties to the social compact, and no government, in whatever form constituted, can accomplish the lawful ends of its institution but in proportion as it improves the condition of those over whom it is established. Roads and canals, by multiplying and facilitating the communications and intercourse between distant regions and multitudes of men, are among the most important means of improvement. But moral, political, intellectual improvement are duties assigned by the Author of our existence to social no less than to individual man. For the fulfillment of those duties governments are invested with power, and to the attainment of the end—the progressive improvement of the condition of the governed—the exercise of delegated powers is a duty as sacred and indispensable as the usurpation of powers not granted is criminal and odious. Among the first, perhaps the very first, instrument for the improvement of the condition of men is knowledge, and to the acquisition of much of the knowledge adapted to the wants, the comforts, and enjoyments of human life public institutions and seminaries of learning are essential. . . .

In inviting the attention of Congress to the subject of internal improvements upon a view thus enlarged it is not my design to recommend the equipment of an expedition for circumnavigating the globe for purposes of scientific research and inquiry. We have objects of useful investigation nearer home, and to which our cares may be more beneficially applied. The interior of our own territories has yet been very imperfectly explored. Our coasts along many degrees of latitude upon the shores of the Pacific Ocean, though much frequented by our spirited commercial navigators, have been barely visited by our public ships. The River of the West, first fully discovered and navigated by a countryman of our own, still bears the name of the ship in which he ascended its waters, and claims the protection of our armed national flag at its mouth. With the establishment of a military post there or at some other point of that coast, recommended by my predecessor and already matured in the deliberations of the last Congress, I would suggest the expediency of connecting the equipment of a public ship for the exploration of the whole northwest coast of this continent.

The establishment of an uniform standard of weights and measures was one of the specific objects contemplated in the formation of our Constitution, and to fix that standard was one of the powers delegated by express terms in that instrument to Congress. The Governments of Great Britain and France have scarcely ceased to be occupied with inquiries and speculations on the same subject since the existence of our Constitution, and with them it has expanded into profound, laborious, and expensive researches into the figure of the earth and the comparative length of the pendulum vibrating seconds in various latitudes from the equator to the pole. These researches have resulted in the composition and publication of several works highly interesting to the cause of science. The experiments are yet in the process of performance. Some of them have recently been made on our own shores, within the walls of one of our own colleges, and partly by one of our own fellow-citizens. It would be honorable to our country if the sequel of the same experiments should be countenanced by the patronage of our Government, as they have hitherto been by those of France and Britain.

Connected with the establishment of an university, or separate from it, might be undertaken the erection of an astronomical observatory, with provision for the support of an astronomer, to be in constant attendance of observation upon the phenomena of the heavens, and for the periodical publication of his observations. . . .

The Constitution under which you are assembled is a charter of limited powers. After full and solemn deliberation upon all or any of the objects which, urged by an irresistible sense of my own duty, I have recommended to your attention should you come to the conclusion that, however desirable in themselves, the enactment of laws for effecting them would transcend the powers committed to you by that venerable instrument which we are all bound to support, let no consideration induce you to assume the exercise of powers not granted to you by the people. But if the power to exercise exclusive legislation in all cases whatsoever over the District of Columbia; if the power to lay and collect taxes, duties, imposts, and excises, to pay the debts and provide for the common defense and general welfare of the United States; if the power to regulate commerce with foreign nations and among the several States and with the Indian tribes, to fix the standard of weights and measures, to establish post-offices and post-roads, to declare war, to raise and support armies, to provide and maintain a navy, to dispose of and make all needful rules and regulations respecting the territory or other property belonging to the United States, and to make all laws which shall be necessary and proper for carrying these powers into execution—if these powers and others enumerated in the Constitution may be effectually brought into action by laws promoting the improvement of agriculture, commerce, and manufactures, the cultivation and encouragement of the mechanic and of the elegant arts, the advancement of literature, and the progress of the sciences, ornamental and profound, to refrain from exercising them for the benefit of the people themselves would be to hide in the earth the talent committed to our charge—would be treachery to the most sacred of trusts.

The spirit of improvement is abroad upon the earth. It stimulates the hearts and sharpens the faculties not of our fellow-citizens alone, but of the nations of Europe and of their rulers. While dwelling with pleasing satisfaction upon the superior excellence of our political institutions, let us not be unmindful that liberty is power; that the nation blessed with the largest portion of liberty must in proportion to its numbers be the most powerful nation upon earth, and that the tenure of power by man is, in the moral purposes of his Creator, upon condition that it shall be exercised to ends of beneficence, to improve the condition of himself and his fellow-men. While foreign nations less blessed with that freedom which is power than ourselves are advancing with gigantic strides in the career of public improvement, were we to slumber in indolence or fold up our arms and proclaim to the world that we are palsied by the will of our constituents, would it not be to cast away the bounties of Providence and doom ourselves to perpetual inferiority? In the course of the year now drawing to its close we have beheld, under the auspices and at the expense of one State of this Union, a new university unfolding its portals to the sons of science and holding up the torch of human improvement to eyes that seek the light. We have seen under the persevering and enlightened enterprise of another State the waters of our Western lakes mingle with those of the ocean. If undertakings like these have been accomplished in the compass of a few years by the authority of single members of our Confederation, can we, the representative authorities of the whole Union, fall behind our fellow-servants in the exercise of the trust committed to us for the benefit of our common sovereign by the accomplishment of works important to the whole and to which neither the authority nor the resources of any one State can be adequate? . . .

CHAPTER IV. THE RISE OF DEMOCRACY

Within four years after Jefferson was elected President, the Republicans took complete command of American politics, dominating all the state governments except Connecticut's, and winning overwhelming majorities in both houses of Congress. Yet they left the political order more or less as they found it, even though in ousting the Federalists in 1800 they claimed to have brought about a second revolution. While there were new administrations and new policies at the state and federal levels, there were no attempts to introduce significant changes in the form of government. Jefferson did persuade congressional Republicans to bring impeachment proceedings against some reactionary judges, with a view to rendering the federal judiciary more responsible to public opinion, but the effort failed and the whole matter was dropped. This was as far as the Republicans went in attacking the system that the Federalists had created.

The people, then, were no closer to exercising direct political power than they had been before 1800. The President was still chosen by electors; the Senators were still chosen by the legislatures; the voting franchise was still restricted to owners of property; the eastern districts of the states were still overrepresented in the legislatures; candidates for federal, state and often local offices were still selected by social elites, usually of well-connected Eastern families, who met in closed caucuses; and appointees to office, whatever their politics, were generally secure in their jobs and unaccountable to the electorate. Moreover, Republican leaders accepted these checks on democracy, provided the scales were not weighted in favor of monopoly and "consolidation," as they appeared to have been before 1800.

The Republicans had come to power when America was a nation of isolated communities and self-sufficient farmers. Roads everywhere were poor; in bad weather they were impassable. It took weeks to travel by coach from the new capital in Washington to New York. Months elapsed before goods shipped from Western settlements such as Cincinnati reached the East, and between the extremities of the North and South there was hardly any overland communication at all. After 1800, however, America began to feel the effects of the English industrial revolution. Vast new markets for American staples, in particular cotton and wheat, suddenly opened up. Farmers poured over the Alleghenies and down the Ohio and Mississippi rivers. An extensive network of turn-pikes and canals was built, connecting the burgeoning West to the ports of the Eastern seaboard.

Subject to the conditions of an open and competitive mar-ket, more and more Americans became producers of cash crops. America was no longer a nation of separate and inte-gral localities; it had developed into a country with an expand-ing money economy, national and even international in scope. To a corresponding degree, the private fortunes and economic freedoms of Americans depended increasingly on their con-trol of public policies. The farmer who raised wheat in Ohio, to take an obvious example, was necessarily concerned about such questions as internal improvements, which gave him ac-cess to the markets; or banking laws, which determined how much he would have to pay for his credit; or tariffs, which influenced the price of his wheat and the goods he bought. Of course, manufacturers, merchants, exporters and other groups had their own reasons for being concerned about these questions.

Americans were thus forced to make politics their everyday preoccupation. The decisions of government affected their lives too intimately, too insistently, to be entrusted to politi-cians or officials who did not answer to them directly. It was under these imperatives that the Federalist-Republican order rapidly gave way to democracy. The distance between leaders and electorate was narrowed by various measures. Fol-lowing the War of 1812 one Eastern state after another re-formed its constitution under pressure from the swelling port cities and the western districts. By 1830 only Delaware and South Carolina among the original thirteen states of the Union had failed to enfranchise all adult white males and to equalize the legislative districts on the principle of one (white) man, one vote. The constitutions of all eight Western states that entered the Union between 1803 and 1821 already included these features.

This rise of democracy was accompanied by the transformation of the party system, the only means through which the vote could become an effective instrument of power, elections something more than formal procedures, and even the most distant offices accountable to the majority. The Republican party, as we have seen, was, despite its agrarian ideology, directed by the established elites of the states; these men decided, in closed caucuses, who the candidates should be. Republican insurgents began to challenge their authority in some states even before the franchise was enlarged, creating local political clubs that were open to all party members irrespective of social status. As these clubs spread, they sent delegates to conventions who nominated their own candidates for office. In time, conventions embraced all political offices, federal, state and local. By the early 1830s presidential candidates, too, were chosen by conventions. The system of democratic parties had become national.

In managing the very complicated business of arranging conventions, recruiting voters and accommodating the various interests, the Republican party developed an elaborate organization, or machine, with its own rules and division of labor. Political office, of course, was the reward of party loyalty and service. For the higher functionary, the reward was elective office; for the lower it was appointive. And so professionalization and patronage came to be the distinguishing features of the democratic party system. Politics ceased to be the avocation of the rich and well-born. The new political man was a full-time operative who came from the lower ranks, accepted the discipline of the organization and made his way up in the world via the convention ladder. After the 1820s the professionals—the Van Burens, the Polks, the Douglases, the Lincolns—completely dominated American politics.

The growing army of party functionaries lived on the spoils of politics, the "loaves and fishes" of office, and it was no coincidence that Jackson, the first democratically elected President, was also the first to introduce patronage to the federal government as a deliberate policy of rewarding his friends and punishing his enemies. To justify the policy, he argued, as had the leaders of the state parties who had already instituted the system in their own bailiwicks, that appointive office was not a "species of property" but a form of public service; that "men of intelligence," whatever their station in life, were qualified to hold office; and that any other assumption was indefensibly anti-republican. Jackson himself was modest in distributing patronage; but by the end of the 1860s hundreds of thousands of federal jobs were available to the party faithful, and spoils had degenerated into plunder.

One of the party's central tasks was to work out the program under which the interests of a given constituency could unite and form a majority. The broader the constituency and the more numerous and disparate the interests, the more comprehensive the program had to be. Democratic conventions were incomparably better equipped than caucuses to perform the work of laying down party platforms, effecting compromises between different groups and defining the issues that would win elections. The new-fashioned party acted as a unifying force in an economy that was growing increasingly diverse, competitive and national.

This was demonstrated in the way it dealt with the rise of sectionalism. Production for the open market meant specialized production, and this in turn meant the increasing concentration of an interest in a particular section. The nation's cotton and sugar and tobacco were raised in the South; its wheat was raised mainly in the Northwest; almost all its commerce, banking and manufacturing were carried on in the Northeast. The emergence of sectional politics in the 1820s and '30s divided the party while forcing it to arrive at a formula for achieving national unity. This was no simple matter. For a politician to succeed in his locality and state he of course had to represent his constituency. But his success in doing so tended to disqualify him from national leadership. Such master politicians and prominent sectional spokesmen as Daniel Webster, John C. Calhoun and Thomas Hart Benton could not count on receiving support from the voters or interests of the other sections, and so did not become serious presidential candidates. The party, however, found a way of overcoming the problem of sectional politics: it chose as its presidential candidate a national hero who could not be identified with a particular interest or section, or a "dark horse," who was unknown to the public at large. With the exception of Van Buren all the men elected to the presidency from Jackson through Lincoln were either heroes or dark horses.

By an ironic twist, then, the party system fulfilled the hopes of the Federalists who had framed the Constitution. Though they had created an "extensive republic" to restrain local democracy and thus factional discord, it was precisely democracy, working through a hierarchic order of party conventions, that held together the component parts of the nation. Party cohesion, Union and democracy were an inseparable triumvirate.

It was the conflict over Andrew Jackson's presidential candidacy in the 1820s that first brought the various issues of democracy into national focus. In 1821, when Jackson was first mentioned as a presidential possibility, he stood outside the Republican establishment that was dominated by Speaker of the House Henry Clay and by three members of Monroe's cabinet: Secretary of State John Quincy Adams, Secretary of War John C. Calhoun, and Secretary of the Treasury William H. Crawford. Since Jefferson's time the Secretary of State had traditionally moved up to the presidency. But the tradition had prevailed only because the Virginia dynasty controlled the congressional caucus system. That dynasty was expiring, and it was taking the caucus system with it to the grave.

Accordingly, the contest for the presidency during this era of good feeling quickly developed into a free-for-all. Jackson's entry into the race with his nomination by the Tennessee legislature in 1822 disturbed the other contestants primarily because he was the most popular man in the country. His humble backwater origins, his struggle against poverty and adversity as a youth, his success as a self-made man in law and business, his rough-and-tumble habits, above all his command of the ragtail force that defeated the British at New Orleans in 1815, followed soon after by his audacious conduct of the Seminole campaign—these achievements had made him a legend. If he seemed uncouth, that was all the more to his advantage in an age of democracy. Moreover, he was not saddled with political liabilities. He could come forward as the unexampled champion of the national good. Calhoun and Crawford were Southerners and Adams a New Englander; only Clay could claim to rival Jackson in national appeal. Clay's "American System," fully worked out by the early 1820s, was an attempt to unite all the sections and major interests of the country under a program of neo-Hamiltonian nationalism: higher tariffs to encourage manufacturing, and increased internal improvements and easier credit through a network of federally chartered banks to help small farmers and businessmen. But despite this program, and despite his personal popularity, Clay lacked any solid strength in New England and the South, and even in the West, where he was best liked, he had alienated many small farmers with his support of the Second Bank of the United States.

Jackson's campaign of 1824 was shrewdly calculated to win maximum favor from the emergent democracy. He avoided quarreling with the other candidates on specific issues, but rather lumped his opponents together as products of "King Caucus," which he denounced as a device by which privileged groups surreptitiously put forward their own men. As expected, Jackson received a plurality of the electoral votes: 99 to Adams's 84, Crawford's 41 and Clay's 37. As no candidate had won a majority, the election went to the House of Representatives, where according to the Constitution, each state delegation was to cast one vote. Clay, realizing it was hopeless for himself, used his enormous influence as Speaker to persuade state delegations to vote for Adams. Adams thus became President, promptly appointing Clay his Secretary of State. Immediately, the cry went up that the two men had struck a "corrupt bargain" and that the special interests were seeking to wrest the country from the people. The Jacksonians had found their issue: it was democracy versus oligarchy.

Jackson's supporters kept this issue continually before the public during Adams's tenure of office. Adams made matters easier for them by his paternalistic policies, which a hostile Congress rejected out of hand, and by his ineptitude as a politician, so that by the time the 1828 campaign began, the most powerful political machine in the country—New York's Albany Regency, headed by Martin Van Buren—had lined up behind Jackson. So too had Calhoun, who agreed to become Jackson's running mate. Jackson had thus gathered around his candidacy a durable coalition of sections and groups. But his decisive strength lay in his appeal to the common people: the small farmer, the urban mechanic, the small businessman, who saw in him the symbol of equalitarian virtue (though he himself happened to be wealthy); in their view, he was the only authentic legatee of Jeffersonian ideals.

Jackson's victory over Adams, following a bitter and vituperative campaign, officially announced the arrival of American democracy. Jackson's votaries proudly appropriated the Democratic party label, thereby emphasizing their break with the oligarchic Republicanism of Adams and Clay. Equal rights and majority rule, emblazoned on the Democratic banner, summed up the triumphant credo of the Jacksonian epoch.

Above all it was the credo of Jackson's own administration. His primary object as President was to rid the federal government of the Hamiltonian cast that it had acquired over the years. To Jackson and the Democrats the government had become too closely identified with special and parochial interests over and against the interests of the country as a whole. For example, it had been subscribing in the stocks of private road building companies for the laudable purpose of aiding internal improvements. The problem became which companies, which among the competing local communities should it support? Federal involvement in internal improvements threatened to create immense inequities. Accordingly, in 1830 Jackson vetoed the Maysville Road Bill, which provided that the federal government buy $117,000 worth of stock in a Kentucky road building company. It was improper, he maintained, for the government to subsidize a project that lay wholly within one state, would enrich a private contractor, and would serve the welfare of the few at the expense of the public.

The most blatant form of federal Hamiltonianism was the Second Bank of the United States. Chartered in 1816 by Republicans to stabilize the chaotic money and credit conditions brought on by the War of 1812, the Bank had been making enemies among small farmers and businessmen by its prudent, but in their view grossly overrestrictive, credit policies. They denounced the Bank as an awesome monopoly, in league with the moneyed aristocracy and the federal government, whose deposits comprised its main source of capital. Equally galling to the Bank's critics was the fact that its director, Nicholas Biddle, openly meddled in politics and distributed fees to his friends, among whom were counted some of the most highly placed men in public life.

Jackson condemned the Bank on old-fashioned Jeffersonian grounds—as concentrated wealth, as the enemy of social and economic equality, as a breeder of factions and conflicts—and he determined to destroy it. His opportunity came in 1832 when anti-Jacksonians, hoping to force the question, passed a bill in Congress to recharter the Bank, even though the old charter had four years to run. Jackson vetoed the bill. Clay, his opponent in the 1832 presidential election, made the veto the central issue of the campaign. Jackson won by a landslide, and interpreting the vote as a command, removed the government's deposits from the Bank and later placed them in favored state banks. Bereft of most of its capital, the Bank, with the help of a special charter from Pennsylvania, lingered on under Biddle's management. But five years later, in 1841, it was bankrupt and had to shut its doors.

The irreducible premise of Jacksonian democracy was this: that while minorities have constitutional rights, they must ultimately yield to the will of the majority. No standard of justice—neither the courts, nor natural law, nor custom—could stand higher than the people. In this sense, Jackson's conflict with South Carolina over nullification was akin to his struggle against the Bank: both were tests of national sovereignty, both asserted that the people were superior to any group or interest or state that dared set itself above them. To Jackson the reasons for the conflict with South Carolina were unimportant; his sole concern was to uphold federal law.

For some time South Carolina and other Southern states, as

exporters of agricultural commodities, had been chafing under the increasingly high tariffs enacted since 1816. By the time Congress passed the tariff of 1832, the forces advocating nullification had come to dominate South Carolina politics. Their chief philosopher and strategist, John C. Calhoun, had been an ardent Republican Unionist but was now convinced that the Union favored the industrial North—inevitably the majority section—at the expense of the agricultural sections, in particular the South. Raising these beliefs to the level of high theory, he argued that a new constitution should be framed, resting on the sovereignty of the three sections North, South and West—each of which would have the power to veto decisions by the national government. This would effectively end the twofold threat of Union and democracy.

Late in 1832 South Carolina did three things: it issued the ordinance nullifying the high tariffs of 1828 and 1832; prevented the collection of duties in the state; and vowed to secede should the federal government resist. The nullifiers backed up their threat by providing for the creation of an army. Jackson answered with his great "Proclamation to the People of South Carolina," drafted by an old Jeffersonian, Edward Livingston. At the heart of Jackson's argument lay the assertion that the Union was sovereign over the states, a point that had many precedents, Federalist and Republican alike. In effect (and anticipating Lincoln's argument against the South in 1861) what he said was that Union and majority rule were inseparable, and that the process of fission, once begun, would not stop until the country disintegrated. Nullification, in a word, was "an impractical absurdity."

To back up his argument, Jackson asked Congress for the power to collect revenue from South Carolina. Congress complied, passing a force bill by an overwhelming majority. Though many Southerners voted against the bill, South Carolina discovered that it stood alone against the federal government; no other state legislature supported it. The conflict was eventually settled by compromise, Congress lowering the tariff in return for South Carolina's rescinding its ordinance of nullification; but the issues it raised concerning the viability of democracy and the Union gave America a fearful preview of events to come.

When Jackson left office in 1837, equal rights was the established ideology of the country and the motive force of reform everywhere. Insurgent elements in the Democratic party wanted to go further than Jackson or his followers in attacking monopolies and corporations. Radical Jacksonians in New York City, for example, concluding that the state Democratic party had opposed the Bank of the United States only in order to advance the interests of local bankers, formed the Equal Rights, or Locofoco, party, whose chief defenders were William Leggett and William Cullen Bryant of the New York *Evening Post*. In the 1840s the Locofocos were joined by upstate farmers, the so-called Barnburner faction of the Democratic party, to create a powerful dissident movement. Eventually, differences between conservative and radical Jacksonians split the Democrats and brought about a political realignment within the state that was to have far-reaching national consequences.

The anti-Jacksonians, or Whigs, as they came to be known in the 1830s, were a disparate group of Southern planters, rich Northern bankers, merchants and manufacturers, and a minority of small farmers and businessmen who, for one reason or another, were not served by Democratic administrations. Apart from their opposition to Jackson and his followers, the Whigs had no definite policies of their own. They were content to rely on Clay's "American System," with its overtones of Hamiltonian nationalism and its promise to protect American industries, build roads and canals and clear harbors and rivers, and maintain a central banking system. The term Whig, then, was appropriate, for Whiggery in Britain and America meant the defense of property rights against the twin threats of strong government on the one hand and the upsurge of the masses on the other. To the Whigs, Jackson, "King Andrew," was at once despot and demagogue, strong leader and popular tribune.

Yet even the Whigs found themselves paying the necessary obsequies to democracy. They had no choice but to imitate the Jacksonians in this respect. Whig party conventions and organizations were hardly different from Democratic ones. Whigs outdid Jacksonians in representing themselves as common men, humble in origins, simple in needs and egalitarian in ideals. This was the price the Whig party had to pay to uphold its vocation as the party of conservatism, of established order, of class prerogatives. But it was too fragile to survive the great struggles of the 1850s, and it went the way of its Federalist predecessor.

Debates in the Virginia Constitutional Convention 1829–30

[Among the famous participants in the Virginia constitutional convention were two ex-Presidents, Madison and Monroe, and the Chief Justice of the Supreme Court, John Marshall. The convention was typical of those that took place in most of the Eastern states after 1816. The two demands made by the democratic insurgents—the "Memorialists" of the convention—were the extension of suffrage to all adult white males and the equitable distribution of seats in the legislature. Both were intended to break the political monopoly held by the Tidewater aristocracy.]

[Excerpt from a Memorial drawn up by the non-freeholders of Richmond asking the convention to extend the franchise]

. . . If we are sincerely republican, we must give our confidence to the principles we profess. We have been taught by our fathers, that all power is vested in, and derived from, the people; not the freeholders: that the majority of the community, in whom abides the physical force, have also the political right of creating and remoulding at will, their civil institutions. Nor can this right be any where more safely deposited. The generality of mankind, doubtless, desire to become owners of property: left free to reap the fruit of their labours, they will seek to acquire it honestly. It can never be their interest to overburthen, or render precarious, what they themselves desire to enjoy in peace. But should they ever prove as base as the argument supposes, force alone; arms, not votes, could effect their designs; and when that shall be attempted, what virtue is there in Constitutional restrictions,

in mere wax and paper, to withstand it? To deny to the
great body of the people all share in the Government; on
suspicion that they may deprive others of their property, to
rob them, in advance of their rights; to look to a privileged
order as the fountain and depository of all power; is to depart
from the fundamental maxims, to destroy the chief beauty,
the characteristic feature, indeed, of Republican Government. Nor is the danger of abuse thereby diminished, but
greatly augmented. No community can exist, no representative body be formed, in which some one division of persons or
section of country, or some two or more combined, may not
preponderate and oppress the rest. The east may be more
powerful than the west, the lowlanders than the highlanders,
the agricultural than the commercial or manufacturing
classes. To give all power, or an undue share, to one, is obviously not to remedy but to insure the evil. Its safest check,
its best corrective, is found in a general admission of all upon
a footing of equality. So intimately are the interests of each
class in society blended and interwoven, so indispensible is
justice to all, that oppression in that case becomes less probable from any one, however powerful. Nor is this mere speculation. In our ecclesiastical polity it has been reduced to
practice; and the most opposed in doctrine, the most bitter
in controversy, have forgotten their angry conflicts for power,
and now mingle in harmony. . . .

Your memorialists do not, perhaps, sufficiently comprehend the precise import of this language, so often used. The
enjoyment of all other rights, whether of person or property,
they will not deny, may be as perfect among those deprived
of the privilege of voting, as among those possessing it. It
may be as great under a despotism, as under any other form
of Government. But they alone deserve to be called free or
have a guarantee for their rights, who participate in the formation of their political institutions, and in the control of
those who make and administer the laws. To such as may be
disposed to surrender this, or any other immunity, to the
keeping of others, no practical mischief may ensue from its
abandonment; or if any, none that will not be justly merited.
Not so with him who feels as a freeman should; who would
think for himself and speak what he thinks; who would not

commit his conscience or his liberty to the uncontrolled direction of others. To him the privation of right, of that especially, which is the only safeguard of freedom, is practically wrong. So thought the fathers of the republic. It was not the oppressive weight of the taxes imposed by England on America: it was the assertion of a right to impose any burthens whatever upon those who were not represented; to bind by laws those who had no share, personal or delegated, in their enactment, that roused this continent to arms. Have the principles and feelings that then prevailed, perished with the conflict to which they gave birth? If not, are they not now grossly outraged? The question is submitted to your candor and justice. . . .

[Mr. John R. Cooke, speaking for the Memorialists]

. . . I say, then, that arguing *a priori*, or taking for our guide the conduct of the slave-holders of Virginia, we are led to the conclusion, that the property of the wealthy would not be imperilled, as gentlemen imagine, by entrusting the powers of Government to *numbers*, without regard to their wealth. That property would be abundantly secure, without investing its holders with a factitious power, derived from its possession. And that there is not the least necessity for the proposed innovation on the great principles of Government, asserted by our ancestors at the æra of the revolution.

But it is not in Virginia alone, that we see evidences of the futility of the apprehensions that are entertained for the safety of property. We have in the history of our Sister-Commonwealths, a rich fund of experience from whence we can draw arguments to illustrate the utter futility of these apprehensions. In *fifteen States of the Union,* representation is apportioned according to numbers alone, and wholly without reference to property, or the wealth of the electors. In eight of these States citizenship is the sole qualification of the elector, and in the remaining seven the payment of any tax, either local or general, is the only qualification superadded. The *numbers,* the needy *many,* have had the supreme control over the wealthy *few,* in some of those States for forty years, in some thirty, in some twenty, and in some ten, in some five. And what has been the practical result? Look at *their* situation, Sir, and look at *ours*. Do we not see among them the richest and most prosperous States of the Union? Has a single instance occurred of a Legislative invasion, by the poor, of the rights of the wealthy? Not one. The machine of Government has rolled smoothly on, and property has been found, as it ever will be found, able to protect itself, without *constitutional barriers* in the shape of *odious privileges*. So much for the *general question*, whether property is endangered by leaving the people in possession of their *natural and equal rights.* . . .

[*Mr. John Randolph of Roanoke, speaking against the Memorialists*]

. . . Mr. Chairman, I am a practical man. I go for solid security, and I never will, knowingly, take any other. But, if the security on which I have relied, is insufficient, and my property is in danger, it is better that I should know it in time, and I may prepare to meet the consequences, while it is yet called to-day, than to rest on a security that is fallacious and deceptive. Sir, I would not give a button for your mixed basis in the Senate. Give up this question, and I have nothing more to lose. This is the entering wedge, and every thing else must follow. We are told, indeed, that we must rely on a restriction of the Right of Suffrage; but, gentlemen, know, that after you shall have adopted the report of the Select Committee, you can place no restriction upon it. When this principle is in operation, the waters are out. It is as if you would ask an industrious and sagacious Hollander, that you may cut his dykes, provided you make your cut only of a certain width. A rat hole will let in the ocean. Sir, there is an end to the security of all property in the Commonwealth, and he will be unwise, who shall not abandon the ship to the underwriters. It is the first time in my life, that I ever heard of a Government, which was to divorce property from power. Yet, this is seriously and soberly proposed to us. Sir, I know it is practicable, but it can be done only by a violent divulsion, as in France—but the moment you have separated the two, that very moment property will go in search of power, and power in search of property. "Male and female created he them;" and the two sexes do not more certainly, nor by a more unerring law, gravitate to each other, than power and property. You can only cause them to change hands. I could almost wish, indeed, for the accommodation of the gentleman from Augusta, that God had ordained it otherwise; but so it is, and so it is obliged to be. It is of the nature of man. Man always has been in society—we always find him in possession of property, and with a certain appetite for it, which leads him to seek it, if not *per fas*, sometimes *per nefas*; and hence the need of laws to protect it, and to punish its invaders.

But, I am subjecting myself, I know, to a most serious reproach. It will be said that I am not a friend to the poor. Sir, the gentleman from Chesterfield and the gentleman from Spottsylvania, have dealt with the "friends of the people" to my entire satisfaction. I wish to say a word as to the "friends of the poor." Whenever I see a man, especially a rich man, endeavoring to rise and to acquire consequence in society, by standing out as the especial champion of the poor, I am always reminded of an old acquaintance of mine, one Signor Manuel Ordonez, who made a comfortable living, and amassed an opulent fortune by administering the funds of the poor. Among the strange notions which have been broached since I have been on the political theatre, there is one which has lately seized the minds of men, that all things must be done for them by the Government, and that they are to do nothing for themselves: The Government is not only to attend to the great concerns which are its province, but it must step in and ease individuals of their natural and moral obligations. A more pernicious notion cannot prevail. Look at that ragged fellow staggering from the whiskey shop, and see that slattern who has gone there to reclaim him; where are their children? Running about, ragged, idle, ignorant, fit candidates for the penitentiary. Why is all this so? Ask the man and he will tell you, "Oh, the Government has undertaken to educate our children for us. It has given us a premium for idleness, and I now spend in liquor, what I should otherwise be obliged to save to pay for their schooling. My neighbor there, that is so hard at work in his field yonder with his son, can't spare that boy to attend, except in the winter months, the school which he is taxed to support for mine. He has to scuffle hard to make both ends meet at the end of the year, and keep the wolf from the door. His children can't go to this school, yet he has to pay a part of the tax to maintain it." Sir, is it like friends of the poor to absolve them from what Nature, what God himself has made their first and most sacred duty? For the education of their children is the first and most obvious duty of every parent, and one which the worthless alone are ever known wholly to neglect. . . .

Andrew Jackson, First Annual Message
December 8, 1829

[This was Jackson's first official pronouncement on the patronage system.]

. . . There are, perhaps, few men who can for any great length of time enjoy office and power without being more or less under the influence of feelings unfavorable to the faithful discharge of their public duties. Their integrity may be proof against improper considerations immediately addressed to themselves, but they are apt to acquire a habit of looking with indifference upon the public interests and of tolerating conduct from which an unpracticed man would revolt. Office is considered as a species of property, and government rather as a means of promoting individual interests than as an instrument created solely for the service of the people. Corruption in some and in others a perversion of correct feelings and principles divert government from its legitimate ends and make it an engine for the support of the few at the expense of the many. The duties of all public officers are, or at least admit of being made, so plain and simple that men of intelligence may readily qualify themselves for their performance; and I can not but believe that more is lost by the long continuance of men in office than is generally to be gained by their experience. I submit, therefore, to your consideration whether the efficiency of the Government would not be promoted and official industry and integrity better secured by a general extension of the law which limits appointments to four years.

In a country where offices are created solely for the benefit of the people no one man has any more intrinsic right to official station than another. Offices were not established to give support to particular men at the public expense. No individual wrong is, therefore, done by removal, since neither appointment to nor continuance in office is matter of right. The incumbent became an officer with a view to public benefits, and when these require his removal they are not to be sacrificed to private interests. It is the people, and they alone, who have a right to complain when a bad officer is substituted for a good one. He who is removed has the same means of obtaining a living that are enjoyed by the millions who never held office. The proposed limitation would destroy the idea of property now so generally connected with official station, and although individual distress may be sometimes produced, it would, by promoting that rotation which constitutes a leading principle in the republican creed, give healthful action to the system. . . .

Henry Clay, Speech on the "American System" February 2, 3, 6, 1832

[Clay had worked out his neo-Hamiltonian "American System" in the early 1820s. He gave his best exposition of it in a very long Senate speech in 1832, excerpts from which follow.]

. . . The question, therefore, which we are now called upon to determine, is not whether we shall establish a new and doubtful system of policy, just proposed, and for the first time presented to our consideration; but whether we shall break down and destroy a long established system, patiently and carefully built up and sanctioned, during a series of years, again and again, by the nation and its highest and most revered authorities. And are we not bound deliberately to consider whether we can proceed to this work of destruction without a violation of the public faith? The people of the United States have justly supposed that the policy of protecting their industry against foreign legislation and foreign industry, was fully settled, not by a single act, but by repeated and deliberate acts of Government, performed at distant and frequent intervals. In full confidence that the policy was firmly and unchangeably fixed, thousands upon thousands have invested their capital, purchased a vast amount of real and other estate, made permanent establishments, and accommodated their industry. Can we expose to utter and irretrievable ruin this countless multitude, without justly incurring the reproach of violating the national faith? . . .

When gentlemen have succeeded in their design of an immediate or gradual destruction of the American System, what is their substitute? Free trade! Free trade! The call for free trade is as unavailing as the cry of a spoiled child, in its nurse's arms, for the moon or the stars that glitter in the firmament of heaven. It never has existed, it never will exist. Trade implies, at least two parties. To be free, it should be fair, equal and reciprocal. But if we throw our ports wide open to the admission of foreign productions, free of all duty, what ports of any other foreign nation shall we find open to the free admission of our surplus produce? We may break down all barriers to free trade on our part, but the work will not be complete until foreign powers shall have removed theirs. There would be freedom on one side, and restrictions, prohibitions and exclusions on the other. The bolts, and the bars, and the chains of all other nations will remain undisturbed. . . .

But, it is argued that if, by the skill, experience, and perfection which we have acquired in certain branches of manufacture, they can be made as cheap as similar articles abroad, and enter fairly into competition with them, why not repeal the duties as to those articles? And why should we? Assuming the truth of the supposition the foreign article would not be introduced in the regular course of trade, but would remain excluded by the possession of the home market, which the domestic article had obtained. The repeal, therefore, would have no legitimate effect. But might not the foreign article be imported in vast quantities, to glut our markets, break down our establishments, and ultimately to enable the foreigner to monopolize the supply of our consumption? . . .

[U]nder the operation of the American System, the products of our agriculture command a higher price than they would do without it, by the creation of a home market; and by the augmentation of wealth produced by manufacturing industry, which enlarges our powers of consumption, both of domestic and foreign articles. The importance of the home market is among the established maxims which are universally recognized by all writers and all men. However some may differ as to the relative advantages of the foreign and the home market, none deny to the latter great value and high consideration. It is nearer to us, beyond the control of foreign legislation, and undisturbed by those vicissitudes to which all international intercourse is more or less exposed. The most stupid are sensible of the benefit of a residence in the vicinity of a large manufactory, or of a market town, of a good road, or of a navigable stream, which connects their farms with some great capital. . . . It is only in the diversity of the vocations of the members of a community that the means can be found for those salutary exchanges which conduce to the general prosperity; and the greater that diversity, the more extensive and the more animating is the circle of exchange. . . .

Let us then adopt the measure before us, which will benefit all classes: the farmer, the professional man, the merchant, the manufacturer, the mechanic, and the cotton planter more than all. A few months ago, there was no diversity of opinion as to the expediency of this measure. All, then, seemed to unite in the selection of these objects for a repeal of duties which were not produced within the country. Such a repeal did not touch our domestic industry, violated no principle, offended no prejudice.

Can we not all, whatever may be our favorite theories, cordially unite on this neutral ground? When that is occupied, let us look beyond it, and see if anything can be done in the field of protection, to modify, or improve it, or to satisfy those who are opposed to the system. Our southern brethren believe that it is injurious to them, and ask its repeal. We believe that its abandonment will be prejudicial to them, and ruinous to every other section of the Union. However strong their convictions may be, they are not stronger than ours. Between the points of the preservation of the system and its absolute repeal, there is no principle of union. If it can be shown to operate immoderately on any quarter; if the measure of protection to any article can be demonstrated to be undue and inordinate, it would be the duty of Congress to interpose and apply a remedy. And none will co-operate more heartily than I shall in the performance of that duty. It is quite probable that beneficial modifications of the system may be made without impairing its efficacy. But to make it fulfill the purposes of its institution, the measure of protection ought to be adequate. If it be not, all interests will be injuriously affected. The manufacturer, crippled in his exertions, will produce less perfect and dearer fabrics, and the consumer will feel the consequence. This is the spirit, and these are the principles only, on which, it seems to me, that a settlement of the great question can be made, satisfactorily to all parts of our Union.

Andrew Jackson, Veto of the Bank Bill
July 10, 1832

[Jackson knew that his veto of the bill to renew the Bank of United States charter would dominate the 1832 presidential campaign. His opponents were so confident of prevailing that they distributed thousands of copies of the veto message.]

The present corporate body, denominated the president, directors, and company of the Bank of the United States, will have existed at the time this act is intended to take effect twenty years. It enjoys an exclusive privilege of banking under the authority of the General Government, a monopoly of its favor and support, and, as a necessary consequence, almost a monopoly of the foreign and domestic exchange. The powers, privileges, and favors bestowed upon it in the original charter, by increasing the value of the stock far above its par value, operated as a gratuity of many millions to the stockholders. . . .

Every monopoly and all exclusive privileges are granted at the expense of the public, which ought to receive a fair equivalent. The many millions which this act proposes to bestow on the stockholders of the existing bank must come directly or indirectly out of the earnings of the American people. . . .

But this act does not permit competition in the purchase of this monopoly. It seems to be predicated on the erroneous idea that the present stockholders have a prescriptive right not only to the favor but to the bounty of Government. It appears that more than a fourth part of the stock is held by foreigners and the residue is held by a few hundred of our own citizens, chiefly of the richest class. For their benefit does this act exclude the whole American people from competition in the purchase of this monopoly and dispose of it for many millions less than it is worth. This seems the less excusable because some of our citizens not now stockholders petitioned that the door of competition might be opened, and offered to take a charter on terms much more favorable to the Government and country.

But this proposition, although made by men whose aggregate wealth is believed to be equal to all the private stock in the existing bank, has been set aside, and the bounty of our Government is proposed to be again bestowed on the few who have been fortunate enough to secure the stock and at this moment wield the power of the existing institution. I can not perceive the justice or policy of this course. If our Government must sell monopolies, it would seem to be its duty to take nothing less than their full value, and if gratuities must be made once in fifteen or twenty years let them not be bestowed on the subjects of a foreign government nor upon a designated and favored class of men in our own country. It is but justice and good policy, as far as the nature of the case will admit, to confine our favors to our own fellow-citizens, and let each in his turn enjoy an opportunity to profit by our bounty. In the bearings of the act before me upon these points I find ample reasons why it should not become a law. . . .

Is there no danger to our liberty and independence in a bank that in its nature has so little to bind it to our country? The president of the bank has told us that most of the State banks exist by its forbearance. Should its influence become concentered, as it may under the operation of such an act as this, in the hands of a self-elected directory whose interests are identified with those of the foreign stockholders, will there not be cause to tremble for the purity of our elections in peace and for the independence of our country in war? Their power would be great whenever they might choose to exert it; but if this monopoly were regularly renewed every fifteen or twenty years on terms proposed by themselves, they might seldom in peace put forth their strength to influence elections or control the affairs of the nation. But if any private citizen or public functionary should interpose to curtail its powers or prevent a renewal of its privileges, it can not be doubted that he would be made to feel its influence. . . .

The bank is professedly established as an agent of the executive branch of the Government, and its constitutionality is maintained on that ground. Neither upon the propriety of present action nor upon the provisions of this act was the Executive consulted. It has had no opportunity to say that it neither needs nor wants an agent clothed with such powers and favored by such exemptions. There is nothing in its legitimate functions which makes it necessary or proper. Whatever interest or influence, whether public or private, has given birth to this act, it can not be found either in the wishes or necessities of the executive department, by which present action is deemed premature, and the powers conferred upon its agent not only unnecessary, but dangerous to the Government and country.

It is to be regretted that the rich and powerful too often bend the acts of government to their selfish purposes. Distinctions in society will always exist under every just government. Equality of talents, of education, or of wealth can not

be produced by human institutions. In the full enjoyment of
the gifts of Heaven and the fruits of superior industry,
economy, and virtue, every man is equally entitled to protection by law; but when the laws undertake to add to these
natural and just advantages artificial distinctions, to grant
titles, gratuities, and exclusive privileges, to make the rich
richer and the potent more powerful, the humble members
of society—the farmers, mechanics, and laborers—who have
neither the time nor the means of securing like favors to
themselves, have a right to complain of the injustice of their
Government. There are no necessary evils in government. Its
evils exist only in its abuses. If it would confine itself to
equal protection, and, as Heaven does its rains, shower its favors alike on the high and the low, the rich and the poor, it
would be an unqualified blessing. In the act before me there
seems to be a wide and unnecessary departure from these
just principles.

Nor is our Government to be maintained or our Union
preserved by invasions of the rights and powers of the several
States. In thus attempting to make our General Government strong we make it weak. Its true strength consists in
leaving individuals and States as much as possible to themselves—in making itself felt, not in its power, but in its beneficence; not in its control, but in its protection; not in binding
the States more closely to the center, but leaving each to
move unobstructed in its proper orbit.

Experience should teach us wisdom. Most of the difficulties
our Government now encounters and most of the dangers
which impend over our Union have sprung from an abandonment of the legitimate objects of Government by our national
legislation, and the adoption of such principles as are em
bodied in this act. Many of our rich men have not been content with equal protection and equal benefits, but have be-
sought us to make them richer by act of Congress. By
attempting to gratify their desires we have in the results
of our legislation arrayed section against section, interest
against interest, and man against man, in a fearful commotion
which threatens to shake the foundations of our Union. It
is time to pause in our career to review our principles, and if
possible revive that devoted patriotism and spirit of com-

promise which distinguished the sages of the Revolution and the fathers of our Union. If we can not at once, in justice to interests vested under improvident legislation, make our Government what it ought to be, we can at least take a stand against all new grants of monopolies and exclusive privileges, against any prostitution of our Government to the advancement of the few at the expense of the many, and in favor of compromise and gradual reform in our code of laws and system of political economy. . . .

South Carolina Ordinance of Nullification
November 24, 1832

[This ordinance was approved by a special convention called for the purpose. The tariff of 1832, against which it was directed, had been passed on July 14.]

An Ordinance to Nullify certain acts of the Congress of the United States, purporting to be laws laying duties and imposts on the importation of foreign commodities.

. . . [The] *people of the State of South Carolina in Convention assembled, do declare and ordain,* . . . That the several acts and parts of acts of the Congress of the United States, purporting to be laws for the imposing of duties and imposts on the importation of foreign commodities, . . . are unauthorized by the Constitution of the United States, and violate the true meaning and intent thereof, and are null, void, and no law, nor binding upon this State, its officers or citizens; and all promises, contracts, and obligations, made or entered into, or to be made or entered into, with purpose to secure the duties imposed by the said acts, and all judicial proceedings which shall be hereafter had in affirmance thereof, are and shall be held utterly null and void.

And it is further Ordained, That it shall not be lawful for any of the constituted authorities, whether of this State or of the United States, to enforce the payment of duties imposed by the said acts within the limits of this State; . . .

And it is further Ordained, That all persons now holding any office of honor, profit, or trust, civil or military, under this State, (members of the Legislature excepted), shall, within such time, and in such manner as the Legislature shall prescribe, take an oath, well and truly to obey, execute, and enforce, this Ordinance, . . .

And we, the People of South Carolina, to the end that it may be fully understood by the Government of the United States, and the people of the co-States, that we are determined to maintain this, our Ordinance and Declaration, at every hazard, *Do further Declare* that we will not submit to the application of force, on the part of the Federal Government, to reduce this State to obedience; but that we will consider the passage, by Congress, of any act . . . to coerce the State, shut up her ports, destroy or harass her commerce, or to enforce the acts hereby declared to be null and void, otherwise than through the civil tribunals of the country, as inconsistent with the longer continuance of South Carolina in the Union: and that the people of this State will thenceforth hold themselves absolved from all further obligation to maintain or preserve their political connexion with the people of the other States, and will forthwith proceed to organize a separate Government, and do all other acts and things which sovereign and independent States may of right do.

Andrew Jackson, Proclamation to the People of South Carolina December 10, 1832

[Jackson answered the South Carolina Ordinance of Nullification with this proclamation. He had already ordered General Winfield Scott to take command of the Union forces in South Carolina. On January 16 Jackson asked Congress for permission to enforce the revenue laws. Both houses of Congress passed the force bill by large majorities.]

. . . To preserve this bond of our political existence from destruction, to maintain inviolate this state of national honor and prosperity, and to justify the confidence my fellow-citizens have reposed in me, I, Andrew Jackson, President of the United States, have thought proper to issue this my proclamation, stating my views of the Constitution and laws applicable to the measures adopted by the convention of South Carolina and to the reasons they have put forth to sustain them, declaring the course which duty will require me to pursue, and, appealing to the understanding and patriotism of the people, warn them of the consequences that must inevitably result from an observance of the dictates of the convention. . . .

The ordinance is founded, not on the indefeasible right of resisting acts which are plainly unconstitutional and too oppressive to be endured, but on the strange position that any one State may not only declare an act of Congress void, but prohibit its execution; that they may do this consistently with the Constitution; that the true construction of that instrument permits a State to retain its place in the Union and yet be bound by no other of its laws than those it may choose to consider as constitutional. It is true, they add, that to justify this abrogation of a law it must be palpably contrary to the Constitution; but it is evident that to give the right of resisting laws of that description, coupled with the uncontrolled right to decide what laws deserve that character, is to give the power of resisting all laws; for as by the theory there is no appeal, the reasons alleged by the State, good or bad, must prevail. If it should be said that public opinion is a sufficient check against the abuse of this power, it may be asked why it is not deemed a sufficient guard against the passage of an unconstitutional act by Congress? There is, however, a restraint in this last case which makes the assumed power of a State more indefensible, and which does not exist in the other. There are two appeals from an unconstitutional act passed by Congress—one to the judiciary, the other to the people and the States. There is no appeal from the State decision in theory, and the practical illustration shows that the courts are closed against an application to review it, both judges and jurors being sworn to decide in its favor. But reasoning on this subject is superfluous when our social compact, in express terms, declares that the laws of the United States, its Constitution, and treaties made under it are the supreme law of the land, and, for greater caution, adds "that the judges in every State shall be bound thereby, anything in the constitution or laws of any State to the contrary notwithstanding." And it may be asserted without fear of refutation that no federative government could exist without a similar provision. Look for a moment to the consequence. If South Carolina considers the revenue laws unconstitutional and has a right to prevent their execution in the port of Charleston, there would be a clear constitutional objection to their collection in every other port; and no revenue could be collected anywhere, for all imposts must be equal. It is no answer to repeat that an unconstitutional law is no law so long as the question of its legality is to be decided by the State itself, for every law operating injuriously upon any local interest will be perhaps thought, and certainly represented, as unconstitutional, and, as has been shown, there is no appeal.

If this doctrine had been established at an earlier day, the Union would have been dissolved in its infancy. The excise law in Pennsylvania, the embargo and nonintercourse law in the Eastern States, the carriage tax in Virginia, were all deemed unconstitutional, and were more unequal in their operation than any of the laws now complained of; but, fortunately, none of those States discovered that they had the right now claimed by South Carolina. The war into which we were forced to support the dignity of the nation and the rights of our citizens might have ended in defeat and disgrace, instead of victory and honor, if the States who supposed it a ruinous and unconstitutional measure had thought they possessed the right of nullifying the act by which it was declared and denying supplies for its prosecution. Hardly and unequally as those measures bore upon several members of the Union, to the legislatures of none did this efficient and peaceable remedy, as it is called, suggest itself. The discovery of this important feature in our Constitution was reserved to the present day. To the statesmen of South Carolina belongs the invention, and upon the citizens of that State will unfortunately fall the evils of reducing it to practice.

If the doctrine of a State veto upon the laws of the Union carries with it internal evidence of its impracticable absurdity, our constitutional history will also afford abundant proof that it would have been repudiated with indignation had it been proposed to form a feature in our Government. . . .

I consider, then, the power to annul a law of the United States, assumed by one State, *incompatible with the existence of the Union, contradicted expressly by the letter of the Constitution, unauthorized by its spirit, inconsistent with every principle on which it was founded, and destructive of the great object for which it was formed.*

After this general view of the leading principle, we must examine the particular application of it which is made in the ordinance.

The preamble rests its justification on these grounds: It assumes as a fact that the obnoxious laws, although they purport to be laws for raising revenue, were in reality intended for the protection of manufactures, which purpose it asserts to be unconstitutional; that the operation of these laws is unequal; that the amount raised by them is greater than is required by the wants of the Government; and, finally, that the proceeds are to be applied to objects unauthorized by the Constitution. These are the only causes alleged to justify an open opposition to the laws of the country and a threat of seceding from the Union if any attempt should be made to enforce them. The first virtually acknowledges that the law in question was passed under a power expressly given by the Constitution to lay and collect imposts; but its constitutionality is drawn in question from the *motives* of those who passed it. However apparent this purpose may be in the present case, nothing can be more dangerous than to admit the position that an unconstitutional purpose entertained by the members who assent to a law enacted under a constitutional power shall make that law void. For how is that purpose to be ascertained? Who is to make the scrutiny? How often may bad purposes be falsely imputed, in how many cases are they concealed by false professions, in how many is no declaration of motive made?

Admit this doctrine, and you give to the States an uncontrolled right to decide, and every law may be annulled under this pretext. If, therefore, the absurd and dangerous doctrine should be admitted that a State may annul an unconstitutional law, or one that it deems such, it will not apply to the present case. . . .

On such expositions and reasonings the ordinance grounds not only an assertion of the right to annul the laws of which it complains, but to enforce it by a threat of seceding from the Union if any attempt is made to execute them.

This right to secede is deduced from the nature of the Constitution, which, they say, is a compact between sovereign States who have preserved their whole sovereignty and therefore are subject to no superior; that because they made the compact they can break it when in their opinion it has been departed from by the other States. Fallacious as this course of reasoning is, it enlists State pride and finds advocates in the honest prejudices of those who have not studied the nature of our Government sufficiently to see the radical error on which it rests. . . .

The Constitution of the United States, then, forms a *government*, not a league; and whether it be formed by compact between the States or in any other manner, its character is the same. It is a Government in which all the people are represented, which operates directly on the people individually, not upon the States; they retained all the power they did not grant. But each State, having expressly parted with so many powers as to constitute, jointly with the other States, a single nation, can not, from that period, possess any right to secede, because such secession does not break a league, but destroys the unity of a nation; and any injury to that unity is not only a breach which would result from the contravention of a compact, but it is an offense against the whole Union. To say that any State may at pleasure secede from the Union is to say that the United States are not a nation, because it would be a solecism to contend that any part of a nation might dissolve its connection with the other parts, to their injury or ruin, without committing any offense. Secession, like any other revolutionary act, may be morally justified by the extremity of oppression; but to call it a constitutional right is confounding the meaning of terms, and can only be done through gross error or to deceive those who are willing to assert a right, but would pause before they made a revolution or incur the penalties consequent on a failure.

Because the Union was formed by a compact, it is said the parties to that compact may, when they feel themselves aggrieved, depart from it; but it is precisely because it is a compact that they can not. A compact is an agreement or binding obligation. It may by its terms have a sanction or penalty for its breach, or it may not. If it contains no sanction, it may be broken with no other consequence than moral guilt; if it have a sanction, then the breach incurs the designated or implied penalty. A league between independent nations generally has no sanction other than a moral one; or if it should contain a penalty, as there is no common superior it can not be enforced. A government, on the contrary, always has a sanction, express or implied; and in our case it is both necessarily implied and expressly given. An attempt, by force of arms, to destroy a government is an offense, by whatever means the constitutional compact may have been formed; and such government has the right by the law of self-defense to pass acts for punishing the offender, unless that right is modified, restrained, or resumed by the constitutional act. In our system, although it is modified in the case of treason, yet authority is expressly given to pass all laws necessary to carry its powers into effect, and under this grant provision has been made for punishing acts which obstruct the due administration of the laws.

It would seem superfluous to add anything to show the nature of that union which connects us, but as erroneous opinions on this subject are the foundation of doctrines the most destructive to our peace, I must give some further development to my views on this subject. . . .

This, then, is the position in which we stand: A small majority of the citizens of one State in the Union have elected delegates to a State convention; that convention has ordained that all the revenue laws of the United States must be repealed, or that they are no longer a member of the Union. The governor of that State has recommended to the legislature the raising of an army to carry the secession into effect, and that he may be empowered to give clearances to vessels in the name of the State. No act of violent opposition to the laws has yet been committed, but such a state of things is hourly apprehended. And it is the intent of this instrument to *proclaim*, not only that the duty imposed on me by the Constitution "to take care that the laws be faithfully executed" shall be performed to the extent of the powers already vested in me by law, or of such others as the wisdom of Congress shall devise and intrust to me for that purpose, but to warn the citizens of South Carolina who have been deluded into an opposition to the laws of the danger they will incur by obedience to the illegal and disorganizing ordinance of the convention; to exhort those who have refused to support it to persevere in their determination to uphold the Constitution and laws of their country; and to point out to all the perilous situation into which the good people of that State have been led, and that the course they are urged to pursue is one of ruin and disgrace to the very State whose rights they affect to support. . . .

If your leaders could succeed in establishing a separation, what would be your situation? Are you united at home? Are you free from the apprehension of civil discord, with all its fearful consequences? Do our neighboring republics, every day suffering some new revolution or contending with some new insurrection, do they excite your envy? But the dictates of a high duty oblige me solemnly to announce that you can not succeed. The laws of the United States must be executed. I have no discretionary power on the subject; my duty is emphatically pronounced in the Constitution. Those who told you that you might peaceably prevent their execution deceived you; they could not have been deceived themselves. They know that a forcible opposition could alone prevent the execution of the laws, and they know that such opposition must be repelled. Their object is disunion. But be not deceived by names. Disunion by armed force is *treason*. Are you really ready to incur its guilt? If you are, on the heads of the instigators of the act be the dreadful consequences; on their heads be the dishonor, but on yours may fall the punishment. On your unhappy State will inevitably fall all the evils of the conflict you force upon the Government of your country. It can not accede to the mad project of disunion, of which you would be the first victims. Its First Magistrate can not, if he would, avoid the performance of his duty. The consequence must be fearful for you, distressing to your fellow-citizens here and to the friends of good government throughout the world. Its enemies have beheld our prosperity with a vexation they could not conceal; it was a standing refutation of their slavish doctrines, and they will point to our discord with the triumph of malignant joy. It is yet in your power to disappoint them. . . .

William Leggett, "The Division of the Parties" November 4, 1834

[Leggett, the Jacksonian radical and inveterate opponent of the banking interests, wrote this as an editorial for William Cullen Bryant's New York *Evening Post*.]

This original line of separation between the two great political parties of the Republic, though it existed under the old Confederation and was distinctly marked in the controversy which preceded the formation and adoption of the present Constitution, was greatly widened and strengthened by the project of a National Bank, brought forward in 1791. This was the first great question which occurred under the new Constitution to test whether the provisions of that instrument were to be interpreted according to their strict and literal meaning; or whether they might be stretched to include objects and powers which had never been delegated to the General Government and which consequently still resided with the States as separate sovereignties. . . .

The Bank question stands now on precisely the same footing that it originally did; it is now, as it was at first, a matter of controversy between the two great parties of this country, between parties as opposite as day and night, between parties which contend, one for the consolidation and enlargement of the powers of the General Government, and the other for strictly limiting that Government to the objects for which it was instituted and to the exercise of the means with which it was entrusted. The one party is for a popular government; the other for an aristocracy. The one party is composed, in a great measure, of the farmers, mechanics, laborers, and other producers of the middling and lower classes, according to the common gradation by the scale of wealth, and the other of the consumers, the rich, the proud, the privileged, of those who, if our Government were converted into an aristocracy, would become our dukes, lords, marquises, and baronets. The question is still disputed between these two parties; it is ever a new question; and whether the democracy or the aristocracy shall succeed in the present struggle, the fight will be renewed whenever the defeated party shall be again able to muster strength enough to take the field. The privilege of self-government is one which the people will never be permitted to enjoy unmolested. Power and wealth are continually stealing from the many to the few. There is a class continually gaining ground in the community who desire to monopolize the advantage of the Government, to hedge themselves round with exclusive privileges and elevate themselves at the expense of the great body of the people. These, in our society, are emphatically the aristocracy; and these, with all such as their means of persuasion or corruption or intimidation can move to act with them, constitute the party which are now struggling against the democracy for the perpetuation of an odious and dangerous moneyed institution. . . .

William Leggett, "Rich and Poor"
December 6, 1834

[Leggett's hostility to the rich was a frequent subject of his editorials for the New York *Evening Post*. Here is a sample.]

The rich perceive, acknowledge, and act upon a common interest, and why not the poor? Yet the moment the latter are called upon to combine for the preservation of their rights, forsooth the community is in danger. Property is no longer secure and life in jeopardy. This cant has descended to us from those times when the poor and laboring classes had no stake in the community and no rights except such as they could acquire by force. But the times have changed though the cant remains the same. The scrip nobility of this Republic have adopted towards the free people of this Republic the same language which the feudal barons and the despot who contested with them the power of oppressing the people used towards their serfs and villains, as they were opprobriously called.

These would-be lordlings of the Paper Dynasty cannot or will not perceive that there is some difference in the situation and feelings of the people of the United States and those of the despotic governments of Europe. They forget that at this moment our people—we mean emphatically the class which labors with its own hands—is in possession of a greater portion of the property and intelligence of this country, ay, ten times over, than all the creatures of the "paper credit system" put together. This property is indeed more widely and equally distributed among the people than among the phantoms of the paper system, and so much the better. And as to their intelligence, let any man talk with them, and if he does not learn something it is his own fault. They are as well acquainted with the rights of person and property and have as just a regard for them as the most illustrious lordling of the scrip nobility. And why should they not? Who and what are the great majority of the wealthy people of this city, we may say of this country? Are they not—we say it not in disparagement, but in high commendation—are they not men who began the world comparatively poor with ordinary education and ordinary means? And what should make them so much wiser than their neighbors? Is it because they live in better style, ride in carriages, and have more money or at least more credit than their poorer neighbors? Does a man become wiser, stronger, or more virtuous and patriotic because he has a fine house over his head? Does he love his country the better because he has a French cook and a box at the opera? Or does he grow more learned, logical, and profound by intense study of the daybook, ledger, bills of exchange, bank promises, and notes of hand?

Of all the countries on the face of the earth or that ever existed on the face of the earth, this is the one where the claims of wealth and aristocracy are the most unfounded, absurd, and ridiculous. With no claim to hereditary distinctions, with no exclusive rights except what they derive from monopolies, and no power of perpetuating their estates in their posterity, the assumption of aristocratic airs and claims is supremely ridiculous. Tomorrow they themselves may be beggars for aught they know, or at all events their children may become so. Their posterity in the second generation will have to begin the world again and work for a living as did their forefathers. And yet the moment a man becomes rich among us, he sets up for wisdom; he despises the poor and ignorant; he sets up for patriotism; he is your only man who has a stake in the community and therefore the only one who ought to have a voice in the state. What folly is this? And how contemptible his presumption? He is not a whit wiser, better, or more patriotic than when he commenced the world, a wagon driver. Nay, not half so patriotic, for he would see his country disgraced a thousand times rather than see one fall of the stocks; unless perhaps he had been speculating on such a contingency. To him a victory is only of consequence as it raises, and a defeat only to be lamented as it depresses a loan. His soul is wrapped up in a certificate of scrip or a bank note. Witness the conduct of these pure patriots during the late war, when they, at least a large proportion of them, not only withheld all their support from the Government but used all their influence to prevent others from giving their assistance. Yet these are the people who alone have a stake in the community and, of course, exclusively monopolize patriotism.

But let us ask what and where is the danger of a combination of the laboring classes in vindication of their political principles or in defense of their menaced rights? Have they not the right to act in concert when their opponents act in concert? Nay, is it not their bounden duty to combine against the only enemy they have to fear as yet in this free country: monopoly and a great paper system that grinds them to the

dust? Truly, this is strange republican doctrine, and this is a
strange republican country, where men cannot unite in one
common effort, in one common cause, without rousing the
cry of danger to the rights of person and property. Is not this
a government of the people, founded on the rights of the
people, and instituted for the express object of guarding them
against the encroachments and usurpations of power? And
if they are not permitted the possession of common interest,
the exercise of a common feeling, if they cannot combine to
resist by constitutional means these encroachments, to what
purpose were they declared free to exercise the right of suffrage in the choice of rulers and the making of laws? . . .

Locofoco Platform
January 12, 1836

[In a New York Democratic party meeting held at Tam-
many Hall on October 29, 1835, the militantly Jeffersonian
Equal Rights bloc refused to accept the slate of delegates put
forward by the machine. The machine men then resorted to
an old trick: they adjourned the meeting and turned out
the gaslights. But the insurgents were prepared. Having
brought along candles, which they lit with new friction
matches called locofocos, they went on to nominate their own
candidates and frame their own platform. Hence the name
of the radical Jacksonian party of New York City.]

We hold these truths to be self-evident, that all men are
created free and equal; that they are endowed by their Creator with certain inalienable rights, among which are life,
liberty, and the pursuit of happiness; that the true foundation of republican government is the equal rights of every
citizen in his person and property, and in their management;
that the idea is quite unfounded that on entering into society
we give up any natural right; that the rightful power of all
legislation is to declare and enforce only our natural rights
and duties, and to take none of them from us; that no man
has the natural right to commit aggressions on the equal rights

of another, and this is all from which the law ought to restrain him; that every man is under the natural duty of contributing to the necessities of society, and this all the law should enforce on him; that when the laws have declared and enforced all this, they have fulfilled their functions.

We declare unqualified hostility to bank notes and paper money as a circulating medium, because gold and silver is the only safe and constitutional currency; hostility to any and all monopolies by legislation, because they are violations of equal rights of the people; hostility to the dangerous and unconstitutional creation of vested rights or prerogatives by legislation, because they are usurpations of the people's sovereign rights; no legislative or other authority in the body politic can rightfully, by charter or otherwise, exempt any man or body of men, in any case whatever, from trial by jury and the jurisdiction or operation of the laws which govern the community.

We hold that each and every law or act of incorporation, passed by preceding legislatures, can be rightfully altered and repealed by their successors; and that they should be altered or repealed, when necessary for the public good, or when required by a majority of the people.

Horace Mann, Common School Journal
1842

[The establishment of a decent public school system for all was the most important social consequence of Jacksonian democracy. It was Horace Mann above all others who was responsible for bringing about such a system—in the Northern states at least. Mann served as secretary of the Massachusetts Board of Education, where he instituted many of his proposed reforms, as a radical Congressman, as the (unsuccessful) Free-Soil candidate for Governor of Massachusetts, and finally, as the first president of Antioch College.]

. . . O, save the myriads of innocent beings who are just landing upon the shores of time;—save them from the contaminations of the world into which they are sent; teach not their unpolluted lips to utter curses, nor their hands to uphold injustice, nor their feet to wander in forbidden paths. Even those who take the darkest views of human nature, and who proclaim the most fearful auguries concerning its ultimate destiny,—even they will admit that the young are less vicious than the old; that childhood had a simplicity and an ingenuousness which intercourse with the world corrupts and debauches. They will admit that there is a guilelessness, an uncalculating affection, a sensibility to wrong, in the breasts of the young, which the arts and customs of the world deprave and harden. It is we, who by our ignorances, and our apathy, by our parsimony and our pride, create in them diseases which even the brute creation do not suffer, because they do not abuse the natures which God has given them. Why should we, who, in our considerate moments, would not punish even the wretch suspected of crime, until guilt is fastened upon him by indubitable proof, and who, even then, profess to pity him, as he meets the just retributions of a violated law,—why should we lead children astray by our evil customs and practices, and bring down upon them those penalties, which, in the self-executing law of God, will assuredly follow transgression? To punish the innocent has been regarded with abhorrence and execration in all ages of the world; but to tempt innocence to the commission of those offences which incur punishment, is far more cruel, because guilt is infinitely worse than the punishment which avenges it. Why should innocent childhood be tormented with pains not of its own procuring,—with pains which the follies and the vices of ancestors seem to have prepared, and made ready against its coming? Why should the new-born generations be ushered into a world worse than themselves; to breathe in physical and moral contaminations which they did not scatter; to die of maladies engendered by those who should have been their protectors and guardian spirits?

It is in our power to rescue children from these calamities. It is in our power to guard them from the contagion of guilt, from that subtilist of poisons, an evil example. They can be restrained from entering paths where others have fallen and perished. No rude child of ignorance, left to himself in the wild wilderness where he was born, ever reached to a thousandth part of that depravity, which has been achieved as a common thing, by those whose birthplace was in a land of boasted civilization. Civilization, then, has not accomplished its object. It has given more power than rectitude,—the ability to perform great things without that moral sovereignty, before which the greatest and grandest achievements stand condemned, if not consecrated by goodness.

And here we would inquire what sphere of patriotic exertion is left open for the lover of his country, but the sphere of improving the rising generation through the instrumentality of a more perfect and efficient system for their education? . . . The only sphere, then, left open for our patriotism, is the improvement of our children,—not the few, but the many; not a part of them, but all. This is but one field of exertion, but it opens an infinite career; for the capacities of mankind can go on developing, improving, perfecting, as long as the cycles of eternity revolve. For this improvement of the race, a high, a generous, an expansive education is the true and efficient means. There is not a good work which the hand of man has ever undertaken, which his heart has ever conceived, which does not require a good education for its helper. There is not an evil afflicting the earth, which can be extirpated, until the auxiliary of education shall lend its mighty aid. If an angel were to descend from heaven to earth, on an errand of mercy and love, he would hasten to accomplish his mission by illuminating the minds and purifying the hearts of children. The Saviour took little children in his arms and blessed them; he did not, by any miraculous exertion of power, bar up all passages to sin and error, and at once make mankind the passive recipients of perfection. He left it for us to be agents and co-workers with him in their redemption. He gave to us, not so much the boon of being blessed, as the more precious, the heavenly boon of blessing others. For this end, an instrument has been put into our hands, fully adequate to the accomplishment of so divine a purpose. We have the power to train up children in accordance with those wise and benign laws which the Creator has stamped upon their physical, their intellectual, and their moral nature; and of this stewardship we must assuredly give account. May it be rendered with joy, and not with sorrow!

Dorothea Lynde Dix, *Memorial to the Legislature of Massachusetts*
1843

[Dorothea Dix was one of the great humanitarian reformers of the Jacksonian era. She had started out as a teacher and author of children's books until she discovered the sufferings of those condemned to punitive institutions: jails, poorhouses and especially insane asylums. After two years of intensive investigation, during which time she visited hundreds of institutions, she presented her *Memorial*. For more than forty years she continued to be active in humanitarian reform.]

. . . About two years since leisure afforded opportunity and duty prompted me to visit several prisons and almshouses in the vicinity of this metropolis. I found, near Boston, in the jails and asylums for the poor, a numerous class brought into unsuitable connection with criminals and the general mass of paupers. I refer to idiots and insane persons, dwelling in circumstances not only adverse to their own physical and moral improvement, but productive of extreme disadvantages to all other persons brought into association with them. I applied myself diligently to trace the causes of these evils, and sought to supply remedies. As one obstacle was surmounted, fresh difficulties appeared. Every new investigation has given depth to the conviction that it is only by decided, prompt, and vigorous legislation the evils to which I refer, and which I shall proceed more fully to illustrate, can be remedied. I shall be obliged to speak with great plainness, and to reveal many things revolting to the taste, and from which my woman's nature shrinks with peculiar sensitiveness. But truth is the highest consideration. *I tell what I have seen*—painful and shocking as the details often are—that from them you may feel more deeply the imperative obligation which lies upon you to prevent the possibility of a repetition or continuance of such outrages upon humanity. If I inflict pain upon you, and move you to horror, it is to acquaint you with sufferings which you have the power to alleviate, and make you hasten to the relief of the victims of legalized barbarity.

I come to present the strong claims of suffering humanity. I come to place before the Legislature of Massachusetts the condition of the miserable, the desolate, the outcast. I come as the advocate of helpless, forgotten, insane, and idiotic men and women; of beings sunk to a condition from which the most unconcerned would start with real horror; of beings wretched in our prisons, and more wretched in our almshouses. And I cannot suppose it needful to employ earnest persuasion, or stubborn argument, in order to arrest and fix attention upon a subject only the more strongly pressing in its claims because it is revolting and disgusting in its details.

I must confine myself to few examples, but am ready to furnish other and more complete details, if required. If my pictures are displeasing, coarse, and severe, my subjects, it must be recollected, offer no tranquil, refined, or composing features. The condition of human beings, reduced to the extremest states of degradation and misery, cannot be exhibited in softened language, or adorn a polished page.

I proceed, gentlemen, briefly to call your attention to the *present* state of insane persons confined within this Commonwealth, in *cages, closets, cellars, stalls, pens! Chained, naked, beaten with rods,* and *lashed* into obedience.

As I state cold, severe *facts,* I feel obliged to refer to persons, and definitely to indicate localities. But it is upon my subject, not upon localities or individuals, I desire to fix attention; and I would speak as kindly as possible of all wardens, keepers, and other responsible officers, believing that most of these have erred not through hardness of heart and wilful cruelty so much as want of skill and knowledge, and want of consideration. Familiarity with suffering, it is said, blunts the sensibilities, and where neglect once finds a footing other injuries are multiplied. This is not all, for it may justly and strongly be added that, from the deficiency of adequate means to meet the wants of these cases, it has been an absolute impossibility to do justice in this matter. Prisons are not constructed in view of being converted into county hospitals, and almshouses are not founded as receptacles for the insane. And yet, in the face of justice and common sense, wardens are by law compelled to receive, and the masters of almshouses not to refuse, insane and idiotic subjects in all stages of mental disease and privation.

It is the Commonwealth, not its integral parts, that is accountable for most of the abuses which have lately and do still exist. I repeat it, it is defective legislation which perpetuates and multiplies these abuses. In illustration of my subject, I offer the following extracts from my Note-book and Journal. . . .

CHAPTER V. SLAVERY AND THE FALL OF THE DEMOCRATIC PARTY

Almost from the start of American history there had been pronounced distinctions between the North and the South. Yet it was not until the 1840s that these sections began to confront each other as enemies. The most obvious explanation for their rising animosity, and the one most often given, is that their economic systems had diverged too far, had grown too antagonistic to coexist peacefully under the same body of laws. On the eve of the Civil War the North was on the verge of an industrial revolution that promised to eclipse England's, while the South depended entirely on the production of agricultural commodities. The rivalry between these industrial and agricultural sections was too intense to be settled any longer by conventional political means.

This explanation falls down for two reasons: first, the great divisive issue arose over slavery in the territories and involved no clear conflict of economic interests; and second, when the crisis broke in the 1840s the predominantly agricultural West sided with the industrial and commercial East, not, as predicted, with the South. The causes of sectional conflict should be sought not in narrow economic differences—though these were important—but in the radically opposing ways of life and social institutions that developed in the North and South. The North was mobile, competitive, diverse, innovative. Its economy rested on free labor and, in principle at least, on equal opportunity for all men. It had carried the ideals of liberalism and democracy further than any other society in the world. The South, shackled to its four million Negro slaves, whom it could neither free nor assimilate, was increasingly conservative, hierarchic and repressive, increasingly hostile to the currents of change that were sweeping through Europe and the North. Two systems of value, two moralities, two cultures, had grown up side by side in the same country.

The South had ceased to honor its Jeffersonian inheritance. Once the heartland of American liberalism, the South disallowed criticism, or reform agitation of any sort, that touched on slavery following the Nat Turner revolt of 1831. Thereafter, Southern spokesmen, citing Scripture and Greek philosophy as sources of incontrovertible authority, defended slavery as an ideal mode of labor in general and as an absolutely necessary one for Negroes. These apologists contrasted the paternalistic care and the spiritual benefits that slaves received from their Christian masters with the destitution, insecurity and lack of religious guidance suffered by Northern workers under a system of free labor. Who were the defenders of equality, they asked, but demagogues, anarchists, free thinkers and rich capitalists?

The South felt beleaguered and threatened. It knew it stood alone in the world, and thus it embraced its "peculiar institution" all the more tightly and flaunted its uniqueness all the more proudly. This attitude of defiant nationalism naturally redounded to the advantage of the rich planters, in whose hands an increasingly large share of the wealth and power was concentrated. Less than 5 per cent of all Southerners owned slaves, and most of these owned only a few. But as slavery came to define the character of the whole South, so the average poor white equated criticism of the institution with criticism of himself and his region. Southerners were outraged when, in 1857, Hinton Helper of North Carolina, in his book *The Impending Crisis*, argued that slavery was ruining the white yeoman farmer. The South banned the book as seditious, and outlawed Helper—who was certainly no friend of the Negro—as a traitor.

As Northern power and prosperity mounted, as the population of the North leaped ahead, Southern fears for the future deepened. The portents were clear. With the annexation of Texas in 1845 the South, meaning the slave system, just about reached the limits of its possibilities for future expansion. The North, on the other hand, was striding across the continent in seven-league boots. In 1848 the two sections were evenly balanced at fifteen states each; thereafter, the new states would all be free. Inevitably, if matters were allowed to run their course, the North would completely dominate Congress and national affairs. And what had been only a paper agreement when it was made—namely the Missouri Compromise of 1820, which had confined slavery to the territory below the 36° 30′ line of the Louisiana Purchase—would become a band of steel. Southern civilization would be at the North's mercy. This eventuality the South refused to accept.

Before the mid-1840s there had been only sporadic hints of the gravity of sectional differences, and those Cassandras who called attention to them—such "extremists" as Calhoun in the South and the abolitionists in the North—went unheeded. In fact, the triumph of Jacksonian democracy reflected the opposite temper. Both the Democratic and Whig parties were national in scope and policies and commanded support from every section and, more or less, from every interest. Both parties embraced the principles of nationalism and democracy that Jackson had enunciated in word and deed. No issue between Whigs and Democrats threatened these principles: neither the bank issue, nor the tariff issue, nor the internal improvements issue. South Carolina's attempt to nullify federal law in 1832, potentially such a threat, had found little support in the South. And so, when the great sectional issue did arise it caught the public unawares, and its effect was the greater for having been unanticipated.

Between 1844 and 1850 the country was rocked by three crises: the proposal to annex the huge slave republic of Texas; the war with Mexico; and the disposition of new territories acquired in that war. These crises were strung together by a single question: should slavery be allowed to spread beyond the limits already set for it by the Missouri Compromise of 1820? In the belief that it should not, a minority in the North opposed annexation, war and expansion. Politically, this minority was significant because it held the balance of power between the two parties. In 1844 a number of New York Whigs refused to vote for Clay, the Whig presidential candidate, after he had equivocated on Texas annexation; they voted instead for the abolitionist Liberty party, thereby giving the state, and hence the election, to James K. Polk, the

Democratic candidate. Four years later radical Democrats voted for Van Buren, who was the choice of the Free-Soil party (which ran on the issue of excluding slavery from the territories won in the Mexican War), thus securing the presidency for the Whig candidate, Zachary Taylor.

In other words, slavery split both parties. But the Whigs found themselves in a much more vulnerable position than the Democrats. Their strength was unevenly distributed. In the New England and Middle Atlantic states they could generally count on securing a majority of the votes. In the West the Whigs were a minority, and in the South the slaveowners provided their main source of support. Accordingly, when a large segment of the party—led by such "conscience" Whigs as William Seward of New York—attacked the policies of annexation, war and expansion, the Southerners defected to the Democrats. The Whig party then became exclusively a Northern party, and as such was reduced to permanent minority status in American politics. There was no longer any hope that it could obtain national power, and it rapidly disintegrated. This left the Democrats, who had the advantage of an even distribution of strength in every section, and who easily weathered the loss of their Northern anti-slavery or Free-Soil faction, in undisputed command of national affairs by 1853.

Meanwhile, the events of the 1840s had thoroughly transformed the Democratic party. Its ideological center of gravity shifted from its radical strongholds in the North and West, from the farmers, workers and small businessmen who formed the Jacksonian coalition, to the South, and in particular to the slave-owning class, whose great power was now concentrated on the single, inflexible task of protecting its interests, or privileges, at all costs. By the early 1850s the party had become for all practical purposes a Southern party; it was determined not to suffer the fate of Whiggery and divide into hostile factions by alienating the slaveowners. The administrations of Polk, Pierce and Buchanan relentlessly drove down tariffs and checked all attempts by Northern majorities in Congress to have the government sponsor internal improvements, settlement of the West, and a more centralized credit system, all of these being measures that the South opposed. States' rights, carried to the extreme, became the dogma of the Democratic party (its 1852 platform actually endorsed the Virginia and Kentucky resolutions as its ideal of the national good), while presidential authority was reduced to the exercise of the veto power.

But the Democratic party paid a price for its unity. A slow hemorrhage was sapping its Northern strength. The Southern or negative cast that the government took on in domestic affairs was alienating more and more Democrats who otherwise had no quarrel with its position on slavery. Pierce's exceptional victory in 1852, when he won 254 electoral votes to the Whig candidate's 42, was achieved with proportionately fewer Northern popular votes than had been given to Democrats in previous elections. Rather, it was the Whig collapse that accounted for the one-sidedness of his victory. The measures that Democratic Presidents were vetoing were those that the North was coming increasingly to depend upon for its prosperity. Harbors and rivers needed to be cleared for commerce; land grants were needed for railroads; tariff protection was needed for burgeoning young industries and for the workers engaged in them; a homestead act was needed to permit unrestricted occupation of Western lands; and a rational banking system was needed to secure the flow of credit, as state and local banks had proved notoriously unreliable. By the 1850s it was apparent to the North that the policies of the government, or lack of them, inhibited economic development and thus constituted a denial of equal rights, that nothing could be done without the slavocracy's consent. This was exactly what Calhoun had advocated.

There were Democratic statesmen who realized that the nation was coming to an impasse, and they sought a way out of it. Their dilemma was acute: what policies could they bring forward which would allow the North to move ahead and at the same time not alienate the South? What policies could command national against merely sectional support? The man best equipped to propose the formula that would answer these questions was Senator Stephen Douglas of Illinois, who represented the deeply rooted agrarian tradition that Jefferson and Jackson had called upon in times of trouble. Young, boundlessly energetic, enormously talented as a politician and legislator, Douglas had a large following in the Democratic party, and had been a contender for presidential nominations since he entered the Senate in 1847. Douglas knew that his future depended on his ability to come up with a formula on which all sections could unite.

As we have seen, the one intractable question that divided the sections pertained to the extension of slavery in the territories. The South and the Democratic administrations would not permit the remaining territories of the Louisiana Purchase, which lay above the 36° 30′ line, to be settled and organized, knowing that free states would be carved out of them. And yet they had to be settled and organized if Northern development was to proceed. It was imperative to Douglas and the Midwestern Democrats for whom he spoke that a trans-continental railroad be built connecting the Ohio and Mississippi valleys with the Pacific coast. But to get the South to allow the rest of Louisiana to be organized Douglas had to make a momentous concession: he had to agree to a repeal of the Missouri Compromise, thereby removing the ban on slavery above the 36° 30′ line. This was the condition under which the act to organize the territories of Kansas and Nebraska was passed in May 1854.

To Douglas, revoking the Missouri Compromise was only a formality, or simply the recognition of a fact, since Kansas and Nebraska were to be organized on the principle of popular sovereignty anyway. Under this principle the settlers themselves, in their territorial legislatures, would decide on whether to have slavery. Once taken out of the hands of the federal government, the issue would cease to divide the nation, and Americans could go about their paramount business of prospering and expanding and filling the vacant lands of the West without a sword hanging over their heads. The Missouri Compromise, with its artificial line drawn by men in Washington, was simply legal legerdemain, and as such an impediment to progress.

Douglas maintained that it had always been an impediment. The feasibility of slavery, he held, depended on climate and geography and other local conditions, and therefore all the federal laws together could not force it upon a people who did not want it. Conversely, he reasoned, the federal government could not prevent slavery if natural conditions and the will of a people favored it. Douglas himself claimed to have no preference one way or the other. He assumed slavery to be a system of labor suitable for the South, and not the North. He was completely indifferent to its moral implications, for he never doubted that the Negro was racially inferior to the white. What was more, he failed to understand how any white man, unless he were a perverse abolitionist, could think otherwise. As an agrarian Democrat he professed a strong belief in the ideal of equality and the Declaration of Independence. But, with fine casuistry, he argued that equality pertained only to whites, and American whites at that. The blind spot in Douglas's moral retina was to prove fatal to him and to his cause.

Astonishingly, Douglas, skilled politician that he was, failed to gauge Northern public opinion. Passage of the Kansas-Nebraska Act did not have its intended effect on the North. Far from being settled, the slavery issue was now thrown open as never before; the conflict of 1819–20 was to be re-enacted. And what was worse, it was a *free* territory that was now placed in doubt, that was now exposed to the aggressions of the slave power. Suddenly, an issue had been found around which all the disaffected, homeless groups flung up by the events of the 1840s–abolitionists, Free-Soilers, Whigs, radical Democrats–could gather. By the summer of 1854 a new party had come into being: the anti-Nebraska or Republican party. It was still rather formless, still in the process of gestation, but there was no question of its strength and its long-term possibilities. Douglas's calculations could not have been more disastrously wrong. Popular sovereignty did not neutralize the slavery problem; it placed it in the forefront of public controversy and so gave rise to the first large sectional party in American history.

Moreover, popular sovereignty became precisely the issue that dismembered the Democratic party, for as far as Southern slaveholders were concerned it had failed its decisive test. That had come very soon after the Act was passed, when pro- and anti-slavery groups flocked into the Kansas Territory. The violent and protracted struggle that followed is too complex to be detailed here. It is enough to point out that two facts had emerged from events in "Bleeding Kansas": first, the Free-Soilers constituted a clear majority there; and second, the South, abetted by the administrations of Pierce and Buchanan, refused to recognize the Free-Soilers' claims. Southern Democrats, along with the federal government, tolerated popular sovereignty only as long as it favored slavery. Douglas, whose honesty and integrity were above reproach, upheld the Kansas Free-Soilers, but in doing so found himself at odds with the leaders of the Democratic party and the federal government. The Southern, or administration, view received formal sanction in the Supreme Court's Dred Scott decision of 1857. The case concerned the question of whether a slave was freed if taken to a territory from which slavery had been excluded by the Missouri Compromise. According to the majority, for whom Chief Justice Taney spoke, the Missouri Compromise had been unconstitutional, since federal law could not interfere with property rights—that is, with slavery—in the territories. Southern Democrats took this to mean that the territorial legislatures could not enact anti-slavery laws, which of course struck at the heart of the popular sovereignty doctrine.

Douglas interpreted the Dred Scott decision differently, insisting that it applied only to federal law, not to the states or territories. After all, he argued, the settlers had the power to restrict the sale of liquor or the practice of prostitution, and these limited property rights. Why, then, could they not outlaw slavery? His differences with the Southern Democrats had grown irreconcilable. For by 1857 they had bypassed popular sovereignty altogether and were calling for nothing less than federal protection of slavery in the territories. They were raising their price for remaining in the Union beyond the bidding point, and they were demanding the unconditional control of the federal government.

The break between the Northern and Southern wings of the Democratic party awaited only the seal of formality. This was given in the spring of 1860 at the party's presidential nominating convention in Charleston. Refusing to support Douglas, who commanded a majority of the votes, almost all of them from Northern and border states, the delegations from the deep South bolted. A second convention, held in

Baltimore, nominated Douglas. A third, held also in Baltimore, nominated the South's man, John Breckinridge of Kentucky. The schism in the Democratic party assured a Republican victory in the election. Secession followed.

John C. Calhoun, Senate Speech on Slavery
February 6, 1837

[By the 1830s Calhoun had emerged as the chief spokesman of the Southern cause. His life's work consisted in seeking to preserve Southern privileges, which meant opposing majority rule and nationalism. And like most Southern patriots at this time Calhoun justified slavery as a good in itself, contrasting it to the Northern system of free labor. The occasion of the following speech was a Senate debate over whether to prohibit the acceptance of abolitionist petitions.]

. . . We of the South will not, cannot surrender our institutions. To maintain the existing relations between the two races, inhabiting that section of the Union, is indispensable to the peace and happiness of both. It cannot be subverted without drenching the country in blood, and extirpating one or the other of the races. Be it good or bad, it has grown up with our society and institutions, and is so interwoven with them, that to destroy it would be to destroy us as a people. But let me not be understood as admitting, even by implication, that the existing relations between the two races in the slaveholding States is an evil:—far otherwise; I hold it to be a good, as it has thus far proved itself to be to both, and will continue to prove so if not disturbed by the fell spirit of abolition. I appeal to facts. Never before has the black race of Central Africa, from the dawn of history to the present day, attained a condition so civilized and so improved, not only physically, but morally and intellectually. It came among us in a low, degraded, and savage condition, and in the course of a few generations it has grown up under the fostering care of our institutions, reviled as they have been, to its present comparatively civilized condition. This, with the rapid increase of numbers, is conclusive proof of the general happiness of the race, in spite of all the exaggerated tales to the contrary.

In the mean time, the white or European race has not degenerated. It has kept pace with its brethren in other sections of the Union where slavery does not exist. It is odious to make comparison; but I appeal to all sides whether the South is not equal in virtue, intelligence, patriotism, courage, disinterestedness, and all the high qualities which adorn our nature. I ask whether we have not contributed our full share of talents and political wisdom in forming and sustaining this political fabric; and whether we have not constantly inclined most strongly to the side of liberty, and been the first to see and first to resist the encroachments of power. In one thing only are we inferior—the arts of gain; we acknowledge that we are less wealthy than the Northern section of this Union, but I trace this mainly to the fiscal action of this Government, which has extracted much from, and spent little among us. Had it been the reverse,—if the exaction had been from the other section, and the expenditure with us, this point of superiority would not be against us now, as it was not at the formation of this Government.

But I take higher grounds. I hold that in the present state of civilization, where two races of different origin, and distinguished by color, and other physical differences, as well as intellectual, are brought together, the relation now existing in the slaveholding States between the two, is, instead of an evil, a good—a positive good. I feel myself called upon to speak freely upon the subject where the honor and interests of those I represent are involved. I hold then, that there never has yet existed a wealthy and civilized society in which one portion of the community did not, in point of fact, live on the labor of the other. Broad and general as is this assertion, it is fully borne out by history. This is not the proper occasion, but if it were, it would not be difficult to trace the various devices by which the wealth of all civilized communities has been so unequally divided, and to show by what means so small a share has been allotted to those by whose labor it was produced, and so large a share given to the nonproducing classes. The devices are almost innumerable, from the brute force and gross superstition of ancient times, to the subtle and artful fiscal contrivances of modern. I might well challenge a comparison between them and the more direct, simple, and patriarchal mode by which the labor of the African race, is, among us, commanded by the European. I may say with truth, that in few countries so much is left to the share of the laborer, and so little exacted from him, or where there is more kind attention paid to him in sickness or infirmities of age. Compare his condition with the tenants of the poor houses in the more civilized portions of Europe—look at the sick, and the old and infirm slave, on one hand, in the midst of his family and friends, under the kind superintending care of his master and mistress, and compare it with the forlorn and wretched condition of the pauper in the poor house. But I will not dwell on this aspect of the question; I turn to the political; and here I fearlessly assert that the existing relation between the two races in the South, against which these blind fanatics are waging war, forms the most solid and durable foundation on which to rear free and stable political institutions. It is useless to disguise the fact. There is and always has been in an advanced stage of wealth and civilization, a conflict between labor and capital. The condition of society in the South exempts us from the disorders and dangers resulting from this conflict; and which explains why it is that the political condition of the slave-holding States has been so much more stable and quiet than that of the North. The advantages of the former, in this respect, will become more and more manifest if left undisturbed by interference from without, as the country advances in wealth and numbers. We have, in fact, but just entered that condition of society where the strength and durability of our political institutions are to be tested; and I venture nothing in predicting that the experience of the next generation will fully test how vastly more favorable our condition of society is to that of other sections for free and stable institutions, provided we are not disturbed by the interference of others, or shall have sufficient intelligence and spirit to resist promptly and successfully such interference. It rests with ourselves to meet and repel them. I look not for aid to this Government, or to the other States;

not but there are kind feelings towards us on the part of the great body of the non-slaveholding States; but as kind as their feelings may be, we may rest assured that no political party in those States will risk their ascendency for our safety. If we do not defend ourselves none will defend us; if we yield we will be more and more pressed as we recede; and if we submit we will be trampled under foot. Be assured that emancipation itself would not satisfy these fanatics:—that gained, the next step would be to raise the negroes to a social and political equality with the whites; and that being effected, we would soon find the present condition of the two races reversed. They and their northern allies would be the masters, and we the slaves; the condition of the white race in the British West India Islands, bad as it is, would be happiness to ours. There the mother country is interested in sustaining the supremacy of the European race. It is true that the authority of the former master is destroyed, but the African will there still be a slave, not to individuals but to the community,—forced to labor, not by the authority of the overseer, but by the bayonet of the soldiery and the rod of the civil magistrate. . . .

Stephen A. Douglas to the Concord, New Hampshire *State Capitol Reporter* February 16, 1854

[Douglas introduced the Kansas-Nebraska bill in Congress on January 23, 1854. The reaction of Northern Free-Soil Democrats—whose support he expected to receive—was as swift as it was adverse. A typical Free-Soil Democratic organ was the Concord *State Capitol Reporter*, whose article on the Kansas-Nebraska bill provoked the following letter from Douglas. In it he explains the advantages of popular sovereignty.]

SIR: I am under obligation to you for your paper which has come to hand regularly from the commencement of the session. I saw with pleasure that you took a bold stand in favor of the Nebraska bill, and spoke in favorable terms of my speech in its support. In this you did no more than what might have been reasonably expected from a sound democratic paper. The bill rests upon, and proposes to carry into effect, the great fundamental principle of self-government upon which our republican institutions are predicated. It does not propose to legislate slavery into the Territories, nor out of the Territories. It does not propose to establish institutions for the people, nor to deprive them of the right of determining for themselves what kind of domestic institutions they may have. It presupposes that the people of the Territories are as intelligent, as wise, as patriotic, as conscientious as their brethren and kindred whom they left behind them in the States, and as they were before they emigrated to the Territories. By creating a territorial government we acknowledge that the people of the Territory ought to be erected into a distinct political organization. By giving them a territorial legislation, we acknowledge their capacity to legislate for themselves. Now, let it be borne in mind that every abolitionist and freesoiler, who opposes the Nebraska bill, avows his willingness to support it, provided that slavery shall be forever prohibited therein. The objection, therefore, does not consist in a denial of the necessity for a territorial government, nor of the capacity of the people to govern themselves, so far as white men are concerned. They are willing to allow the people to legislate for themselves in relation to husband and wife, parent and child, master and servant, and guardian and ward, so far as white persons are to be affected; but seem to think that it requires a higher degree of civilization and refinement to legislate for the negro race, than can reasonably be expected the people of a Territory to possess. Is this position well founded? Does it require any greater capacity or keener sense of moral rectitude to legislate for the black man than for the white man? Not being able to appreciate the force of this theory on the part of the abolitionists, I propose, by the express terms of the Nebraska bill, to leave the people of the Territories "perfectly free to form and regulate their domestic institutions in their own way, subject only to the constitution of the United States."

While I have understood you to support these principles,

and to defend the Nebraska bill upon these grounds in former numbers of your paper, I have observed with regret and amazement a leading article in your paper of the 14th instant, this moment received, in which the whole object, meaning, principles, provisions, and legal effect of the bill are so grossly and wickedly perverted and misrepresented, as to leave no doubt that the article was prepared by a deadly enemy, under the hypocritical guise of friendship, for the purpose of furnishing "aid and comfort" to the northern whigs and abolitionists in their warfare upon this great measure of pacification and the Democratic party in New Hampshire and throughout the Union, and especially upon that great fundamental principle which declares that every people capable of self-government ought to be permitted to regulate their domestic concerns in their own way. It is but justice to you to remark, that the article in question, although appearing under the editorial head, has the sign at the end of it which would indicate that it was not written by the editor, but was furnished as a communication. Trusting that such may be the case, and that you will promptly vindicate yourself by exposing the fraud and its author, I will quote a single paragraph as a specimen of the whole article, which contains incontestable proof that the writer is an enemy to the bill, and to the great principle involved in it, and to its friends, and that he has assumed the garb of friendship in order to destroy, by fatal admissions, perversions, and misrepresentations, what he could not accomplish by direct opposition over his own signature:

"The Nebraska bill, if it shall pass both houses of Congress and become a law, repeals the Missouri Compromise. And what will be the effect of such repeal? *Unquestionably to revive and re-establish slavery over that whole region.* When Louisiana was ceded to the United States the law of slavery existed over that whole vast territory. It required no law to establish the institution—it then existed in fact and by law. And out of that territory already three slave States have been carved, and admitted into the Union, viz., Louisiana, Arkansas, and Missouri. When they came into the possession of the Union as Territories, slavery had been planted and was flourishing upon their soil; and the whole territory of Louisiana was under the dominion of the law which established and legalized the institution. Therefore, when those States came into the Union, the people did not have to establish and ordain slavery. The Missouri Compromise *repealed and excluded* the institution above the line of 36° 30′. *The repeal of that Compromise revives and re-establishes slavery in all the remaining territory of the Louisiana purchase.* Therefore, the law which permits slavery will be revived, and slavery will exist in Nebraska and Kansas the very moment the Nebraska bill receives the sanction of the President. This is the only deduction which can be logically drawn from the premises.

"The proposition, therefore, which northern men are to look fully in the face, and to meet without the possibility of evasion, is this: *Shall slavery be revived and re-established in Nebraska and Kansas?* And, as a necessary consequence, shall the slave States regain that political preponderance in the Senate of the United States which they have lost by the more rapid multiplication, of late, of free States? These are the propositions which northern men must meet, and which they cannot now dodge or evade."

Now, Mr. Editor, you must bear in mind that the italics are yours and not mine. When a newspaper writer italicises particular passages in an article, he has an object in doing so. We all know that the object is to invite the attention of the reader especially to passages thus designated. What are the passages thus italicised? The first is, that the effect of the Nebraska bill will be "UNQUESTIONABLY TO REVIVE AND RE-ESTABLISH SLAVERY OVER THAT WHOLE REGION!" The second is, that "THE REPEAL OF THE MISSOURI COMPROMISE REVIVES AND RE-ESTABLISHES SLAVERY IN ALL THE REMAINING TERRITORY OF THE LOUISIANA PURCHASE."

The third is, that the whole question involved in the passage of the Nebraska bill is: "SHALL SLAVERY BE REVIVED AND RE-ESTABLISHED IN NEBRASKA AND KANSAS?"

Now, Mr. Editor, did you not know, when you read the "proof" of this article, that each of these passages, thus italicised, contains a wicked and unpardonable slander against every friend and supporter of the bill, whether he be a northern or a southern man? Do you not know that the southern men deny the constitutional power of Congress to "establish slavery in the Territories?" Yet in the teeth of this undeniable fact, which is well known to every man, woman, and child who has ever read a newspaper, your paper represents these gentlemen as proposing to violate not only the constitution, but their own oaths, by voting to "*establish*" slavery in Nebraska and Kansas? After attempting to fix this brand of infamy on the brow of more than two-thirds of the members of the United States Senate, the writer of the article in question proceeds to show the kindness of his heart and the purity of his motives, by assuring your readers that he is no better than those whom he assails, and therefore he approves the act and advises its consummation.

Three times in the short paragraph I have quoted has the writer of that article repeated the statement that it was not only the legal effect, but the object of the Nebraska bill, to "revive and establish" slavery in those Territories.

Now, sir, if you be a true friend of the bill, as your paper professes, you will correct these misrepresentations, and vindicate the measure, and the motives and conduct of its supporters, by publishing the bill itself, and especially that portion which relates to the act of 1820, and which your paper represents as being designed to establish slavery in the Territories. For fear that you may not have a copy of the bill, I will transcribe so much as bears upon this point, with the request that during the pendency of this discussion you will keep it standing in your paper under the editorial head, in as conspicuous a place and italicised in the same manner in which the misrepresentation was published. I quote from the 14th section of the bill:

"That the constitution and laws of the United States, which are not locally inapplicable, shall have the same force and effect within the said Territory of Nebraska as elsewhere within the United States, except the eighth section of the act preparatory to the admission of Missouri into the Union, approved March 6, 1820, which being inconsistent with the *principle* of NON-INTERVENTION BY CONGRESS *with slavery in the States and Territories as recognised by the legislation of* 1850, (commonly called the Compromise measure) is hereby declared inoperative and void, IT BEING THE TRUE IN-

TENT AND MEANING *of this act,* NOT *to legislate slavery into any Territory or State,* NOR *to exclude it therefrom, but to leave the people thereof perfectly* FREE TO FORM AND REGULATE THEIR DOMESTIC INSTITUTIONS IN THEIR OWN WAY, SUBJECT ONLY *to the constitution of the United States."* Now, sir, inasmuch as you are the editor of a democratic paper, and claim to be the friend of the bill, you will excuse me for repeating the suggestion that you keep this clause standing under the editorial head as a notice to your readers, that whoever shall hereafter say that the object of the bill is to "revive or establish slavery" in the Territories may be branded as he deserves, as a falsifier of the record, and a calumniator of those whom he professes to cherish as friends.

The bill provides, in words as specific and unequivocal as our language affords, that the *true intent and meaning* of the act is NOT to legislate slavery into any Territory or State. The bill, therefore, does not introduce slavery; does not revive it; does not establish it; does not contain any clause designed to produce that result, or which by any possible construction can have that legal effect.

"Non-intervention by Congress with slavery in the States and Territories" is expressly declared to be the principle upon which the bill is constructed. The great fundamental principle of self-government, which authorizes the people to regulate their own domestic concerns, as recognised in the Compromise measure of 1850, and affirmed by the Democratic national convention, and reaffirmed by the Whig convention at Baltimore, is declared in this bill to be the rule of action in the formation of territorial governments. The two great political parties of the country are solemnly pledged to a strict adherence to this principle as a final settlement of the slavery agitation. How can that settlement be final, unless the principle be preserved and carried out in all new territorial organizations?

But the professed friend of the measure in the article referred to follows the lead of his abolition confederates in this city, and declares that this bill opens that whole country to slavery! Why do they not state the matter truly, and say that it opens the country to *freedom* by leaving the people *perfectly free* to do as they please? Is it true, as these professed advocates of freedom would wish to make the world believe, that the people of northern latitudes are so adverse to free institutions, and so much in love with slavery, that it is necessary to have Congress appointed their guardian in order to preserve that freedom of which they boast so much? Were not the people of New Hampshire left free to decide this question for themselves? Did not all the New England States become free States under the operation of the principle upon which the Nebraska bill is predicated? If this be so—and every child knows that it is true—by what authority are we told that a country, lying between the same parallels of latitude which embrace all of the New England States, is to be doomed to slavery if we intrust them with the same rights, privileges, and immunities which the constitution guarantees to the people of New England? Are the sons of New England any less capable of judging for themselves when they emigrate to Minnesota, Nebraska, or Kansas, than they were before they ever passed beyond that circle which circumscribed their vision with their native valleys? Is it wise to violate the great principle of self-government, which lies at the foundation of all free institutions, by constituting ourselves the officious guardians of a people we do not know, and of a country we never saw? May we not safely leave them to form and regulate their domestic institutions in the same manner, and by virtue of the same principle, which enabled New York, New Jersey, and Pennsylvania, to exclude slavery from their limits and establish free institutions for themselves?

But, sir, I fear I have already made this letter too long. If so, my apology therefor is to be found in the great importance of the subject, and my earnest desire that no honest mind be misled with regard to the provisions of the bill or the principles involved in it. Every intelligent man knows that it is a matter of no practical importance, so far as the question of slavery is concerned. The cry of the extension of slavery has been raised for mere party purposes by the abolition confederates and disappointed office-seekers. All candid men who understand the subject admit that the laws of climate, and production, and of physical geography, (to use the language of one of New England's greatest statesmen,) have excluded slavery from that country. This was admitted by Mr. Everett in his speech against the bill, and because slavery could not go there, he appealed to southern Senators not to insist upon applying the provisions of the Utah bill to Nebraska, when they would derive no advantages from it. The same admission and appeal were made by Mr. Smith, of Connecticut, in his speech against the bill. To-day Mr. Badger, of North Carolina, replied to these appeals by the distinct declaration that he and his southern friends did not expect that slavery would go there; that the climate and productions were not adapted to slave labor; but they insisted upon it as a matter of principle, and of principle alone. In short, all candid and intelligent men make the same admission, and present the naked question as a matter of principle, whether the people shall be allowed to regulate their domestic concerns in their own way or not. In conclusion, I may be permitted to add, that the Democratic party, as well as the country, have a deep interest in this matter. Is our party to be again divided and rent asunder upon this vexed question of slavery? . . .

Franklin Pierce, Veto Message
May 3, 1854

[This veto of a land-grant bill exemplifies Pierce's, and the Democratic party's, states' rights conception of federal responsibilities in the 1850s.]

The bill entitled "An act making a grant of public lands to the several States for the benefit of indigent insane persons," which was presented to me on the 27th ultimo, has been maturely considered, and is returned to the Senate, the House in which it originated, with a statement of the objections which have required me to withhold from it my approval.

In the performance of this duty, prescribed by the Constitution, I have been compelled to resist the deep sympathies of my own heart in favor of the humane purpose sought to be accomplished and to overcome the reluctance with which I dissent from the conclusions of the two Houses of Congress, and present my own opinions in opposition to the action of a coordinate branch of the Government which possesses so fully my confidence and respect. . . .

The question presented, therefore, clearly is upon the constitutionality and propriety of the Federal Government assuming to enter into a novel and vast field of legislation, namely, that of providing for the care and support of all those among the people of the United States who by any form of calamity become fit objects of public philanthropy.

I readily and, I trust, feelingly acknowledge the duty incumbent on us all as men and citizens, and as among the highest and holiest of our duties, to provide for those who, in the mysterious order of Providence, are subject to want and to disease of body or mind; but I can not find any authority in the Constitution for making the Federal Government the great almoner of public charity throughout the United States. To do so would, in my judgment, be contrary to the letter and spirit of the Constitution and subversive of the whole theory upon which the Union of these States is founded. And if it were admissible to contemplate the exercise of this power for any object whatever, I can not avoid the belief that it would in the end be prejudicial rather than beneficial in the noble offices of charity to have the charge of them transferred from the States to the Federal Government. Are we not too prone to forget that the Federal Union is the creature of the States, not they of the Federal Union? We were the inhabitants of colonies distinct in local government one from the other before the Revolution. By that Revolution the colonies each became an independent State. They achieved that independence and secured its recognition by the agency of a consulting body, which, from being an assembly of the ministers of distinct sovereignties instructed to agree to no form of government which did not leave the domestic concerns of each State to itself, was appropriately denominated a Congress. When having tried the experiment of the Confederation, they resolved to change that for the present Federal Union, and thus to confer on the Federal Government more ample authority, they scrupulously measured such of the functions of their cherished sovereignty as they chose to delegate to the General Government. With this aim and to this end the fathers of the Republic framed the Constitution, in and by which the independent and sovereign States united themselves for certain specified objects and purposes, and for those only, leaving all powers not therein set forth as conferred on one or another of the three great departments—the legislative, the executive, and the judicial—indubitably with the States. And when the people of the several States had in their State conventions, and thus alone, given effect and force to the Constitution, not content that any doubt should in future arise as to the scope and character of this act, they ingrafted thereon the explicit declaration that "the powers not delegated to the United States by the Constitution nor prohibited by it to the States are reserved to the States respectively or to the people." Can it be controverted that the great mass of the business of Government—that involved in the social relations, the internal arrangements of the body politic, the mental and moral culture of men, the development of local resources of wealth, the punishment of crimes in general, the preservation of order, the relief of the needy or otherwise unfortunate members of society—did in practice remain with the States; that none of these objects of local concern are by the Constitution expressly or impliedly prohibited to the States, and that none of them are by any express language of the Constitution transferred to the United States? Can it be claimed that any of these functions of local administration and legislation are vested in the Federal Government by any implication? I have never found anything in the Constitution which is susceptible of such a construction. No one of the enumerated powers touches the subject or has even a remote analogy to it. The powers conferred upon the United States have reference to federal relations, or to the means of accomplishing or executing things of federal relation. So also of the same character are the powers taken away from the States by enumeration. In either case the powers granted and the powers restricted were so granted or so restricted only where it was requisite for the maintenance of peace and harmony between the States or for the purpose of protecting their common interests and defending their common sovereignty against aggression from abroad or insurrection at home.

I shall not discuss at length the question of power sometimes claimed for the General Government under the clause of the eighth section of the Constitution, which gives Congress the power "to lay and collect taxes, duties, imposts, and excises, to pay debts and provide for the common defense and general welfare of the United States," because if it has not already been settled upon sound reason and authority it never will be. I take the received and just construction of that article, as if written to lay and collect taxes, duties, imposts, and excises *in order* to pay the debts and *in order* to provide for the common defense and general welfare. It is not a substantive general power to provide for the welfare of the United States, but is a limitation on the grant of power to raise money by taxes, duties, and imposts. If it were otherwise, all the rest of the Constitution, consisting of carefully enumerated and cautiously guarded grants of specific powers, would have been useless, if not delusive. It would be impossible in that view to escape from the conclusion that these were inserted only to mislead for the present, and, instead of enlightening and defining the pathway of the future, to involve its action in the mazes of doubtful construction. Such a conclusion the character of the men who framed that sacred instrument will never permit us to form. Indeed, to suppose it susceptible of any other construction would be to consign all the rights of the States and of the people of the States to the mere discretion of Congress, and thus to clothe the Federal Government with authority to control the sovereign States, by which they would have been dwarfed into provinces or departments and all sovereignty vested in an absolute consolidated central power, against which the spirit of liberty has so often and in so many countries struggled in vain. In my judgment you can not by tributes to humanity make any adequate compensation for the wrong you would inflict by removing the sources of power and political action from those who are to be thereby affected. If the time shall ever arrive when, for an object appealing, however strongly, to our sympathies, the dignity of the States shall bow to the dictation of Congress by conforming their legislation thereto, when the power and majesty and honor of those who created shall become subordinate to the thing of their creation, I but feebly utter my apprehensions when I express my firm conviction that we shall see "the beginning of the end." . . .

Robert C. Toombs, Speech on Slavery
January 24, 1856

[Toombs of Georgia was a Southern moderate. Here, in these remarks before an audience at Tremont Temple, Boston, he attempts to give a reasoned defense of the South's "peculiar institution." What it owes to Calhoun is readily apparent.]

. . . In 1790 there were less than seven hundred thousand slaves in the United States; in 1850 the number exceeded three and one quarter millions. The same authority shows their increase, for the ten years preceding the last census, to have been above twenty-eight per cent., or nearly three per cent. per annum, an increase equal, allowing for the element of foreign immigration, to the white race, and nearly three times that of the free blacks of the North. But these legal rights of the slave embrace but a small portion of the privileges actually enjoyed by him. He has, by universal custom, the control of much of his own time, which is applied, at his own choice and convenience, to the mechanic arts, to agriculture, or to some other profitable pursuit, which not only gives him the power of purchase over many additional necessaries of life, but over many of its luxuries, and in numerous cases, enables him to purchase his freedom when he desires it. Besides, the nature of the relation of master and slave begets kindnesses, imposes duties (and secures their performance), which exist in no other relation of capital and labor. Interest and humanity co-operate in harmony for the well-being of slave labor. Thus the monster objection to our institution of slavery, that it deprives labor of its wages, cannot stand the test of a truthful investigation. . . .

In this division of the earnings of labor between it and capital, the southern slave has a marked advantage over the English laborer, and is often equal to the free laborer of the North. Here again we are furnished with authentic data from which to reason. The census of 1850 shows that, on the cotton estates of the South, which is the chief branch of our agricultural industry, one-half of the arable lands are annually put under food crops. This half is usually wholly consumed on the farm by the laborers and necessary animals; out of the other half must be paid all the necessary expenses of production, often including additional supplies of food beyond the produce of the land, which usually equals one-third of the residue, leaving but one-third for net rent. The average rent of land in the older non-slaveholding states is equal to one-third of the gross product, and it not unfrequently amounts to one-half of it (in England it is sometimes even greater), the tenant, from his portion, paying all expenses of production and the expenses of himself and family. From this statement it is apparent that the farm laborers of the South receive always as much, and frequently a greater portion of the produce of the land, than the laborer in the New or Old England. Besides, here the portion due the slave is a charge upon the whole product of capital and the capital itself; it is neither dependent upon seasons nor subject to accidents, and survives his own capacity for labor, and even the ruin of his master.

But it is objected that religious instruction is denied the slave—while it is true that religious instruction and privileges are not enjoined by law in all of the states, the number of slaves who are in connection with the different churches abundantly proves the universality of their enjoyment of those privileges. And a much larger number of the race in slavery enjoy the consolations of religion than the efforts of the combined Christian world have been able to convert to Christianity out of all the millions of their countrymen who remained in their native land.

The immoralities of the slaves, and of those connected with slavery, are constant themes of abolition denunciation. They are lamentably great; but it remains to be shown that they are greater than with the laboring poor of England, or any other country. And it is shown that our slaves are without the additional stimulant of want to drive them to crime—we have at least removed from them the temptation and excuse of hunger. Poor human nature is here at least spared the wretched fate of the utter prostration of its moral nature at the feet of its physical wants. Lord Ashley's report to the British Parliament shows that in the capital of that empire, perhaps within the hearing of Stafford House and Exeter Hall, hunger alone daily drives its thousands of men and women into the abyss of crime.

It is also objected that our slaves are debarred the benefits of education. This objection is also well taken, and is not without force. And for this evil the slaves are greatly indebted to the abolitionists. Formerly in none of the slaveholding states was it forbidden to teach slaves to read and write; but the character of the literature sought to be furnished them by the abolitionists caused these states to take counsel rather of their passions than their reason, and to lay the axe at the root of the evil; better counsels will in time prevail, and this will be remedied. It is true that the slave, from his protected position, has less need of education than the free laborer, who has to struggle for himself in the warfare of society; yet it is both useful to him, his master, and society.

The want of legal protection to the marriage relation is also a fruitful source of agitation among the opponents of slavery. The complaint is not without foundation. This is an evil not yet removed by law; but marriage is not inconsistent with the institution of slavery as it exists among us, and the objection, therefore, lies rather to an incident than to the essence of the system. But in the truth and fact marriage does exist to a very great extent among slaves, and is encouraged and protected by their owners; and it will be found, upon careful investigation, that fewer children are born out of wedlock among slaves than in the capitals of two of the most civilized countries of Europe—Austria and France; . . . The general happiness, cheerfulness, and contentment of slaves attest both the mildness and humanity of the system and their natural adaptation to their condition. They require no standing armies to enforce their obedience; while the evidence of discontent, and the appliances of force to repress it, are everywhere visible among the toiling millions of the earth; even in the northern states of this Union, strikes and mobs, unions and combinations against employers, attest at once the misery and discontent of labor among them. England keeps one hundred thousand soldiers in time of peace, a large navy, and an innumerable police, to secure obedience to her social institutions; and physical force is the sole guarantee of her social order, the only cement of her gigantic empire.

I have briefly traced the condition of the African race through all ages and all countries, and described it fairly and truly under American slavery, and I submit that the proposition is fully proven, that his position in slavery among us is superior to any which he has ever attained in any age or country. The picture is not without shade as well as light; evils and imperfections cling to man and all of his works, and this is not exempt from them.

Hinton Rowan Helper, *The Impending Crisis of the South*
1857

[Helper, who was a North Carolinian, wrote this book in behalf of the small farmers, mechanics and workers of the South who disliked both the slavocracy and the Negroes. He prophesied the enslavement of the poor white unless slavery was abolished. Republicans distributed *The Impending Crisis* en masse as campaign literature. The South banned it.]

. . . And now that we have come to the very heart and soul of our subject, we feel no disposition to mince matters, but mean to speak plainly, and to the point, without any equivocation, mental reservation, or secret evasion whatever. The son of a venerated parent, who, while he lived, was a considerate and merciful slaveholder, a native of the South, born and bred in North Carolina, of a family whose home has been in the valley of the Yadkin for nearly a century and a half, a Southerner by instinct and by all the influences of thought, habits, and kindred, and with the desire and fixed purpose to reside permanently within the limits of the South, and with the expectation of dying there also—we feel that we have the right to express our opinion, however humble or unimportant it may be, on any and every question that affects the public good; and, so help us God, "sink or swim, live or die, survive or perish," we are determined to exercise that right with manly firmness, and without fear, favor or affection.

And now to the point. In our opinion, an opinion which has been formed from data obtained by assiduous researches, and comparisons, from laborious investigation, logical reasoning, and earnest reflection, the causes which have impeded the progress and prosperity of the South, which have dwindled our commerce, and other similar pursuits, into the most contemptible insignificance; sunk a large majority of our people in galling poverty and ignorance, rendered a small minority conceited and tyrannical, and driven the rest away from their homes; entailed upon us a humiliating dependence on the Free States; disgraced us in the recesses of our own souls, and brought us under reproach in the eyes of all civilized and enlightened nations—may all be traced to one common source, and there find solution in the most hateful and horrible word, that was ever incorporated into the vocabulary of human economy—*Slavery!*

Reared amidst the institution of slavery, believing it to be wrong both in principle and in practice, and having seen and felt its evil influences upon individuals, communities and states, we deem it a duty, no less than a privilege, to enter our protest against it, and to use our most strenuous efforts to overturn and abolish it! Then we are an abolitionist? Yes! not merely a freesoiler, but an abolitionist, in the fullest sense of the term. We are not only in favor of keeping slavery out of the territories, but, carrying our opposition to the institution a step further, we here unhesitatingly declare ourself in favor of its immediate and unconditional abolition, in every state in this confederacy, where it now exists! Patriotism makes us a freesoiler; state pride makes us an emancipationist; a profound sense of duty to the South makes us an abolitionist; a reasonable degree of fellow feeling for the negro, makes us a colonizationist. With the free state men in Kansas and Nebraska, we sympathize with all our heart. We love the whole country, the great family of states and territories, one and inseparable, and would have the word Liberty engraved as an appropriate and truthful motto, on the escutcheon of every member of the confederacy. We love freedom, we hate slavery, and rather than give up the one or submit to the other, we will forfeit the pound of flesh nearest our heart. Is this sufficiently explicit and categorical? If not, we hold ourself in readiness at all times, to return a prompt reply to any proper question that may be propounded. . . .

It is against slavery on the whole, and against slaveholders as a body, that we wage an exterminating war. Those persons who, under the infamous slave-laws of the South—laws which have been correctly spoken of as a "disgrace to civilization," and which must be annulled simultaneously with the abolition of slavery—have had the vile institution entailed on them contrary to their wills, are virtually on our side; we may, therefore, very properly strike them off from the black list of three hundred and forty-seven thousand slaveholders, who, as a body, have shocked the civilized world with their barbarous conduct, and from whose conceited and presumptuous ranks are selected the officers who do all the legislation, town, county, state and national, for (against) five millions of poor outraged whites, and three millions of enslaved negroes.

Non-slaveholders of the South! farmers, mechanics and workingmen, we take this occasion to assure you that the slaveholders, the arrogant demagogues whom you have elected to offices of honor and profit, have hoodwinked you, trifled with you, and used you as mere tools for the consummation of their wicked designs. They have purposely kept you in ignorance, and have, by moulding your passions and prejudices to suit themselves, induced you to act in direct opposition to your dearest rights and interests. By a system of the grossest subterfuge and misrepresentation, and in order to avert, for a season, the vengeance that will most assuredly overtake them ere long, they have taught you to hate the abolitionists, who are your best and only true friends. Now, as one of your own number, we appeal to you to join us in our patriotic endeavors to rescue the generous soil of the South from the usurped and desolating control of these political vampires. Once and forever, at least so far as this country is concerned, the infernal question of slavery must be disposed of; a speedy and perfect abolishment of the whole institution is the true policy of the South—and this is the policy which we propose to pursue. Will you aid us, will you assist us, will you be freemen, or will you be slaves? These are questions of vital importance; weigh them well in your minds; come to a prudent and firm decision, and hold yourselves in readiness to act in accordance therewith. You must either be for us or against us—anti-slavery or pro-slavery; it is impossible for you to occupy a neutral ground; it is as certain as fate itself, that if you do not voluntarily oppose the usurpations and outrages of the slavocrats, they will force you into involuntary compliance with their infamous measures. . . .

Stephen A. Douglas, Debate in the Senate
May 17, 1860

[The debate that follows pointed up Douglas's break with the Southern wing of the Democratic party. It took place two weeks after the Democratic nominating convention at Charleston had failed to select a presidential candidate. The party was now split beyond reconciliation.]

Mr. Davis. What now disturbs our country? The court have decided the question so far as the court could decide any legal question. A case arose in relation to property in a slave held within a Territory, where a law of Congress declared that such property should not be held. The whole case was before them; everything, except the mere technical point that the law was not enacted by a Territorial Legislature. Why, then, if we are to abide by the decision of the Supreme Court in any future case, do we maintain this controversy now on this last point which to-day divides, disturbs, distracts, and destroys the efficiency and the power, because it disintegrates the Democratic party? To the Senator, I know, as a question of property, it is a matter of consequence. I should do him injustice if I left any one to infer that I treated his argument as one made by a man prejudiced against the character of property involved in the question. That is not his position; but I claim that he is pursuing an *ignis fatuus*, a thing which has no existence under the Constitution, and which has arisen from the corrupting strifes of political faction and the rivalry of individuals. Measured by any standard of common sense, its magnitude would be too small to disturb the adjustment of the balance between the political parties of our country. There can be no appeal to humanity made upon this basis. Least of all could it be made to one who, like the Senator and myself, has seen this species of property in its sparse condition on the northwestern frontier, and seen it go out without disturbing the harmony of the community, as it had previously existed to the benefit of the individual who held it. He has no apprehension, he can have none, that it is to retard the political prosperity of the future States—now the Territories. He can have no apprehension that in that country to which they never would be carried except from necessity, and for domestic purposes, they could ever so accumulate as to constitute a great political element. He knows, and every man who has experience and judgment must admit, that the few who may be so carried have nothing to fear but the climate, and that living in that close relation which belongs to one or two of them connected together, the kindest relations which it is possible to exist between master and dependent would exist between these domestics and their owners.

There is a relation belonging to this species of property, not connected with the apprentice, not connected with the hired man, which awakens whatever there is of kindness or of nobility of soul in the heart of him who owns it; and this can only be alienated, can only be obscured or destroyed, by collecting this species of property into such masses that the owner himself becomes ignorant of the individuals who compose it. In the relation, however, which can exist in the northwestern Territories, the mere domestic connection of one, two, or, at most, half a dozen servants in a family, associating with the children as they grow up, attending upon age as it declines, there can be nothing against which either philanthropy or humanity can make an appeal. Not even the emancipationist could raise his voice, for this is the high road and the open gate for the emancipation of every one who may thus be taken to the frontier. . . .

We believe now, as we have asserted on former occasions, that the best hope for the perpetuity of our Government depends upon the coöperation, the harmony, the zealous action of the Democratic party. We cling to that party from conviction, as we cling to the Union for the purpose for which it was formed. Whenever we shall be taught that the Democratic party is recreant to its principles; whenever we shall learn that it cannot be relied upon to maintain the great measures which constitute its vitality, I, for one, shall be ready to leave it. And so, sir, when we declare our tenacious adherence to the Union, it is the Union of the Constitution. If the compact between the States is to be trampled into the dust; if anarchy is to be substituted for the usurpation which threatened the Government at an earlier period; if the Union is to become powerless for the purposes for which it was established, and we are vainly to appeal to it for protection, then, sir, conscious in the rectitude of our course, and self-reliant within ourselves, we look beyond the confines of the Union for the maintenance of our rights. A habitual reverence and cherished affection for the Government of our fathers will hold us to it much longer than our interest; but he is a poor statesman who does not understand that communities at last must yield to the dictates of their interests. That the affection which existed without stint or denial among our fathers may be weakened in succeeding generations by the constant denial of right, until equality will be asserted within or without the Union, must be evident. It is time to be up and doing. There is yet time to remove all these causes of dissension and alienation which are now distracting, and have for years past divided, the country.

If the Senator correctly described me as having, at a former period, against my own tendencies and opinions, acquiesced in the decision of my party; and if, when I had more of youth, and of youth's vigor, and the future was painted in the colors of hope, which youth always furnishes, I could thus surrender my own convictions, my own prejudices, and coöperate with my political friends for the public good; now, when the years of the future may not be so hopeful; when I approach the evening of life, and the shadows are reversed, and the mind turns to the retrospective, it is not to be supposed that I would be disposed lightly to desert, or idly to put upon trial, the party to which I have adhered. It is rather to be supposed that that conservatism which belongs to the timidity of increasing years would lead me to cling to it; to be supported by, rather than to cast off, the organization with which I have been so long connected. If I am driven to consider the necessity of separating myself from those old and dear relations, from this support, under circumstances such as I have described, might not my friends who differed from me pause and inquire whether there is not something real involved?

I desire no divided flag for the Democratic party. I seek not to depreciate the power of the Senator, or take from him anything of that confidence he feels in the large army at his back. I prefer that his banner should lie in its silken folds; but if it impatient rustles to be unfurled in opposition to ours, then, sir, we will plant our own on every hill; it shall overlook the Atlantic and welcome the sun as it rises; it shall give its last graceful dismissal to the sun as he sinks in the quiet Pacific. Our principles are national; they belong to every State in the Union; and though elections may be lost by their assertion, they constitute the only foundation on which we can maintain power, on which we can again rise to the dignity the Democracy once professed. Does not my friend from Illinois—he will permit me to call him so because of so many years of kind relations—does he not see in the sectional character of the vote he received, that his opinions are not welcome to every portion of the country? Is not the fact that the resolutions adopted by seventeen States on which the greatest reliance must be placed for Democratic support, are in opposition to the dogma to which he still clings, a warning that if he persists and succeeds in planting his theory upon the Democratic party, its days are numbered? We ask only for the Constitution. We ask of the Democracy

only from time to time to declare with current events what
the Constitution was intended to secure and provide. Our
flag bears no new device. All its folds, in living light, proclaim the constitutional Union, justice, equality, and frater-
nity, now and forever.

Mr. Douglas . . . The Senator says he loves his party; but
he loves to have the party agree with him, and then he will
fight for them. I wish him to bear in mind that the party
never did indorse this new article of faith which he is now
threatening to use for the disruption of the party unless it
can be admitted. The party rejected it in 1848, scouted it in
1852, denounced it in 1856, and again in 1860. The party
stands under its old flag; under its old organization; proclaiming its time-honored creed; making no variation whatever. Is that sufficient cause to disrupt the only party that
can save the Union? I think we all profess to believe that
the Democratic party is the only political organization now
adequate to the preservation of the Union. He who attempts
to break up that organization looks with complacency to the
only alternative which we are told is to follow—to wit: disunion. The simple question then is, whether it is better to
have a Democratic Administration on the same platform
that brought Mr. Buchanan into power, or dissolve the
Union. If this platform was so fearfully bad, so vicious, so
fatal to southern interests, and destructive of southern rights,
how happened it that every man of you indorsed it in 1856?
Did you not know what your rights were then? Were you not
as much devoted to the interest and honor of your States then
as now? How happened it that every delegate from every State
of the Union voted for it then, if it is sufficient cause for
disruption now? . . .

Now, sir, are these dissensions a sufficient cause for the
disruption of the party? What has been done? What new
question has arisen since 1856 that makes the platform then
adopted unworthy of the support of patriotic men now? We
are told that the Supreme Court have made a decision in the
Dred Scott case, and that is the cause. Is that decision hostile
to the southern States? Is there anybody in the Democratic
party that does not propose to abide by it, and carry it out in
good faith? No; but you want us to declare, first, what that

decision means, and then that we will carry it out according to that construction. . . .

I should like to know how many States will be "certain," if you repudiate the Cincinnati platform, strike away the flag-staff, pull down the old Democratic banner, and run up this new one; this Yancey flag of intervention by Congress for slavery in the Territories in all cases where the people do not want it. How many do you think you will get? You tell us, too, that the South cannot be carried on the Charleston platform; at any rate, we are told so by others. If they cannot, then are those States not certainly Democratic. You want to change the platform from what it was, because the South cannot be carried on the same issues upon which we triumphed in 1856! Then they are not "certainly Democratic States." If Mississippi will not go for a candidate on the same platform now that she did in 1856, I reckon that Mississippi is either not Democratic now, or she was not then. Alabama voted for Buchanan, in 1856, on the Cincinnati platform. All we ask is the same platform, and a candidate holding the same opinions. Will not Alabama stand by him now? She was a Democratic State in 1856; and if Democracy has not changed, she ought to be now. If she will not stand by the organization, by what right do you call her a Democratic State? So with Georgia; so with South Carolina; so with every one of these States whose delegates seceded because we did not change the platform, and repudiated our time-honored principles. Sir, I do not believe those people have changed. I believe the people of every one of those States are now as much attached to the old principles of the party and its organization as they ever were. I believe they will repudiate the action of those men who are willing to divide and destroy the party merely because they cannot carry out their peculiar views. . . .

Mr. Yancey's plan was, to remain in the organization of the Democratic party; form the Southern League, bound by secrecy for a southern confederacy—involving disunion, of course; wait in the Democratic party until the proper moment came; and then, by a sudden movement, disrupt the party, and plunge the cotton States into revolution. The proof is here clear that disunion was Mr. Yancey's object. A separate southern confederacy was his whole end. He believed the South could not find safety anywhere else. His plan was to keep in the Democratic party until the proper moment came for revolution; then plunge the cotton States into it; break up the party, and with the party the Confederacy. Sir, I cannot doubt but that this was Mr. Yancey's plan. I submit to the Senate and the country whether "the proper moment" selected by him was not the Charleston convention; and whether the secession of these same States at Charleston was not in obedience to that plan? I do not mean to say, nor do I believe, that all the men who approved or defended that secession were disunionists; but I do believe that disunion was the prompting motive that broke up that convention. It is a disunion movement, and intervention is a disunion platform. Congressional intervention South for slavery, congressional intervention North against slavery, brings the two sections into hostile array, renders a conflict inevitable, and forces them either to a collision or a separation; for neither party can back out with honor. This action has been taken, by some at least, solemnly, deliberately; seeking to make this new test a *sine qua non* at the risk of disrupting or destroying the only political party in existence that can save the Union.

I submit, then, whether this new change of platform does not carry with it not only a dissolution of the party, but a disruption of all those ties which bind the country together? I believe that it does. I believe that my friend from Mississippi is himself following a mere phantom in trying to get a recognition of the right of Congress to intervene for the protection of slavery in the Territories, when the people do not want it. He, in effect, confesses that it is a mere phantom, an abstract theory, without results, without fruits; and why? He says that he admits that slavery cannot be forced on a hostile people. He says he has always regarded it as a question of soil and climate and political economy. I so regard it.

Mr. DAVIS. I say we have a constitutional right to try it.

Mr. DOUGLAS. He says they have a constitutional right to try it—just such a right as he says the soldier had when he was going to Concord, who declared he had a right to go, and he was going because he had the right. Statesmen do not always act on the principle that they will do whatever they have a right to do. A man has a right to do a great many silly things; a statesman has a right to perpetrate acts of consummate folly; but I do not know that it is a man's duty to do all that he may have a right to do. Let me put the case to you again. When this compromise was made of taking non-intervention by Congress with slavery in the Territories, the object was to defeat the Wilmot proviso. A majority of the North, and a good many of the South, believed that the Wilmot proviso was constitutional. Some southern men said they believed it was; but whether it was or not, they would not submit to it anyhow, because it was morally wrong. . . .

Now, suppose the Supreme Court should decide hereafter that the Wilmot proviso was constitutional: would that justify me, after my compact with you to abide by non-intervention, in going for the proviso merely because the court had decided that I had a right to it? Would not you say that I was faithless to the compact? Would you not say that, while the court had settled the question of power in my favor, it had not released my conscience from the obligations that bound me as an honest and honorable man never to go for it? If that would have been true in the event of the decision having been the other way, what moral right have you to go for intervention, even if the court decides that you may? It is one thing to have the right; it is another thing to exercise it. We came together, a portion believing in the right, a portion not believing in it, a portion taking a third view; we shook hands, all pledging our honors that we would abandon all our claims on either side to intervention, and go for non-intervention. I care not how the court decide as to the power. I may have the right to make a speech here of two hours every day, but I do not think I am bound to inflict it on the Senate merely because I have a constitutional right to do it. We have the right to do a great many foolish things, a great many silly things; but I hold that the path of duty and wisdom is to stand by the doctrine of non-intervention; quit quarreling on these abstruse theories about the power of a Territorial Legislature; leave that to the courts, where we agreed to leave it, and where the Constitution has left it. When we do that, there will be peace and harmony in the whole country.

James Buchanan, Fourth Annual Message
December 3, 1860

[In his last four months as President, Buchanan faced the problem of dealing with the impending secession of at least seven Southern states. As the message below indicates, Buchanan, true to his states' rights philosophy of government, felt that he was powerless to do anything and that the decision to maintain or break up the Union must be made by the people of the separate states.]

Throughout the year since our last meeting the country has been eminently prosperous in all its material interests. The general health has been excellent, our harvests have been abundant, and plenty smiles throughout the land. Our commerce and manufactures have been prosecuted with energy and industry, and have yielded fair and ample returns. In short, no nation in the tide of time has ever presented a spectacle of greater material prosperity than we have done until within a very recent period.

Why is it, then, that discontent now so extensively prevails, and the Union of the States, which is the source of all these blessings, is threatened with destruction?

The long-continued and intemperate interference of the Northern people with the question of slavery in the Southern States has at length produced its natural effects. The different sections of the Union are now arrayed against each other, and the time has arrived, so much dreaded by the Father of his Country, when hostile geographical parties have been formed.

I have long foreseen and often forewarned my countrymen of the now impending danger. This does not proceed solely from the claim on the part of Congress or the Territorial legislatures to exclude slavery from the Territories, nor from the efforts of different States to defeat the execution of the fugitive-slave law. All or any of these evils might have been endured by the South without danger to the Union (as others have been) in the hope that time and reflection might apply the remedy. The immediate peril arises not so much from these causes as from the fact that the incessant and violent agitation of the slavery question throughout the North for the last quarter of a century has at length produced its malign influence on the slaves and inspired them with vague notions of freedom. Hence a sense of security no longer exists around the family altar. This feeling of peace at home has given place to apprehensions of servile insurrections. Many a matron throughout the South retires at night in dread of what may befall herself and children before the morning. Should this apprehension of domestic danger, whether real or imaginary, extend and intensify itself until it shall pervade the masses of the Southern people, then disunion will become inevitable. Self-preservation is the first law of nature, and has been implanted in the heart of man by his Creator for the wisest purpose; and no political union, however fraught with blessings and benefits in all other respects, can long continue if the necessary consequence be to render the homes and the firesides of nearly half the parties to it habitually and hopelessly insecure. Sooner or later the bonds of such a union must be severed. It is my conviction that this fatal period has not yet arrived, and my prayer to God is that He would preserve the Constitution and the Union throughout all generations.

But let us take warning in time and remove the cause of danger. It can not be denied that for five and twenty years the agitation at the North against slavery has been incessant. In 1835 pictorial handbills and inflammatory appeals were circulated extensively throughout the South of a character to excite the passions of the slaves, and, in the language of General Jackson, "to stimulate them to insurrection and produce all the horrors of a servile war." This agitation has ever since been continued by the public press, by the proceedings of State and county conventions and by abolition sermons and lectures. The time of Congress has been occupied in violent speeches on this never-ending subject, and appeals, in pamphlet and other forms, indorsed by distinguished names, have been sent forth from this central point and spread broadcast over the Union.

How easy would it be for the American people to settle the slavery question forever and to restore peace and harmony to this distracted country! They, and they alone, can do it. All that is necessary to accomplish the object, and all for which the slave States have ever contended, is to be let alone and permitted to manage their domestic institutions in their own way. As sovereign States, they, and they alone, are responsible before God and the world for the slavery existing among them. For this the people of the North are not more responsible and have no more right to interfere than with similar institutions in Russia or in Brazil.

Upon their good sense and patriotic forbearance I confess I still greatly rely. Without their aid it is beyond the power of any President, no matter what may be his own political proclivities, to restore peace and harmony among the States. Wisely limited and restrained as is his power under our Constitution and laws, he alone can accomplish but little for good or for evil on such a momentous question.

And this brings me to observe that the election of any one of our fellow-citizens to the office of President does not of itself afford just cause for dissolving the Union. This is more especially true if his election has been effected by a mere plurality, and not a majority of the people, and has resulted from transient and temporary causes, which may probably never again occur. In order to justify a resort to revolutionary resistance, the Federal Government must be guilty of "a deliberate, palpable, and dangerous exercise" of powers not granted by the Constitution. The late Presidential election, however, has been held in strict conformity with its express provisions. How, then, can the result justify a revolution to destroy this very Constitution? Reason, justice, a regard for the Constitution, all require that we shall wait for some overt and dangerous act on the part of the President elect before resorting to such a remedy. It is said, however, that the antecedents of the President elect have been sufficient to justify the fears of the South that he will attempt to invade their constitutional rights. But are such apprehensions of contingent danger in the future sufficient to justify the immediate destruction of the noblest system of government ever devised by mortals? From the very nature of his office and its high responsibilities he must necessarily be conservative. The stern duty of administering the vast and complicated concerns of this Government affords in itself a guaranty that he will not attempt any violation of a clear constitutional right.

After all, he is no more than the chief executive officer of the Government. His province is not to make but to execute the laws. And it is a remarkable fact in our history that, notwithstanding the repeated efforts of the antislavery party, no single act has ever passed Congress, unless we may possibly except the Missouri compromise, impairing in the slightest degree the rights of the South to their property in slaves; and it may also be observed, judging from present indications, that no probability exists of the passage of such an act by a majority of both Houses, either in the present or the next Congress. Surely under these circumstances we ought to be restrained from present action by the precept of Him who spake as man never spoke, that "sufficient unto the day is the evil thereof." The day of evil may never come unless we shall rashly bring it upon ourselves.

It is alleged as one cause for immediate secession that the Southern States are denied equal rights with the other States in the common Territories. But by what authority are these denied? Not by Congress, which has never passed, and I believe never will pass, any act to exclude slavery from these Territories; and certainly not by the Supreme Court, which has solemnly decided that slaves are property, and, like all other property, their owners have a right to take them into the common Territories and hold them there under the protection of the Constitution.

So far then, as Congress is concerned, the objection is not to anything they have already done, but to what they may do hereafter. It will surely be admitted that this apprehension of future danger is no good reason for an immediate dissolution of the Union. It is true that the Territorial legislature of Kansas, on the 23d February, 1860, passed in great haste an act over the veto of the governor declaring that

slavery "is and shall be forever prohibited in this Territory."
Such an act, however, plainly violating the rights of property
secured by the Constitution, will surely be declared void by
the judiciary whenever it shall be presented in a legal
form. . . .

The fact is that our Union rests upon public opinion, and
can never be cemented by the blood of its citizens shed in
civil war. If it can not live in the affections of the people, it
must one day perish. Congress possesses many means of preserving it by conciliation, but the sword was not placed in
their hand to preserve it by force.

But may I be permitted solemnly to invoke my countrymen to pause and deliberate before they determine to destroy
this the grandest temple which has ever been dedicated to
human freedom since the world began? It has been consecrated by the blood of our fathers, by the glories of the
past, and by the hopes of the future. The Union has already
made us the most prosperous, and ere long will, if preserved,
render us the most powerful, nation on the face of the earth.
In every foreign region of the globe the title of American
citizen is held in the highest respect, and when pronounced
in a foreign land it causes the hearts of our countrymen to
swell with honest pride. Surely when we reach the brink of
the yawning abyss we shall recoil with horror from the last
fatal plunge.

By such a dread catastrophe the hopes of the friends of
freedom throughout the world would be destroyed, and a
long night of leaden despotism would enshroud the nations.
Our example for more than eighty years would not only be
lost, but it would be quoted as a conclusive proof that man
is unfit for self-government.

It is not every wrong—nay, it is not every grievous wrong
—which can justify a resort to such a fearful alternative. This
ought to be the last desperate remedy of a despairing people, after every other constitutional means of conciliation had
been exhausted. We should reflect that under this free Government there is an incessant ebb and flow in public opinion.
The slavery question, like everything human, will have its
day. I firmly believe that it has reached and passed the cul-
minating point. But if in the midst of the existing excite-

ment the Union shall perish, the evil may then become irreparable.

Congress can contribute much to avert it by proposing and recommending to the legislatures of the several States the remedy for existing evils which the Constitution has itself provided for its own preservation. This has been tried at different critical periods of our history, and always with eminent success. It is to be found in the fifth article, providing for its own amendment. Under this article amendments have been proposed by two-thirds of both Houses of Congress, and have been "ratified by the legislatures of three-fourths of the several States," and have consequently become parts of the Constitution. To this process the country is indebted for the clause prohibiting Congress from passing any law respecting an establishment of religion or abridging the freedom of speech or of the press or of the right of petition. To this we are also indebted for the bill of rights which secures the people against any abuse of power by the Federal Government. Such were the apprehensions justly entertained by the friends of State rights at that period as to have rendered it extremely doubtful whether the Constitution could have long survived without those amendments. . . .

This is the very course which I earnestly recommend in order to obtain an "explanatory amendment" of the Constitution on the subject of slavery. This might originate with Congress or the State legislatures, as may be deemed most advisable to attain the object. The explanatory amendment might be confined to the final settlement of the true construction of the Constitution on three special points:

1. An express recognition of the right of property in slaves in the States where it now exists or may hereafter exist.

2. The duty of protecting this right in all the common Territories throughout their Territorial existence, and until they shall be admitted as States into the Union, with or without slavery, as their constitutions may prescribe.

3. A like recognition of the right of the master to have his slave who has escaped from one State to another restored and "delivered up" to him, and of the validity of the fugitive-slave law enacted for this purpose, together with a declaration that all State laws impairing or defeating this right are viola-

tions of the Constitution, and are consequently null and void. It may be objected that this construction of the Constitution has already been settled by the Supreme Court of the United States, and what more ought to be required? The answer is that a very large proportion of the people of the United States still contest the correctness of this decision, and never will cease from agitation and admit its binding force until clearly established by the people of the several States in their sovereign character. Such an explanatory amendment would, it is believed, forever terminate the existing dissensions, and restore peace and harmony among the States. . . .

Alexander H. Stephens, Speech on the Confederate Constitution
March 12, 1861

[Stephens was a Georgia moderate who had opposed secession but who nonetheless had been elected provisional Vice-President of the Confederacy. In this speech delivered at Atlanta soon after his election he discusses the virtues of the Confederate Constitution.]

Taking the whole of the new constitution, I have no hesitancy in giving it as my judgment that it is decidedly better than the old. Allow me briefly to allude to some of these improvements. . . .

This old thorn of the tariff, which was the cause of so much irritation in the old body politic, is removed forever from the new.

Again, the subject of internal improvements, under the power of Congress to regulate commerce, is put at rest under our system. The power claimed by construction, under the old Constitution, was at least a doubtful one—it rested solely upon construction. We of the South, generally apart from considerations of constitutional principles, opposed its exercise upon grounds of expediency and justice. . . .

The true principle is, to subject the commerce of every locality to whatever burdens may be necessary to facilitate it.

If Charleston harbor needs improvement, let the commerce of Charleston bear the burden. If the mouth of the Savannah river has to be cleared out, let the seagoing navigation which is benefited by it bear the burden. So with the mouths of the Alabama and Mississippi rivers. Just as the products of the interior—our cotton, wheat, corn, and other articles—have to bear the necessary rates of freight over our railroads to reach the seas. This is again the broad principle of perfect equality and justice. And it is specially held forth and established in our new constitution.

Another feature to which I will allude is, that the new constitution provides that cabinet ministers and heads of departments shall have the privilege of seats upon the floor of the Senate and House of Representatives,—shall have the right to participate in the debates and discussions upon the various subjects of administration. I should have preferred that this provision should have gone further, and allowed the President to select his constitutional advisers from the Senate and House of Representatives. That would have conformed entirely to the practice in the British Parliament, which in my judgment is one of the wisest provisions in the British constitution. It is that which gives its stability, in its facility to change its administration. Ours, as it is, is a great approximation to the right principle. . . .

Another change in the constitution relates to the length of the tenure of the presidential office. In the new constitution it is six years instead of four, and the President is rendered ineligible for re-election. This is certainly a decidedly conservative change. It will remove from the incumbent all temptation to use his office or exert the powers confided to him for any objects of personal ambition. The only incentive to that higher ambition which should move and actuate one holding such high trusts in his hands, will be the good of the people, the advancement, prosperity, happiness, safety, honor, and true glory of the Confederacy.

But not to be tedious in enumerating the numerous changes for the better, allow me to allude to one other—though last, not least: The new constitution has put to rest, *forever*, all agitating questions relating to our peculiar institution, African slavery as it exists among us,—the proper status of the negro in our form of civilization. This was the immediate cause of the late rupture and present revolution. Jefferson, in his forecast, had anticipated this as the "rock upon which the old Union would split." He was right. What was conjecture with him is now a realized fact. But whether he fully comprehended the great truth upon which that rock *stood* and *stands* may be doubted. The prevailing ideas entertained by him and most of the leading statesmen at the time of the formation of the old Constitution were that the enslavement of the African was in violation of the laws of nature; that it was wrong in *principle*, socially, morally, and politically. It was an evil they knew not well how to deal with, but the general opinion of the men of that day was that somehow or other, in the order of Providence, the institution would be evanescent and pass away. This idea, though not incorporated in the Constitution, was the prevailing idea at the time. The Constitution, it is true, secured every essential guaranty to the institution while it should last, and hence no argument can be justly used against the constitutional guaranties thus secured, because of the common sentiment of the day. Those ideas, however, were fundamentally wrong. They rested upon the assumption of the equality of races. This was an error. It was a sandy foundation, and the idea of the government built upon it; when the "storm came and the wind blew, it *fell*."

Our new government is founded upon exactly the opposite idea; its foundations are laid, its corner-stone rests, upon the great truth that the negro is not equal to the white man; that slavery—subordination to the superior race—is his natural and normal condition.

CHAPTER VI. THE REPUBLICAN REVOLUTION

Formal political opposition to slavery began in 1840 when the Liberty party nominated James G. Birney, an abolitionist, as its presidential candidate. He received only seven thousand votes in the election, compared to more than a million each for the Democratic and Whig candidates. The results accurately reflected the indifference or downright hostility of the North to any anti-slavery crusade at that time. Four years later the conflict over Texas annexation brought the slavery issue to the fore in American politics, and this time the Liberty party scored heavily in the presidential election, winning over sixty thousand votes—enough to take the victory from Clay, the Whig candidate, who had equivocated over Texas annexation and so had alienated anti-slavery Whigs.

In 1848 the Liberty party merged with a group of anti-slavery Whigs and Democrats to form the Free-Soil party. The issue that united them was support for the Wilmot Proviso, which proposed to keep slavery out of the territory recently won from Mexico. The Free-Soil party went beyond mere opposition to the extension of slavery, however, and attempted to become a viable and permanent political force. Putting up Martin Van Buren as its presidential candidate, it offered a program which was calculated to have wide appeal in the North, including federal aid for local internal improvements and a homestead act to encourage settlement, exclusively by free men, in the Western territories. Though he won no states in the election, Van Buren did exceptionally well in securing votes, receiving almost three hundred thousand and thereby depriving the Democratic party of the presidency. By 1848, then, the signs were unmistakable: more and more Northerners had become convinced that something must be done to stop the slavocracy and the expansion of the South.

Northern anxieties mounted during the years of prosperity that followed the Compromise of 1850. While most Northerners accepted the Compromise, it had one feature that they could not easily abide: the Fugitive Slave Act, which gave federal authorities sweeping powers to issue warrants and hunt down runaway slaves. The Act empowered special commissioners to call together a *posse comitatus* in any local community to aid them in the hunt. Any citizen refusing to serve could be fined severely; anyone actively helping a fugitive was subject to a prison term and suits for civil damages. The fugitives themselves were totally without rights or redress, so that free Negroes had no way of protecting themselves against false accusation and arrest. Northerners responded angrily to the Act. They disliked the blatant intrusion of federal police officials in their local affairs, and they had no wish to bear witness to, even to co-operate in, the grossest violations of personal liberty, all in behalf of the slavocracy.

The election of Democrat Franklin Pierce in 1852 marked a turning point in the North's attitude toward the South, though the change was not at once apparent. Pierce was himself a Northerner, yet his administration went further than had any previous one in defending the Southern interest. Committed to the principle of states' rights, in accordance with the dictates of his party, Pierce fought off successive attempts by Northern majorities in Congress to enlarge federal responsibilities. Applying his veto power freely, he rebuffed Northern demands for higher tariffs, immediate settlements of the territories and aid for rivers and harbors. Resentment against the administration, however, failed to congeal into political opposition because the Whig party had collapsed following the defection of Southern planters to the Democratic party. Northern Whigs were split into factions: the conservatives, led by ex-President Millard Fillmore, who gravitated toward the American, or Know-Nothing, party in the belief that antipathy to Catholics and immigrants would unite the sections; the liberals, led by William Seward, who awaited an issue that would fuse all the anti-slavery groups into a new party; and the middle-of-the-roaders, like Lincoln, who clung to the sinking ship as long as they could.

The issue for which the liberals were waiting suddenly arose in 1854 with the passage of the Kansas-Nebraska Act. This Act, it will be remembered, opened the Kansas and Nebraska territories to settlement on the principle of popular sovereignty, according to which the settlers themselves would determine, through their territorial legislatures, whether to permit slavery. It fixed the northern boundary of the Nebraska Territory at the 40th parallel, thereby nullifying the Missouri Compromise of 1820, which had confined slavery to the area below the 36° 30' parallel. By the time the Act passed Congress on May 30, three months after it had been introduced, the North was seething with protest. Anti-Nebraska groups had sprung up spontaneously in every free state. Whigs, Know-Nothings, Wilmot Proviso Democrats, Free-Soilers, abolitionists, people who had not been concerned with politics before—all joined the burgeoning anti-Nebraska movement.

Stephen Douglas and the other advocates of popular sovereignty could not fathom the reason for the uprising in the North. Supposing that they had found the basis of sectional reconciliation, they expected to be congratulated, not reviled. The climate and terrain of Kansas and Nebraska, they maintained, were uncongenial to the development of a slave economy. Moreover, no Southerner, not even the hottest of the firebrands, proposed extending slavery to the free states. To Douglas and his followers, all the sound and fury stirred up by abolitionists and other such demagogues was quite pointless.

But Douglas failed to perceive that a large segment of the North did not want the slavery question reopened. The Missouri Compromise had definitively settled it so far as they were concerned. They regarded the Compromise as a national commitment to the containment of slavery and an implicit assertion of the supremacy of freedom in the scale of national values. The Kansas-Nebraska Act cast doubts on this commitment. What were the nation's ideals now? Were slavery and freedom equal in value? Were they comparable to other public choices, as the doctrine of popular sovereignty implied, to be voted up or down on every occasion? The Kansas-Nebraska Act forced the North to take a moral stand, to draw the line beyond which there could be no compromise. At stake was the meaning and purpose of the nation as a whole.

The anti-Nebraska movement soon crystallized around the Republican party. Exactly where and when the party was founded is not known, but the best evidence is that it first appeared as a formal organization in Jackson, Michigan, in early July 1854, with a platform demanding repeal of the Kansas-Nebraska and Fugitive Slave acts and the abolition of slavery in the District of Columbia. Before long, Republican organizations in the other Northern states were putting forward similar sets of demands. The party's rise to power was spectacular. Within two years of its founding it had clearly established itself as the Democratic party's only rival; within four it had won over the majority in all but two Northern states; and within six it had captured the presidency.

These six years of insurgency shaped the party's character and ideology. Republicans thought of themselves as revolutionists, reliving the experiences of 1776, struggling, as their forebears had, against privilege and monopoly and in behalf of the rights of man. Republicans were thoroughgoing Jeffersonians, and the Declaration of Independence served as the text of their crusade against the "slave oligarchy." Republicans wanted America to return to the ideals of free labor and human equality.

The Democrats, as well, laid claim to the Jeffersonian legacy. Their Jefferson, however, was not the author of the Declaration, but the patron saint of states' rights and nullification and author of the Kentucky Resolutions. Few Democrats willingly admitted that *all* men were created equal, and possessed inalienable rights. Even Democratic agrarians, like Hinton Helper and Andrew Johnson, who opposed the slavocracy, assumed that the Declaration referred to whites alone, Negroes being naturally inferior. Stephen Douglas, professing neutrality toward slavery, felt that the Declaration applied to nations, not individuals; and the defenders of slavery contended that the South's "peculiar institution" should be adopted by the ruling classes everywhere. In short, the Democratic party had banished the spirit of Jefferson, even as it invoked his name to justify its policies.

The Republican party brought nationalism as well as Jeffersonian ideals back to the center of American politics, though it was not the conservative nationalism that the Federalists and Whigs had espoused, but the democratic nationalism of Jackson. The states' rights policies of successive Democratic administrations had consistently excluded federal assistance to the mechanics and skilled workers, immigrants, farmers and small businessmen who populated the North. Accordingly, the Republican party fashioned a comprehensive national program to aid these groups and draw them together into a new coalition. As worked out in party conventions, this program included federal supervision of the territories, federal subsidies to clear harbors and rivers and build railroads, a federal homestead act and federal encouragement to industry. The 1860 platform commended "that policy of national exchanges which secures to the workingman liberal wages, to agriculture remunerative prices, to mechanics and manufacturers an adequate reward for their skill, labor and enterprise and to the nation commercial prosperity and independence."

Republican nationalism, however, did not especially appeal to the large commercial interests of the North before the Civil War. This should be emphasized, since it has often been assumed that the party attracted, or was dominated by, big business from the start. In fact, most members of the business elite opposed the Republican party throughout the 1850s. They feared its radical tendencies, and to a greater degree, the effects of its antipathy toward the South. Northern capitalists stood to lose heavily from sectional conflict. The South raised cotton for Northern mills, provided a substantial market for Northern shippers and manufacturers, and owed hundreds of millions of dollars to Northern bankers. When weighed against these facts, how much could the issue of freedom in the territories count in the balance? "Cotton thread," Emerson wrote, "holds the Union together, unites John C. Calhoun and Abbot Lawrence." After the demise of the Whig party, Northern businessmen supported the Know-Nothing, the Constitutional Union and the Democratic parties—any party but the Republican. It was the Civil War that finally severed the cotton thread of the Union and brought capitalists into Republican ranks en masse.

But as the Republican party grew in size during the 1850s, it increasingly played down its Jeffersonian radicalism in the attempt to convey an image of responsibility and sobriety. Carefully distinguishing themselves from abolitionists, Republicans repeatedly emphasized that they were proposing only to contain slavery, not extinguish it. At all costs they had to avoid alarming farmers and workers, who feared competition from free Negroes almost as much as from the owners of enslaved ones. The slightest overtones of abolitionism might prove fatal to the chances of Republicans who aspired to office, and in particular to the presidency, as William Seward discovered in 1860. Lincoln was nominated because no one could accuse him of radicalism, much less of abolitionism.

Lincoln himself embodied all the strains and tensions in the Republican character. He was simultaneously a Jeffersonian defender of universal equality and the rights of labor, a nationalist who believed in large-scale federal economic intervention, and a shrewd, cautious politician. He started out in Illinois in the 1830s as a devoted follower of Henry Clay and opponent of the Jacksonians. He rose rapidly in the Whig hierarchy, having married into one of the best families in the state, and was elected to the House of Representatives in 1846. At that point he suffered a setback, losing the support of his constituency because he condemned the Mexican War. His political career seemed to be over, and he was apparently just another casualty of the ripening conflict between North and South. In 1849 Lincoln retired from politics, apparently forever, and turned his full attention to the practice of law.

The Kansas-Nebraska Act suddenly thrust him into the center of Illinois politics. The Lincoln who emerged from five years of obscurity was no longer the conservative Whig to whom obedience to the Constitution and respect for the established order represented the supreme good. He was now a committed Jeffersonian liberal. He had learned that the Constitution alone, separated from the Declaration, could not command obedience, and that the Union would break down unless it rested firmly on the ideal of equality and freedom for all men. Clay, he had come to realize, had temporized too long with the South, forgetting why the nation was worth preserving. The time for temporizing was over, Lincoln felt. Slavery had to be prevented from spreading into the territories; Douglas's program of popular sovereignty had to be decisively rejected.

Driving home these themes in speech after speech, Lincoln soon established himself as Douglas's most effective opponent in Illinois. No one else was so eloquent, lucid, or well informed, nor defined the issues so sharply as Lincoln. But he remained in the Whig party until he was convinced that all hope for it was futile. It was not until 1856 that he became a Republican. Two years later he ran against Douglas for the Senate. In the course of the campaign he and Douglas held their famous debates, which were followed attentively by the country at large. While Lincoln lost the election by a narrow margin, he gained a national reputation.

Lincoln, it should be noted, attributed his defeat to the animosity of the Illinois aristocracy toward Republicans. "Nearly all the old exclusive silk-stocking Whiggery is against us," he said after the election. "I don't mean nearly all the old Whig party but nearly all the nice, exclusive sort." And so, for the next two years he admonished Republicans to show restraint, to jettison such terms as "the higher law" and "irrepressible conflict," to promise to obey the Fugitive Slave Act, and, above all, to keep their distance from abolitionists. Lincoln carried out his own injunctions exceedingly well. In 1859 he delivered a speech at Cooper Union in New York City which satisfied Eastern conservatives that this Free-Soiler from the West—who impressed them enormously—constituted no threat to order or property.

But while Lincoln tacked and veered to win over groups who were suspicious of Republicans, he never did so at the expense of his Jeffersonian principles or his commitment to the Republican cause. Free labor had no better friend than he; he even defended the right of workers to strike, a radical position for a politician to take in 1860. "I am glad to see that a system of labor exists," he informed a group of striking workers in New Haven, "under which laborers can strike when they want to, where they are not obliged to work under all circumstances. . . . I like a system that lets a man quit when he wants to, and wish it might prevail everywhere. One of the reasons I am opposed to slavery is here." He refused to yield an inch on the one position—refusal to allow slavery into the territories—that distinguished the Republican party from the other parties and that alone defined its sectional character. Republicans, he stated firmly, must not "demoralize" themselves and their cause "by entertaining propositions for compromise on slavery extension. There is no possible compromise upon it but which puts us under again and leaves us all our work to do over again . . . on that point hold firm, as with a chain of steel."

With Lincoln's victory in 1860 Republicans looked forward to the regeneration of American life. Practically speaking, however, the results of the election meant little. The new administration, whatever its ideology, posed no immediate threat to slavery or to the South. The Republican party wanted merely to confine slavery to the states in which it already existed, on the assumption that it would eventually wither away. But that assumption was apocryphal. In 1860 slavery was more solidly entrenched than ever. How—and when—could the South free four million slaves, with a combined value of four billion dollars? How could these Negroes be integrated in a society that was profoundly hostile to them? Moreover, the South's influence in the federal government remained considerable. The Supreme Court was pro-Southern; most Northern Democrats, despite the schism in their party, would undoubtedly co-operate with Southerners against a common enemy; Congress would certainly be a thorn in Lincoln's side; and Eastern commercial interests would continue to oppose the Free-Soilers.

In short, the new Republican administration augured no significant change in the status quo—provided the Southern states stayed in the Union. But by June 1861 eleven of them had seceded and had formed a republic of their own, under a constitution that rested on state sovereignty and the unrestricted right of slavery. Their departure set in motion a train of events that swiftly altered the course of American history. A little more than four years after Lincoln took office, the slave system, and with it Southern power, lay in ruins. The Civil War thus settled the questions that had perplexed and divided the country since its independence, and that had hopelessly deadlocked it since the 1840s. The Republican party had carried out a revolution. Its ideology based on democratic nationalism, its belief in the virtues of free labor and industrial progress, had become the undisputed law of the land. But it was the improvidence of the South in pulling out of the Union that had made it all possible.

The first issue to be settled by the Civil War concerned the nature of the Union, which now, for the first time, faced the immediate possibility of dissolution. According to Jefferson Davis, speaking for the Confederacy, dissolution was legal, the Constitution being merely a contract between the states which they could break at any time. Davis's argument contained nothing new; it was as old as the Union itself and had been advanced repeatedly by states dissatisfied with federal policies, in North and South alike. The traditional nationalist answer was that the contract to form the Union had been drawn up not by the states but by "the people," meaning the aggregate of individuals in the country as a whole. In other words, the constitutional controversy over the years had turned on the question of who had brought the nation into being, the people or the states, both sides agreeing implicitly that there had been no nation before the social contract.

Lincoln shifted the entire ground of the controversy. The Union, he held, transcended the rational limits of contract theory and therefore could not be reduced to individuals or states. To Lincoln, the Union was a mystical thing, an indefinable substance, an organic whole greater than the sum of its parts. As such, it preceded any formal agreement as to its exact nature. The Constitution, it followed, could not be broken, since it embodied the nation's "perpetuity." "It is safe to assert," Lincoln said in his First Inaugural, "that no government proper ever had a provision in its organic law for its own termination. Continue to execute all the express provisions of our national Constitution and the Union will endure forever, it being impossible to destroy it except by some action not provided for in the instrument itself."

No other important politician had ever gone as far as Lincoln in asserting the authority of the national government over the states. He categorically denied the South's "assumption that there is some omnipotent and sacred supremacy pertaining to a State." "The Union," he explained, "is older than any of the States, and, in fact, it created them. . . . Not one of them ever had a State constitution independent of the Union." His words reflected the feelings of most Northerners during the secession crisis. They would not have pressed on against the South had they not been fired by the mystique of the Union. The South, after all, demanded only the right to withdraw in peace.

But if, as Lincoln maintained, the Union was indestructible, what precisely was secession? Lincoln was hard put to define it. Secession was not revolution, he insisted, because revolutions aim to depose the government, and this the South was not aiming to do. Nor was secession a declaration of war, since war implied separate nations, and the Confederacy was no nation. The seceders, Lincoln finally concluded, were "discontented individuals" engaged in a conspiracy or rebellion. The Confederacy represented a minority's disobedience of the law. It was a form of anarchy. Should this conspiratorial minority succeed, Lincoln reasoned, then nothing could prevent a faction of that minority from seceding, and so on indefinitely. The end result must be tyranny, the obverse side of anarchy. "Is there in all republics," Lincoln asked, "this inherent and fatal weakness? Must a government, of necessity, be too strong for the liberties of its own people, or too *weak* to maintain its own existence?"

His final answer was that majority rule alone reconciled liberty and order. The Civil War was being fought so that the nation would be governed democratically and not anarcho-despotically. This was the second great issue decided by the war. It was one, moreover, that concerned not only America but the whole of mankind. If the Union were defeated, Lincoln was certain, it would convince the world that America's experiment in democracy had failed, that the people could not govern themselves, the burden of freedom being too heavy for common men to bear. "On the side of the Union," Lincoln declared, "it is a struggle for maintaining in the world that form and substance of government whose leading object is to elevate the condition of men—to lift artificial weight from all shoulders; to clear the path of laudable pursuits for all; to afford all an unfettered start and a fair chance in the race for life."

Slavery was the third issue decided by the Civil War. Lincoln at first tried to keep this issue separate from and subordinate to the issues of Union and democracy, hoping thereby to maintain the broadest grounds of support for his war policies. He was particularly concerned to avoid alienating the border states—Delaware, Maryland, Kentucky and Missouri—which were at once pro-Union and pro-slavery. In addition, Northern public opinion was sharply divided on the moral right of slavery in the early stages of the war. There were few abolitionists, but many Democrats and conservative Republicans supported the administration only out of sympathy for the Union.

Of course, Lincoln knew that slavery was the root cause of secession, and that the old problems would inevitably recur unless the South's "peculiar institution" was extirpated once and for all. As the war progressed, and as hatred of the South mounted, the North came around to the abolitionist viewpoint. There were additional pressures to turn the Civil War into a crusade for freedom. Politically, the promise of emancipation would make it more difficult for the governments of Britain and France to recognize the South. And militarily, it would induce Negroes to enlist in the Union army and encourage slave defections and uprisings, thereby seriously disrupting the Southern economy. Accordingly, on January 1, 1863, Lincoln issued his Emancipation Proclamation, which declared slaves in rebellious areas to be "then, henceforth, and forever free." The next step was actually to free them; this awaited the conquering Northern armies. The last step was to outlaw slavery permanently; this was done by the Thirteenth Amendment to the Constitution, ratified in 1865.

The triumph of Union arms completed the second phase of the Republican revolution; Reconstruction marked the third: it preserved the revolution. The main facts of Reconstruction may be briefly mentioned. The problem was how and under whose authority, the President's or Congress's, the Southern states should be brought back into the Union. Lincoln, after appointing military governors for several captured states, introduced his reconstruction plan in December 1863. It would have pardoned all Southerners, except the leaders of the rebellion, who took a loyalty oath to the Union, and allowed the oath takers to form a government when their members equaled a tenth of the 1860 electorate. Republican Radicals, who dominated Congress, rejected Lincoln's plan out of hand and presented one of their own, the so-called Wade-Davis Bill. The Wade-Davis Bill demanded that a majority of the electorate, not just 10 per cent, declare loyalty to the Union, that no man who had fought for the Confederacy be permitted to vote, and that Negro rights be guaranteed. Lincoln pocket-vetoed the Bill. Matters thus stood at an impasse when Lincoln died.

It has generally been taken for granted that Lincoln and the Congressional Radicals were enemies, that Lincoln was merciful and statesmanlike toward the South while the Radicals were vindictive and hardhearted. The fact is, Lincoln was moving closer and closer to the Radical position, first, because Northern public opinion insisted on it, and second, because the Republican party organization required it. The North was determined to prevent the South from challenging its hegemony, the Democratic party from regrouping and taking power again, and the emasculation of beneficent laws passed by Congress since 1861 on tariffs, homesteads, railroad grants, internal improvements, etc., from taking place. The Republican party, moreover, had an incalculable stake in office. By the end of the war several hundred thousand federal jobs had bound the party very closely to every community, village, ward and precinct in the North. Under no circumstances would the party yield up this advantage. Responding to these imperatives, Lincoln's ideas on restoring the South changed markedly between 1863 and 1865.

It is therefore a fallacy to assume that Andrew Johnson was Lincoln's true legatee, and, by extension, to argue that if Lincoln had lived he too would have fallen victim to Radical assaults. Johnson was a Southerner and a Democrat, and while he was also a staunch Union man and long-time foe of the slavocracy, he continued to regard Negroes as congenitally inferior and incapable of becoming citizens. He was therefore content to see the Southern states return to the Union practically under their own terms. By the end of 1865 it was clear what those terms were: the re-election of many of the secessionist leaders, and the enactment of "Black Codes" by most Southern states. Intended to regulate the movement and activities of nearly four million ex-slaves, these codes varied in severity from state to state, some going as far as to re-impose involuntary servitude. It was under these conditions that Johnson, in December 1865, called the South restored.

But Republicans felt that if the South were restored in this way everything would be lost; the war would have been fought in vain. And so, at the very time Johnson announced the restoration of the Union, the Republicans were laying plans in Congress, through their special Joint Committee of Fifteen, headed by the most militant of the Radicals, Thaddeus Stevens, to thwart the President's program and institute their own. The congressional election of 1866 settled the conflict. The North overwhelmingly repudiated Johnson. The Radicals had their mandate, and neither the President nor the courts would be permitted to stand in their way.

Between 1866 and 1868 the Republican party brought the South under direct national or military control. The passage of the Fourteenth Amendment provided the basis of this so-called Radical Reconstruction. Applying the Constitution to the states, the Amendment declared, in its crucial first section, that "all persons" born in the United States were citizens and that therefore no state could "make or enforce any law which shall abridge" their "privilege and immunities," "deprive any person of life, liberty, or property without due process of law," or deny him "equal protection of the laws." The Amendment's other sections detailed the penalties for failing to observe the rights of citizens and prohibited ex-Confederates from holding federal or state office. Radical Reconstruction was to bring profound social changes to the South and give the lower classes access to political office. The military occupation of the South, ordered by Congress in a series of punitive Reconstruction acts in 1867, compelled the Southern states to ratify the Fourteenth Amendment as the condition for returning to the Union. In the course of doing so they were forced to jettison the governments previously set up under the Johnson plan and form Radical ones based on universal male suffrage (something rarely found in the North, where Negroes were still not enfranchised), and to enact a wide-ranging body of reform legislation—improving schools, hospitals, asylums, etc.—primarily in behalf of Negroes and poor whites.

But so far as Northern Republicans were concerned, the main object of Radical Reconstruction was not to reform the South but to prevent the Democrats from obtaining national power. This object they achieved. In the elections of 1868 and 1872 the Republican party, behind its figurehead leader, Ulysses S. Grant, easily retained control of the federal government and with it the spoils of office. Gradually, the party relaxed its grip on the South. Federal troops were withdrawn from the reconstructed states, and everywhere the conservatives, or "Bourbons," ousted the Radicals. By 1876 only Florida, Louisiana, and South Carolina remained occupied. Reconstruction officially ended in April 1877, when President Hayes, making good his agreement with the Democrats, removed the final contingents of federal troops from these states. Before long, Southern Negroes were disfranchised, and by the end of the century they had become second-class citizens. For them the fruits of Reconstruction were bitterest of all.

The Republicans abandoned Southern Negroes for two reasons. First, they realized that they no longer needed Negro votes, control of the populated Northern states alone being sufficient to ensure the party's national supremacy. And second, it was obvious even before the Compromise of 1877 that the South had finally come to accept the verdict of the Civil War and would not again attempt to institute a system of involuntary servitude. As for the actual condition of the Southern Negro—the North could not have been less concerned. By the 1870s the North wanted to be done with wars and armies and militant ideologies. The Radical idealism of the 1860s gave way to the cupidity, jobbery and corruption of the Gilded Age. The Republican revolution that had begun with the uprising against the Kansas-Nebraska Act had run its course.

Liberty Party Platform
August 30, 1843

[The abolitionists who framed the Liberty party platform in Buffalo had no reason to hope that the party would do any better in 1844 than it had done in 1840, when it had polled only seven thousand votes. But then there arose the issue of Texas annexation, which involved the possibility that several slave states would enter the Union. In the 1844 election the Liberty party vote increased ninefold, and it suddenly became an important factor in American politics.]

1. *Resolved,* That human brotherhood is a cardinal principle of true democracy, as well as of pure Christianity, which spurns all inconsistent limitations; and neither the political party which repudiates it, nor the political system which is not based upon it, can be truly democratic or permanent.

2. *Resolved,* That the Liberty party, placing itself upon this broad principle, will demand the absolute and unqualified divorce of the general government from slavery, and also the restoration of equality of rights among men, in every state where the party exists, or may exist.

3. *Resolved,* That the Liberty party has not been organized for any temporary purpose by interested politicians, but has arisen from among the people in consequence of a conviction, hourly gaining ground, that no other party in the country represents the true principles of American liberty, or the true spirit of the constitution of the United States.

4. *Resolved,* That the Liberty party has not been organized merely for the overthrow of slavery; its first decided effort must, indeed, be directed against slaveholding as the grossest and most revolting manifestation of despotism, but it will also carry out the principle of equal rights into all its practical consequences and applications, and support every just measure conducive to individual and social freedom.

5. *Resolved,* That the Liberty party is not a sectional party but a national party; was not originated in a desire to accomplish a single object, but in a comprehensive regard to the great interests of the whole country; is not a new party, nor a third party, but is the party of 1776, reviving the principles of that memorable era, and striving to carry them into practical application. . . .

10. *Resolved,* That we recognize as sound the doctrine maintained by slaveholding jurists, that slavery is against natural rights, and strictly local, and that its existence and continuance rests on no other support than state legislation, and not on any authority of Congress.

11. *Resolved,* That the general government has, under the constitution, no power to establish or continue slavery anywhere, and therefore that all treaties and acts of Congress establishing, continuing or favoring slavery in the District of Columbia, in the territory of Florida, or on the high seas, are unconstitutional, and all attempts to hold men as property within the limits of exclusive national jurisdiction ought to be prohibited by law. . . .

18. *Resolved,* That this convention recommend to the friends of liberty in all those free states where any inequality of rights and privileges exists on account of color, to employ their utmost energies to remove all such remnants and effects of the slave system.

Whereas, The constitution of these United States is a series of agreements, covenants or contracts between the people of the United States, each with all, and all with each; and,

Whereas, It is a principle of universal morality, that the moral laws of the Creator are paramount to all human laws; or, in the language of an Apostle, that "we ought to obey God rather than men;" and, . . .

Whereas, The third clause of the second section of the fourth article of the constitution of the United States, when construed as providing for the surrender of a fugitive slave . . . is a contract to rob a man of a natural right—namely, his natural right to his own liberty—and is therefore absolutely *void.* Therefore,

19. *Resolved,* That we hereby give it to be distinctly un-

derstood by this nation and the world, that, as abolitionists, considering that the strength of our cause lies in its righteousness, and our hope for it in our conformity to the laws of God, and our respect for the rights of man, we owe it to the Sovereign Ruler of the Universe, as a proof of our allegiance to Him, in all our civil relations and offices, whether as private citizens, or public functionaries sworn to support the constitution of the United States, to regard and to treat the third clause of the fourth article of that instrument, whenever applied to the case of a fugitive slave, as utterly null and void, and consequently as forming no part of the constitution of the United States, whenever we are called upon or sworn to support it. . . .

Free-Soil Platform
June 22, 1848

[Radical New York Democrats bolted from the party's national convention, which had been held in late May, because it had failed to approve the Wilmot Proviso (which, it will be recalled, proposed that Congress outlaw slavery from territory captured in the Mexican War). A month later the radicals met in Utica, formed a Democratic faction of their own, and nominated Martin Van Buren as their presidential candidate. On August 9 the Free-Soil party was launched. Repeating the Utica platform, it drew support from antislavery Whigs and Liberty party abolitionists.]

Whereas, We have assembled in convention as a union of freemen, for the sake of freedom, forgetting all past political difference, in a common resolve to maintain the rights of free labor against the aggression of the slave power, and to secure free soil to a free people. . . .

1. *Resolved, therefore,* That we, the people here assembled, remembering the example of our fathers in the days of the first Declaration of Independence, putting our trust in God for the triumph of our cause, and invoking His guidance in our endeavors to advance it, do now plant ourselves upon

the national platform of freedom, in opposition to the sectional platform of slavery.

2. *Resolved*, That slavery in the several states of this Union which recognize its existence, depends upon the state laws alone, which can not be repealed or modified by the Federal government, and for which laws that government is not responsible. We therefore propose no interference by Congress with slavery within the limits of any state.

3. *Resolved*, That the proviso of Jefferson, to prohibit the existence of slavery, after 1800, in all the territories of the United States, southern and northern; the votes of six states and sixteen delegates in Congress of 1784, for the proviso, to three states and seven delegates against it; the actual exclusion of slavery from the Northwestern Territory, by the Ordinance of 1787, unanimously adopted by the states in Congress; and the entire history of that period, clearly show that it was the settled policy of the nation not to extend, nationalize or encourage, but to limit, localize and discourage, slavery; and to this policy, which should never have been departed from, the government ought to return.

4. *Resolved*, That our fathers ordained the constitution of the United States, in order, among other great national objects, to establish justice, promote the general welfare, and secure the blessings of liberty; but expressly denied to the Federal government, which they created, all constitutional power to deprive any person of life, liberty, or property, without due legal process.

5. *Resolved*, That in the judgment of this convention, Congress has no more power to make a slave than to make a king; no more power to institute or establish slavery than to institute or establish a monarchy; no such power can be found among those specifically conferred by the constitution, or derived by just implication from them.

6. *Resolved*, That it is the duty of the Federal government to relieve itself from all responsibility for the existence or continuance of slavery wherever the government possesses constitutional power to legislate on that subject, and it is thus responsible for its existence.

7. *Resolved*, That the true, and, in the judgment of this convention, the only safe means of preventing the extension

of slavery into territory now free, is to prohibit its extension in all such territory by an act of Congress.

8. *Resolved*, That we accept the issue which the slave power has forced upon us; and to their demand for more slave states, and more slave territory, our calm but final answer is, no more slave states and no more slave territory. Let the soil of our extensive domains be kept free for the hardy pioneers of our own land, and the oppressed and banished of other lands, seeking homes of comfort and fields of enterprise in the new world. . . .

13. *Resolved*, That river and harbor improvements, when demanded by the safety and convenience of commerce with foreign nations, or among the several states, are objects of national concern, and that it is the duty of Congress, in the exercise of its constitutional power, to provide therefor.

14. *Resolved*, That the free grant to actual settlers, in consideration of the expenses they incur in making settlements in the wilderness, which are usually fully equal to their actual cost, and of the public benefits resulting therefrom, of reasonable portions of the public lands, under suitable limitations, is a wise and just measure of public policy, which will promote in various ways the interests of all the states of this Union; and we, therefore, recommend it to the favorable consideration of the American People.

15. *Resolved*, That the obligations of honor and patriotism require the earliest practical payment of the national debt, and we are, therefore, in favor of such a tariff of duties as will raise revenue adequate to defray the expenses of the Federal government, and to pay annual installments of our debt and the interest thereon.

16. *Resolved*, That we inscribe on our banner, "Free Soil, Free Speech, Free Labor, and Free Men," and under it we will fight on, and fight ever, until a triumphant victory shall reward our exertions.

Senate Debate
June 26, 1854

[Below is an exchange—typical of the kind that was taking place in Congress from 1854 on—between Charles Sumner of Massachusetts, the militant Free-Soiler and Republican, and several Southern Democrats.]

Mr. BUTLER. . . . If we repeal the fugitive slave law, will the honorable Senator tell me that Massachusetts will execute the provision of the Constitution without any law of Congress? Suppose we should take away all laws, and devolve upon the different States the duties that properly belong to them, I would ask that Senator whether, under the prevalence of public opinion there, Massachusetts would execute that provision as one of the constitutional members of this Union? Would they send fugitives back to us after trial by jury, or any other mode? Will this honorable Senator (Mr. Sumner) tell me that he will do it?

Mr. SUMNER. Does the honorable Senator ask me if I would personally join in sending a fellow-man into bondage? "Is thy servant a dog, that he should do this thing?"

Mr. BUTLER. These are the prettiest speeches that I ever heard. [Laughter.] He has them turned down in a book by him, I believe, and he has them so elegantly fixed that I cannot reply to them. [Laughter.] They are too delicate for my use. [Renewed laughter.] They are beautiful things; made in a factory of rhetoric somewhat *of a peculiar shape.* But, I must be permitted to say, not of a definite texture. Now, what does he mean by talking about his not being a dog? [Continued laughter.] What has that to do with the Constitution, or the constitutional obligations of a State? [Laughter.] Well, sir, it was a beautiful sentiment, no doubt, as he thought, and perhaps he imagined he expressed it with Demosthenian abruptness and eloquence. [Laughter.] I asked him whether he would execute the Constitution of the United States without any fugitive slave law, and he answered me, is he a dog—

Mr. SUMNER. The Senator asked me if I would help to reduce a fellow-man to bondage? I answered him.

Mr. BUTLER. Then you would not obey the Constitution. Sir, [turning to Mr. SUMNER,] standing here before this tribunal, where you swore to support it, you rise and tell me that you regard it the office of a dog to enforce it. You stand in my presence, as a coequal Senator, and tell me that it is a dog's office to execute the Constitution of the United States?

Mr. PRATT. Which he has sworn to support.

Mr. SUMNER. I recognize no such obligation.

Mr. BUTLER. I know you do not. But nobody cares about your recognitions as an individual; but as a Senator, and a constitutional representative, you stand differently related to this body. But enough of this. . . .

Mr. MASON. . . . I do not know whether the Senator claims to be a jurist; I know not his position at home; but I know something of his associations there from his language here. Sir, he has denounced a gentleman from Virginia who goes under the protection of the Constitution, and the sanction of the law into his State, to reclaim his property. He has the boldness to speak here of such a man as "a slave-hunter from Virginia." Sir, my constituents need no vindication from me from such a charge, coming from such a quarter. The Senator from Massachusetts, in the use of such vulgar language here, betrays the vulgarity of his associations at home; and shall it be tolerated in the American Senate? Yes, sir, a gentleman from the South, who goes under the protection of that Constitution which the Senator has sworn to support, and which he just now declared he would be a dog to execute or to recognize; a gentleman from Virginia who goes to his State under the protection of the Constitution and the sanction of the law, to reclaim his property, may be subject to vulgar denunciation, but only by vulgar men. . . .

Mr. President, I did not think I could have been drawn into a debate on this subject. I should not have engaged in it but that I thought it right to vindicate the law from the misconstruction which was placed on it by the honorable Senator, before the country, in reference to the *habeas corpus*. But, sir, I may say neither that law nor any other law could require vindication from attacks made by one mad enough to announce to the American Senate and the American people, that although the Constitution provides that fugitives from service shall be surrendered up, he would recognize himself as a dog were he to execute that provision. He has said so in the presence of that American Senate who witnessed his oath to support, protect, and defend that same Constitution, and his appeal to his God to witness the truth and sincerity of his purpose. Why, sir, am I speaking of a fanatic, one whose reason is dethroned! Can such a one expect to make impressions upon the American people from his vapid, vulgar declamation here, accompanied by a declaration that he would violate his oath now recently taken? . . .

Mr. PETTIT. . . . Sir, the Senator named an African who was among the first that was slain in the contest for freedom in the streets of Boston. I will not pretend to say whether that African was the superior of the Senator from Massachusetts, or the Senator his superior; but they were not, in my judgment, equals in life or equals in death. They were not harmonious and beautiful in life, nor will they be equally beautiful in death.

Now, sir, to give this clause of the Declaration of Independence any other construction than that which I have given it, is an evident, a self-evident, a palpable lie. What is the language? That "all men are created equal." Are they created equally tall, equally broad, equally long, equally short? Are they created politically equal? Are they created physically equal? Are they created mentally equal? Are they created morally equal? I say, in no one of these several instances are all men created equal. You cannot go beyond the moment when they first respire their native air. At that time you see presented to you the imbecile in mind, weak in body, dwarf in size; while, beside him, the same day's birth, you see power, greatness, strength, wisdom, and beauty. In no one instance, therefore, is there perfect equality among men, if you regard them as individuals. As nations, as collections of men, they have a right to perfect equality as to the formation of their government, and the rights and domestic duties that shall be established among them. I ask that Senator—you, who to-day have stultified yourself—you, who have said that the solemn oath which you took at that stand, administered by the President of this body upon the holy Evangelists of God, kissing the book, giving seal and sanction to your asseveration—you, who have said to-day that you would spit upon that oath, would disregard its obligations—

Mr. Sumner. Never! Never!

Mr. Pettit. You, who denied it; denied its power to bind you; you, who said you would not maintain the Constitution of the United States—

Mr. Sumner. I said I recognized no obligation in the Constitution of the United States to bind me to help to reduce a man to slavery.

Mr. Pettit. I ask you, do you claim to be the equal of your revolutionary sires?

The Presiding Officer. The Senator must address the Chair, not the Senator from Massachusetts.

Mr. Pettit. I ask the Chair, then, whether the Senator from Massachusetts, with this odium on his lips, is the equal of his revolutionary sires? I do not know that he had any, properly speaking, but I take it in a State point of view. Is he the equal of Adams, of Hancock, of Warren, who was the first martyr in the great cause of liberty, of freedom, and union; whose blood was the first to cement the union of these States, on Bunker's hill, to which he has referred? Are you the equal of those men? Is he, sir, the equal of those men? I had rather ask you, Mr. President, for I think you would answer "no," and he might answer "yes." . . .

Sir, men come to the earth, they make their appearance upon it, with mental powers, but with no political rights, and I may therefore say with more propriety that Jefferson intended to say they were created mentally instead of politically equal. At the earliest creation there are evidences of mentality without any political rights whatever. Then is the Senator the equal of Webster, who has left a name, a monument, and a fame, I will not say unsurpassable, but unequaled in strength, and power, and durability by any other American Senator? I believe that as a mere mental man—and I speak of him in no other capacity—Webster had not his equal on this continent, if he had in Europe, or upon any other continent. Is that Senator his equal? He might as well say that the jackal is the equal of the lion, or that the buzzard is the equal of the eagle.

When you, sir, [addressing Mr. SUMNER] find no man beneath you; when those who are near you—your own class of men—can find no man beneath you; when you shall claim as your equal the man who rolls in the gutter, whom God has deprived in his own organization and creation of all mental power and capacity; when you shall claim that he who wallows in the gutter with the vilest and most worthless is your equal, then your interpretation of the doctrine is true. Let me go further. If the Almighty even intended to create the Senator the equal with mighty and lamented Webster, I must be allowed to say that He made a gross blunder and a most egregious mistake. . . .

Abraham Lincoln, Speech on Republicanism
September 11, 1858

[In the intervals between his debates with Douglas Lincoln spoke several times on the slavery issue. Following is an admirable statement of his Republican principles, presented at Edwardsville, Illinois.]

. . . The difference between the Republican and the Democratic parties on the leading issue of this contest, as I understand it, is, that the former consider slavery a moral, social and political wrong, while the latter *do not* consider it either a moral, social or political wrong; and the action of each, as respects the growth of the country and the expansion of our population, is squared to meet these views. I will not allege that the Democratic party consider slavery morally, socially and politically *right*; though their tendency to that view has, in my opinion, been constant and unmistakable for the past five years. I prefer to take, as the accepted maxim of the party, the idea put forth by Judge Douglas, that he "don't care whether slavery is voted down or voted up." I am quite willing to believe that many Democrats would prefer that slavery be always voted down, and I am sure that some prefer that it be always "voted up"; but I have a right to insist that their action, especially if it be their *constant and unvarying* action, shall determine their ideas and preferences on the subject. Every measure of the Democratic party of late years, bearing directly or indirectly on the slavery question, has corresponded with this notion of utter indifference whether slavery or freedom shall outrun in the race of empire across the Pacific—every measure, I say, up to the Dred Scott decision, where, it seems to me, the idea is boldly suggested that slavery is *better* than freedom. The Republican party, on the contrary, hold that this government was instituted to secure the blessings of freedom, and that slavery is an unqualified evil to the negro, to the white man, to the soil, and to the State. Regarding it an evil, they will not molest it in the States where it exists; they will not overlook the constitutional guards which our forefathers have placed around it; they will do nothing which can give proper offence to those who hold slaves by legal sanction; but they will use every constitutional method to prevent the evil from becoming larger and involving more negroes, more white men, more soil, and more States in its deplorable consequences. They will, if possible, place it where the public mind shall rest in the belief that it is in course of ultimate peaceable extinction, in God's own good time. And to this end, they will, if possible, restore the government to the policy of the fathers —the policy of preserving the new territories from the baneful influence of human bondage, as the Northwestern territories were sought to be preserved by the ordinance of 1787 and the compromise act of 1820. They will oppose, in all its length and breadth, the modern Democratic idea that slavery is as good as freedom, and ought to have room for expansion all over the continent, if people can be found to carry it. All, or very nearly all, of Judge Douglas' arguments about "Popular Sovereignty," as he calls it, are logical if you admit that slavery is as good and as right as freedom; and not one of them is worth a rush if you deny it. This is the difference, as I understand it, between the Republican and the Democratic parties. . . .

Lincoln-Douglas Debates
1858

[Following are excerpts from the famous debates. Douglas's remarks were made at Ottawa, Illinois, on August 21, 1858; Lincoln's at Galesburg on October 7. Douglas's strategy was to identify Lincoln and the Republican party with the abolitionists; Lincoln's strategy was to widen the breach between Douglas and the Southern Democrats.]

DOUGLAS

. . . In the remarks I have made on this platform, and the position of Mr. Lincoln upon it, I mean nothing personally disrespectful or unkind to that gentleman. I have known him for nearly twenty-five years. There were many points of sympathy between us when we first got acquainted. We were both comparatively boys, and both struggling with poverty in a strange land. I was a school-teacher in the town of Winchester, and he a flourishing grocery-keeper in the town of Salem. [Applause and laughter.] He was more successful in his occupation than I was in mine, and hence more fortunate in this world's goods. Lincoln is one of those peculiar men who perform with admirable skill everything which they undertake. I made as good a school-teacher as I could and when a cabinet maker I made a good bedstead and tables, although my old boss said I succeeded better with bureaus and secretaries than anything else; [Cheers.] but I believe that Lincoln was always more successful in business than I, for his business enabled him to get into the Legislature. I met him there, however, and had a sympathy with him, because of the up hill struggle we both had in life. He was then just as good at telling an anecdote as now. ["No doubt."] He could beat any of the boys wrestling, or running a foot race, in pitching quoits or tossing a copper, could ruin more liquor than all the boys of the town together, [uproarious laughter.] I sympathised with him, because he was struggling with difficulties and so was I. Mr. Lincoln served with me in the Legislature in 1836, when we both retired, and he subsided, or became submerged, and he was lost sight of as a public man for some years. In 1846, when Wilmot introduced his celebrated proviso, and the Abolition tornado swept over the country, Lincoln again turned up as a member of Congress from the Sangamon district. I was then in the Senate of the United States, and was glad to welcome my old friend and companion. Whilst in Congress, he distinguished himself by his opposition to the Mexican war, taking the side of the common enemy against his own country; ["that's true,"] and when he returned home he found that the indignation of the people followed him everywhere, and he was again submerged or obliged to retire into private life, forgotten by his former friends. . . .

We are told by Lincoln that he is utterly opposed to the Dred Scott decision, and will not submit to it, for the reason that he says it deprives the negro of the rights and privileges of citizenship. [Laughter and applause.] That is the first and main reason which he assigns for his warfare on the Supreme Court of the United States and its decision. I ask you, are you in favor of conferring upon the negro the rights and privileges of citizenship? ["No, no."] Do you desire to strike out of our State Constitution that clause which keeps slaves and free negroes out of the State, and allow the free negroes to flow in, ["never,"] and cover your prairies with black settlements? Do you desire to turn this beautiful State into a free negro colony, ["no, no,"] in order that when Missouri abolishes slavery she can send one hundred thousand emancipated slaves into Illinois, to become citizens and voters, on an equality with yourselves? ["Never," "no,"] If you desire negro citizenship, if you desire to allow them to come into the State and settle with the white man, if you desire them to vote on an equality with yourselves, and to make them eligible to office, to serve on juries, and to adjudge your rights, then support Mr. Lincoln and the Black Republican party, who are in favor of the citizenship of the negro. ["Never, never."] For one, I am opposed to negro citizenship in any and every form. [Cheers.] I believe this government was made on the white basis. ["Good."] I believe it was made by white men, for the benefit of white men and their posterity for ever, and I am in favor of confining citizenship to white men, men of European birth and descent, instead of conferring it upon negroes, Indians and other inferior races. ["Good for you." "Douglas forever."] . . .

LINCOLN

The judge has also detained us awhile in regard to the distinction between his party and our party. His he assumes to be a national party—ours a sectional one. He does this in asking the question whether this country has any interest in the maintenance of the Republican party? He assumes that our party is altogether sectional—that the party to which he adheres is national; and the argument is that no party can be a rightful party—can be based upon rightful principles—unless it can announce its principles everywhere. I presume that Judge Douglas could not go into Russia and announce the doctrine of our national Democracy; he could not denounce the doctrine of kings and emperors and monarchies in Russia; and it may be true of this country, that in some places we may not be able to proclaim a doctrine as clearly true as the truth of Democracy, because there is a section so directly opposed to it that they will not tolerate us in doing so. Is it the true test of the soundness of a doctrine, that in some places people won't let you proclaim it? [No, no, no.] Is that the way to test the truth of any doctrine? [No, no, no.] . .

I ask his attention also to the fact that by the rule of nationality he is himself fast becoming sectional. [Great cheers and laughter.] I ask his attention to the fact that his speeches would not go as current now south of the Ohio River as they have formerly gone there. [Loud cheers.] I ask his attention to the fact that he felicitates himself today that all the Democrats of the free States are agreeing with him, [applause,] while he omits to tell us that the Democrats of any slave State agree with him. If he has not thought of this, I commend to his consideration the evidence in his own declaration, on this day, of his becoming sectional too. [Immense cheering.] I see it rapidly approaching. Whatever may be the result of this ephemeral contest between Judge Douglas and myself, I see the day rapidly approaching when his pill of sectionalism, which he has been thrusting down the throats of Republicans for years past, will be crowded down his own throat. [Tremendous applause.] . . .

The judge tells us, in proceeding, that he is opposed to making any odious distinctions between free and slave States. I am altogether unaware that the Republicans are in favor of making any odious distinctions between the free and slave States. But there still is a difference, I think, between Judge Douglas and the Republicans in this. I suppose that the real difference between Judge Douglas and his friends and the Republicans, on the contrary, is that the judge is not in favor of making any difference between slavery and liberty—that he is in favor of eradicating, of pressing out of view, the questions of preference in this country for free or slave institutions; and consequently every sentiment he utters discards the idea that there is any wrong in slavery. Everything that emanates from him or his coadjutors in their course of policy carefully excludes the thought that there is anything wrong in slavery. All their arguments, if you will consider them, will be seen to exclude the thought that there is anything whatever wrong in slavery. If you will take the judge's speeches, and select the short and pointed sentences expressed by him—as his declaration that he "don't care whether slavery is voted up or down"—you will see at once that this is perfectly logical, if you do not admit that slavery is wrong. If you do admit that it is wrong, Judge Douglas cannot logically say he don't care whether a wrong is voted up or voted down. Judge Douglas declares that if any community wants slavery they have a right to have it. He can say that logically, if he says that there is no wrong in slavery; but if you admit that there is a wrong in it, he cannot logically say that anybody has a right to do wrong. He insists that, upon the score of equality, the owners of slaves and owners of property—of horses and every other sort of property—should be alike, and hold them alike in a new Territory. That is perfectly logical, if the two species of property are alike, and are equally founded in right. But if you admit that one of them is wrong, you cannot institute any equality be-

tween right and wrong. And from this difference of sentiment—the belief on the part of one that the institution is
wrong, and a policy springing from that belief which looks
to the arrest of the enlargement of that wrong; and this other
sentiment, that it is no wrong, and a policy sprung from that
sentiment which will tolerate no idea of preventing that
wrong from growing larger, and looks to there never being
an end of it through all the existence of things—arises the
real difference between Judge Douglas and his friends on the
one hand, and the Republicans on the other. Now, I confess
myself as belonging to that class in the country who contemplate slavery as a moral, social, and political evil, having due
regard for its actual existence amongst us, and the difficulties of getting rid of it in any satisfactory way, and to all
the constitutional obligations which have been thrown about
it; but who, nevertheless, desire a policy that looks to
the prevention of it as a wrong, and looks hopefully to the
time when as a wrong it may come to an end. [Great
applause.] . . .

In these general maxims about liberty—in his assertions
that he "don't care whether Slavery is voted up or voted
down"; that "whoever wants Slavery has a right to have it";
that "upon principles of equality it should be allowed to go
everywhere;" that "there is no inconsistency between free
and slave institutions." In this he is also preparing (whether
purposely or not), the way for making the institution of Slavery national! [Cries of "Yes," "Yes," "That's so."] I repeat
again, for I wish no misunderstanding, that I do not charge
that he means it so; but I call upon your minds to inquire,
If you were going to get the best instrument you could, and
then set it to work in the most ingenious way, to prepare
the public mind for this movement, operating in the free
States, where there is now an abhorrence of the institution
of Slavery, could you find an instrument so capable of
doing it as Judge Douglas? or one employed in so apt a way
to do it? [Great cheering. Cries of "Hit him again," "That's
the doctrine."]

I have said once before, and I will repeat it now, that Mr.
Clay, when he was once answering an objection to the Colonization Society, that it had a tendency to the ultimate eman-

cipation of the slaves, said that "those who would repress all tendencies to liberty and ultimate emancipation must do more than put down the benevolent efforts of the Colonization Society—they must go back to the era of our liberty and independence, and muzzle the cannon that thunders its annual joyous return—they must blot out the moral lights around us—they must penetrate the human soul, and eradicate the light of reason and the love of liberty!" And I do think—I repeat, though I said it on a former occasion—that Judge Douglas, and whoever like him teaches that the negro has no share, humble though it may be, in the Declaration of Independence, is going back to the era of our liberty and independence, and, so far as in him lies, muzzling the cannon that thunders its annual joyous return; ["That's so."] that he is blowing out the moral lights around us, when he contends that whoever wants slaves has a right to hold them; that he is penetrating, so far as lies in his power, the human soul, and eradicating the light of reason and the love of liberty, when he is in every possible way preparing the public mind, by his vast influence, for making the institution of slavery perpetual and national. [Great applause, and cries of "Hurrah for Lincoln," "That's the true doctrine."] . . .

Abraham Lincoln to H. L. Pierce and Others
April 6, 1859

[Lincoln wrote this letter to a group of Boston Republicans who had invited him to attend a festival commemorating Jefferson's birthday.]

Gentlemen:

Your kind note inviting me to attend a festival in Boston, on the 28th instant, in honor of the birthday of Thomas Jefferson, was duly received. My engagements are such that I cannot attend.

Bearing in mind that about seventy years ago two great political parties were first formed in this country, that Thomas Jefferson was the head of one of them and Boston the headquarters of the other, it is both curious and interesting that those supposed to descend politically from the party opposed to Jefferson should now be celebrating his birthday in their own original seat of empire, while those claiming political descent from him have nearly ceased to breathe his name everywhere.

Remembering, too, that the Jefferson party were formed upon their supposed superior devotion to the *personal* rights of men, holding the rights of *property* to be secondary only, and greatly inferior, and assuming that the so-called Democracy of today are the Jefferson, and their opponents the anti-Jefferson parties, it will be equally interesting to note how completely the two have changed hands as to the principle upon which they were originally supposed to be divided. The Democracy of today hold the *liberty* of one man to be absolutely nothing, when in conflict with another man's right of *property*. Republicans, on the contrary, are for both the *man* and the *dollar*; but in case of conflict, the man *before* the dollar.

I remember being once much amused at seeing two partially intoxicated men engaged in a fight with their greatcoats on, which fight, after a long and rather harmless contest, ended in each having fought himself *out* of his own coat and *into* that of the other. If the two leading parties of this day are really identical with the two in the days of Jefferson and Adams, they have performed the same feat as the two drunken men.

But, soberly, it is now no child's play to save the principles of Jefferson from total overthrow in this nation. One would state with great confidence that he could convince any sane child that the simpler propositions of Euclid are true; but nevertheless, he would fail, utterly, with one who should deny the definitions and axioms. The principles of Jefferson are the definitions and axioms of free society. And yet they are denied and evaded, with no small show of success. One dashingly calls them "glittering generalities;" another bluntly calls them "self-evident lies;" and others insidiously argue that they apply to "superior races." These expressions, differing in form, are identical in object and effect—the supplanting the principles of free government, and restoring those of classification, caste, and legitimacy. They would delight a convocation of crowned heads, plotting against the people. They are the vanguard—the miners and sappers—of returning despotism. We must repulse them, or they will subjugate us. This is a world of compensations; and he who would *be* no slave must consent to *have* no slave. Those who deny freedom to others deserve it not for themselves, and, under a just God, cannot long retain it.

All honor to Jefferson—to the man, who, in the concrete pressure of a struggle for national independence by a single people, had the coolness, forecast, and capacity to introduce into a merely revolutionary document, an abstract truth, applicable to all men and all times, and so to embalm it there, that today and in all coming days, it shall be a rebuke and a stumbling-block to the very harbingers of reappearing tyranny and oppression.

Abraham Lincoln, Speech to Wisconsin
Agricultural Society
September 30, 1859

[These remarks indicate what Lincoln and the Republican party meant by equal rights and free labor—essentially the right or freedom to become an independent property owner.]

. . . The world is agreed that *labor* is the source from which human wants are mainly supplied. There is no dispute upon this point. From this point, however, men immediately diverge. Much disputation is maintained as to the best way of applying and controlling the labor element. By some it is assumed that labor is available only in connection with capital—that nobody labors, unless somebody else, owning capital, somehow, by the use of that capital, induces him to do it. Having assumed this, they proceed to consider whether it is best that capital shall *hire* laborers, and thus induce them to work by their own consent; or *buy* them, and drive them to it without their consent. Having proceeded so far, they naturally conclude that all laborers are naturally either *hired* laborers, or *slaves*. They further assume that whoever is once a *hired* laborer, is fatally fixed in that condition for life; and hence again that his condition is as bad as, or worse than that of a slave. This is the *"mud-sill"* theory. But another class of reasoners hold the opinion that there is no *such* relation between capital and labor, as assumed; and that there is no such thing as a free man being fatally fixed for life, in the condition of a hired laborer, that both these assumptions are false, and all inferences from them groundless. They hold that labor is prior to, and independent of, capital; that, in fact, capital is the fruit of labor, and could never have existed if labor had not *first* existed—that labor can exist without capital, but that capital could never have existed without labor. Hence they hold that labor is the superior—greatly the superior—of capital.

They do not deny that there is, and probably always will be, *a* relation between labor and capital. The error, as they hold, is in assuming that the *whole* labor of the world exists within that relation. A few men own capital; and that few avoid labor themselves, and with their capital, hire, or buy, another few to labor for them. A large majority belong to neither class—neither work for others, nor have others working for them. Even in all our slave States, except South Carolina, a majority of the whole people of all colors, are neither slaves nor masters. In these free States, a large majority are neither *hirers* nor *hired*. Men, with their families—wives, sons and daughters—work for themselves, on their farms, in their houses, and in their shops, taking the whole product to themselves, and asking no favors of capital on the one hand, nor of hirelings or slaves on the other. It is not forgotten that a considerable number of persons mingle their own labor with capital; that is, labor with their own hands, and also buy slaves or hire free men to labor for them; but this is only a *mixed*, and not a *distinct* class. No principle stated is disturbed by the existence of this mixed class. Again, as has already been said, the opponents of the *"mud-sill"* theory insist that there is not, of necessity, any such thing as the free hired laborer being fixed to that condition for life. There is demonstration for saying this. Many independent men, in this assembly, doubtless a few years ago were hired laborers. And their case is almost, if not quite, the general rule.

The prudent, penniless beginner in the world, labors for wages awhile, saves a surplus with which to buy tools or land for himself; then labors on his own account another while, and at length hires another new beginner to help him. This, say its advocates, is *free* labor—the just, and generous, and prosperous system, which opens the way for all—gives hope to all, and energy, and progress, and improvement of condition to all. If any continue through life in the condition of the hired laborer, it is not the fault of the system, but because of either a dependent nature which prefers it, or improvidence, folly, or singular misfortune. I have said this much about the elements of labor generally, as introductory to the consideration of a new phase which that element is in process of assuming. The old general rule was that *educated* people did not perform manual labor. They managed to eat their bread, leaving the toil of producing it to the uneducated. This was not an unsupportable evil to the working bees, so long as the class of drones remained very small. But *now*, especially in these free States, nearly all are educated—quite too nearly all, to leave the labor of the uneducated, in any wise adequate to the support of the whole. It follows from this that henceforth educated people must labor. Otherwise, education itself would become a positive and intolerable evil. No country can sustain, in idleness, more than a small percentage of its numbers. The great majority must labor at something productive. From these premises the problem springs, "How can *labor* and *education* be the most satisfactorily combined?"

By the "*mud-sill*" theory it is assumed that labor and education are incompatible; and any practical combination of them impossible. According to that theory, a blind horse upon a tread-mill, is a perfect illustration of what a laborer should be—all the better for being blind, that he could not kick understandingly. According to that theory, the education of laborers is not only useless but pernicious, and dangerous. In fact, it is, in some sort, deemed a misfortune that laborers should have heads at all. Those same heads are regarded as explosive materials, only to be safely kept in damp places, as far as possible from that peculiar sort of fire which ignites them. A Yankee who could invent a strong-*handed* man without a head would receive the everlasting gratitude of the "mud-sill" advocates.

But free labor says, "No." Free labor argues that as the Author of man makes every individual with one head and one pair of hands, it was probably intended that heads and hands should co-operate as friends; and that that particular head, should direct and control that pair of hands. As each man has one mouth to be fed, and one pair of hands to furnish food, it was probably intended that that particular pair of hands should feed that particular mouth—that each head is the natural guardian, director, and protector of the hands and mouth inseparably connected with it; and that being so, every head should be cultivated, and improved, by whatever will add to its capacity for performing its charge. In one word, free labor insists on *universal education*.

I have so far stated the opposite theories of "*mud-sill*" and "free labor," without declaring any preference of my own between them. On an occasion like this, I ought not to declare any. I suppose, however, I shall not be mistaken, in assuming as a fact, that the people of Wisconsin prefer free labor, with its natural companion, education. . . .

Republican Party Platform
May 16, 1860

[It was a foregone conclusion that the Republican party would win the presidential election in 1860. But as it approached national power it grew increasingly cautious and conservative. Only reluctantly did the Chicago convention, which nominated Lincoln and wrote the following platform, reassert the party's commitment to the egalitarian ideals of the Declaration of Independence.]

Resolved, That we, the delegated representatives of the Republican electors of the United States, in Convention assembled, in discharge of the duty we owe to our constituents and our country, unite in the following declarations:

1. That the history of the nation, during the last four years, has fully established the propriety and necessity of the organization and perpetuation of the Republican party, and that the causes which called it into existence are permanent in their nature, and now, more than ever before, demand its peaceful and constitutional triumph.

2. That the maintenance of the principles promulgated in the Declaration of Independence and embodied in the Federal Constitution, "That all men are created equal; that they are endowed by their Creator with certain inalienable rights; that among these are life, liberty and the pursuit of happiness; that, to secure these rights, governments are instituted among men, deriving their just powers from the consent of the governed," is essential to the preservation of our Republican institutions; and that the Federal Constitution, the Rights of the States, and the Union of the States, must and shall be preserved.

3. That to the Union of the States this nation owes its unprecedented increase in population, its surprising development of material resources, its rapid augmentation of wealth, its happiness at home and its honor abroad; and we hold in abhorrence all schemes for Disunion, come from whatever source they may; And we congratulate the country that no Republican member of Congress has uttered or countenanced the threats of Disunion so often made by Democratic members, without rebuke and with applause from their political associates; and we denounce those threats of Disunion, in case of a popular overthrow of their ascendency, as denying the vital principles of a free government, and as an avowal of contemplated treason, which it is the imperative duty of an indignant People sternly to rebuke and forever silence.

4. That the maintenance inviolate of the rights of the States, and especially the right of each State to order and control its own domestic institutions according to its own judgment exclusively, is essential to that balance of powers on which the perfection and endurance of our political fabric depends; and we denounce the lawless invasion by armed

force of the soil of any State or Territory, no matter under what pretext, as among the gravest of crimes.

5. That the present Democratic Administration has far exceeded our worst apprehensions, in its measureless subserviency to the exactions of a sectional interest, as especially evinced in its desperate exertions to force the infamous Lecompton constitution upon the protesting people of Kansas; in construing the personal relation between master and servant to involve an unqualified property in persons; in its attempted enforcement, everywhere, on land and sea, through the intervention of Congress and of the Federal Courts of the extreme pretensions of a purely local interest; and in its general and unvarying abuse of the power intrusted to it by a confiding people. . . .

7. That the new dogma that the Constitution, of its own force, carries Slavery into any or all of the Territories of the United States, is a dangerous political heresy, at variance with the explicit provisions of that instrument itself, with contemporaneous exposition, and with legislative and judicial precedent; is revolutionary in its tendency, and subversive of the peace and harmony of the country.

8. That the normal condition of all the territory of the United States is that of freedom; That as our Republican fathers, when they had abolished slavery in all our national territory, ordained that "no person should be deprived of life, liberty, or property, without due process of law," it becomes our duty, by legislation, whenever such legislation is necessary, to maintain this provision of the Constitution against all attempts to violate it; and we deny the authority of Congress, of a territorial legislature, or of any individuals, to give legal existence to Slavery in any Territory of the United States.

9. That we brand the recent re-opening of the African slave-trade, under the cover of our national flag, aided by perversions of judicial power, as a crime against humanity and a burning shame to our country and age; and we call upon Congress to take prompt and efficient measures for the total and final suppression of that execrable traffic.

10. That in the recent vetoes, by their Federal Governors, of the acts of the Legislatures of Kansas and Nebraska, pro-

hibiting Slavery in those Territories, we find a practical illustration of the boasted Democratic principle of Non-Intervention and Popular Sovereignty embodied in the Kansas-Nebraska bill, and a demonstration of the deception and fraud involved therein.

11. That Kansas should, of right, be immediately admitted as a State under the Constitution recently formed and adopted by her people, and accepted by the House of Representatives.

12. That, while providing revenue for the support of the General Government by duties upon imports, sound policy requires such an adjustment of these imposts as to encourage the development of the industrial interests of the whole country; and we commend that policy of national exchanges which secures to the working men liberal wages, to agriculture remunerating prices, to mechanics and manufacturers an adequate reward for their skill, labor and enterprise, and to the nation commercial prosperity and independence.

13. That we protest against any sale or alienation to others of the Public Lands held by actual settlers, and against any view of the Homestead policy which regards the settlers as paupers or supplicants for public bounty; and we demand the passage by Congress of the complete and satisfactory Homestead measure which has already passed the house.

14. That the Republican Party is opposed to any change in our Naturalization Laws or any State legislation by which the rights of our citizenship hitherto accorded to immigrants from foreign lands shall be abridged or impaired; and in favor of giving a full and efficient protection to the rights of all classes of citizens, whether native or naturalized, both at home and abroad.

15. That appropriations by Congress for River and Harbor improvements of a National character, required for the accommodation and security of an existing commerce, are authorized by the Constitution, and justified by the obligations of Government to protect the lives and property of its citizens.

16. That a Railroad to the Pacific Ocean is imperatively demanded by the interests of the whole country; that the

Federal Government ought to render immediate and efficient aid in its construction; . . .

Abraham Lincoln, First Inaugural Address
March 4, 1861

[The Confederacy had already been formed when Lincoln took office. Still hoping that the issue could be settled peacefully, he was as moderate as possible in this his first speech as President. But of course his extreme Unionist arguments were unpalatable to all but a few slave-owning states.]

. . . Apprehension seems to exist among the people of the Southern States that by the accession of a Republican administration their property and their peace and personal security are to be endangered. There has never been any reasonable cause for such apprehension. Indeed, the most ample evidence to the contrary has all the while existed and been open to their inspection. It is found in nearly all the published speeches of him who now addresses you. I do but quote from one of those speeches when I declare that "I have no purpose, directly or indirectly, to interfere with the institution of slavery in the States where it exists. I believe I have no lawful right to do so, and I have no inclination to do so." . . .

A disruption of the Federal Union, heretofore only menaced, is now formidably attempted.

I hold that, in contemplation of universal law and of the Constitution, the Union of these States is perpetual. Perpetuity is implied, if not expressed, in the fundamental law of all national governments. It is safe to assert that no government proper ever had a provision in its organic law for its own termination. Continue to execute all the express provisions of our national Constitution, and the Union will endure forever—it being impossible to destroy it except by some action not provided for in the instrument itself.

Again, if the United States be not a government proper, but an association of States in the nature of contract merely, can it as a contract be peaceably unmade by less than all the parties who made it? One party to a contract may violate it—break it, so to speak; but does it not require all to lawfully rescind it?

Descending from these general principles, we find the proposition that in legal contemplation the Union is perpetual confirmed by the history of the Union itself. The Union is much older than the Constitution. It was formed, in fact, by the Articles of Association in 1774. It was matured and continued by the Declaration of Independence in 1776. It was further matured, and the faith of all the then thirteen States expressly plighted and engaged that it should be perpetual, by the Articles of Confederation in 1778. And, finally, in 1787 one of the declared objects for ordaining and establishing the Constitution was "to form a more perfect Union."

But if the destruction of the Union by one or by a part only of the States be lawfully possible, the Union is less perfect than before the Constitution, having lost the vital element of perpetuity.

It follows from these views that no State upon its own mere motion can lawfully get out of the Union; that resolves and ordinances to that effect are legally void; and that acts of violence, within any State or States, against the authority of the United States, are insurrectionary or revolutionary, according to circumstances.

I therefore consider that, in view of the Constitution and the laws, the Union is unbroken; and to the extent of my ability I shall take care, as the Constitution itself expressly enjoins upon me, that the laws of the Union be faithfully executed in all the States. Doing this I deem to be only a simple duty on my part; and I shall perform it so far as practicable, unless my rightful masters, the American people, shall withhold the requisite means, or in some authoritative manner direct the contrary. I trust this will not be regarded as a menace, but only as the declared purpose of the Union that it will constitutionally defend and maintain itself.

In doing this there needs to be no bloodshed or violence; and there shall be none, unless it be forced upon the national authority. The power confided to me will be used to hold, occupy, and possess the property and places belonging to the Government, and to collect the duties and imposts; but beyond what may be necessary for these objects, there will be no invasion, no using of force against or among the people anywhere. Where hostility to the United States, in any interior locality, shall be so great and universal as to prevent competent resident citizens from holding the Federal offices, there will be no attempt to force obnoxious strangers among the people for that object. While the strict legal right may exist in the government to enforce the exercise of these offices, the attempt to do so would be so irritating, and so nearly impracticable withal, that I deem it better to forego for the time the uses of such offices.

The mails, unless repelled, will continue to be furnished in all parts of the Union. So far as possible, the people everywhere shall have that sense of perfect security which is most favorable to calm thought and reflection. The course here indicated will be followed unless current events and experience shall show a modification or change to be proper, and in every case and exigency my best discretion will be exercised according to circumstances actually existing, and with a view and a hope of a peaceful solution of the national troubles and the restoration of fraternal sympathies and affections.

That there are persons in one section or another who seek to destroy the Union at all events, and are glad of any pretext to do it, I will neither affirm nor deny; but if there be such, I need address no word to them. To those, however, who really love the Union may I not speak?

Before entering upon so grave a matter as the destruction of our national fabric, with all its benefits, its memories, and its hopes, would it not be wise to ascertain precisely why we do it? Will you hazard so desperate a step while there is any possibility that any portion of the ills you fly from have no real existence? Will you, while the certain ills you fly to are greater than all the real ones you fly from—will you risk the commission of so fearful a mistake?

All profess to be content in the Union if all constitutional rights can be maintained. Is it true, then, that any right, plainly written in the Constitution, has been denied? I think not. Happily the human mind is so constituted that no party can reach to the audacity of doing this. Think, if you can, of a single instance in which a plainly written provision of the Constitution has ever been denied. If by the mere force of numbers a majority should deprive a minority of any clearly written constitutional right, it might, in a moral point of view, justify revolution—certainly would if such a right were a vital one. But such is not our case. All the vital rights of minorities and of individuals are so plainly assured to them by affirmations and negations, guaranties and prohibitions, in the Constitution, that controversies never arise concerning them. But no organic law can ever be framed with a provision specifically applicable to every question which may occur in practical administration. No foresight can anticipate, nor any document of reasonable length contain, express provisions for all possible questions. Shall fugitives from labor be surrendered by national or by State authority? The Constitution does not expressly say. *May* Congress prohibit slavery in the Territories? The Constitution does not expressly say. *Must* Congress protect slavery in the Territories? The Constitution does not expressly say.

From questions of this class spring all our constitutional controversies, and we divide upon them into majorities and minorities. If the minority will not acquiesce, the majority must, or the Government must cease. There is no other alternative; for continuing the Government is acquiescence on one side or the other.

If a minority in such case will secede rather than acquiesce, they make a precedent which in turn will divide and ruin them; for a minority of their own will secede from them whenever a majority refuses to be controlled by such minority. For instance, why may not any portion of a new confederacy a year or two hence arbitrarily secede again, precisely as portions of the present Union now claim to secede from it? All who cherish disunion sentiments are now being educated to the exact temper of doing this.

Is there such perfect identity of interests among the States to compose a new Union as to produce harmony only, and prevent renewed secession?

Plainly, the central idea of secession is the essence of anarchy. A majority held in restraint by constitutional checks and limitations, and always changing easily with deliberate changes of popular opinions and sentiments, is the only true sovereign of a free people. Whoever rejects it does, of necessity, fly to anarchy or to despotism. Unanimity is impossible; the rule of a minority, as a permanent arrangement, is wholly inadmissible; so that, rejecting the majority principle, anarchy or despotism in some form is all that is left.

I do not forget the position assumed by some, that constitutional questions are to be decided by the Supreme Court; nor do I deny that such decisions must be binding, in any case, upon the parties to a suit, as to the object of that suit, while they are also entitled to a very high respect and consideration in all parallel cases by all other departments of the government. And, while it is obviously possible that such decision may be erroneous in any given case, still the evil effect following it, being limited to that particular case, with the chance that it may be overruled and never become a precedent for other cases, can better be borne than could the evils of a different practice. At the same time, the candid citizen must confess that if the policy of the government, upon vital questions affecting the whole people, is to be irrevocably fixed by decisions of the Supreme Court, the instant they are made, in ordinary litigation between parties in personal actions, the people will have ceased to be their own rulers, having to that extent practically resigned the government into the hands of that eminent tribunal. Nor is there in this view any assault upon the court or the judges. It is a duty from which they may not shrink to decide cases properly brought before them, and it is no fault of theirs if others seek to turn their decisions to political purposes.

One section of our country believes slavery is right, and ought to be extended, while the other believes it is wrong, and ought not to be extended. This is the only substantial dispute. The fugitive slave clause of the Constitution and the law for the suppression of the foreign slave trade are each as well enforced, perhaps, as any law can ever be in a community where the moral sense of the people imperfectly supports the law itself. The great body of the people abide by the dry legal obligation in both cases, and a few break over in each. This, I think, cannot be perfectly cured; and it would be worse in both cases after the separation of the sections than before. The foreign slave trade, now imperfectly suppressed, would be ultimately revived, without restriction, in one section, while fugitive slaves, now only partially surrendered, would not be surrendered at all by the other.

Physically speaking, we cannot separate. We cannot remove our respective sections from each other, nor build an impassable wall between them. A husband and wife may be divorced and go out of the presence and beyond the reach of each other; but the different parts of our country cannot do this. They cannot but remain face to face, and intercourse, either amicable or hostile, must continue between them. Is it possible, then, to make that intercourse more advantageous or more satisfactory after separation than before? Can aliens make treaties easier than friends can make laws? Can treaties be more faithfully enforced between aliens than laws can among friends? Suppose you go to war, you cannot fight always; and when, after much loss on both sides, and no gain on either, you cease fighting, the identical old questions as to terms of intercourse are again upon you.

This country, with its institutions, belongs to the people who inhabit it. Whenever they shall grow weary of the existing government, they can exercise their constitutional right of amending it, or their revolutionary right to dismember or overthrow it. I cannot be ignorant of the fact that many worthy and patriotic citizens are desirous of having the national Constitution amended. While I make no recommendation of amendments, I fully recognize the rightful authority of the people over the whole subject, to be exercised in either of the modes prescribed in the instrument itself, and I should, under existing circumstances, favor rather than oppose a fair opportunity being afforded the people to act upon it. I will venture to add that to me the convention mode seems preferable, in that it allows amendments to originate with the people themselves, instead of only permitting them to take or reject propositions originated by others not especially chosen for the purpose, and which might not be precisely such as they would wish to either accept or refuse.

I understand a proposed amendment to the Constitution—which amendment, however, I have not seen—has passed Congress, to the effect that the Federal Government shall never interfere with the domestic institutions of the States, including that of persons held to service. To avoid misconstruction of what I have said, I depart from my purpose not to speak of particular amendments so far as to say that, holding such a provision to now be implied constitutional law, I have no objection to its being made express and irrevocable. . . .

Abraham Lincoln, Message to Congress
July 4, 1861

[On April 15 Lincoln requested that Congress meet in special session. By the time it met ten weeks later full-scale war had broken out with the Confederacy, which was now made up of eleven, not seven states. In this message Lincoln goes further than he went in his inaugural speech in subordinating the states to the Union.]

. . . The purpose to sever the Federal Union was openly avowed. In accordance with this purpose, an ordinance had been adopted in each of these States, declaring the States respectively to be separated from the national Union. A formula for instituting a combined government of these States had been promulgated; and this illegal organization, in the character of confederate States, was already invoking recognition, aid, and intervention from foreign powers. . . .

And this issue embraces more than the fate of these United States. It presents to the whole family of man the question whether a constitutional republic or democracy—a government of the people by the same people—can or cannot maintain its territorial integrity against its own domestic foes. It presents the question whether discontented individuals, too few in number to control administration according to organic laws in any case, can always, upon the pretenses made in this case, or on any other pretenses, or arbitrarily without any pretense, break up their government, and thus practically put an end to free government upon the earth. It forces us to ask: Is there in all republics this inherent and fatal weakness? Must a government, of necessity, be too strong for the liberties of its own people, or too weak to maintain its own existence?

So viewing the issue, no choice was left but to call out the war power of the government, and so to resist force employed for its destruction by force for its preservation. . . .

It might seem, at first thought, to be of little difference whether the present movement at the South be called "secession" or "rebellion." The movers, however, well understand the difference. At the beginning they knew they could never raise their treason to any respectable magnitude by any name which implies violation of law. They knew their people possessed as much of moral sense, as much of devotion to law and order, and as much pride in and reverence for the history and government of their common country as any other civilized and patriotic people. They knew they could make no advancement directly in the teeth of these strong and noble sentiments. Accordingly, they commenced by an insidious debauching of the public mind. They invented an ingenious sophism which, if conceded, was followed by perfectly logical steps, through all the incidents, to the complete destruction of the Union. The sophism itself is that any State of the Union may consistently with the national Constitution, and therefore lawfully and peacefully, withdraw from the Union without the consent of the Union or of any other State. . . .

This sophism derives much, perhaps the whole, of its currency from the assumption that there is some omnipotent and sacred supremacy pertaining to a State—to each State of our Federal Union. Our States have neither more nor less power than that reserved to them in the Union by the Constitution —no one of them ever having been a State out of the Union. The original ones passed into the Union even before they cast off their British colonial dependence; and the new ones each came into the Union directly from a condition of dependence, excepting Texas. And even Texas in its temporary independence was never designated a State. The new ones only took the designation of States on coming into the Union, while that name was first adopted for the old ones in and by the Declaration of Independence. . . . Having never been States either in substance or in name outside of the Union, whence this magical omnipotence of "State rights," asserting a claim of power to lawfully destroy the Union itself? Much is said about the "sovereignty" of the States; but the word even is not in the national Constitution, nor, as is believed, in any of the State constitutions. What is "sovereignty" in the political sense of the term? Would it be far wrong to define it as "a political community without a political superior"? Tested by this, no one of our States except Texas ever was a sovereignty. . . . The States have their status in the Union, and they have no other legal status. If they break from this, they can only do so against law and by revolution. The Union, and not themselves separately, procured their independence and their liberty. By conquest or purchase the Union gave each of them whatever of independence or liberty it has. The Union is older than any of the States, and, in fact, it created them as States. Originally some dependent colonies made the Union, and, in turn, the Union threw off their old dependence for them, and made them States, such as they are. Not one of them ever had a State constitution independent of the Union. Of course, it is not forgotten that all the new States framed their constitutions before they entered the Union—nevertheless, dependent upon and pre paratory to coming into the Union. . . .

What is now combated is the position that secession is consistent with the Constitution—is lawful and peaceful. It is not contended that there is any express law for it; and nothing should ever be implied as law which leads to unjust or absurd consequences. . . .

The seceders insist that our Constitution admits of secession. They have assumed to make a national constitution of their own, in which of necessity they have either discarded or retained the right of secession as they insist it exists in ours. If they have discarded it, they thereby admit that on principle it ought not to be in ours. If they have retained it, by their own construction of ours, they show that to be consistent they must secede from one another whenever they shall find it the easiest way of settling their debts, or effecting any other selfish or unjust object. The principle itself is one of disintegration and upon which no government can possibly endure. . . .

This is essentially a people's contest. On the side of the Union it is a struggle for maintaining in the world that form and substance of government whose leading object is to elevate the condition of men—to lift artificial weights from all shoulders; to clear the paths of laudable pursuit for all; to afford all an unfettered start, and a fair chance in the race of life. Yielding to partial and temporary departures, from necessity, this is the leading object of the government for whose existence we contend. . . .

Our popular government has often been called an experiment. Two points in it our people have already settled—the successful establishing and the successful administering of it. One still remains—its successful maintenance against a formidable internal attempt to overthrow it. It is now for them to demonstrate to the world that those who can fairly carry an election can also suppress a rebellion; that ballots are the rightful and peaceful successors of bullets; and that when ballots have fairly and constitutionally decided, there can be no successful appeal back to bullets; that there can be no successful appeal, except to ballots themselves, at succeeding elections. Such will be a great lesson of peace: teaching men that what they cannot take by an election, neither can they take it by war; teaching all the folly of being the beginners of a war. . . .

Abraham Lincoln to Horace Greeley
August 22, 1862

[On August 19, 1862, Horace Greeley, the Radical Republican publisher of the New York *Tribune*, wrote an open letter to Lincoln, demanding, in his typically imperious manner, that Lincoln immediately order the emancipation of all slaves within Union control. Lincoln had been reluctant to do this for fear of antagonizing the crucial border states (Kentucky, Missouri, Maryland and Delaware), which were at once Unionist and slave. Following is his answer to Greeley, asserting, at this stage of the conflict, the primacy of union over liberty.]

DEAR SIR: I have just read yours of the nineteenth, addressed to myself through the New-York *Tribune*. If there be in it any statements or assumptions of fact which I may know to be erroneous, I do not now and here controvert them. If there be in it any inferences which I may believe to be falsely drawn, I do not now and here argue against them. If there be perceptible in it an impatient and dictatorial tone, I waive it in deference to an old friend, whose heart I have always supposed to be right.

As to the policy I "seem to be pursuing," as you say, I have not meant to leave any one in doubt.

I would save the Union. I would save it the shortest way under the Constitution. The sooner the National authority can be restored, the nearer the Union will be "the Union as it was." If there be those who would not save the Union unless they could at the same time *save* Slavery, I do not agree with them. If there be those who would not save the Union unless they could at the same time *destroy* Slavery, I do not agree with them. My paramount object in this struggle *is* to save the Union, and is *not* either to save or destroy Slavery. If I could save the Union without freeing *any* slave, I would do it; and if I could save it by freeing *all* the slaves, I would do it; and if I could do it by freeing some and leaving others alone, I would also do that. What I do about Slavery and the colored race, I do because I believe it helps to save this Union; and what I forbear, I forbear because I do *not* believe it would help to save the Union. I shall do *less* whenever I shall believe what I am doing hurts the cause, and I shall do *more* whenever I shall believe doing more will help the cause. I shall try to correct errors when shown to be errors; and I shall adopt new views so fast as they shall appear to be true views. I have here stated my purpose according to my view of *official* duty, and I intend no modification of my oft-expressed *personal* wish that all men, everywhere, could be free.

Yours,

A. LINCOLN.

Abraham Lincoln, Second Inaugural Address
March 4, 1865

[There is no more just or eloquent appraisal of the cause of the Civil War than Lincoln's great second inaugural.]

Fellow Countrymen:

At this second appearing to take the oath of the presidential office, there is less occasion for an extended address than there was at the first. Then a statement, somewhat in detail, of a course to be pursued, seemed fitting and proper. Now, at the expiration of four years, during which public declarations have been constantly called forth on every point and phase of the great contest which still absorbs the attention, and engrosses the energies of the nation, little that is new could be presented. The progress of our arms, upon which all else chiefly depends, is as well known to the public as to myself; and it is, I trust, reasonably satisfactory and encouraging to all. With high hope for the future, no prediction in regard to it is ventured.

On the occasion corresponding to this four years ago, all thoughts were anxiously directed to an impending civil-war. All dreaded it—all sought to avert it. While the inaugural address was being delivered from this place, devoted altogether to *saving* the Union without war, insurgent agents were in the city seeking to *destroy* it without war—seeking to dissolve the Union, and divide effects, by negotiation. Both parties deprecated war; but one of them would *make* war rather than let the nation survive; and the other would *accept* war rather than let it perish. And the war came.

One eighth of the whole population were colored slaves, not distributed generally over the Union, but localized in the Southern part of it. These slaves constituted a peculiar and powerful interest. All know that this interest was, somehow, the cause of the war. To strengthen, perpetuate, and extend this interest was the object for which the insurgents would rend the Union, even by war; while the government claimed

no right to do more than to restrict the territorial enlargement of it. Neither party expected for the war, the magnitude, or the duration, which it has already attained. Neither
anticipated that the *cause* of the conflict might cease with,
or even before, the conflict itself should cease. Each looked
for an easier triumph, and a result less fundamental and
astounding. Both read the same Bible, and pray to the same
God; and each invokes His aid against the other. It may seem
strange that any men should dare to ask a just God's assistance in wringing their bread from the sweat of other men's
faces; but let us judge not that we be not judged. The prayers
of both could not be answered; that of neither has been answered fully. The Almighty has His own purposes. "Woe unto
the world because of offences! for it must needs be that
offences come; but woe to that man by whom the offence
cometh!" If we shall suppose that American Slavery is one of
those offences which, in the providence of God, must needs
come, but which, having continued through His appointed
time, He now wills to remove, and that He gives to both
North and South, this terrible war, as the woe due to those
by whom the offence came, shall we discern therein any departure from those divine attributes which the believers in
a Living God always ascribe to Him? Fondly do we hope—
fervently do we pray—that this mighty scourge of war may
speedily pass away. Yet, if God wills that it continue, until
all the wealth piled by the bond-man's two hundred and fifty
years of unrequited toil shall be sunk, and until every drop
of blood drawn with the lash, shall be paid by another drawn
with a sword, as was said three thousand years ago, so still it
must be said "the judgments of the Lord, are true and righteous altogether."

With malice toward none; with charity for all; with firmness in the right, as God gives us to see the right, let us strive
on to finish the work we are in; to bind up the nation's
wounds; to care for him who shall have borne the battle, and
for his widow, and his orphan—to do all which may achieve
and cherish a just, and a lasting peace, among ourselves, and
with all nations.

Louisiana Regulations for Freedmen
July 1865

[In 1865 such regulations are these sprang up in parishes and towns throughout Louisiana.]

WHEREAS it was formerly made the duty of the police jury to make suitable regulations for the police of slaves within the limits of the parish; and whereas slaves have become emancipated by the action of the ruling powers; and whereas it is necessary for public order, as well as for the comfort and correct deportment of said freedmen, that suitable regulations should be established for their government in their changed condition, the following ordinances are adopted with the approval of the United States military authorities commanding in said parish, viz:

Sec. 1. *Be it ordained by the police jury of the parish of St. Landry,* That no negro shall be allowed to pass within the limits of said parish without special permit in writing from his employer. Whoever shall violate this provision shall pay a fine of two dollars and fifty cents, or in default thereof shall be forced to work four days on the public road, or suffer corporeal punishment as provided hereinafter.

Sec. 2. . . . Every negro who shall be found absent from the residence of his employer after ten o'clock at night, without a written permit from his employer, shall pay a fine of five dollars, or in default thereof, shall be compelled to work five days on the public road, or suffer corporeal punishment as hereinafter provided.

Sec. 3. . . . No negro shall be permitted to rent or keep a house within said parish. Any negro violating this provision shall be immediately ejected and compelled to find an employer; and any person who shall rent, or give the use of any house to any negro, in violation of this section, shall pay a fine of five dollars for each offence. . . .

Sec. 5. . . . No public meetings or congregations of negroes shall be allowed within said parish after sunset; but such public meetings and congregations may be held between the hours of sunrise and sunset, by the special permission in writing of the captain of patrol, within whose beat such meetings shall take place. This prohibition, however, is not to prevent negroes from attending the usual church services, conducted by white ministers and priests. Every negro violating the provisions of this section shall pay a fine of five dollars, or in default thereof shall be compelled to work five days on the public road, or suffer corporeal punishment as hereinafter provided.

Sec. 6. . . . No negro shall be permitted to preach, exhort, or otherwise declaim to congregations of colored people, without a special permission in writing from the president of the police jury. Any negro violating the provisions of this section shall pay a fine of ten dollars, or in default shall be forced to work ten days on the public road, or suffer corporeal punishment as hereinafter provided. . . .

Sec. 8. . . . No negro shall sell, barter, or exchange any articles of merchandise or traffic within said parish without the special written permission of his employer, specifying the article of sale, barter or traffic. Any one thus offending shall pay a fine of one dollar for each offence, and suffer the forfeiture of said articles, or in default of the payment of said fine shall work one day on the public road, or suffer corporeal punishment as hereinafter provided. . . .

Sec. 9. . . . Any negro found drunk, within the said parish shall pay a fine of five dollars, or in default thereof work five days on the public road, or suffer corporeal punishment as hereinafter provided. . . .

Sec. 11. . . . It shall be the duty of every citizen to act as a police officer for the detection of offences and the apprehension of offenders, who shall be immediately handed over to the proper captain or chief of patrol. . . .

Sec. 14. . . . The corporeal punishment provided for in the foregoing sections shall consist in confining the body of the offender within a barrel placed over his or her shoulders, in the manner practiced in the army, such confinement not to continue longer than twelve hours, and for such time within the aforesaid limit as shall be fixed by the captain or chief of patrol who inflicts the penalty.

Mississippi Apprentice Law
November 22, 1865

[Such laws were enacted by most states of the deep South following emancipation. Some states made no distinction between Negro and white apprentices.]

Sec. 1. . . . . It shall be the duty of all sheriffs, justices of the peace, and other civil officers of the several counties in this State, to report to the probate courts of their respective counties semi-annually, at the January and July terms of said courts, all freedmen, free negroes, and mulattoes, under the age of eighteen, in their respective counties, beats, or districts, who are orphans, or whose parent or parents have not the means or who refuse to provide for and support said minors; and thereupon it shall be the duty of said probate court to order the clerk of said court to apprentice said minors to some competent and suitable person, on such terms as the court may direct, having a particular care to the interest of said minor: *Provided*, that the former owner of said minors shall have the preference when, in the opinion of the court, he or she shall be a suitable person for that purpose.

Sec. 2. . . . . The said court shall be fully satisfied that the person or persons to whom said minor shall be apprenticed shall be a suitable person to have the charge and care of said minor, and fully to protect the interest of said minor. The said court shall require the said master or mistress to execute bond and security, payable to the State of Mississippi, conditioned that he or she shall furnish said minor with sufficient food and clothing; to treat said minor humanely; furnish medical attention in case of sickness; teach, or cause to be taught, him or her to read and write, if under fifteen years old, and will conform to any law that may be hereafter passed for the regulation of the duties and relation of master and apprentice. . . .

Sec. 3. . . . . in the management and control of said apprentices, said master or mistress shall have the power to inflict such moderate corporal chastisement as a father or guardian is allowed to inflict on his or her child or ward at common law: *Provided*, that in no case shall cruel or inhuman punishment be inflicted.

Sec. 4. . . . if any apprentice shall leave the employment of his or her master or mistress, without his or her consent, said master or mistress may pursue and recapture said apprentice, and bring him or her before any justice of the peace of the county, whose duty it shall be to remand said apprentice to the service of his or her master or mistress; and in the event of a refusal on the part of said apprentice so to return, then said justice shall commit said apprentice to the jail of said county, on failure to give bond, to the next term of the county court; and it shall be the duty of said court at the first term thereafter to investigate said case, and if the court shall be of opinion that said apprentice left the employment of his or her master or mistress without good cause, to order him or her to be punished, as provided for the punishment of hired freedmen, as may be from time to time provided for by law for desertion, until he or she shall agree to return to the service of his or her master or mistress: . . . if the court shall believe that said apprentice had good cause to quit his said master or mistress, the court shall discharge said apprentice from said indenture, and also enter a judgment against the master or mistress for not more than one hundred dollars, for the use and benefit of said apprentice. . . .

Thaddeus Stevens, Speech on the Fourteenth Amendment
May 8, 1866

[Here the leader of the Radical Republicans in the House comments on the Fourteenth Amendment, which the Southern states—"conquered provinces," he called them—were required to ratify as the condition for re-entering the Union.]

. . . Upon a careful survey of the whole ground, we did not believe that nineteen of the loyal States could be induced to ratify any proposition more stringent than this. I say nineteen, for I utterly repudiate and scorn the idea that any State not acting in the Union is to be counted on the question of ratification. It is absurd to suppose that any more than three fourths of the States that propose the amendment are required to make it valid; that States not here are to be counted as present. Believing then, that this is the best proposition that can be made effectual, I accept it. . . .

The first section prohibits the States from abridging the privileges and immunities of citizens of the United States, or unlawfully depriving them of life, liberty, or property, or of denying to any person within their jurisdiction the "equal" protection of the laws.

I can hardly believe that any person can be found who will not admit that every one of these provisions is just. They are all asserted, in some form or other, in our DECLARATION or organic law. But the Constitution limits only the action of Congress, and is not a limitation on the States. This amendment supplies that defect, and allows Congress to correct the unjust legislation of the States, so far that the law which operates upon one man shall operate *equally* upon all. Whatever law punishes a white man for a crime shall punish the black man precisely in the same way and to the same degree. Whatever law protects the white man shall afford "equal" protection to the black man. Whatever means of redress is afforded to one shall be afforded to all. Whatever law allows the white man to testify in court shall allow the man of color to do the same. These are great advantages over their present codes. Now different degrees of punishment are inflicted, not on account of the magnitude of the crime, but according to the color of the skin. Now color disqualifies a man from testifying in courts, or being tried in the same way as white men. I need not enumerate these partial and oppressive laws. Unless the Constitution should restrain them, those States will all, I fear, keep up this discrimination, and crush to death the hated freedmen. Some answer, "Your civil rights bill secures the same things." That is partly true, but a law is repealable by a majority. And I need hardly say that the first time that the South with their copperhead allies obtain the command of Congress it will be repealed. The veto of the

President and their votes on the bill are conclusive evidence of that. And yet I am amazed and alarmed at the impatience of certain well-meaning Republicans at the exclusion of the rebel States until the Constitution shall be so amended as to restrain their despotic desires. This amendment once adopted cannot be annulled without two thirds of Congress. That they will hardly get. And yet certain of our distinguished friends propose to admit State after State before this becomes a part of the Constitution. What madness! Is their judgment misled by their kindness; or are they unconsciously drifting into the haven of power at the other end of the avenue? I do not suspect it, but others will.

The second section I consider the most important in the article. It fixes the basis of representation in Congress. If any State shall exclude any of her adult male citizens from the elective franchise, or abridge that right, she shall forfeit her right to representation in the same proportion. The effect of this provision will be either to compel the States to grant universal suffrage or so to shear them of their power as to keep them forever in a hopeless minority in the national Government, both legislative and executive. If they do not enfranchise the freedmen, it would give to the rebel States but thirty-seven Representatives. Thus shorn of their power, they would soon become restive. Southern pride would not long brook a hopeless minority. True, it will take two, three, possibly five years before they conquer their prejudices sufficiently to allow their late slaves to become their equals at the polls. That short delay would not be injurious. In the mean time the freedmen would become more enlightened, and more fit to discharge the high duties of their new condition. In that time, too, the loyal Congress could mature their laws and so amend the Constitution as to secure the rights of every human being, and render disunion impossible. Heaven forbid that the southern States, or *any one of them,* should be represented on this floor until such muniments of freedom are built high and firm. Against our will they have been absent for four bloody years; against our will they must not come back until we are ready to receive them. Do not tell me that there are loyal representatives waiting for admission

—until their States are loyal they can have no standing here. They would merely *mis*represent their constituents.

I admit that this article is not as good as the one we sent to death in the Senate. In my judgment, we shall not approach the measure of justice until we have given every adult freedman a homestead on the land where he was born and toiled and suffered. Forty acres of land and a hut would be more valuable to him than the immediate right to vote. Unless we give them this we shall receive the censure of mankind and the curse of Heaven. That article referred to provided that if *one* of the injured race was excluded the State should forfeit the right to have any of them represented. That would have hastened their full enfranchisement. This section allows the States to discriminate among the same class, and receive proportionate credit in representation. This I dislike. But it is a short step forward. The large stride which we in vain proposed is dead; the murderers must answer to the suffering race. I would not have been the perpetrator. A load of misery must sit heavy on their souls. . . .

The Civil Rights Act
March 1, 1875

[This act, the final gesture of Republican generosity toward Southern Negroes, was struck down by the Supreme Court in 1883. In 1964 Congress passed a similar act, which the Court validated.]

Whereas it is essential to just government we recognize the equality of all men before the law, and hold that it is the duty of government in its dealings with the people to mete out equal and exact justice to all, of whatever nativity, race, color, or persuasion, religious or political; and it being the appropriate object of legislation to enact great fundamental principles into law: Therefore,

Be it enacted, That all persons within the jurisdiction of the United States shall be entitled to the full and equal enjoyment of the accommodations, advantages, facilities, and privileges of inns, public conveyances on land or water, theaters, and other places of public amusement; subject only to the conditions and limitations established by law, and applicable alike to citizens of every race and color, regardless of any previous condition of servitude.

SEC. 2. That any person who shall violate the foregoing section by denying to any citizen, except for reasons by law applicable to citizens of every race and color, and regardless of any previous condition of servitude, the full enjoyment of any of the accommodations, advantages, facilities, or privileges in said section enumerated, or by aiding or inciting such denial, shall, for every such offense, forfeit and pay the sum of five hundred dollars to the person aggrieved thereby, . . . and shall also, for every such offense, be deemed guilty of a misdemeanor, and, upon conviction thereof, shall be fined not less than five hundred nor more than one thousand dollars, or shall be imprisoned not less than thirty days nor more than one year . . .

SEC. 3. That the district and circuit courts of the United States shall have, exclusively of the courts of the several States, cognizance of all crimes and offenses against, and violations of, the provisions of this act . . .

SEC. 4. That no citizen possessing all other qualifications which are or may be prescribed by law shall be disqualified for service as grand or petit juror in any court of the United States, or of any State, on account of race, color, or previous condition of servitude. . . .

CHAPTER VII. THE AGE
OF NEO-HAMILTONIANISM

The Compromise of 1877, it becomes obvious, reflected the desire of both parties and most Americans to close the book on the Negro problem. Fundamentally, the Compromise meant that the federal government would defer to the states on matters of civil rights. The Republican party was no longer interested in supporting, much less enforcing, the legislation passed since 1866, and in particular the Fourteenth Amendment. The Republican position on civil rights was foreshadowed as early as 1873 by the Supreme Court's decision in the Slaughterhouse case. Called upon to interpret the first section of the Fourteenth Amendment, the predominantly Republican Court then declared that the states alone had the authority to define the privileges and immunities of citizenship pertaining to voting rights, elections, holding office, etc. The Court thus served notice that the states were free to begin disfranchising Negroes.

Ten years later the Court went further in denying Negroes the federal protection that should have been theirs under the Fourteenth Amendment when it overturned the Civil Rights Act of 1875. This Act had guaranteed Negroes equal treatment in places of public accommodation (hotels, theaters, means of transportation, etc.). The Court struck down the law by giving an absurdly narrow construction to the Fourteenth Amendment. According to the majority, the Amendment was intended to protect civil rights from interference by state governments, not by individual persons—as though it were possible for individuals to act without the acquiescence of state laws. The Court made an unusual, and quite incomprehensible, distinction between political rights, which the Fourteenth Amendment could regulate, and social rights, which they maintained it could not. The last obstacle in the path to Jim Crowism had been cleared.

With the removal of sectional and racial issues from public life, until the second half of the twentieth century at least, the major political parties resumed their original function of mediating between interest groups, seeking out bases of mutual agreement and reciprocal advantage. By the mid-1870s the Republican and Democratic parties had between them arrived at an approximately even balance in regional and economic power and in the over-all distribution of votes. The Republican party drew its strength primarily from Eastern bankers and manufacturers and Northern farmers; the Democratic party represented merchants, shippers and the solid South; the urban vote was divided.

The issues that agitated American politics from the early 1870s to the early 1890s corresponded to this rough economic and regional alignment. The two most persistent issues were high versus low tariffs and easy versus hard money. In general, farmers and merchants plumped for free trade; manufacturers and workers, on the other hand, favored protection of industries. Farmers and small-business men called for easy money policies, particularly during periods of depression, when the cost of paying off debts rose in direct proportion to the fall in the price of goods. The East, being predominantly a region of creditors and consumers, advocated strict adherence to the gold standard to underpin the value of the dollar. For two decades both parties uneasily maintained their internal balance in the face of these conflicting interests. Both adopted nearly similar policies, even though the Democrats appeared to be identified with low tariffs and hard money, and the Republicans with high tariffs and easy money. Ideologically, there was little to enable one to distinguish between them.

Throughout the period the most powerful interest of all remained the political party. Historians often mistakenly assume that politics invariably subserves economics or is merely the reflex of a social class. In point of fact, the political system has its own imperatives and its own sanctions, which are independent of, and often superior to, any class or group. This was certainly true in the decades following the Civil War. The primary responsibility of the federal government then was to supply patronage for the party machine; to act in behalf of economic interests was only its secondary responsibility. The government passed laws or granted favors because the party in power stood to benefit from them. The party struck a *quid pro quo* with both the poor and the rich, the people and the special interests—the one for their votes, the other for their money. To businessmen, of course, this was an unhappy arrangement, but they had no choice except to comply since they still lacked the power and the organization to lay down their own terms.

The spoils system had become the cement of the Union. The hundreds of thousands of federal offices that the Republican party had been distributing since 1861—mostly postmasterships, court clerks and marshals—reached into every community in the country. The political party might be likened to a feudal society, its members bound to each other by a hierarchy of duties and benefices. The lower vassals at the county and ward levels received their fiefs in the form of appointive offices, in return for their support of the higher vassals who served in Congress and who obtained patronage from the government. United States Senators were the vassals-in-chief because they commanded the greatest number of jobs for their particular states. From the late 1860s on, these medieval barons, governing with all the panoply and prerogatives of their class, dominated the nation's political life. Individually they ran their own states, governors being mere local functionaries, and collectively they ran the federal government. The President was their chosen titular head. The Republican presidents from Lincoln to Theodore Roosevelt—Grant, Hayes, Garfield, Arthur, Harrison, and McKinley—were chief executives only in name. Real authority resided in the Senate.

The supremacy of the party organization rested on its capacity to fill its own financial needs. When it ceased to be self-sufficient it fell from its seat of power. The main source of party funds, so necessary to bring out the votes, keep the endless number of caucuses and conventions running, maintain a permanent staff of workers, etc., came from contributions by the faithful in the form of kickbacks. Each local, state and federal job had its monetary price. After the Pendleton Act was passed in January 1883, however, thousands of high-echelon federal offices were brought under the civil service. Chester A. Arthur, one of the notorious spoilsmen of the age, was the first President to make use of this Act. His motive was not to advance the cause of good government—for nothing could have been further from his mind—but to give his appointments permanent status in the civil service, thereby protecting them from the Democrats, who were about to take office. Whatever the motive, however, the precedent was established, and future chief executives similarly applied the Act in behalf of their appointees. The effect of this reform was to deplete party coffers at a time of rising costs, forcing the politicos to look elsewhere for revenue.

As soon as the party organization began depending on voluntary contributions from the rich, a new *quid pro quo* emerged: it was now the businessman who laid down the terms to the politicos. Actually, the relations between them were even closer than this, for businessmen had themselves become entrenched in the higher reaches of the party apparatus. Nothing reveals this fact so clearly as the composition of the Senate in the 1890s. The old feudal barons had by then been replaced by members of the *haute bourgeoisie*, millionaires who had entered politics in their middle years, having first made their fortunes in business. The Shermans, the Mortons, the Chandlers, the Logans, the Morrills—the men who had joined the Republican party at its birth, had seen it grow into a revolutionary movement and subsequently develop into a gigantic spoils machine—these were replaced by the new men of power, the Aldriches, the Platts, the Spooners, the Penroses, the Hannas, who made up the "Millionaires' Club," as the Senate was called in the 1890s.

This change in the party organization reflected the extraordinary shift in the distribution of national wealth and power that had been taking place since the 1860s. By the turn of the century—the story is too well known to need retelling here—empires of industry and finance, centered in the great cities of the Northeast, had come to dominate the economic life of the nation, shattering the balance of regional and class interests that both parties had more or less successfully maintained since Reconstruction. But the political effects of this vast concentration of power were not felt in all their vehemence and wrath until the plutocratic leaders of the Democratic and Republican parties were confronted by a serious challenge to their authority.

When the challenge did emerge in the 1890s it came from two quarters: from the farmers of the West and South, and from a segment of the urban working class. We need not discuss the nature of the Populist movement. It is enough to note here that, by 1890, the cotton and wheat farmers, groaning under the burden of increasingly heavy debts and finding no redress from the existing parties, had decided to create their own party and draw up a bold plan of social and economic reform, involving large-scale federal intervention. Specifically, these men wanted the government to own the systems of transportation and communication, control national banking facilities, issue easier terms of credit, and enact shorter work week schedules in factories and mines. Politically, they demanded the direct election of Senators, the direct primary, the secret ballot, initiative and referendum. In short, the Populists declared war both on the party machines and on the plutocratic interests that now controlled them.

Many Southern Populists, moreover, voted for Grover Cleveland in 1892 in the belief that he understood their problems and would assist them. But Cleveland's faith in the gold standard, or hard money, was invincible, his belief in states' rights and laissez-faire liberalism unconquerable. He could not see how the federal government could possibly help the farmers, nor the workers thrown into the streets by the Depression of 1893, without violating these principles. If the individual could not help himself, reasoned Cleveland, nobody could help him, least of all the state. His Secretary of Agriculture, J. S. Morton, advised the people to read Adam Smith to understand why the laws of nature forbade the government from coming to their aid. By 1894, the lines of conflict had been drawn in the Democratic party, with Cleveland representing, not its rank and file, but its Eastern oligarchy.

Definitive proof of this fact was given when he intervened to break the great Pullman strike of 1894. In late June of that year, the American Railway Union, led by Eugene Debs, struck against the Pullman Company of Chicago for cutting wages despite the high profits the company itself was making. The workers refused to work on Pullman cars, detaching them from the rest of the trains and thereby tying up the whole Middle Western railroad network. In its early stages the strike was notably peaceful. But Cleveland's Attorney General, Richard Olney, himself a prominent railroad lawyer, was determined to send the mails through and conceived a three-point plan for forcing the union to submit: first, thousands of marshals (many of them toughs deputized off the streets) were to be sent to Chicago to move the trains; second, a court injunction to stop the strike was to be sought; and third, in the event of conflict, federal troops were to be called in. Olney's plan worked to perfection. Violence broke out, the injunction was granted, and federal troops came in to crush the strike. Debs was jailed and the union broken. But in the end the Democratic party paid a high price for Cleveland's triumph; it lost the support of the working class.

Cleveland's anti-agrarian, anti-labor policies precipitated important changes in both major political parties. A majority of Democrats, representing the South and West, were sympathetic to the Populist cause, and in 1896 they captured the Democratic party organization. In the famous convention held in St. Louis that year they nominated William Jennings Bryan for the presidency. Immediately, the followers of Cleveland, or the "Gold Democrats," bolted the convention and formed a rump conservative party of their own.

Bryan was the furthest left of any Democratic candidate since Jackson. And though the party platform was not as radical as the Populist platform of 1892, it was radical enough in the context of the times. For not since the emergence of Republicanism in the 1850s had a major party come out so defiantly against the special interests and in defense of free labor. Once again Jeffersonian ideals were broadcast throughout the land. The trusts and monopolies were execrated, the Court's use of injunctions against labor was decried, high tariffs were condemned, and free and unlimited coinage of silver, intended to provide cheap credit to farmers already mortgaged over their heads, was declared a necessity.

The Populists, finding Bryan's position worthy of support in the election, ran him on their ticket as well.

The Republican party, meanwhile, had become the avowed defender of the great industrial and financial combines. This was clear from the platform that it framed in 1896. One has to go back to the rise of the slavocracy to find a party so emphatically Hamiltonian in its subservience to powerful economic groups and its affirmation of conservatism. It had cast off whatever was left of its Jeffersonian heritage as refracted through Lincoln and the Radicals. Its 1896 program called for unlimited protection for manufacturing and unreserved support for the gold standard, an announcement of its solidarity with the industrialists, the bankers and the bondholders of the country.

But the Republicans could not have hoped to win if they had appealed exclusively to the tiny minority of the rich and privileged, and in fact, the party in 1896 put together a majority coalition. Urban workers had scant interest in free silver; but they had a compelling interest in high tariffs, which promised to benefit their industries. Despite Bryan's pro-labor and pro-union campaign, moreover, workers still identified the Democratic party with Cleveland and the Depression of 1893. The Republicans also had the backing of Midwestern farmers, the prosperous corn and dairy producers, who were not at the mercy of fluctuating world prices, since their market was entirely domestic. To them, Bryan's radicalism was more a threat than a promise, and they had no intention of cutting their historic ties to the Grand Old Party for his will-o'-the-wisp. The Republican coalition that was forged in 1896 thus countered the Democratic-Populist philosophy of class conflict by promulgating a philosophy of class harmony, under the aegis of enlightened business enterprise.

The genius who presided over the fortunes of the Republican party at this time was Mark Hanna of Ohio. He secured the nomination for William McKinley, drew together the party's coalition, and brilliantly organized the campaign that won the election. One of the new breed of millionaires who were entering politics after a successful career in business, he had been McKinley's sponsor in Ohio since the 1880s, and as such, thanks to his money and business methods, had overcome the resistance thrown up by the Republican machine in that state. These methods he introduced to national politics in the 1896 campaign. The same rational procedures, the same consolidation of power that had transformed industry, Hanna now employed to transform the party organization. He received a staggering sum of money from Eastern financiers and industrialists, who trembled at the prospect that the Tiberius Gracchus of the West might become President. With an overflowing war chest at his disposal, Hanna set up a remarkable apparatus for distributing propaganda, subsidizing local candidates, and buying votes in crucial states. It was the best-organized campaign in American political history.

The Republican triumph was the most decisive any party had enjoyed in twenty-five years. McKinley received a half million votes and nearly a hundred electoral votes more than Bryan did. And more significantly, both houses of Congress went Republican by huge majorities. Republican strength was concentrated in the urban and industrial Northeastern states. Bryan won no electoral votes east of the Mississippi and above the Mason-Dixon line. His entire support lay in the South and far West. The "anarchist" challenge represented by Bryan was thus turned back; the established order could now rest secure, for the nation had overwhelmingly vindicated the Republicans' Hamiltonian program. So, apparently, had the inscrutable laws of political economy, as the Depression lifted in the very year of the election. Prosperity soon returned, money was abundant, and land values, along with the price of all agricultural commodities, rose sharply. The Republican party promptly made good its promise. In 1897 Congress enacted the Dingley Tariff, which raised rates to an all-time high, and in 1900 it passed the Currency Act, which irrevocably fastened the dollar to the gold standard.

Cleveland had already marked out the course that the Republican party now officially sanctioned. For Republicans, as for conservative Democrats, the federal government was responsible for maintaining the status quo; in plain words, for protecting large corporations from the "anarchists" and "revolutionists" who threatened to regulate, or worse, socialize them. This vulgar form of Hamiltonianism was designed by and for the great possessing classes of the country. It was less a theory of the national good than a rationalization of power.

The new federalism of the late nineteenth century rested on two contradictory assumptions. The first was that there must be no state interference in the economy; individual freedom of contract was the categorical imperative of progress and happiness. This assumption was buttressed by the myth of social Darwinism, according to which distinctions of wealth and power, however marked, resulted from the natural competition, or process of selection, between the strong and the weak; such distinctions, being both right and necessary, were unalterable. The second assumption was that the state had to interfere in the economy not only to protect property rights, but actively to promote business enterprise, through high tariffs, for example. The new federalism used whatever ideological instruments were available, depending on the problem and the occasion.

The decisions of the Supreme Court from the early 1880s on give a clear indication of how the doctrine of the new federalism was applied. The Court, for the first time since the days of John Marshall, unhesitatingly struck down legislation it thought undesirable. Invoking the Fourteenth Amendment, it invalidated scores of state laws, most of which regulated factories and mines, hours of work, etc., on the grounds that property rights could not be abridged without "due process of law"—the meaning of due process being left for the Court's majority to define.

The Fourteenth Amendment was thus turned on its head. The Amendment originally had been framed by Radical Republicans to protect Negro rights, and for this reason it had given the federal government sweeping powers over the states. But from the 1870s on, the Court allowed the states plenary authority to deal with Negroes. The final act of federal withdrawal came in the famous *Plessy* v. *Ferguson* decision of 1896, in which the Court upheld the right of states to segregate Negroes by interpreting "the equal protection" clause of the Fourteenth Amendment to mean "separate but equal." Under the Court's guidance, then, the

Amendment served not the human rights of Negroes, but the property rights of corporations. The fate of the Amendment since its enactment precisely corresponded to the course traveled by the Republican party since its inception.

Thomas Jenckes, Speech on Civil Service Reform
January 29, 1867

[Representative Jenckes of Rhode Island was one of the few critics of patronage in the 1860s who was himself a politician. Here he speaks to the House about his bill to reform the civil service.]

Mr. JENCKES. Mr. Speaker, the bill just reported, and to which I am instructed by the committee to invite the favorable attention of the House, is intended to work an entire reformation in the method of making appointments to the subordinate offices in the civil service of the United States. It has been framed, and is now proposed, for no political or partisan purpose. It has no regard to the existing condition and relations of parties in the Republic, and no bearing upon the controversies between the different departments of the Government. . . .

It may be questioned whether a more vicious system, or rather want of system, than that now existing can be devised or imagined. The public sale of offices could hardly be worse, for in such case the tenure of the office would be required to be defined and its emoluments made certain before the office could have any marketable price. Something definite must be offered for sale before a sale can be effected. But at present nearly every one of these subordinate offices is filled by some person who gained his appointment by the recommendation of personal and political friends, and not by the application of any test to discover his fitness for the place he occupies. His compensation is subject to assessments or forced contributions to pay the expenses of conducting elections in which he is not a candidate for office. If he should show any decided ability or special aptitude for the service he has no assurance of promotion, or even of retention. His term of office is limited by the pleasure, caprice, or interest of his superior.

In the corruption of our politics all these places have become the rewards of partisanship. At every change of administration which brings a different political party into power, the time within which a clean sweep can be made depends upon the industry and zeal with which the incoming authorities can hear and decide upon the claims of the new horde of office-seekers clamorous for the reward of their partisan services. The good of the service is seldom consulted in making appointments, and more rarely in making removals, and the applicants care far less for the public interest than for their own. There is little or no scrutiny into the character and antecedents of the applicant other than as to his political services; no examination to test his qualifications; no probation even during which his fitness or unfitness for the office might be discovered. . . .

Very few who feel themselves competent to attain eminence or even reputable positions in the learned professions or in business, ever enter the subordinate grades of the civil service. It has no rewards or honors to stimulate ambition; it gives the individual no position either in society or in the State. It must be confessed that this service has sunk into a sort of disrepute. Those active, energetic, and capable men who are scattered among its places feel called upon to give some reason for their being found there, whenever the character of their employment is the subject of conversation in their presence. The employés in the public service have not an equal standing in the community with those in corresponding positions employed by private persons or corporations. The merchant's bookkeepers and clerks, the bank cashiers, clerks, and tellers, the agents of express and insurance companies, and others who, although in subordinate capacities, urge forward the business of the world, stand higher in public esteem than those who have dropped into this treadmill of the public service. Even the great but more poorly paid class of teachers, with lives as monotonous, and with as slight rewards for successful toil, are much more respected. The reason is plain. In the pursuits of active life there is no place for the idle, the corrupt, the ignorant, the dissolute, or the dishonest.

If a man be an inferior lawyer or noisy primary-meeting politician, or both, no presumption is raised thereby in his favor that he will make a good bank-teller or accountant; although these qualities seem to avail him if he aspires to similar employment in a post office or custom-house. As a general rule, those who from some defect or incorrect habit in mind or character have been unable to succeed in the open competition of business, are quartered by their relations and political friends, as occasion may offer, upon the public service; and although, taken as a whole, the pay is greater and the labor lighter under Government than in other employment, yet the work is done with less promptitude and thoroughness. The Government runs every custom-house and considerable post offices with more men and greater pay and with greater loss from inefficiency and dishonesty than every successful individual or corporation manages an equal amount of business. . . .

The measure now before the House is an approximation to a remedy for these evils. The systems regulating the civil service of other nations have been examined, and the results of their experience have been embodied in this bill. The principle is not new, nor is the mode in which it is to be wrought out. The attempt has been to adapt it to the wants of this country, and therein is its merit, if it has any. This principle is to place practically in the hands of the Government the power of employing the services of the capable and of dispensing with the services of the incapable in every subordinate place and every executive department. In other words, "let the best attainable talent, the greatest attainable fitness, in every case be placed in office," and thus approximate as near as possible to having the right man in the right place. Let merit be the sole title to office, and we work a thorough reformation in our mode of appointments, and infuse new life and vigor into every branch of the executive service. . . .

This measure proposes to extirpate, eradicate, or, in plain Saxon, dig up, root out, and throw aside any, every, and all kinds of "patronage" in appointments to the public service.

The word, the thing, the act, have no place in a republic. In other countries and in past ages Government was the patrimony of princes, the heritage of kings; here and now it is the inheritance of the people. Unto every man who casts a ballot in this country is remitted at every election day his portion of the sovereignty of this great nation. The political career is open to all; the public service should be a career equally accessible. There is no place for "patronage" in our system; it is a solecism in itself. In practice it is a great public injury: "It 'curseth' him that gives and him that takes." The assumed right of control by one class of public servants over another on other than meritorious grounds ought not to be tolerated. The people do not elect a man President in order that he may have the privilege, the "patronage" of quartering all his relations and personal and political friends upon the Treasury, but because they believe that their Government will be best administered by him. Inherent in the common sense of the people is the maxim concerning government, "That which is best administered is best," and the people demand that in their Government, which this is, all obstructions to the best administration shall be removed. The best way of doing this has seemed to us to be the securing of the services of the best administrators. When merit is the key that opens the gate to a career in the public service, the "patronage" which has introduced dullness, mediocrity, laziness, and profligacy into it, becomes extinct. . . .

John A. Logan, Speech on Civil Service Reform
January 8, 1869

[Senator Logan of Illinois was one of the great Republican spoilsmen of the age. Here he defends patronage before the Senate, giving the classic Jacksonian arguments.]

Mr. LOGAN. . . . Mr. Chairman, I rise to oppose the bill known as Mr. JENCKES's "civil service bill," which provides for a new department of Government and a "life tenure for all civil offices of the United States, except those wherein the

Senate must consent to the appointment;" and in opposing this bill I desire to say I am in favor of having the business of this Government, in every department, transacted with the utmost intelligence, fidelity, and dispatch. I believe that all employés in the service of the Government should have intelligence and capacity sufficient to enable them to perform their duties in a satisfactory manner, and that they receive such compensation as will make them proof against dishonesty and ambitious of promotion. I am in favor of governmental economy, but I do not regard that to be a wise economy which pinches a subordinate to lavish on a superior. In a word, sir, I desire to see the affairs of the nation transacted by all its participants with the utmost attainable precision, aptitude, and integrity; and whenever it is shown to me that a reform is needed in any point and it can be effected by any proper legislation I will cheerfully vote for it.

I think it is proper that I should thus express my views in order that I may not be misunderstood in my motives or feelings when I say that I cannot vote for this bill nor advocate the system which is embodied in it. I think that the bill is bad in theory, wrong in principle, opposed to the genius and spirit of our institutions and our people, and probably unconstitutional in its legal aspect. I regard the introduction of a bill like this, and the favor with which it has been thus far received by both parties and the press of the country, as one of the most positive, and, therefore, one of the most alarming signs of the inauguration of a policy which if persisted in will end in the obliteration of all that is republican in this Government and the substitution of that which is monarchical in its stead. If I had had nothing but the bill itself before me I might have hesitated before expressing this opinion; but when I read, as I have done with great care, the report of the committee and the exhibits attached to their report, and find their whole plan is taken openly, boldly, and without disguise from monarchical Governments, I cannot doubt what its results will be if I could doubt the intention. . . .

Every Administration is justly held responsible by the country for the policy it pursues, the measures which it upholds, and the good or evil which springs therefrom. It happens not unfrequently that the success or failure of an administrative design is caused by the acts of those who are intrusted with its execution. A whole scheme has often been thwarted by some insignificant subordinate and the fate of a party has turned upon an accident.

An incoming Administration has, therefore, clearly a right to demand that any person who may be known to harbor hostility to its wholesome measures or enmity to our institutions shall not be retained in the public service. The right to demand this rests not alone upon the necessity of unanimity in all departments of public service; not alone upon the right of the officers-elect to chose those agents whom they may deem to be the best to carry out their views; not alone upon the principle that a spy shall not be tolerated in military or civil pursuits, but upon the broader ground that the Administration represents the country for the time being and is the embodiment of the country's welfare and prosperity, unless it has proved treacherous to the principles upon which the people placed it there; and that he who does not unite in its views is not to be intrusted with its employment. I recognize this principle, sir, as a wise and salutary one; I do not say I would apply it in all instances, but I insist that the right to apply it shall not be taken away. . . .

I have adverted to this incidentally before, when it fell in with another topic. But I wish now to call the most earnest attention of the House to that which stares us in the face. This bill is the opening wedge to an aristocracy in this country. It is first to be created by law, and then to maintain itself by its own power, which will increase from day to day until finally it will become irresistible. I say this deliberately, and after giving the bill the most careful attention. It will lead us to the point where there will be two national schools in this country—one for the military and the other for civil education. Those schools will monopolize all avenues of approach to the Government. Unless a man can pass one or the other of those schools and be enrolled upon their lists he cannot receive employment under this Government, no matter how great may be his capacity, how indisputable may be his qualifications. When once he does pass his school and fixes himself for life his next care will be to get his children there also. In these schools the scholars will soon come to believe that they are the only persons qualified to administer the Government, and soon come to resolve that the Government shall be administered by them and by none others.

Combinations will come. They may be at first nothing more than unity of feeling and purpose, which comes of simple association. It will be possibly only the feeling which the man of the world has for his *Alma Mater*. It may not take shape or purpose until some favorite candidate brings it together. Then it will learn its strength; afterward it will use its strength, and soon its strength will be so great as to overcome all organized opposition.

The two schools will combine, for they will have sentiments, hopes, and ambitions alike. Their tone, habits, and manner, will soon be distinctive. It will stamp itself upon society. It will arrogate to itself to be the "cream of the cream" of society. It will assume foreign airs, and shoddy will ape it and them. It will toady to titles and long for them, and if not swept away too soon will have them.

Let any man stand in the great cities of the East and see how, with our boasted wealth and refinement, we have imported European vices and monarchical customs. Look at the liveried servants, the emblazoned equipages, the coats of arms, and crests of heraldry—pages, tigers, outriders. That which is foreign is fashionable, and that which is fashionable is baleful and demoralizing. Who will not say that this moment titles and all the paraphernalia of royalty would not be hailed by these? Alas! for the days of republican simplicity. If the essential differences which prevail between our form of government and those of Europe were remembered it would be seen that the same reasons which make this system a good one there make it a bad one here. In this country every man has a political opinion and a vote. The vote of the poorest and humblest man counts as much as that of the richest and most distinguished.

Every man is interested in politics and uses his political influence whether or not he be employed in the service of the Government. There is no man in office, no matter how high, who is beyond the reach of the vote cast by one, no matter how low. There is no measure of State policy which may not be changed by a single vote. Every man here is a part of the Government. If he disagrees with the administration of the Government his vote will assist to change it. There is no class, save the United States judges, not amenable to his censure or not removable by his vote. . . .

This is a new danger to the country, and it comes not with the bold front of revolution, but with the pleasing show of reform. It appeals to our protection with a special plea, now that the finances of the country are suffering from the shock of war. It invokes our patriotism by declaring itself for the purification of party and the just disposition of the nation's patronage. The disguise is thin, and he who looks beneath may see the true lineaments of a monster which will destroy us all. . . .

Civil Rights Cases
1883

[Following is the decision, delivered by Justice Joseph P. Bradley, that struck down the Civil Rights Act of 1875.]

Bradley, J. . . . It is true that slavery cannot exist without law any more than property in lands and goods can exist without law, and therefore the Thirteenth Amendment may be regarded as nullifying all state laws which establish or uphold slavery. But it has a reflex character also, establishing and decreeing universal civil and political freedom throughout the United States; and it is assumed that the power in Congress to enforce the articles by appropriate legislation, clothes Congress with power to pass all laws necessary and proper for abolishing all badges and incidents of slavery in the United States; and upon this assumption it is claimed that this is sufficient authority for declaring by law that all persons shall have equal accommodations and privileges in all inns, public conveyances, and places of public amusement; the argument being that the denial of such equal accommodations and privileges is in itself a subjection to a species of servitude within the meaning of the amendment. Conceding the major proposition to be true, that Congress has a right to enact all necessary and proper laws for the obliteration and prevention of slavery with all its badges and incidents, is the minor proposition also true, that the denial to any person of admission to the accommodations and privileges of an inn, a public conveyance, or a theatre, does subject that person to any form of servitude, or tend to fasten upon him any badge of slavery? If it does not, then power to pass the law is not found in the Thirteenth Amendment. . . .

But is there any similarity between such servitudes and a denial by the owner of an inn, a public conveyance, or a theatre, of its accommodations and privileges to an individual, even though the denial be founded on the race or color of that individual? Where does any slavery or servitude, or badge of either, arise from such an act of denial? . . .

The long existence of African slavery in this country gave us very distinct notions of what it was, and what were its necessary incidents. Compulsory service of the slave for the benefit of the master, restraint of his movements except by the master's will, disability to hold property, to make contracts, to have a standing in court, to be a witness against a white person, and such like burdens and incapacities were the inseparable incidents of the institution. . . . Can the act of a mere individual, the owner of the inn, the public conveyance, or place of amusement, refusing the accommodation, be justly regarded as imposing any badge of slavery or servitude upon the applicant, or only as inflicting an ordinary civil injury, properly cognizable by the laws of the State, and presumably subject to redress by those laws until the contrary appears?

After giving to these questions all the consideration which their importance demands, we are forced to the conclusion that such an act of refusal has nothing to do with slavery or involuntary servitude, and that if it is violative of any right of the party, his redress is to be sought under the laws of the State; or, if those laws are adverse to his rights and do not protect him, his remedy will be found in the corrective legislation which Congress has adopted, or may adopt, for counteracting the effect of state laws, or state action, prohibited by the Fourteenth Amendment. It would be running the slavery argument into the ground to make it apply to every act of discrimination which a person may see fit to make as to the guests he will entertain, or as to the people he will take into his coach or cab or car, or admit to his concert or theatre, or deal with in other matters of intercourse or business. . . .

When a man has emerged from slavery, and by the aid of beneficent legislation has shaken off the inseparable concomitants of that state, there must be some stage in the progress of his elevation when he takes the rank of a mere citizen, and ceases to be the special favorite of the laws, and when his rights as a citizen, or a man, are to be protected in the ordinary modes by which other men's rights are protected. There were thousands of free colored people in this country before the abolition of slavery, enjoying all the essential rights of life, liberty and property the same as white citizens; yet no one, at that time, thought that it was any invasion of his personal status as a freeman because he was not admitted to all the privileges enjoyed by white citizens, or because he was subjected to discriminations in the enjoyment of accommodations in inns, public conveyances and places of amusement. Mere discriminations on account of race or color were not regarded as badges of slavery. If, since that time, the enjoyment of equal rights in all these respects has become established by constitutional enactment, it is not by force of the Thirteenth Amendment (which merely abolishes slavery), but by force of the Fourteenth and Fifteenth Amendments.

On the whole we are of the opinion that no countenance of authority for the passage of the law in question can be found in either the Thirteenth or Fourteenth Amendment of the Constitution; and no other ground of authority for its passage being suggested, it must necessarily be declared void, at least so far as its operation in the several States is concerned. . . .

The Farmers' Association of South Carolina, "The Coming Campaign" January 23, 1890

[Typical of the agrarian movements that were rising up in the South was the one led by "Pitchfork Ben" Tillman of South Carolina. This movement was particularly significant because the Tidewater aristocracy had controlled that state since pre-Revolutionary days. Tillman's movement, like most of the others in the South, was at once radical and racist. When, finally, it took power it proceeded to disfranchise Negroes and pass Jim Crow laws. Below is the manifesto, printed in the Charleston *News and Courier*, put out by the Tillman forces shortly before they carried nearly all the state offices in the Democratic primary. Tillman himself was elected governor.]

To the Democracy of South Carolina: For four years the Democratic party in the State has been deeply agitated, and efforts have been made at the primaries and conventions to secure retrenchments and reform, and a recognition of the needs and rights of the masses. The first Farmers' Convention met in April, 1886. Another in November of the same year perfected a permanent organization under the name of the "Farmers' Association of South Carolina." This Association, representing the reform element in the party, has held two annual sessions since, and at each of these four conventions, largely attended by representative farmers from nearly all of the counties, the demands of the people for greater economy in the Government, greater efficiency in its officials, and a fuller recognition of the necessity for cheaper and more practical education have been pressed upon the attention of our Legislature.

In each of the two last Democratic State Conventions the "Farmers' Movement" has had a large following and we only failed of controlling the Convention of 1888 by a small vote—less than twenty-five—and that, too, in the face of the active opposition of nearly every trained politician in the State. We claim that we have always had a majority of the people on our side, and have only failed by reason of the superior political tactics of our opponents and our lack of organization. . . .

The executive committee of the Farmers' Association did not deem it worth while to hold any convention last November, but we have watched closely every move of the enemies of economy—the enemies of true Jeffersonian Democracy—and we think the time has come to show the people what it is they need and how to accomplish their desires. We will draw up the indictment against these who have been and are still governing our State, because it is at once the cause and justification of the course we intend to pursue.

South Carolina has never had a real Republican Government. Since the days of the "Lords Proprietors" it has been an aristocracy under the forms of Democracy, and whenever a champion of the people has attempted to show them their rights and advocated those rights an aristocratic oligarchy has bought him with an office, or failing in that turned loose the floodgates of misrepresentation and slander in order to destroy his influence.

The peculiar situation now existing in the State, requiring the united efforts of every true white man to preserve white supremacy and our very civilization even has intensified and tended to make permanent the conditions which existed before the war. Fear of a division among us and consequent return of a negro rule has kept the people quiet, and they have submitted to many grievances imposed by the ruling faction because they dreaded to risk such a division.

The "Farmers' Movement" has been hampered and retarded in its work by this condition of the public mind, but we have shown our fealty to race by submitting to the edicts of the party and we intend, as heretofore, to make our fight inside the party lines, feeling assured that truth and justice must finally prevail. The results of the agitation thus far are altogether encouraging. Inch by inch and step by step true Democracy—the rule of the people—has won its way. We have carried all the outposts. Only two strongholds remain to be taken, and with the issues fairly made up and plainly put to the people we have no fear of the result. The House of Representatives has been carried twice, and at last held after a desperate struggle.

The advocates of reform and economy are no longer sneered at as "Three for a quarter statesmen." They pass measures of economy which four years ago would have excited only derision, and with the Farmers' Movement to strengthen their backbone have withstood the cajolery, threats and impotent rage of the old "ring bosses." The Senate is now the main reliance of the enemies of retrenchment and reform, who oppose giving the people their rights. The Senate is the stronghold of "existing institutions" and the main dependence of those who are antagonistic to all progress. As we captured the House we can capture the Senate; but we must control the Democratic State Convention before we can hope to make economy popular in Columbia, or be assured of no more pocket votes.

The General Assembly is largely influenced by the idea and policy of the State officers, and we must elect those before we can say the Farmers' Movement has accomplished its mission. It is true that we have wrenched from the aristocratic coterie who were educated at and sought to monopolize everything for the South Carolina College, the right to control the land script and Hatch fund and a part of the privilege tax on fertilizers for one year, and we have $40,000 with which to commence building a separate agricultural college, where the sons of poor farmers can get a practical education at small expense.

We cannot elaborate the other counts in this indictment. We can only point briefly to the mismanagement of the Penitentiary, which is a burden on the taxpayers, even while engaged in no public works which might benefit the State. To the wrong committed against the people of many counties (strongholds of Democracy) by the failure to reapportion representation according to the population, whereby Charleston has five votes in the House and ten votes in the State Convention, which choose our State officers, to which it is not entitled.

To the zeal and extravagance of this aristocratic oligarchy, whose sins we are pointing out, in promising higher education for every class except farmers, while it neglects the free schools which are the only chance for an education to thousands of poor children, whose fathers bore the brunt in the struggle for our redemption in 1876. To the continued recurrence of horrible lynchings—which we can but attribute to bad laws and their inefficient administration. To the impotence of justice to punish criminals who have money. To the failure to call a constitutional convention that we may have an organic law framed by South Carolinians for South Carolinians and suited to our wants, thereby lessening the burdens of taxation and giving us better government.

Fellow Democrats, do not all these things cry out for a change? Is it not opportune, when there is no national election, for the common people who redeemed the State from Radical rule to take charge of it? Can we afford to leave it longer in the hands of those who, wedded to antebellum ideas, but possessing little of ante-bellum patriotism and honor, are running it in the interest of a few families and for the benefit of a selfish ring of politicians? As real Democrats and white men, those who here renew our pledge to make the fight inside the Democratic party and abide the result, we call upon every true Carolinian, of all classes and callings, to help us purify and reform the Democratic party and give us a government of the people, by the people and for the people.

If we control the State Democratic Convention, a Legislature in sympathy will naturally follow; failing to do this, we risk losing all we have gained, and have no hope of any change for the better. . . .

Populist Party Platform
July 4, 1892

[Sentiment for a third party had been germinating in the West and South since the late 1880s. In the South, however, most agrarian groups—e.g., Tillman's in South Carolina —struggled for power within the Democratic party. Populism, therefore, was overwhelmingly a Western movement, and it was appropriate that it held its national convention in Omaha. Among the delegates to the convention were some of the veterans of previous campaigns against Eastern plutocrats—Ignatius Donnelly of Minnesota, General James Weaver of Iowa, "Sockless" Jerry Simpson of Kansas, and others. The Populists drew up the following notable platform after choosing General Weaver as their presidential candidate. He received over a million votes in the election.]

Assembled upon the 116th anniversary of the Declaration of Independence, the People's Party of America, in their first national convention, invoking upon their action the blessing of Almighty God, put forth in the name and on behalf of the people of this country, the following preamble and declaration of principles:

PREAMBLE

The conditions which surround us best justify our co-operation; we meet in the midst of a nation brought to the verge of moral, political, and material ruin. Corruption dominates the ballot-box, the Legislatures, the Congress, and touches even the ermine of the bench. The people are demoralized; most of the States have been compelled to isolate the voters at the polling places to prevent universal intimidation and bribery. The newspapers are largely subsidized or muzzled, public opinion silenced, business prostrated, homes covered with mortgages, labor impoverished, and the land concentrating in the hands of capitalists. The urban workmen are denied the right to organize for self-protection, imported pauperized labor beats down their wages, a hireling standing army, unrecognized by our laws, is established to shoot them down, and they are rapidly degenerating into European conditions. The fruits of the toil of millions are boldly stolen to build up colossal fortunes for a few, unprecedented in the history of mankind; and the possessors of these, in turn, despise the Republic and endanger liberty. From the same prolific womb of governmental injustice we breed the two great classes—tramps and millionaires.

The national power to create money is appropriated to enrich bond-holders; a vast public debt payable in legal-tender currency has been funded into gold-bearing bonds, thereby adding millions to the burdens of the people.

Silver, which has been accepted as coin since the dawn of history, has been demonetized to add to the purchasing power of gold by decreasing the value of all forms of property as well as human labor, and the supply of currency is purposely abridged to fatten usurers, bankrupt enterprise, and enslave industry. A vast conspiracy against mankind has been organized on two continents, and it is rapidly taking possession of the world. If not met and overthrown at once it forebodes terrible social convulsions, the destruction of civilization, or the establishment of an absolute despotism.

We have witnessed for more than a quarter of a century the struggles of the two great political parties for power and plunder, while grievous wrongs have been inflicted upon the suffering people. We charge that the controlling influences dominating both these parties have permitted the existing dreadful conditions to develop without serious effort to prevent or restrain them. Neither do they now promise us any substantial reform. They have agreed together to ignore, in the coming campaign, every issue but one. They propose to drown the outcries of a plundered people with the uproar of a sham battle over the tariff, so that capitalists, corporations, national banks, rings, trusts, watered stock, the demonetization of silver and the oppressions of the usurers may all be lost sight of. They propose to sacrifice our homes, lives, and children on the altar of mammon; to destroy the multitude in order to secure corruption funds from the millionaires.

Assembled on the anniversary of the birthday of the nation, and filled with the spirit of the grand general and chief who established our independence, we seek to restore the government of the Republic to the hands of the "plain people," with which class it originated. We assert our purposes to be identical with the purposes of the National Constitution; to form a more perfect union and establish justice, insure domestic tranquillity, provide for the common defence, promote the general welfare, and secure the blessings of liberty for ourselves and our posterity. . . .

PLATFORM

We declare, therefore—

First.—That the union of the labor forces of the United States this day consummated shall be permanent and perpetual; may its spirit enter into all hearts for the salvation of the Republic and the uplifting of mankind.

Second.—Wealth belongs to him who creates it, and every dollar taken from industry without an equivalent is robbery. "If any will not work, neither shall he eat." The interests of rural and civil labor are the same; their enemies are identical.

Third.—We believe that the time has come when the railroad corporations will either own the people or the people must own the railroads; and should the government enter upon the work of owning and managing all railroads, we should favor an amendment to the constitution by which all persons engaged in the government service shall be placed under a civil-service regulation of the most rigid character, so as to prevent the increase of the power of the national administration by the use of such additional government employes.

FINANCE.—We demand a national currency, safe, sound, and flexible issued by the general government only, a full legal tender for all debts, public and private, and that without the use of banking corporations; a just, equitable, and efficient means of distribution direct to the people, at a tax not to exceed 2 per cent, per annum, to be provided as set forth in the sub-treasury plan of the Farmers' Alliance, or a better system; also by payments in discharge of its obligations for public improvements.

1. We demand free and unlimited coinage of silver and gold at the present legal ratio of 16 to 1.
2. We demand that the amount of circulating medium be speedily increased to not less than $50 per capita.
3. We demand a graduated income tax.
4. We believe that the money of the country should be kept as much as possible in the hands of the people, and hence we demand that all State and national rev-

enues shall be limited to the necessary expenses of the government, economically and honestly administered.

5. We demand that postal savings banks be established by the government for the safe deposit of the earnings of the people and to facilitate exchange.

TRANSPORTATION.—Transportation being a means of exchange and a public necessity, the government should own and operate the railroads in the interest of the people. The telegraph and telephone, like the post-office system, being a necessity for the transmission of news, should be owned and operated by the government in the interest of the people.

LAND.—The land, including all the natural sources of wealth, is the heritage of the people, and should not be monopolized for speculative purposes, and alien ownership of land should be prohibited. All land now held by railroads and other corporations in excess of their actual needs, and all lands now owned by aliens should be reclaimed by the government and held for actual settlers only.

EXPRESSION OF SENTIMENTS

Your Committee on Platform and Resolutions beg leave unanimously to report the following:

Whereas, Other questions have been presented for our consideration, we hereby submit the following, not as a part of the Platform of the People's Party, but as resolutions expressive of the sentiment of this Convention.

1. RESOLVED, That we demand a free ballot and a fair count in all elections, and pledge ourselves to secure it to every legal voter without Federal intervention, through the adoption by the States of the unperverted Australian or secret ballot system.

2. RESOLVED, That the revenue derived from a graduated income tax should be applied to the reduction of the burden of taxation now levied upon the domestic industries of this country.

3. RESOLVED, That we pledge our support to fair and liberal pensions to ex-Union soldiers and sailors.

4. RESOLVED, That we condemn the fallacy of protect-

ing American labor under the present system, which opens our ports to the pauper and criminal classes of the world and crowds out our wage-earners; and we denounce the present ineffective laws against contract labor, and demand the further restriction of undesirable emigration.

5. RESOLVED, That we cordially sympathize with the efforts of organized workingmen to shorten the hours of labor, and demand a rigid enforcement of the existing eight-hour law on Government work, and ask that a penalty clause be added to the said law.

6. RESOLVED, That we regard the maintenance of a large standing army of mercenaries, known as the Pinkerton system, as a menace to our liberties, and we demand its abolition; and we condemn the recent invasion of the Territory of Wyoming by the hired assassins of plutocracy, assisted by Federal officers.

7. RESOLVED, That we commend to the favorable consideration of the people and the reform press the legislative system known as the initiative and referendum.

8. RESOLVED, That we favor a constitutional provision limiting the office of President and Vice-President to one term, and providing for the election of Senators of the United States by a direct vote of the people.

9. RESOLVED, That we oppose any subsidy or national aid to any private corporation for any purpose.

10. RESOLVED, That this convention sympathizes with the Knights of Labor and their righteous contest with the tyrannical combine of clothing manufacturers of Rochester, and declare it to be a duty of all who hate tyranny and oppression to refuse to purchase the goods made by the said manufacturers, or to patronize any merchants who sell such goods.

David J. Brewer, "The Movement of Coercion"
January 17, 1893

[Brewer was a conservative judge on a very conservative Supreme Court during the years it was defending property rights against unruly majorities. In this speech to the New York Bar Association Brewer explains his, and by implication the Court's, political philosophy.]

. . . I wish rather to notice that movement which may be denominated the movement of 'coercion,' and which by the mere force of numbers seeks to diminish protection to private property. It is a movement which in spirit, if not in letter, violates both the Eighth and Tenth Commandments; a movement, which, seeing that which a man has, attempts to wrest it from him and transfer it to those who have not. It is the unvarying law, that the wealth of a community will be in the hands of a few; and the greater the general wealth, the greater the individual accumulations. The large majority of men are unwilling to endure that long self-denial and saving which makes accumulation possible; they have not the business tact and sagacity which bring about large combinations and great financial results; and hence it always has been, and until human nature is remodeled always will be true, that the wealth of a nation is in the hands of a few, while the many subsist upon the proceeds of their daily toil. But security is the chief end of government; and other things being equal, that government is best which protects to the fullest extent each individual, rich or poor, high or low, in the possession of his property and the pursuit of his business. . . .

This movement expresses itself in two ways: First, in the improper use of labor organizations to destroy the freedom of the laborer, and control the uses of capital. . . . That which I particularly notice is the assumption of control over the employer's property, and blocking the access of laborers to it. The common rule as to strikes is this: Not merely do the employees quit the employment, and thus handicap the employer in the use of his property, and perhaps in the discharge of duties which he owes to the public; but they also forcibly prevent others from taking their places. It is useless to say that they only advise—no man is misled. When a thousand laborers gather around a railroad track, and say to those who seek employment that they had better not, and when that advice is supplemented every little while by a terrible assault on one who disregards it, every one knows that something more than advice is intended. It is coercion, force; it is the effort of the many, by the mere weight of numbers, to compel the one to do their bidding. It is a proceeding outside of the law, in defiance of the law, and in spirit and effect—an attempt to strip from one that has that which of right belongs to him—the full and undisturbed use and enjoyment of his own. It is not to be wondered at, that deeds of violence and cruelty attend such demonstrations as these; nor will it do to pretend that the wrongdoers are not the striking laborers, but lawless strangers who gather to look on. Were they strangers who made the history of the 'Homestead' strike one of awful horror? Were they women from afar who so maltreated the surrendered guards, or were they the very ones who sought to compel the owners of that property to do their bidding? . . .

What, then, ought to be done? My reply is, strengthen the judiciary. How? Permanent tenure of office accomplishes this. . . .

It may be said that this is practically substituting government by the judges for government by the people, and thus turning back the currents of history. The world has seen government by chiefs, by kings, and emperors, by priests and by nobles. All have failed, and now government by the people is on trial. Shall we abandon that and try government by judges? But this involves a total misunderstanding of the relations of judges to government. There is nothing in this power of the judiciary detracting in the least from the idea of government of and by the people. The courts hold neither purse nor sword; they cannot corrupt nor arbitrarily control. They make no laws, they establish no policy, they never enter into the domain of popular action. They do not govern.

Their functions in relation to the State are limited to seeing that popular action does not trespass upon right and justice as it exists in written constitutions and natural law. So it is that the utmost power of the courts and judges works no interference with true liberty, no trespass on the fullest and highest development of government of and by the people; it only means security to personal rights—the inalienable rights, life, liberty and the pursuit of happiness; it simply nails the Declaration of Independence, like Luther's theses against indulgences upon the doors of the Wittenburg church of human rights, and dares the anarchist, the socialist and every other assassin of liberty to blot out a single word. . . .

The other form of this movement assumes the guise of a regulation of the charges for the use of property subjected, or supposed to be, to a public use. This acts in two directions: One by extending the list of those things, charges for whose use the government may prescribe; until now we hear it affirmed that whenever property is devoted to a use in which the public has an interest, charges for that use may be fixed by law. And if there be any property in the use of which the public or some portion of it has no interest, I hardly know what it is or where to find it. And second, in so reducing charges for the use of property, which in fact is subjected to a public use, that no compensation or income is received by those who have so invested their property. By the one it subjects all property and its uses to the will of the majority; by the other it robs property of its value. Statutes and decisions both disclose that this movement, with just these results, has a present and alarming existence. . . .

There are to-day ten thousand million of dollars invested in railroad property, whose owners in this country number less than two million persons. Can it be that whether that immense sum shall earn a dollar, or bring the slightest recompense to those who have invested perhaps their all in that business, and are thus aiding in the development of the country, depends wholly upon the whim and greed of that great majority of sixty millions who do not own a dollar? It may be said that that majority will not be so foolish, selfish and cruel as to strip that property of its earning capacity. I say that so long as constitutional guaranties lift on American soil their buttresses and bulwarks against wrong, and so long as the American judiciary breathes the free air of courage, it cannot.

It must not be supposed that the forms in which this movement expresses itself are in themselves bad. Indeed, the great danger is in the fact that there is so much of good in them. If the livery of heaven were never stolen, and all human struggles were between obvious right and conceded wrong, the triumph of the former would be sure and speedy. Labor organizations are the needed and proper complement of capital organizations. They often work wholesome restraints on the greed, the unscrupulous rapacity which dominates much of capital; and the fact that they bring together a multitude of tiny forces, each helpless in a solitary struggle with capital, enables labor to secure its just rights. So also, in regulating the charges of property which is appropriated to a public use, the public is but exercising a legitimate function, and one which is often necessary to prevent extortion in respect to public uses. Within limits of law and justice, labor organizations and state regulation of charges for the use of property which is in fact devoted to public uses are commendable. But with respect to the proposition that the public may rightfully regulate the charges for the use of any property in whose use it has an interest, I am like the lawyer who, when declared guilty of contempt, responded promptly that he had shown no contempt, but on the contrary had carefully concealed his feelings.

Now, conceding that there is this basis of wisdom and justice, and that within limits the movement in both directions will work good to society, the question is how can its excesses, those excesses which mean peril to the nation, be stayed? Will the many who find in its progress temporary and apparent advantages, so clearly discern the ultimate ruin which flows from injustice as voluntarily to desist? or must there be some force, some tribunal, outside so far as possible, to lift the restraining hand? . . .

William Graham Sumner, "The Absurd Effort to Make the World Over"
1894

[By the turn of the century it had become fashionable to defend the social order on Darwinian grounds, to reason that the rise of monopoly capitalism was a natural and historic necessity and that the efforts of reformers to bring about government intervention were unrealistic and sentimental. Such a defense was offered by William Graham Sumner, professor at Yale and widely read writer on a host of subjects, from economics to sociology.]

It will not probably be denied that the burden of proof is on those who affirm that our social condition is utterly diseased and in need of radical regeneration. My task at present, therefore, is entirely negative and critical: to examine the allegations of fact and the doctrines which are put forward to prove the correctness of the diagnosis and to warrant the use of the remedies proposed.

The propositions put forward by social reformers nowadays are chiefly of two kinds. There are assertions in historical form, chiefly in regard to the comparison of existing with earlier social states, which are plainly based on defective historical knowledge, or at most on current stock historical dicta which are uncritical and incorrect. Writers very often assert that something never existed before because they do not know that it ever existed before, or that something is worse than ever before because they are not possessed of detailed information about what has existed before. The other class of propositions consists of dogmatic statements which, whether true or not, are unverifiable. This class of propositions is the pest and bane of current economic and social discussion. . . .

When anyone asserts that the class of skilled and unskilled manual laborers of the United States is worse off now in respect to diet, clothing, lodgings, furniture, fuel, and lights; in respect to the age at which they can marry; the number of children they can provide for; the start in life which they can give to their children, and their chances of accumulating capital, than they ever have been at any former time, he makes a reckless assertion for which no facts have been offered in proof. Upon an appeal to facts, the contrary of this assertion would be clearly established. It suffices, therefore, to challenge those who are responsible for the assertion to make it good.

If it is said that the employed class are under much more stringent discipline than they were thirty years ago or earlier, it is true. It is not true that there has been any qualitative change in this respect within thirty years, but it is true that a movement which began at the first settlement of the country has been advancing with constant acceleration and has become a noticeable feature within our time. This movement is the advance in the industrial organization. The first settlement was made by agriculturists, and for a long time there was scarcely any organization. There were scattered farmers, each working for himself, and some small towns with only rudimentary commerce and handicrafts. As the country has filled up, the arts and professions have been differentiated and the industrial organization has been advancing. This fact and its significance has hardly been noticed at all; but the stage of the industrial organization existing at any time, and the rate of advance in its development, are the absolutely controlling social facts. Nine-tenths of the socialistic and semi-socialistic, and sentimental or ethical, suggestions by which we are overwhelmed come from failure to understand the phenomena of the industrial organization and its expansion. It controls us all because we are all in it. It creates the conditions of our existence, sets the limits of our social activity, regulates the bonds of our social relations, determines our conceptions of good and evil, suggests our life-philosophy, molds our inherited political institutions, and reforms the oldest and toughest customs, like marriage and property. I repeat that the turmoil of heterogeneous and antagonistic social whims and speculations in which we live is due to the failure to understand what the industrial organization is and its all-pervading control over human life, while the traditions of our school of philosophy lead us always to approach the industrial organization, not from the side of objective study, but from that of philosophical doctrine. Hence it is that we find that the method of measuring what we see happening by what are called ethical standards, and of proposing to attack the phenomena by methods thence deduced, is so popular. . . .

Now the intensification of the social organization is what gives us greater social power. It is to it that we owe our increased comfort and abundance. We are none of us ready to sacrifice this. On the contrary, we want more of it. We would not return to the colonial simplicity and the colonial exiguity if we could. If not, then we must pay the price. Our life is bounded on every side by conditions. We can have this if we will agree to submit to that. In the case of industrial power and product the great condition is combination of force under discipline and strict coordination. Hence the wild language about wage-slavery and capitalistic tyranny.

In any state of society no great achievements can be produced without great force. Formerly great force was attainable only by slavery aggregating the power of great numbers of men. Roman civilization was built on this. Ours has been built on steam. It is to be built on electricity. Then we are all forced into an organization around these natural forces and adapted to the methods of their application; and although we indulge in rhetoric about political liberty, nevertheless we find ourselves bound tight in a new set of conditions, which control the modes of our existence and determine the directions in which alone economic and social liberty can go.

If it is said that there are some persons in our time who have become rapidly and in a great degree rich, it is true; if it is said that large aggregations of wealth in the control of individuals is a social danger, it is not true.

The movement of the industrial organization which has just been described has brought out a great demand for men capable of managing great enterprises. Such have been called "captains of industry." The analogy with military leaders suggested by this name is not misleading. The great leaders in the development of the industrial organization need those

talents of executive and administrative skill, power to command, courage, and fortitude, which were formerly called for
in military affairs and scarcely anywhere else. The industrial
army is also as dependent on its captains as a military body
is on its generals. One of the worst features of the existing
system is that the employees have a constant risk in their
employer. If he is not competent to manage the business with
success, they suffer with him. Capital also is dependent on
the skill of the captain of industry for the certainty and magnitude of its profits. Under these circumstances there has
been a great demand for men having the requisite ability for
this function. As the organization has advanced, with more
impersonal bonds of coherence and wider scope of operations, the value of this functionary has rapidly increased. The
possession of the requisite ability is a natural monopoly.
Consequently, all the conditions have concurred to give to
those who possessed this monopoly excessive and constantly
advancing rates of remuneration. . . .

But it is repeated until it has become a commonplace
which people are afraid to question, that there is some social
danger in the possession of large amounts of wealth by individuals. I ask, Why? I heard a lecture two years ago by a
man who holds perhaps the first chair of political economy
in the world. He said, among other things, that there was
great danger in our day from great accumulations; that this
danger ought to be met by taxation, and he referred to
the fortune of the Rothschilds and to the great fortunes
made in America to prove his point. He omitted, however,
to state in what the danger consisted or to specify what
harm has ever been done by the Rothschild fortunes or by
the great fortunes accumulated in America. It seemed to me
that the assertions he was making, and the measures he was
recommending, ex-cathedra, were very serious to be thrown
out so recklessly. It is hardly to be expected that novelists,
popular magazinists, amateur economists, and politicians
will be more responsible. It would be easy, however, to show
what good is done by accumulations of capital in a few hands
—that is, under close and direct management, permitting
prompt and accurate application; also to tell what harm is
done by loose and unfounded denunciations of any social

component or any social group. In the recent debates on the income tax the assumption that great accumulations of wealth are socially harmful and ought to be broken down by taxation was treated as an axiom, and we had direct proof how dangerous it is to fit out the average politician with such unverified and unverifiable dogmas as his warrant for his modes of handling the direful tool of taxation.

Great figures are set out as to the magnitude of certain fortunes and the proportionate amount of the national wealth held by a fraction of the population, and eloquent exclamation-points are set against them. If the figures were beyond criticism, what would they prove? Where is the rich man who is oppressing anybody? If there was one, the newspapers would ring with it. The facts about the accumulation of wealth do not constitute a plutocracy, as I will show below. Wealth, in itself considered, is only power, like steam, or electricity, or knowledge. The question of its good or ill turns on the question how it will be used. To prove any harm in aggregations of wealth it must be shown that great wealth is, as a rule, in the ordinary course of social affairs, put to a mischievous use. This cannot be shown beyond the very slightest degree, if at all. . . .

The question, therefore, arises, if it is proposed to reorganize the social system on the principles of American democracy, whether the institutions of industrialism are to be retained. If so, all the virus of capitalism will be retained. It is forgotten, in many schemes of social reformation in which it is proposed to mix what we like with what we do not like, in order to extirpate the latter, that each must undergo a reaction from the other, and that what we like may be extirpated by what we do not like. We may find that instead of democratizing capitalism we have capitalized democracy—that is, have brought in plutocracy. Plutocracy is a political system in which the ruling force is wealth. The denunciation of capital which we hear from all the reformers is the most eloquent proof that the greatest power in the world to-day is capital. They know that it is, and confess it most when they deny it most strenuously. At present the power of capital is social and industrial, and only in a small degree political. So far as capital is political, it is on account of political abuses, such as tariffs and special legislation on the one hand and legislative strikes on the other. These conditions exist in the democracy to which it is proposed to transfer the industries. What does that mean except bringing all the power of capital once for all into the political arena and precipitating the conflict of democracy and plutocracy at once? Can anyone imagine that the masterfulness, the overbearing disposition, the greed of gain, and the ruthlessness in methods, which are the faults of the master of industry at his worst, would cease when he was a functionary of the State, which had relieved him of risk and endowed him with authority? Can anyone imagine that politicians would no longer be corruptly fond of money, intriguing, and crafty when they were charged, not only with patronage and government contracts, but also with factories, stores, ships, and railroads? Could we expect anything except that, when the politician and the master of industry were joined in one, we should have the vices of both unchecked by the restraints of either? In any socialistic state there will be one set of positions which will offer chances of wealth beyond the wildest dreams of avarice; *viz.*, on the governing committees. Then there will be rich men whose wealth will indeed be a menace to social interests, and instead of industrial peace there will be such war as no one has dreamed of yet: the war between the political ins and outs—that is, between those who are on the committee and those who want to get on it. . . .

If this poor old world is as bad as they say, one more reflection may check the zeal of the headlong reformer. It is at any rate a tough old world. It has taken its trend and curvature and all its twists and tangles from a long course of formation. All its wry and crooked gnarls and knobs are therefore stiff and stubborn. If we puny men by our arts can do anything at all to straighten them, it will only be by modifying the tendencies of some of the forces at work, so that, after a sufficient time, their action may be changed a little and slowly the lines of movement may be modified. This effort, however, can at most be only slight, and it will take a long time. In the meantime spontaneous forces will be at work, compared with which our efforts are like those of a man trying to deflect a river, and these forces will have changed the whole problem before our interferences have time to make themselves felt. The great stream of time and earthly things will sweep on just the same in spite of us. It bears with it now all the errors and follies of the past, the wreckage of all the philosophies, the fragments of all the civilizations, the wisdom of all the abandoned ethical systems, the debris of all the institutions, and the penalties of all the mistakes. It is only in imagination that we stand by and look at and criticize it and plan to change it. Everyone of us is a child of his age and cannot get out of it. He is in the stream and is swept along with it. All his sciences and philosophy come to him out of it. Therefore the tide will not be changed by us. It will swallow up both us and our experiments. It will absorb the efforts at change and take them into itself as new but trivial components, and the great movement of tradition and work will go on unchanged by our fads and schemes. The things which will change it are the great discoveries and inventions, the new reactions inside the social organism, and the changes in the earth itself on account of changes in the cosmical forces. These causes will make it just what, in fidelity to them, it ought to be. The men will be carried along with it and be made by it. The utmost they can do by their cleverness will be to note and record their course as they are carried along, which is what we do now, and is that which leads us to the vain fancy that we can make or guide the movement. That is why it is the greatest folly of which a man can be capable, to sit down with a slate and pencil to plan out a new social world.

The Republican Platform of 1896
June 16, 1896

[The Republicans were in an optimistic mood when they met in St. Louis in 1896 to nominate a presidential candidate. A Democratic administration had been in office during the Depression of 1893. The Democratic party, moreover, was hopelessly divided into agrarian and conservative factions.]

. . . We renew and emphasize our allegiance to the policy of protection as the bulwark of American industrial independence and the foundation of American development and prosperity. This true American policy taxes foreign products and encourages home industry. It puts the burden of revenue on foreign goods; it secures the American market for the American producer. It upholds the American standard of wages for the American workingman; it puts the factory by the side of the farm, and makes the American farmer less dependent on foreign demand and price; it diffuses general thrift, and founds the strength of each. In its reasonable application it is just, fair and impartial, equally opposed to foreign control and domestic monopoly, to sectional discrimination and individual favoritism.

We denounce the present tariff as sectional, injurious to the public credit and destructive to business enterprise. We demand such an equitable tariff on foreign imports which come into competition with the American products as will not only furnish adequate revenue for the necessary expense of the Government, but will protect American labor from degradation and the wage level of other lands. We are not pledged to any particular schedules. The question of rates is a practical question, to be governed by the condition of time and of production. The ruling and uncompromising principle is the protection and development of American labor and industries. The country demands a right settlement, and then it wants a rest.

We believe the repeal of the reciprocity arrangements negotiated by the last Republican Administration was a national calamity, and demand their renewal and extension on such terms as will equalize our trade with other nations, remove the restrictions which now obstruct the sale of American products in the ports of other countries, and secure enlarged markets for the products of our farms, forests, and factories.

Protection and Reciprocity are twin measures of American policy and go hand in hand. Democratic rule has recklessly struck down both, and both must be re-established. Protection for what we produce; reciprocal agreement of mutual interests, which gain open markets for us in return for our open markets for others. Protection builds up domestic industry and trade and secures our own market for ourselves; reciprocity builds up foreign trade and finds an outlet for our surplus. . . .

The Republican party is unreservedly for sound money. It caused the enactment of a law providing for the resumption of specie payments in 1879. Since then every dollar has been as good as gold. We are unalterably opposed to every measure calculated to debase our currency or impair the credit of our country. We are therefore opposed to the free coinage of silver, except by international agreement with the leading commercial nations of the earth, which agreement we pledge ourselves to promote, and until such agreement can be obtained the existing gold standard must be maintained. All of our silver and paper currency must be maintained at parity with gold, and we favor all measures designated to maintain inviolable the obligations of the United States, of all our money, whether coin or paper, at the present standard, the standard of most enlightened nations of the world. . . .

William Jennings Bryan, Speech at St. Paul
October 9, 1896

[While McKinley remained on the front porch of his home in Canton, Ohio, receiving delegations from all over the country, Bryan was conducting the most intensive campaign of any candidate in American history. In three and a half months he visited twenty-nine states and delivered six hundred speeches, most of them very much like the one below.]

Before addressing myself to the subject in hand, I desire to express to organized labor my grateful appreciation of the gift just presented. It is a gold pen with a silver holder, and if I am elected by my countrymen to be chief executive of this nation, that pen and holder will be used to sign a free coinage bill. I am glad that the pen with which my signature is to be affixed is the gift of the laboring men, because I believe that the laboring men of this country—aye, more than that, the laboring men of all the world—are interested in the restoration of silver to its ancient place by the side of gold.

I would not favor the free coinage of silver did I not believe that it would be beneficial to those who toil, because my political philosophy teaches me that there can be no prosperity in this nation unless that prosperity begins first among those who create wealth and finds its way afterward to the other classes of society. More than that, civilization itself rests upon the great mass of the people, and it is only by carrying the people upward and onward that we can expect any advance in civilization. There can be no real civilization where a few have more than they can use and the many have not sufficient to give necessary sustenance. Nor do I believe that these great inequalities can exist in a nation where the government observes the old maxim of equal rights to all and special privileges to none.

When government is properly administered, there will be no railroad wreckers to make themselves rich by bankrupting those who put their confidence in them; when government is properly administered there will be no representative of a coal trust sitting by every fireside to exact tribute from those who desire to be protected from the cold of winter; when government is properly administered there will be no syndicates fattening upon the government's adversities, after they have brought the adversities upon the government; when government is properly administered there will be no corporations which will assume to be greater than the power which created them; when government is properly administered it will recognize those fundamental principles set forth in the Declaration of Independence: that all men are created equal, that they are endowed with inalienable rights, that governments are instituted to preserve these rights, and that governments derive their just powers from the consent of the governed. When these four principles are applied, then government will be what it ought to be.

Jackson has well said that there are no necessary evils in government; that evils exist only in its abuses. It is not government against which we raise our hands. It is against the abuses of government that we aim, and we will not be driven from our purpose to eradicate these evils, although every man entrenched behind a special privilege heaps abuse upon us. . . .

I am not going to say one word to prevent any Democrat doing what his conscience tells him to be right, but if any Democrat is going to leave the Democratic party, I want him to find his reason in his head or in his heart, and not in his pocketbook. If he finds his reason in his pocketbook, I want him to be man enough to say that that is where the reason is, and not say that he leaves because all the rest of the Democrats have become anarchists. If a Democrat is connected with a trust and loves the trust more than he does his country, let him say so, and we will bid him Godspeed. If there is any Democrat who is connected with a corporation and prefers to retain his connection with that corporation rather than to stand with the Democratic party in its effort to bring the Government back to the position of Jefferson and Jackson, let him say so.

And more than that, let not the Democrats who go delude themselves with the thought that this is but a temporary disagreement. Let them not delude themselves with the thought that they can separate from us now and come back hereafter to assume positions of command. Let them understand what this contest means. This contest is not for an hour, or for a day. This contest is the beginning of a struggle which will not end until this Government is wrested from the hands of syndicates and trusts, and put back into the hands of the people. Any Democratic son who desires to leave his father's house can do so, but let him understand that when he gets tired and comes back we may not kill the fatted calf for him. When he gets tired of associating with those who would undo what Jefferson and Jackson did, it may be that those whom he left at home will make him saw wood a long while before he gets to the dinner table.

Plessy v. *Ferguson*
1896

[This was the famous decision that permitted the states to establish segregated schools. The Court reasoned that the equal rights guaranteed by the Fourteenth Amendment really meant separate but equal, that Negroes had no cause to complain so long as their *political* freedoms were unimpaired. It might be noted that Justice Henry Brown, who wrote the majority opinion, came from Michigan. The dissenter was John Harlan of Kentucky.]

BROWN, J. . . . The constitutionality of this act is attacked upon the ground that it conflicts both with the 13th Amendment of the Constitution, abolishing slavery, and the 14th Amendment, which prohibits certain restrictive legislation on the part of the states.

1. That it does not conflict with the 13th Amendment, which abolished slavery and involuntary servitude, except as a punishment for crime, is too clear for argument. . . .

A statute which implies merely a legal distinction between the white and colored races—a distinction which is founded in the color of the two races, and which must always exist so long as white men are distinguished from the other race by color—has no tendency to destroy the legal equality of the two races, or re-establish a state of involuntary servitude. Indeed, we do not understand that the 13th Amendment is strenuously relied upon by the plaintiff in error in this connection. . . .

The object of the amendment was undoubtedly to enforce the absolute equality of the two races before the law, but in the nature of things it could not have been intended to abolish distinctions based upon color, or to enforce social, as distinguished from political, equality, or a commingling of the two races upon terms unsatisfactory to either. Laws permitting, and even requiring their separation in places where they are liable to be brought into contact do not necessarily imply the inferiority of either race to the other, and have been generally, if not universally, recognized as within the competency of the state legislatures in the exercise of their police power. The most common instance of this is connected with the establishment of separate schools for white and colored children, which have been held to be a valid exercise of the legislative power even by courts of states where the political rights of the colored race have been longest and most earnestly enforced. . . .

So far, then, as a conflict with the 14th Amendment is concerned, the case reduces itself to the question whether the statute of Louisiana is a reasonable regulation, and with respect to this there must necessarily be a large discretion on the part of the legislature. In determining the question of reasonableness it is at liberty to act with reference to the established usages, customs, and traditions of the people, and with a view to the promotion of their comfort, and the preservation of the public peace and good order. Gauged by this standard, we cannot say that a law which authorizes or even requires the separation of the two races in public conveyances is unreasonable or more obnoxious to the 14th Amendment than the acts of Congress requiring separate schools for colored children in the District of Columbia, the constitutionality of which does not seem to have been questioned, or the corresponding acts of state legislatures.

We consider the underlying fallacy of the plaintiff's argument to consist in the assumption that the enforced separation of the two races stamps the colored race with a badge of inferiority. If this be so, it is not by reason of anything found in the act, but solely because the colored race chooses to put that construction upon it. The argument necessarily assumes that if, as has been more than once the case, and is not unlikely to be so again, the colored race should become the dominant power in the state legislature, and should enact a law in precisely similar terms, it would thereby relegate the white race to an inferior position. We imagine that the white race, at least, would not acquiesce in this assumption. The argument also assumes that social prejudice may be overcome by legislation, and that equal rights cannot be secured to the Negro except by an enforced commingling of the two races. We cannot accept this proposition. If the two races are to meet on terms of social equality, it must be the result of natural affinities, a mutual appreciation of each other's merits and a voluntary consent of individuals. . . . Legislation is powerless to eradicate racial instincts or to abolish distinctions based upon physical differences, and the attempt to do so can only result in accentuating the difficulties of the present situation. If the civil and political right of both races be equal, one cannot be inferior to the other civilly or politically. If one race be inferior to the other socially, the Constitution of the United States cannot put them upon the same plane.

Justice HARLAN, dissenting. . . . In my opinion, the judgment this day rendered will, in time, prove to be quite as pernicious as the decision made by this tribunal in the Dred Scott Case. It was adjudged in that case that the descendants of Africans who were imported into this country and sold as slaves were not included nor intended to be included under the word "citizens" in the Constitution, and could not claim any of the rights and privileges which that instrument provided for and secured to citizens of the United States; that at the time of the adoption of the Constitution they were "considered as a subordinate and inferior class of beings, who had been subjugated by the dominant race, and, whether emancipated or not, yet remained subject to their authority, and had no rights or privileges but such as those who held the power and the government might choose to grant them." The recent amendments of the Constitution, it was supposed, had eradicated these principles from our institutions. But it seems that we have yet, in some of the states, a dominant race, a superior class of citizens, which assumes to regulate the enjoyment of civil rights, common to all citizens, upon the basis of race. The present decision, it may well be apprehended, will not only stimulate aggressions, more or less brutal and irritating, upon the admitted rights of colored citizens, but will encourage the belief that it is possible, by means of state enactments, to defeat the beneficent purposes which the people of the United States had in view when they adopted the recent amendments of the Constitution, by one of which the blacks of this country were made citizens of the United States and of the states in which they respectively reside and whose privileges and immunities, as citizens, the states are forbidden to abridge. Sixty millions of whites are in no danger from the presence here of eight millions of blacks. The destinies of the two races in this country are indissolubly linked together, and the interests of both require that the common government of all shall not permit the seeds of race hate to be planted under the sanction of law. What can more certainly arouse race hate, what more certainly create and perpetuate a feeling of distrust between these races, than state enactments which in fact proceed on the ground that colored citizens are so inferior and degraded that they cannot be allowed to sit in public coaches occupied by white citizens? That, as all will admit, is the real meaning of such legislation as was enacted in Louisiana. . . .

I am of opinion that the statute of Louisiana is inconsistent with the personal liberty of citizens, white and black, in that state, and hostile to both the spirit and letter of the Constitution of the United States. If laws of like character should be enacted in the several states of the Union, the effect would be in the highest degree mischievous. Slavery as an institution tolerated by law would, it is true, have disappeared from our country, but there would remain a power in the states, by sinister legislation, to interfere with the full enjoyment of the blessings of freedom; to regulate civil rights, common to all citizens, upon the basis of race; and to place in a condition of legal inferiority a large body of American citizens, now constituting a part of the political community, called the people of the United States, for whom and by whom, through representatives, our government is administered. Such a system is inconsistent with the guarantee given by the Constitution to each state of a republican form of government, and may be stricken down by Congressional action, or by the courts in the discharge of their solemn duty to maintain the supreme law of the land, anything in the Constitution or laws of any state to the contrary notwithstanding.

For the reasons stated, I am constrained to withhold my assent from the opinion and judgment of the majority.

Thomas J. Semmes, Speech to
the Louisiana Constitutional Convention
May 12, 1898

[The total exclusion of Negroes from the political life of the South was a direct consequence of Northern indifference, or complicity, as symbolized in the *Plessy* v. *Ferguson* decision. Typically, Louisiana adopted a new constitution in May 1898 that contained such devices as literacy and property tests and the infamous "grandfather clause" to keep Negroes from voting. Below is an extract from the speech by the chairman of the convention's judiciary committee.]

Mr. President and Gentlemen of the Convention:

Now we have gotten through with our work. It is about to go forth throughout the length and breadth of this State to be submitted to the criticisms of the people. This is the work of a Democratic Convention. This is the work of the Democratic party of the State, represented by its selected agents appointed to do that work. If we have done any thing wrong, any thing which will involve the dissolution or disintegration or defeat of the Democratic party, then we ought to be condemned. It has been stated in some quarters that we have been actuated to a certain extent by party spirit. Granted. What of it? What is the State? It is the Democratic party. (Applause.) What are the people of the State? They are the Democracy of the State, and when you eliminate the Democratic party or the Democracy of the State from the State, what is there left but that which we came here to suppress? I don't allude to the fragments of what is called the Republican party. We met here to establish the supremacy of the white race, and the white race constitutes the Democratic party of this State. There is, therefore, in my judgment, no separation whatever between the interests of the State and those of the Democratic party, and if we are to be subjected to criticism because our ordinances may have been colored, with the view, in some instances, of promoting the interests of the Democratic party, as those interests are not separated from the State, I feel no hesitancy in saying that we have done no injury to the State.

It is said that we sought to establish our party in power. Wherever there were political questions involved, of course, we looked to the interests of the party, because they are the interests of the State. Whoever heard of a political party being in the ascendancy, and in power and undertaking to do any act to remove that ascendancy or to impair their power? Look throughout the nations of Europe. In all of their political matters; in all of their statesmanship; those who are in power seek to maintain it, and, with that power to promote the interests of the State which they govern. If it is so as to nations, it is so as to parties. Does the Republican party throughout the United States ever do any act without looking to the interests of the party, as well as to the interests of the nation? And have they not remained in the ascendancy for years? Do we, who have obtained the ascendancy but recently in this State, wish the Democratic party to do any act by which its ascendancy shall be impaired? It is absolutely absurd.

Now then, what have we done? is the question. Our mission was, in the first place, to establish the supremacy of the white race in this State to the extent to which it could be legally and constitutionally done, and what has our ordinance on suffrage, the constitutional means by which we hope to maintain that ascendancy, done? We have established throughout the State white manhood suffrage. A great cry went out that there should be a poll tax; that there should be an educational test; that as a qualification for a voter, he should be a property owner. We have in the ordinance established those qualifications which are necessary to be possessed in order to entitle these citizens to vote. . . .

But a hue and cry has been raised by people who are entirely ignorant of the fact which we have shown, against what is called section 5 of the ordinance on suffrage. Now, what is section 5? Very few people know anything about it. Very few people understand its effects. They have taken their ideas from outside criticism and suppose that we have committed some very great wrong. I repeat, what is section

5? It is a declaration on the part of this Convention, that no white man in this State—that's the effect but not the language—that no white man in this State who has heretofore exercised the right of suffrage shall be deprived of it, whether or not he can read or write, or whether he possesses the property qualifications. . . .

Now, why was this exception made? Because, and I am ashamed to say it, Louisiana is one of the most illiterate States in the Union. It is more illiterate than any other State except North Carolina. We, therefore, have in this State a large white population whose right to vote would have been stricken down but for the operation of section 5. And all of these men had aided the white people of the State to wrest from the hands of the Republican party, composed almost exclusively of negroes, the power which, backed by Federal bayonets, they had exercised for many years. Now can we go to them, these men who stood side by side with us in the dark days of reconstruction and say to them that a convention of Louisianians has deprived them of the right to vote? Could we face these men who have always been Democrats; who have always aided us in achieving the ascendancy of the Democratic party in this State with such a record as that?

Lochner v. *New York*
1905

[In this decision the Court threw out a New York law restricting the maximum number of hours that bakers could work. The Court's argument was similar to the one used in numerous other cases from the 1880s on. The decision was especially notable for Justice Holmes's great dissent.]

PECKHAM, J. . . . It must, of course, be conceded that there is a limit to the valid exercise of the police power by the State. There is no dispute concerning this general proposition. Otherwise the Fourteenth Amendment would have no efficacy and the legislatures of the States would have unbounded power, and it would be enough to say that any piece of legislation was enacted to conserve the morals, the health, or the safety of the people; such legislation would be valid, no matter how absolutely without foundation the claim might be. The claim of the police power would be a mere pretext —become another and delusive name for the supreme sovereignty of the State to be exercised free from constitutional restraint. This is not contended for. In every case that comes before this court, therefore, where legislation of this character is concerned, and where the protection of the federal Constitution is sought, the question necessarily arises: Is this a fair, reasonable, and appropriate exercise of the police power of the State, or is it an unreasonable, unnecessary, and arbitrary interference with the right of the individual to his personal liberty or to enter into those contracts in relation to labor which may seem to him appropriate or necessary for the support of himself and his family? Of course the liberty of contract relating to labor includes both parties to it. The one has as much right to purchase as the other to sell labor.

This is not a question of substituting the judgment of the court for that of the legislature. If the act be within the power of the State it is valid, although the judgment of the court might be totally opposed to the enactment of such a law. But the question would still remain: Is it within the police power of the State? and that question must be answered by the court.

The question whether this act is valid as a labor law, pure and simple, may be dismissed in a few words. There is no reasonable ground for interfering with the liberty of person or the right of free contract, by determining the hours of labor, in the occupation of a baker. There is no contention that bakers as a class are not equal in intelligence and capacity to men in other trades or manual occupations, or that they are not able to assert their rights and care for themselves without the protecting arm of the State, interfering with their independence of judgment and of action. They are in no sense wards of the State. Viewed in the light of a purely labor law, with no reference whatever to the question of health, we think that a law like the one before us involves neither the safety, the morals, nor the welfare, of the public, and that the interest of the public is not in the slightest degree affected by such an act. The law must be upheld, if at all, as a law pertaining to the health of the individual engaged in the occupation of a baker. It does not affect any other portion of the public than those who are engaged in that occupation. Clean and wholesome bread does not depend upon whether the baker works but ten hours per day or only sixty hours a week. The limitation of the hours of labor does not come within the police power on that ground. . . .

The act is not, within any fair meaning of the term, a health law, but is an illegal interference with the rights of individuals, both employers and employees, to make contracts regarding labor upon such terms as they may think best, or which they may agree upon with the other parties to such contracts. Statutes of the nature of that under review, limiting the hours in which grown and intelligent men may labor to earn their living, are mere meddlesome interferences with the rights of the individual, and they are not saved from condemnation by the claim that they are passed in the exercise of the police power and upon the subject of the health of the individual whose rights are interfered with, unless there be some fair ground, reasonable in and of itself, to say that there is material danger to the public health, or to the health of the employees, if the hours of labor are not curtailed. . . .

HOLMES, J., dissenting. . . . The case is decided upon an economic theory which a large part of the country does not entertain. If it were a question whether I agreed with that theory, I should desire to study it further and long before making up my mind. But I do not conceive that to be my duty, because I strongly believe that my agreement or disagreement has nothing to do with the right of a majority to embody their opinions in law. It is settled by various decisions of this court that state constitutions and state laws may regulate life in many ways which we as legislators might think as injudicious, or if you like as tyrannical, as this, and which, equally with this, interfere with the liberty to contract. Sunday laws and usury laws are ancient examples. A more modern one is the prohibition of lotteries. The liberty of the citizen to do as he likes so long as he does not interfere with the liberty of others to do the same, which has been a shibboleth for some well-known writers, is interfered with by school laws, by the post-office, by every state or municipal institution which takes his money for purposes thought desirable, whether he likes it or not. The Fourteenth Amendment does not enact Mr. Herbert Spencer's Social Statics. . . . [A] constitution is not intended to embody a particular economic theory, whether of paternalism and the organic relation of the citizen to the state or of *laissez faire*. It is made for people of fundamentally differing views, and the accident of our finding certain opinions natural and familiar, or novel, and even shocking, ought not to conclude our judgement upon the question whether statutes embodying them conflict with the Constitution of the United States.

General propositions do not decide concrete cases. The decision will depend on a judgement or intuition more subtle than any articulate major premise. But I think that the proposition just stated, if it is accepted, will carry us far toward the end. Every opinion tends to become a law. I think that the word "liberty," in the Fourteenth Amendment, is perverted when it is held to prevent the natural outcome of a dominant opinion, unless it can be said that a rational and fair man necessarily would admit that the statute proposed would infringe fundamental principles as they have been understood by the traditions of our people and our law. It does not need research to show that no such sweeping condemnation can be passed upon the statute before us. A reasonable man might think it a proper measure on the score of health. Men whom I certainly could not pronounce unreasonable would uphold it as a first instalment of a general regulation of the hours of work. Whether in the latter aspect it would be open to the charge of inequality I think it unnecessary to discuss.

CHAPTER VIII. INSURGENCY AND REFORM

In the years following the 1896 election the Republican party re-established its hegemony over American politics. As it went from triumph to triumph, taking credit for bringing high levels of prosperity to all sectors of the economy, for resolving the vexatious issues of fiscal management and protective tariffs that had disturbed the country since the 1870s, and for successfully launching the United States on a course of imperial expansion in Asia and Latin America, so the public gratefully gave it increasingly large majorities in local, state and federal elections. By 1900, when McKinley defeated Bryan by a substantially greater margin than in 1896, nearly every state outside the South was going Republican. Congress was overwhelmingly Republican. Furthermore, the tradition of radical protest, which had called forth one third-party movement after another in the past three decades, now lay moribund. Populism, the latest and most promising of these movements, had disappeared in all but name.

Nonetheless, there was a deepening sense of disquietude in the country. The trust problem above all continued to trouble the public mind. Since the Depression of 1893 industry had been consolidating relentlessly. By 1901 the Populist outcry against Wall Street had come to seem like an understatement, for in that year New York investment bankers formed two gigantic holding companies: United States Steel, which embraced twelve iron and steel producers, including the two largest; and the incredible Northern Securities Company (later dissolved by Court order), which brought all the major railroads from Chicago to the Pacific coast into a single combine. Middle-class Americans now felt the threat of monopoly capital as never before, and they began to fear that the Morgans, the Rockefellers, the Harrimans and the other czars of high finance would soon rule over them politically just as they had come to rule over them industrially.

But even before 1901 the middle class in the states west of the Mississippi, especially in the dairy, corn and hog-growing regions, was demonstrating its dissatisfaction with the status quo. Farmers, professionals and small-business men, having beaten back the Populist and Democratic assaults, discovered that the local Republican party, which sub-served the national party and therefore the industrial East, was no longer answering to their own needs. They held the tariff, the pride of the party, responsible for the recent rise in the price of manufactured goods. And farmers complained that the burgeoning prosperity benefited them little in re-lation to the country as a whole, that they were receiving a diminishing share of the national income. More generally, there was the feeling that the Republican party no longer offered humble men of talent limitless opportunities for ad-vance, and that one had to be rich or to represent some special interest in order to rise up in its ranks. And so by the turn of the century factional conflicts between regular and insurgent Republicans were taking place in the states west of the Mississippi.

In the year of McKinley's second triumph, when the na-tional Republican party stood at the summit of its power, Wisconsin elected an insurgent Republican, Robert LaFol-lette, as governor. LaFollette, no mere disgruntled, con-ventionally opportunist office seeker, headed a formidable opposition to the regular Republicans, who had dominated the state since the Civil War. His career was typical of those of the Western insurgent leaders. He started out in politics in the early 1880s as a faithful worker for the Republican organization, and as such served three terms in the House of Representatives. In 1891 he broke with the bosses, charg-ing that one of them had tried to bribe him. Soon after, he offered himself as an insurgent gubernatorial candidate. Every two years he campaigned for the nomination, but every two years the boss-run Republican nominating convention turned him down. Meanwhile he became the best-known politician in the state, famed as the man who was taking on the machine singlehandedly.

At first, LaFollette's insurgency was purely political; ideologically there was little difference between him and the party regulars. But his angry and protracted struggle with them transformed him into a radical. Echoing the classical Populist arguments, he linked the special interests, chief among them the railroads, to the Republican organization. He maintained, just as the Populists had, that a huge syndicate of Eastern plutocrats and corrupt bosses, acting through local officials, really ran the state. LaFollette's charges may have been exaggerated and hyperbolic, but they called attention to the undeniable fact that the state government was controlled by the two federal Senators, both of whom were quite rich and closely connected to the Eastern centers of power. These Senators appointed the state's federal jobholders (marshals, court clerks, postmasters, etc.), who presided over the various party caucuses and conventions and so determined the candidates for all local office.

LaFollette's insurgency rested on the proposal—also taken from the Populists—to abolish the system of nominating conventions altogether and enact in its place a direct primary law under which candidates for office would be chosen by the voters instead of by the machine. Such a law, he claimed in speech after speech, campaign after campaign, would release the governor's office from its bondage to the federal or Senatorial organization, and would simultaneously turn the state legislature from a mere agency for electing Senators into a responsible, indigenous lawmaking body. With the people thus firmly in control the state would at last be able to assert its independence and discipline the predatory interests that were exploiting it.

Having built up a substantial following in the rural communities and small towns, LaFollette finally obtained the Republican nomination for governor in 1900 and was easily elected. Within four years he had made good his extravagant campaign promises. Under his prompting, the legislature enacted extensive political, economic and administrative reforms. A plethora of commissions was established to regulate railroads, utilities, workers' compensations, factories and mines. In setting up and staffing these commissions, LaFollette bypassed the regular party organization and drew upon a new stratum of personnel that comprised the nucleus of the Wisconsin progressive movement: University of Wisconsin professors, assorted reformers, and young lawyers and other professionals who were attracted to his moral crusade.

The direct primary bill was passed in 1903, following a mortal struggle between the insurgents and the "stand-patters." Both sides now assumed that the days of machine rule were over, and that henceforth the people at large would control the political process, from nominations to elections. In any case, the federal organization ceased to run the state. Candidates for office, from the governor down, now looked to the electorate rather than to the two Senators for their mandate. And for the first time since the Civil War and the ascendancy of the machine, the governor of the state commanded power in his own right. The direct primary law became the Magna Charta of home rule.

LaFollette's election and reforms marked a turning point in the political history of the era. One by one the other traditionally Republican states of the West followed Wisconsin's example. Insurgent Republican governors took power in Iowa, Kansas, Nebraska, the Dakotas, Minnesota, California, Oregon and Washington after defeating the federal, or stand-pat, party organizations of their states. The insurgents then proceeded to put through a host of laws regulating the "self-ish" interests, just as Wisconsin had done. Everywhere the crowning reform was the direct primary law. The standpat-ters were willing to compromise on all social and economic issues; the primary law they fought to the death. To Western Progressives the portents were clear: the liquidation of machine politics was at hand.

Progressivism next advanced to the national level, and here again it was LaFollette who pointed the way. In 1905, the Wisconsin legislature, now firmly under his control, elected him United States Senator in the place of the Old Guard incumbent. Once again he confronted a powerful and intransigent Republican machine. This time, however, his cause seemed hopeless; the odds against him and his lonely crusade were too high. The Senate, which consisted of fifty-six Republican regulars, thirty-three Democrats and LaFol-lette, obeyed the wishes of a tiny oligarchy headed by Senator

Nelson Aldrich of Rhode Island, one of the parvenu aristocrats who had risen in politics after making his fortune in business. Aldrich and his little group saw to it that the Republican party as a whole rested safely on the twin pillars of sound money and high tariffs and that no piece of legislation or executive act disturbed the status quo. They would have preferred a weaker and more compliant President than Theodore Roosevelt, whose flamboyance, popularity and criticisms of big business at times annoyed them. But Roosevelt carefully avoided infringing their authority, and no serious intraparty conflicts arose during his administration.

Though LaFollette carried no weight in the Senate or with the leaders of the Republican party, his fame was spreading nationally. The muckraking journals, which throve on their exposés of the great trusts and the corrupt politicians, began to feature articles on him. His career proved definitively that the struggle against the special interests could not be confined to the localities and states, that the road to reform led inexorably to the national government. Lincoln Steffens, the most prominent of the muckrakers, later wrote that LaFollette taught him to understand "the nature of the compulsion which drove city reformers to the State and governors like LaFollette to the Senate at Washington. It was not necessarily ambition; it was a search for the seat of American sovereignty, and probably the bad businessman and the bad politician followed the same pursuit. They were all feeling for the throne where they could wield power and do what they wanted to do."

Muckraking journalists in general arrived at the same conclusion that the Populists, the Bryan Democrats and the Western Progressives had—namely that the trusts and the political machines were engaged in a conspiracy to destroy representative government, and that the United States Senate was at the heart of this conspiracy. The Senate, they maintained in article after article, was part of a central syndicate—a syndicate of syndicates—of Eastern bankers and industrial moguls. The central syndicate controlled local and state governments through the various political machines, which in turn answered to the Senate oligarchy. This view underlay what were probably the most sensational muckraking articles of all: David Graham Phillips's series for *Cosmopolitan,* "The Treason of the Senate." Phillips spared no detail in disclosing the history of perfidies, the reactionary voting records, the awesome power and the personal wealth of leading Senators. The articles appeared in 1906, the year LaFollette went to Washington.

LaFollette was soon joined by other Republican insurgents from Western states. The pattern of their ascent had been similar to his: upon capturing the state houses in Iowa, Kansas, the Dakotas, etc., the insurgent governors went on to replace the standpat Senators. By 1909 there were six Republican insurgents in the Senate, all from states west of the Mississippi. Led by LaFollette, they challenged Aldrich and the Senate hierarchy on every important issue. They attracted wide public notice during the tempestuous debates over the Payne-Aldrich Tariff Bill of 1909. To the insurgents, this bill, though it made some reductions in the 1897 rates, was still outrageous, providing further confirmation that the Republican party leadership cared more for the privileged interests than for the people. High tariffs, they argued, swelled the profits of Eastern plutocrats by forcing the people to pay exorbitant prices for manufactured goods.

The insurgents hoped that President Taft, who took office in 1909 as Theodore Roosevelt's chosen successor, would side with them against the Aldrich faction. But Taft quickly made it clear where his sympathies lay. He welcomed the Payne-Aldrich Tariff, calling it "the best bill the Republican party ever passed." In 1910 he further alienated the Progressives as a result of the famous Ballinger-Pinchot controversy. Gifford Pinchot, who headed the Forest Service, accused Taft's Secretary of the Interior, Richard Ballinger, of seeking to give away public lands to a private mining concern. Though Ballinger was probably innocent of the charge—he was eventually exonerated by a Congressional committee—the publicity attending the controversy proved so adverse to the administration that he had to resign. Taft formally broke with the insurgents when he campaigned for conservative Western Republicans who were up for re-election in 1910. In almost every instance the conservatives lost to the insurgents. By 1911 twelve Republican Senators and more than a score of Representatives stood with LaFollette. They formed the nucleus of the National Republican League, whose object was to wrest the national party organization from the conservatives and nominate an insurgent candidate—namely La-Follette—for President in 1912.

But as the insurgent movement grew in size, and as its prospects of success improved, so its leaders found LaFollette a liability. He had made too many enemies; his radicalism was unacceptable to too many moderates. It was well known that Roosevelt sympathized with the insurgents, and that since 1910, when he returned home from a hunting trip, he had been estranged from Taft, his erstwhile friend and protégé. On February 10, 1912, in a well-publicized letter, seven progressive Republican governors asked him to become the party's presidential candidate. Two weeks later he replied that he would accept the nomination if it were "tendered" to him. That settled the question. With the most popular man in the country at their head, progressives were certain they would capture both the party and the presidency. But they lost LaFollette, who felt he had been betrayed.

Roosevelt had been an enigma during his seven years as President. He had endeared himself to Progressives by his ready application of federal powers, he was the first strong President since Lincoln. Through his actions, and even more through his words, he alerted the public to the danger of monopolies. Though the title of "trust-buster" exaggerated his achievements—his administration filed only forty-four suits against big business, while Taft's filed ninety—he set a precedent that future Presidents were obliged to observe. Also, under his urging, conservative Congresses passed several pieces of significant legislation, chief among them the Hepburn Act (which strengthened the Interstate Commerce Commission), the Pure Food and Drug Act and the Meat Inspection Act. Far more important than these was the great conservation program that he initiated. Taking advantage of little-known laws passed in the 1890s, he set aside a total of 150 million acres of public land as national forest preserves and as water-power sites. With Roosevelt's accession, one era of land giveaways (there would be other kinds later) began drawing to a close.

Yet, as noted, Roosevelt never challenged the conservative leadership of the Republican party. On the commanding issues that divided the country—tariffs and fiscal policy—he deferred entirely to Aldrich and the Senate oligarchy. He gave little or no encouragement to Western insurgents when they were battling the federal machines in their states. Roosevelt's progressivism during his years as President might be defined as negative in purpose and character. He railed against the "malefactors of great wealth" not because he believed in equal rights but because he thought they were acting contrary to their own long-term interests. His task, as he conceived it, was to restrain the malefactors in order to keep down the radicals. He felt a ferocious enmity toward such "anarchists" as Eugene Debs and William Jennings Bryan. At best he distrusted LaFollette. Roosevelt, in short, was an enlightened Hamiltonian.

But by 1912 he had grown radical enough to qualify as a full-blown insurgent. And it was as head of the progressive Republican forces that he confronted President Taft at the party's convention in that year. Though a majority of Republican voters undoubtedly supported Roosevelt—this had been established in every preferential primary—a majority in the party organization did not. The conservatives, who controlled the convention, disqualified the delegates favoring Roosevelt and went on to steam-roller Taft's nomination. The progressives bolted. Later they held their own convention, at which they chose Roosevelt to be their standard-bearer and framed a remarkable platform—a "Contract with the People"—that promised to lower tariffs, eliminate child labor, enact minimum wage laws for women, strictly regulate trusts and railroads and adopt numerous political reforms, among them the direct election of Senators, nationwide primaries, female suffrage and, most controversial of all, the recall of judicial decisions.

The Republican schism set the stage for Woodrow Wilson's triumphant entry. Wilson's political career was as astonishing as any event in that era. A college teacher and president and author of many books on American government and history, he was a staunch Cleveland Democrat until 1910. That year the New Jersey Democratic boss chose Wilson to be the party's gubernatorial candidate. But during the campaign Wilson suddenly and inexplicably emerged as a militant progressive of the Bryan camp. After he won the election, his first act was to repudiate the Democratic machine. In his two years as governor of New Jersey he gained national fame as a reformer and as an uncompromising foe of the trusts. On the strength of his reputation, and with Bryan's help, he secured the presidential nomination in 1912. It was a foregone conclusion that he would win the election.

Nonetheless the 1912 presidential campaign was profoundly significant, for it brought into open conflict the two schools of progressivism that dominated American life. Roosevelt reflected the view of most Northeastern Progressives in maintaining that there was nothing intrinsically wrong with big corporations, given the nature of modern industry, and that a sound policy must distinguish between the good and the bad among them. Roosevelt's "New Nationalism" was an apt title: it assumed that social justice was best obtained by a strong national government regulating competing groups of businessmen, workers and farmers. The New Nationalism thus sought to continue a Republican tradition that went back to Hamilton—a tradition, however, that now rested on the Jeffersonian values of equal rights and popular sovereignty.

Wilson's brand of progressivism was more purely Jeffersonian. It harked back to a better day when each man owned his own capital or tool of production and was neither the master nor the servant of another. Wilson did not distinguish between good and bad trusts; bigness as such was the curse that must be exorcised. According to Wilson's doctrine of the New Freedom, which he first espoused in the 1912 campaign, the country needed a rebirth of individual self-sufficiency and competition. Only then could the ideal of equal rights be realized. For his analysis of the trust problem Wilson relied on Louis Brandeis, the great progressive who had once been a prominent corporation lawyer himself. Brandeis held that large corporations that could not be broken up without endangering the public welfare should be publicly owned. While Wilson did not go that far, his New Freedom, at least in theory, cast a long shadow of socialism across the American landscape.

Wilson was only the second Democrat since the Civil War to win the presidency. And he won it only because the Republicans were divided. He actually received fewer votes than Bryan had in 1908 and nearly one and a half million fewer than Roosevelt and Taft combined. And while Democrats took control of both houses of Congress for the first time since 1893, it was by such a slim margin that no reform legislation would have gone through without the support of insurgent Republicans. Under Wilson's shrewd leadership this Progressive coalition enacted a host of laws, including the Federal Reserve Act, which created a government board to manage the quantity and distribution of credit; the Underwood Tariff, which reduced rates appreciably and moreover imposed a graduated income tax; the Federal Trade Commission Act, which established a commission to regulate unfair business practices; and the Clayton Anti-Trust Act, which supplemented the Sherman Act and explicitly declared that labor and agricultural organizations were not "illegal combinations in restraint of trade." Labor unions hailed the Clayton Act as their "Magna Charta"; but their ebullience proved premature.

Wilson's New Freedom was largely vitiated by his curious appointments. The men he selected to occupy the regulatory commissions were recruited from the ranks of industry. It was soon evident that Wilson was at most a moderate progressive who feared pushing too hard and too far. He abandoned all talk of destroying the trusts. Pragmatically, he adopted Roosevelt's rule of distinguishing between them. Accordingly, by 1916 most Progressives had come to despair of Wilson, and had made it clear that they would not support him again.

But suddenly there arose what amounted to a second New Freedom. Wilson knew that he had to have the support of progressives to win in 1916. The Republicans, after all, still constituted a majority of the electorate, with the insurgents and Bull Moosers among them holding the balance of power between parties. And so Wilson dropped his policy of cautious advance and introduced a series of reforms that put him back in the good graces of the progressive community. In 1916 Congress passed the following laws sponsored by the administration: the Federal Farm Loan Act, which set up a separate banking system to provide easy credit to farmers; the Warehouse Act, which enabled farmers to use their stored-up commodities as collateral for loans; the Adamson Act, which ordered interstate railroads to establish an eight-hour day for their employees; and the Keating-Owen Act (later overturned by the Supreme Court), which banned the interstate commerce in all goods produced by child labor. In 1916, too, Wilson nominated Brandeis to the Supreme Court. This shocked conservatives, especially corporation lawyers, who found it intolerable that a Jew, a reformer and an apostate to their profession should have a position of such high trust, the Court being the sacred Areopagus, the guardian of property and established order. For months the conflict over Brandeis raged in the Senate Judiciary Committee. But Wilson never wavered in his support, and Brandeis was finally approved.

With America's entry into the First World War Wilson prepared to extend the progressive crusade to the entire world, to send it abroad, as it were, with the American troops. In proclaiming the war to be a moral struggle between freedom and autocracy he pointed to a self-evident truth: the major Allied powers, including Russia (thanks to the February 1917 revolution), were democracies, while Germany and Austria-Hungary were not. But when the Bolsheviks seized control of Russia in October 1917 they immediately flung down a revolutionary challenge to Wilsonian progressivism. They declared that both sides in the war were equally imperialistic, that the distinction between autocracy and democracy was a false one, that the real distinction lay between the capitalists and the proletariat, and that the people of all countries should overthrow their governments, end the war, and create a socialist community of nations. Wilson had to meet this bold alternative from the left by stating concretely what the Allied war aims were. He had to spell out precisely what he meant by a democratic peace.

This he did in his Fourteen Points speech of January 8,

1918. Wilson's Fourteen Points were predicated on a single assumption: that relations between sovereign states should be modeled on the relations between individual men in a free, democratic society. Wilson believed that if all nations governed themselves as America governed herself the world would be as peaceful, as just, and as happy as America was. It followed that wars, imperialisms and revolutions were traceable to the machinations of absolute rulers, never to the will of peoples. The Fourteen Points, in short, directly applied the precepts of Jeffersonian democracy to international affairs. This was a unique phenomenon in the history of diplomacy. The strongest nation on earth, instead of embarking on an imperialist crusade, was committing itself to the cause of international law and promoting the self-determination of all men. It was partially on the strength of this commitment that the German people rose up in early November 1918, overthrew the Kaiser's regime, created a democratic republic and ended the war.

The Fourteen Points stated that a "general association of nations must be formed" to provide "mutual guarantees of political independence and territorial integrity to great and small states alike." For Wilson, the chief purpose of the peace treaty negotiations that followed the armistice was precisely to form such a "general association." At the Paris peace conference he personally supervised the framing of the League of Nations Covenant from the first draft to the last. He was willing to make many concessions on matters of territories, reparations, boundaries, etc. to secure agreement on the Covenant. In doing so, however, he went back on some features of his Fourteen Points and compromised his ideal of a non-vindictive peace. Wilson thought that all the problems of the negotiating table would eventually be resolved within the councils of the League. The important thing was to bring the League into existence.

Wilson realized that the League would endure only if the great powers were bound to it by legal obligation. And since the United States had emerged from the war as the greatest of the powers, and was, moreover, the most deeply committed to the League's values, she was expected to assume the greatest obligation. According to Wilson, then, America's role in the organization could not be passive; she had to be its prime mover, its dominant force. And he was convinced that the American people would eagerly grasp the chance to guide the rest of humanity toward democracy and freedom. For this reason he refused to compromise with the Senate Republicans, led by Henry Cabot Lodge. He regarded their attempt to qualify America's obligation to the League as rank betrayal. He preferred to see the treaty turned down rather than emasculated.

We need not pursue the terrible and tragic history of Wilson's breakdown and subsequent defeat in the Senate. His ideal of a progressive world order was dashed when America failed to join the League of Nations. And to the role of martyr was added that of prophet outcast. With the onset of war progressivism at home gave way to repression and, for radical dissenters, to downright terror. In the name of patriotism and unity America abandoned due process of law. Under these circumstances, it was too much to hope that the country would want to keep progressivism alive in the rest of the world. How completely America repudiated everything Wilson stood for —and therefore her own recent past as well—became clear with Warren Gamaliel Harding's nomination and overwhelming victory in the 1920 election.

Robert M. LaFollette, "Menace of the Machine"
February 22, 1897

[LaFollette had already acquired a good deal of public attention in the West when he delivered this speech at Chicago University.]

. . . To enlist the interest of every individual, encourage research, stimulate discussion of measures and of men, prior to the time when the voter should discharge this primary duty of citizenship, offers political organization opportunity for the highest public service. Teaching the principles of the party, reviewing political history, discussing pending and proposed legislation, investigating the fitness of candidates for office, quickening the sense of obligation and personal responsibility in all the duties of citizenship, commanding the continuous, intelligent, personal interest of the individual voter —and when the campaign is on, conducting the canvass—these are the legitimate functions of political organization.

Such organizations cannot be used as political machines for individuals or factions. Whenever such organizations are maintained political slates are shattered and political bargains fail of consummation. Cliques, rings, machines, thrive upon the citizen's indifference to the plain duties of representative government.

There is no likeness or similitude between a political organization that appeals to every voter in the party and a machine that appeals only to the most skilled and unscrupulous workers of the party.

This is the modern political machine. It is impersonal, irresponsible, extra legal. The courts offer no redress for the rights it violates, the wrongs it inflicts. It is without conscience and without remorse. It has come to be enthroned in American politics. It rules caucuses, names delegates, appoints committees, dominates the councils of the party, dictates nominations, makes platforms, dispenses patronage, directs state administrations, controls legislatures, stifles opposition, punishes independence and elects United States senators. In the states where it is supreme, the edict of the machine is the only sound heard, and outside is easily mistaken for the voice of the people. If some particular platform pledge is necessary to the triumph of the hour, the platform is so written and the pledge violated without offering excuse or justification. If public opinion be roused to indignant protest, some scapegoat is put forward to suffer vicariously for the sins of the machine, and subsequently rewarded for his service by the emoluments of machine spoils. If popular revolt against the machine sweeps over the state on rare occasions and the machine finds itself hard pressed to maintain its hold on party organization, control conventions and nominate its candidates—when threats and promises fail—the "barrel" is not wanting and the way is cleared.

It is independent of the people, and fears no reckoning. In extreme cases where it becomes necessary to meet arraignment it has its own press to parry or soften the blow. Having no constituency to serve it serves itself. The machine is its own master. It owes no obligation and acknowledges no responsibility.

Its legislature makes the laws by its schedule. It names their committees. It suppresses bills inimical to its interests, behind the closed doors of its committee rooms. It suppresses rebate by machine rule and the ready gavel of the pliant speaker. It exploits measures with reform titles, designed to perpetuate machine control. It cares for special interests and takes tribute from its willing subjects, the private corporations. There was a time when the corporation lobbyist was an important functionary, and the mercenary legislator a factor with whom it was necessary to make terms. The perfect political machine is fast superseding the lobbyist. The corporation now makes terms direct with the machine and the lobbyist now attends upon the legislature to look after details and spy upon the action of members.

It is as much the interest and as plainly the duty of the state, to as carefully perfect and guard a system of nominating candidates as it perfects and guards the system of electing them.

The reformation affected in our elections by the Australian voting system should inspire us with confidence in advancing the lines of attack. Recall for one moment the change wrought wherever the Australian system has been adopted. Formerly the polling place was the scene of wrangling, dispute, disorder, often of violence and collision; weak men were badgered, corrupt men were bought. The employer often followed his men to the ballot box, voting them in a body, and the political boss was always present. Today the voter, freed from all annoyances, all espionage, all intimidation, goes alone into the quiet of the election booth and exercises his right without fear of punishment or hope of reward, other than his own conscience affords and the general good secures. Here rich and poor, employer and employed, meet on the same level. That which had become mere theory under the old plan of voting is transformed into an assured fact under the new, and the state maintains in this place the quality of its citizens before the law.

Is there any good reason why a plan so successful in securing a free, honest ballot and fair count in the election, will not work equally well in the nomination of candidates?

Then every citizen will share equally in the nomination of the candidates of his party and attend primary elections, as a privilege as well as a duty. It will no longer be necessary to create an artificial interest in the general election to induce voters to attend. Intelligent, well-considered judgment will be substituted for unthinking enthusiasm, the lamp of reason for the torchlight. The voter will not require to be persuaded that he has an interest in the election. He will know that the nominations of the party will not be the result of "compromise," or impulse or vile design—the "barrel" and the machine—but the candidates of the majority honestly and fairly nominated.

To every generation some important work is committed. If this generation will destroy the political machine, will emancipate the majority from its enslavement, will again place the destinies of this nation in the hands of its citizens, then, "Under God, this government of the people, by the people and for the people shall not perish from the earth."

Lincoln Steffens, "Enemies of the Republic" October 1904

[Steffens's article below informed the country of what La-Follette had been doing in Wisconsin. It was part of a series on state governments that Steffens wrote for *McClure's Magazine* in 1904–5.]

The story of Wisconsin is the story of Governor LaFollette. He is the head of the state. Not many governors are that. In all the time I spent studying the government of Missouri, I never once had to see or name the Governor of Missouri, and I doubt if many of my readers know who he is. They need not. He is only the head of a paper government described in the Constitution, and most governors are simply "safe men" set up as figureheads by the System, which is the actual government that is growing up in the United States in place of the "government of the people, by the people, and for the people, which shall not perish from the earth." The System, as we have found it, is a reorganization of the political and financial powers of the state by which, for boodle of one sort or another, the leading politicians of both parties conduct the government in the interest of the leading businesses which seek special privileges and pay for them with bribes and the "moral" support of graft. And a "safe man" is a man who takes his easy honors and orders, lets the boss reign, and makes no trouble for the System. . . .

"They" say in Wisconsin that LaFollette is a Democrat; that "he appeals to Democratic voters." He does. He admits it, but he adds that it is indeed to the Democratic voters that he appeals—not to the Democratic machine. And he gets Democratic votes. "They" complain that he has split the Republican party; he has, and he has split the Democratic party too. When "they" united the two party rings of the bipartisan System against LaFollette in 1902, he went out after the voters of both parties, and those voters combined; they beat Rose, the two rings, and the System. The people of Wisconsin reëlected LaFollette, the "unsafe," and that is why the trouble is so great in Wisconsin. The System there is down.

There is a machine, but it is LaFollette's. When he was reëlected, the Governor organized his party, and I think no other of his offenses is quite so heinous in Stalwart eyes. They wanted me to expose him as a boss who had used state patronage to build up an organization. I reminded "them" that their federal patronage is greater than LaFollette's in the state, and I explained that my prejudice was not against organization; their kind everywhere had been urging me so long to believe that organization was necessary in politics, that I was disposed to denounce only those machines that sold out the party and the people. And as for the "boss"—it is not the boss in an elective office where he is responsible that is so bad, but the irresponsible boss back of a safe figurehead; this is the man that is really dangerous. Then they declared that Governor LaFollette had sacrificed good service to the upbuilding of his machine. This is a serious charge. I did not go thoroughly into it. Cases which I investigated at

Stalwart behest, held, with one exception, very little water, and I put no faith in the rest. But, for the sake of argument, let us admit that the departments are not all that they should be. What then? As in Chicago, the fight in Wisconsin is for self-government, not "good" government; it is a fight to re-establish a government representative of all the people. Given that; remove from control the Big Business and the Bad Politics that corrupt all branches of the government, and "good" government will come easily enough. But Big Business and Bad Politics are hard to beat.

The defeat of Rose did not beat them. The Stalwarts still had the senate, and they manned the lobby to beat the railroad tax and the primary election bills. But Governor La-Follette outplayed them at the great game. He long had been studying the scheme for a state commission to regulate railway freight rates. It was logical. If their taxes were increased the roads could take the difference out of the people by raising freight rates. Other states had such commissions, and in some of them, notably Iowa and Illinois, the rates were lower than in Wisconsin. Moreover, we all know railroads give secret rebates and otherwise discriminate in favor of individuals and localities.

When then, the battle lines were drawn on the old bills in the legislature of 1903, the Governor threw into the fight a bristling message calling for a commission to regulate railway rates. The effect was startling. "Populism," "Socialism," "they" cried, and they turned to rend this new bill. They let the tax bill go through to fight this fresh menace to "business." They held out against the primary election bill also, for, if that passed they feared the people might keep La-Follette in power forever. Even that, however, they let pass finally, with an amendment for a referendum. Concentrating upon the rate commission bill, Big Business organized business men's mass meetings throughout the state, and with the help of favored or timid shippers, sent committees to Madison to protest to the legislature. Thus this bill was beaten by Business and, with the primary election referendum, is an issue in this year's campaign.

As I have tried to show, however, the fundamental issue lies deeper. The people of Wisconsin understand this. The

Stalwarts dread the test at the polls. But what other appeal was there? They knew one. When the Republican state convention met this year, the Stalwarts bolted; whatever the result might have been of a fight in the convention, they avoided it and held a separate convention in another hall, hired in advance. The Halfbreeds renominated LaFollette; the Stalwarts put up another ticket. To the Stalwart convention came Postmaster-General Payne, United States Senators Spooner and Quarles, Stalwart congressmen and federal office holders—the Federal System. The broken State System was appealing to the United States System, and the Republican National Convention at Chicago was to decide the case. And it did decide—for the System. I attended that convention, and heard what was said privately and honestly. The Republicans who decided for Payne-Spooner-Pfister-Babcock, etc., said "LaFollette isn't really a Republican anyhow."

Isn't he? That is a most important question. True, he is very democratic essentially. He helped to draw the McKinley tariff law and he is standing now on the national Republican platform; his democracy consists only in the belief that the citizens elected to represent the people should represent the people, not the corrupt special interests. Both parties should be democratic in that sense. But they aren't. Too often we have found both parties representing graft—big business graft. The people, especially in the West, are waking to a realization of this state of things and (taking a hint from the Big Grafters) they are following leaders who see that the way to restore government representative of the common interests of the city or state, is to restore to public opinion the control of the dominant party. . . .

David Graham Phillips, "The Treason of the Senate"
March, May 1906

[The following are excerpts from the first two instalments of Phillips's remarkable polemic, published by *Cosmopolitan* in 1906.]

I

One morning, during this session of the Congress, the Senate blundered into a discussion of two of its minor disreputables, Burton and Mitchell, who had been caught with their fingers sliding about in the change pocket of the people. The discussion on these change-pocket thieves was a fine exhibition of "senatorial dignity and courtesy," which means, nowadays, regard for the honor and dignity of the American people smugly sacrificed to the Senate's craftily convenient worship of the Mumbo-Jumbo mask and mantle of its own high respectability. In closing the brief debate over his fellow-senators who had been so unluckily caught, Senator Lodge said,

"There is too much tendency to remember the senators, and to forget the Senate."

A profound criticism—profounder far than was intended, or realized, by the senator from the "interests" that center in Massachusetts.

Let us take Mr. Lodge's hint. Let us disregard the senators as individuals; let us for the moment "remember the Senate." The treason of the Senate!

Politics does not determine prosperity. But in this day of concentrations, politics does determine *the distribution of prosperity*. Because the people have neglected politics, have not educated themselves out of credulity to flimsily plausible political lies and liars, because they will not realize that *it is not enough to work, it is also necessary to think*, they remain poor, or deprived of their fair share of the products, though they have produced an incredible prosperity. The people have been careless and unwise enough in electing every kind of public administrator. When it comes to the election of the Senate, how describe their stupidity, how measure its melancholy consequences? The Senate is the most powerful part of our public administration. It has vast power in the making of laws. It has still vaster power through its ability to forbid the making of laws and in its control over the appointment of the judges who say what the laws mean. It is, in fact, *the final arbiter of the sharing of prosperity*. The laws it permits or compels, the laws it refuses to permit, the interpreters of laws it permits to be appointed—these factors determine whether the great forces which modern concentration has produced shall operate to distribute prosperity equally or with shameful inequality and cruel and destructive injustice. The United States Senate is a larger factor than your labor or your intelligence, you average American, in determining your income. And the Senate is a traitor to you.

The treason of the Senate! Treason is a strong word, but not too strong, rather too weak, to characterize the situation in which the Senate is the eager, resourceful, indefatigable agent of interests as hostile to the American people as any invading army could be, and vastly more dangerous; interests that manipulate the prosperity produced by all, so that it heaps up riches to the few; interests whose growth and power can only mean the degradation of the people, of the educated into sycophants, of the masses toward serfdom.

A man cannot serve two masters. The senators are not elected by the people; they are elected by the "interests." A senator obeys him who can punish and dismiss. Except in extreme and rare and negligible instances, can the people either elect or dismiss a senator? The senator, in the dilemma which the careless ignorance of the people thrusts upon him, chooses to be comfortable, placed and honored, and a traitor to oath and people rather than to be true to his oath and poor and ejected into private life. . . .

II
Aldrich, the Head of it All

. . . For the organizer of this treason we must look at Nelson W. Aldrich, senior senator from Rhode Island.

Rhode Island is the smallest of our states in area and thirty-fourth in population—twelve hundred and fifty square miles, less than half a million people, barely seventy thousand voters with the rolls padded by the Aldrich machine. But size and numbers are nothing; it contains as many sturdy Americans proportionately as any other state. Its bad distinction of supplying the enemy with a bold leader is due to its ancient and aristocratic constitution, changed once, away back before the middle of the last century, but still an archaic document for class rule. The apportionment of legislators is such that one-eleventh of the population, and they the most ignorant and most venal, elect a majority of the legislature —which means that they elect the two United States senators. Each city and township counts as a political unit; thus, the five cities that together have two-thirds of the population are in an overwhelming minority before twenty almost vacant rural townships—their total population is not thirty-seven thousand—where the ignorance is even illiterate, where the superstition is mediæval, where tradition and custom have made the vote an article of legitimate merchandising.

The combination of bribery and party prejudice is potent everywhere; but there come crises when these fail "the interests" for the moment. No storm of popular rage, however, could unseat the senators from Rhode Island. The people of Rhode Island might, as a people and voting almost unanimously, elect a governor; but not a legislature. Bribery is a weapon forbidden those who stand for right and justice— who "fights the devil with fire" gives him choice of weapons, and must lose to him, though seeming to win. A few thousand dollars put in the experienced hands of the heelers, and the senatorial general agent of "the interests" is secure for another six years.

The Aldrich machine controls the legislature, the election boards, the courts—the entire machinery of the "republican form of government." In 1904, when Aldrich needed a legislature to reëlect him for his fifth consecutive term, it is estimated that carrying the state cost about two hundred thousand dollars—a small sum, easily to be got back by a few minutes of industrious pocket-picking in Wall Street; but a very large sum for Rhode Island politics, and a happy augury of a future day, remote, perhaps, but inevitable, when the people shall rule in Rhode Island. Despite the bribery, despite the swindling on registration lists and all the chicane which the statute book of the state makes easy for "the interests," Aldrich elected his governor by a scant eight hundred on the face of the returns. His legislature was, of course, got without the least difficulty—the majority for "the interests" is on joint ballot seventy-five out of a total of one hundred and seventeen. The only reason Aldrich disturbed himself about the governorship was that, through the anger of the people and the carelessness of the machine, a people's governor had been elected in 1903 and was up for reëlection; this people's governor, while without any power whatever under the Constitution, still could make disagreeable demands on the legislature, demands which did not sound well in the ears of the country and roused the people everywhere to just what was the source of the most respectable politician's security. So, Aldrich, contrary to his habit in recent years, took personal charge of the campaign and tried to show the people of Rhode Island that they were helpless and might as well quiet down, accept their destiny and spare his henchmen the expense and labor of wholesale bribery and fraud.

But, as a rule, Aldrich no longer concerns himself with Rhode Island's petty local affairs. "Not until about a year or so before it comes time for him to be elected again, does he get active," says his chief henchman, Gen. Charles R. Brayton, the state's boss. "He doesn't pay much attention to details." Why should he? Politically, the state is securely "the interests'" and his; financially, "the interests" and he have incorporated and assured to themselves in perpetuity about all the graft—the Rhode Island Securities Company, capitalized at and paying excellent dividends upon thirty-nine million dollars, representing an actual value of less than nine million dollars, owns, thanks to the munificence of the legislature, the state's street and trolley lines, gas and electric franchises, etc., etc. It began as a street railway company of Providence in which Aldrich, president of the Providence council and afterwards member of the legislature, acquired an interest. The sugar trust's Searles put in a million and a half shortly after the sugar trust got its license to loot through Aldrich at Washington; the legislature passed the necessary laws and gave the necessary franchises; Senator Steve Elkins and his crowd were invited in; more legislation; more franchises, more stocks and bonds, the right to loot the people of the state in perpetuity. Yes, Aldrich is rich, enormously rich, and his mind is wholly free for the schemes he plots and executes at Washington. And, like all the other senators who own large blocks of stocks and bonds in the great drainage companies fastened upon America's prosperity, his service is not the less diligent or adroit because he himself draws huge dividends from the people. . . .

Such is Aldrich, the senator. At the second session of the last Congress his main achievements, so far as the surface shows, were smothering all inquiry into the tariff and the freight-rate robberies, helping Elkins and the group of traitors in the service of the thieves who control the railway corporations to emasculate railway legislation, helping Allison and Bailey to smother the bill against the food poisoners for dividends. During the past winter he has been concentrating on the "defense of the railways"—which means not the railways nor yet the railway corporations, but simply the Rockefeller-Morgan looting of the people by means of their control of the corporations that own the railways.

Has Aldrich intellect? Perhaps. But he does not show it. He has never in his twenty-five years of service in the Senate introduced or advocated a measure that shows any conception of life above what might be expected in a Hungry Joe. No, intellect is not the characteristic of Aldrich—or of any of these traitors, or of the men they serve. A scurvy lot they are, are they not, with their smirking and cringing and voluble palaver about God and patriotism and their eager offerings of endowments for hospitals and colleges whenever the American people so much as looks hard in their direction!

Aldrich is rich and powerful. Treachery has brought him wealth and rank, if not honor, of a certain sort. He must laugh at us, grown-up fools, permitting a handful to bind the might of our eighty millions and to set us all to work for them.

Theodore Roosevelt, "The New Nationalism"
August 31, 1910

[By August 1910, two months after his return from Africa, Roosevelt had begun to gravitate toward the Republican insurgents and, implicitly, to oppose Taft's policies. The speech

below, delivered at Osawatomie, Kansas, anticipated much
of the Progressive party program two years later.]

. . . Nothing is more true than that excess of every kind
is followed by reaction; a fact which should be pondered by
reformer and reactionary alike. We are face to face with
new conceptions of the relations of property to human welfare, chiefly because certain advocates of the rights of property as against the rights of men have been pushing their
claims too far. The man who wrongly holds that every human
right is secondary to his profit must now give way to the
advocate of human welfare, who rightly maintains that every
man hold his property subject to the general right of the
community to regulate its use to whatever degree the public
welfare may require it.

But I think we may go still further. The right to regulate
the use of wealth in the public interest is universally admitted. Let us admit also the right to regulate the terms and
conditions of labor, which is the chief element of wealth,
directly in the interest of the common good. The fundamental thing to do for every man is to give him a chance to
reach a place in which he will make the greatest possible
contribution to the public welfare. Understand what I say
there. Give him a chance, not push him up if he will not be
pushed. Help any man who stumbles; if he lies down, it is a
poor job to try to carry him; but if he is a worthy man, try
your best to see that he gets a chance to show the worth
that is in him. No man can be a good citizen unless he has
a wage more than sufficient to cover the bare cost of living,
and hours of labor short enough so that after his day's work
is done he will have time and energy to bear his share in the
management of the community, to help in carrying the general load. We keep countless men from being good citizens by
the conditions of life with which we surround them. We need
comprehensive workmen's compensation acts, both state and
national laws to regulate child labor and work for women,
and, especially, we need in our common school not merely
education in book learning, but also practical training for
daily life and work. We need to enforce better sanitary conditions for our workers and to extend the use of safety ap-

pliances for our workers in industry and commerce, both within and between the states. Also, friends, in the interest of the workingman himself we need to set our faces like flint against mob violence just as against corporate greed; against violence and injustice and lawlessness by wage workers just as much as against lawless cunning and greed and selfish arrogance of employers. If I could ask but one thing of my fellow countrymen, my request would be that, whenever they go in for reform, they remember the two sides, and that they always exact justice from one side as much as from the other. I have small use for the public servant who can always see and denounce the corruption of the capitalist, but who cannot persuade himself, especially before election, to say a word about lawless mob violence. And I have equally small use for the man, be he a judge on the bench, or editor of a great paper, or wealthy and influential private citizen, who can see clearly enough and denounce the lawlessness of mob violence, but whose eyes are closed so that he is blind when the question is one of corruption in business on a gigantic scale. Also remember what I said about excess in reformer and reactionary alike. If the reactionary man, who thinks of nothing but the rights of property, could have his way, he would bring about a revolution; and one of my chief fears in connection with progress comes because I do not want to see our people, for lack of proper leadership, compelled to follow men whose intentions are excellent, but whose eyes are a little too wild to make it really safe to trust them. . . .

National efficiency has many factors. It is a necessary result of the principle of conservation widely applied. In the end it will determine our failure or success as a nation. National efficiency has to do, not only with natural resources and with men, but it is equally concerned with institutions. The state must be made efficient for the work which concerns only the people of the state; and the nation for that which concerns all the people. There must remain no neutral ground to serve as a refuge for lawbreakers, and especially for lawbreakers of great wealth, who can hire the vulpine legal cunning which will teach them how to avoid both jurisdictions. It is a misfortune when the national legislature fails to do its duty in providing a national remedy, so that the only national activity is the purely negative activity of the judiciary in forbidding the state to exercise power in the premises.

I do not ask for overcentralization; but I do ask that we work in a spirit of broad and far-reaching nationalism when we work for what concerns our people as a whole. We are all Americans. Our common interests are as broad as the continent. I speak to you here in Kansas exactly as I would speak in New York or Georgia, for the most vital problems are those which affect us all alike. The national government belongs to the whole American people, and where the whole American people are interested, that interest can be guarded effectively only by the national government. The betterment which we see must be accomplished, I believe, mainly through the national government.

The American people are right in demanding that New Nationalism, without which we cannot hope to deal with new problems. The New Nationalism puts the national need before sectional or personal advantage. It is impatient of the utter confusion that results from local legislatures attempting to treat national issues as local issues. It is still more impatient of the impotence which springs from overdivision of governmental powers, the impotence which makes it possible for local selfishness or for legal cunning, hired by wealthy special interests, to bring national activities to a deadlock. This New Nationalism regards the executive power as the steward of the public welfare. It demands of the judiciary that it shall be interested primarily in human welfare rather than in property, just as it demands that the representative body shall represent all the people rather than any one class or section of the people.

I believe in shaping the ends of government to protect property as well as human welfare. Normally, and in the long run, the ends are the same; but whenever the alternative must be faced, I am for men and not for property, as you were in the Civil War. I am far from underestimating the importance of dividends; but I rank dividends below human character. Again, I do not have any sympathy with the reformer who says he does not care for dividends. Of course, economic welfare is necessary, for a man must pull his own weight and be able to support his family. I know well that the reformers must not bring upon the people economic ruin, or the reforms themselves will go down in the ruin. But we must be ready to face temporary disaster, whether or not brought on by those who will war against us to the knife. Those who oppose all reforms will do well to remember that ruin in its worst form is inevitable if our national life brings us nothing better than swollen fortunes for the few and the triumph in both politics and business of a sordid and selfish materialism. . . .

Declaration of Principles of the National Progressive Republican League
January 21, 1911

[LaFollette drew up the Declaration in behalf of the now powerful insurgent movement within the Republican party. It was specifically directed against the party's Old Guard organization and against the President, and it looked forward to the nomination of a reform candidate—namely LaFollette —in 1912.]

We, the undersigned, associate ourselves together as The National Progressive Republican League.

The object of the League is the promotion of popular government and progressive legislation.

Popular government in America has been thwarted and progressive legislation strangled by the special interests, which control caucuses, delegates, conventions, and party organizations; and, through this control of the machinery of government, dictate nominations and platforms, elect administrations, legislatures, representatives in Congress, United States Senators, and control cabinet officers.

Under existing conditions legislation in the public interest has been baffled and defeated. This is evidenced by the long struggle to secure laws but partially effective for the control of railway rates and services, the revision of the tariff in the interest of the producer and consumer, statutes dealing with trusts and combinations, based on sound economic principles, as applied to modern industrial and commercial conditions; wise, comprehensive and impartial reconstruction of banking and monetary laws, the conservation of coal, oil, gas, timber, waterpowers, and other natural resources belonging to the people, and for the enactment of all legislation solely for the common good.

Just in proportion as popular government has in certain states superseded the delegate convention system, and the people have assumed control of the machinery of government, has government become responsive to the popular will, and progressive legislation been secured.

The Progressive Republican League believes that popular government is fundamental to all other questions. To this end it advocates:

(1) The election of United States Senators by direct vote of the people.

(2) Direct primaries for the nomination of elective officials.

(3) The direct election of delegates to national conventions with opportunity for the voter to express his choice for President and Vice-President.

(4) Amendment to state constitutions providing for the Initiative, Referendum and Recall.

(5) A thoroughgoing corrupt practices act.

Progressive Party Platform
August 5, 1912

[The Republican national convention, which met on June 18, threw out the pro-Roosevelt contested delegations preparatory to nominating President Taft. The Progressives meanwhile had marched out, vowing to hold their own convention. This they did on August 5 in Chicago. They promptly chose Roosevelt as their presidential candidate and framed the following platform.]

The Old Parties

Political parties exist to secure responsible government and to execute the will of the people.

From these great tasks both of the old parties have turned aside. Instead of instruments to promote the general welfare, they have become the tools of corrupt interests which use them impartially to serve their selfish purposes. Behind the ostensible government sits enthroned an invisible government owing no allegiance and acknowledging no responsibility to the people.

To destroy this invisible government, to dissolve the unholy alliance between corrupt business and corrupt politics is the first task of the statesmanship of the day.

The deliberate betrayal of its trust by the Republican party, the fatal incapacity of the Democratic party to deal with the new issues of the new time, have compelled the people to forge a new instrument of government through which to give effect to their will in laws and institutions. . . .

The Rule of the People

. . . In particular, the party declares for direct primaries for the nomination of State and National officers, for nation-wide preferential primaries for candidates for the presidency; for the direct election of United States Senators by the people; and we urge on the States the policy of the short ballot, with responsibility to the people secured by the initiative, referendum and recall. . . .

Equal Suffrage

The Progressive party, believing that no people can justly claim to be a true democracy which denies political rights on account of sex, pledges itself to the task of securing equal suffrage to men and women alike.

Corrupt Practices

We pledge our party to legislation that will compel strict limitation of all campaign contributions and expenditures, and detailed publicity of both before as well as after primaries and elections.

PUBLICITY AND PUBLIC SERVICE

We pledge our party to legislation compelling the registration of lobbyists; publicity of committee hearings except on foreign affairs, and recording of all votes in committee; and forbidding federal appointees from holding office in State or National political organizations, or taking part as officers or delegates in political conventions for the nomination of elective State or National officials.

THE COURTS

The Progressive party demands such restriction of the power of the courts as shall leave to the people the ultimate authority to determine fundamental questions of social welfare and public policy. To secure this end, it pledges itself to provide:

1. That when an Act, passed under the police power of the State, is held unconstitutional under the State Constitution, by the courts, the people, after an ample interval for deliberation, shall have an opportunity to vote on the question whether they desire the Act to become law, notwithstanding such decision.

2. That every decision of the highest appellate court of a State declaring an Act of the Legislature unconstitutional on the ground of its violation of the Federal Constitution shall be subject to the same review by the Supreme Court of the United States as is now accorded to decisions sustaining such legislation.

ADMINISTRATION OF JUSTICE

. . . We believe that the issuance of injunctions in cases arising out of labor disputes should be prohibited when such injunctions would not apply when no labor disputes existed.

We believe also that a person cited for contempt in labor disputes, except when such contempt was committed in the actual presence of the court or so near thereto as to interfere with the proper administration of justice, should have a right to trial by jury.

SOCIAL AND INDUSTRIAL JUSTICE

The supreme duty of the Nation is the conservation of human resources through an enlightened measure of social and industrial justice. We pledge ourselves to work unceasingly in State and Nation for:

Effective legislation looking to the prevention of industrial accidents, occupational diseases, overwork, involuntary unemployment, and other injurious effects incident to modern industry;

The fixing of minimum safety and health standards for the various occupations, and the exercise of the public authority of State and Nation, including the Federal Control over interstate commerce, and the taxing power, to maintain such standards;

The prohibition of child labor;

Minimum wage standards for working women, to provide a "living wage" in all industrial occupations;

The general prohibition of night work for women and the establishment of an eight hour day for women and young persons;

One day's rest in seven for all wage workers;

The eight hour day in continuous twenty-four-hour industries;

The abolition of the convict contract labor system; substituting a system of prison production for governmental consumption only; and the application of prisoners' earnings to the support of their dependent families;

Publicity as to wages, hours and conditions of labor; full reports upon industrial accidents and diseases, and the opening to public inspection of all tallies, weights, measures and check systems on labor products;

Standards of compensation for death by industrial accident and injury and trade disease which will transfer the burden of lost earnings from the families of working people to the industry, and thus to the community;

The protection of home life against the hazards of sickness, irregular employment and old age through the adoption of a system of social insurance adapted to American use;

The development of the creative labor power of America by lifting the last load of illiteracy from American youth and establishing continuation schools for industrial education under public control and encouraging agricultural education and demonstration in rural schools;

The establishment of industrial research laboratories to put the methods and discoveries of science at the service of American producers;

We favor the organization of the workers, men and women, as a means of protecting their interests and of promoting their progress. . . .

CONSERVATION

. . . We believe that the remaining forests, coal and oil lands, water powers and other natural resources still in State or National control (except agricultural lands) are more likely to be wisely conserved and utilized for the general welfare if held in the public hands.

In order that consumers and producers, managers and workmen, now and hereafter, need not pay toll to private monopolies of power and raw material, we demand that such resources shall be retained by the State or Nation, and opened to immediate use under laws which will encourage development and make to the people a moderate return for benefits conferred. . . .

Woodrow Wilson, "Free Men Need No Guardians" February 1913

[Wilson was about to take office when the following article setting forth his political philosophy appeared in the magazine *Fortnightly Review*.]

There are two theories of government that have been contending with each other ever since government began. One of them is the theory which in America is associated with the name of a very great man, Alexander Hamilton. A great man, but in my judgment, not a great American. He did not think in terms of American life. Hamilton believed that the only people who could understand government, and therefore the only people who were qualified to conduct it, were the men who had the biggest financial stake in the commercial and industrial enterprises of the country.

That theory, though few have now the hardihood to profess it openly, has been the working theory upon which our government has lately been conducted. It is astonishing how persistent it is. It is amazing how quickly the political party which had Lincoln for its first leader—Lincoln, who not only denied, but in his own person, so completely disproved, the aristocratic theory—it is amazing how quickly that party founded on faith in the people forgot the precepts of Lincoln and fell under the delusion that the "masses" needed the guardianship of "men of affairs."

For indeed, if you stop to think about it, nothing could be a further departure from original Americanism, from faith in the ability of a confident, resourceful, and independent people than the discouraging doctrine that somebody has got to provide prosperity for the rest of us. And yet that is exactly the doctrine on which the government of the United States has been conducted lately. Who have been consulted when important measures of government, like tariff acts, and currency acts, and railroad acts were under consideration? The people whom the tariff chiefly affects, the people for whom the currency is supposed to exist, the people who pay the duties and ride on the railroads? Oh! no. What do they know about such matters! The gentlemen whose ideas have been sought are the big manufacturers, the bankers, and the heads of the great railroad combinations. The masters of the government of the United States are the combined capitalists and manufacturers of the United States. It is written over every intimate page of the records of Congress; it is written all through the history of conferences at the White House, that the suggestions of economic policy in this country have come from one source, not from many sources; the benevolent guardians, the kind-hearted trustees who have taken the troubles of government off our hands have become so conspicuous that almost anybody can write out a list of them. They have become so conspicuous that their names are mentioned upon almost every political platform. The men who have undertaken the interesting job of taking care of us do not force us to requite them with anonymously directed gratitude. We know them by name. . . .

The government of the United States at present is a foster-child of the special interests. It is not allowed to have a will of its own. It is told at every move, "Don't do that; you will interfere with our prosperity." And when we ask, "Where is our prosperity lodged?" a certain group of gentlemen say, "With us." The government of the United States in recent years has not been administered by the common people of the United States. You know just as well as I do—it is not an indictment against anybody, it is a mere statement of the facts—that the people have stood outside and looked on at their own government and that all they have had to determine in past years has been which crowd they would look on at; whether they would look on at this little group or that little group who had managed to get the control of affairs in its hands. Have you ever heard, for example, of any hearing before any great committee of the Congress in which the people of the country as a whole were represented, except it may be by the Congressmen themselves? The men who appear at those meetings in order to argue for this schedule in the tariff, for this measure or against that measure, are men who represent special interests. They may represent them very honestly; they may intend no wrong to their fellow citizens, but they are speaking from the point of view always of a small portion of the population. I have sometimes wondered why men, particularly men of means, men who didn't have to work for their living shouldn't constitute themselves attorneys for the people, and every time a hearing is held before a committee of Congress should not go and ask, "Gentlemen, in considering these things suppose you consider the whole country? Suppose you consider the citizens of the United States?" . . .

I am one of those who absolutely reject the trustee theory, the guardianship theory. I have never found a man who knew how to take care of me, and, reasoning from that point out, I conjecture that there isn't any man who knows how to take care of the people of the United States. I suspect that the people of the United States understand their own interests better than any group of men in the confines of the country understand them. The men who are sweating blood to get their foothold in the world of endeavour understand the conditions of business in the United States very much better than the men who have arrived and are at the top. They know what the thing is that they are struggling against. They know how difficult it is to start a new enterprise. They know how far they have to search for credit that will put them upon an even footing with the men who have already built up industry in this country. They know that somewhere by somebody the development of industry in this country is being controlled.

I do not say this with the slightest desire to create any prejudice against wealth; on the contrary, I should be ashamed of myself if I excited class feeling of any kind. But I do mean to suggest this: that the wealth of the country has, in recent years, come from particular sources; it has come from those sources which have built up monopoly. Its point of view is a special point of view. It is the point of view of those men who do not wish that the people should determine their own affairs, because they do not believe that the people's judgment is sound. They want to be commissioned to take care of the United States and of the people of the United States, because they believe that they, better than anybody else, understand the interests of the United States. I do not challenge their character; I challenge their point of view. We cannot afford to be governed as we have been governed in the last generation, by men who occupy so narrow, so prejudiced, so limited a point of view.

The government of our country cannot be lodged in any special class. The policy of a great nation cannot be tied up with any particular set of interests. I want to say, again and again, that my arguments do not touch the character of the men to whom I am opposed. I believe that the very wealthy men who have got their money by certain kinds of corporate enterprises have closed in their horizon, and that they do not see and do not understand the rank and file of the people. It is for that reason that I want to break up the little coterie that has determined what the government of the nation should do. . . .

Woodrow Wilson, Speech Accepting Nomination
September 2, 1916

[Wilson summarizes the progressive reforms that he had brought about in his first four years as President.]

. . . The Republican party was put out of power because of failure, practical failure and moral failure; because it had served special interests and not the country at large; because, under the leadership of its preferred and established guides, of those who still make its choices, it had lost touch with the thoughts and the needs of the Nation and was living in a past age and under a fixed illusion, the illusion of greatness. It had framed tariff laws based upon a fear of foreign trade, a fundamental doubt as to American skill, enterprise, and capacity, and a very tender regard for the profitable privileges of those who had gained control of domestic markets and domestic credits; and yet had enacted antitrust laws which hampered the very things they meant to foster, which were stiff and inelastic, and in part unintelligible. It had permitted the country throughout the long period of its control to stagger from one financial crisis to another under the operation of a national banking law of its own framing which made stringency and panic certain and the control of the larger business operations of the country by the bankers of a few reserve centers inevitable; had made as if it meant to reform the law but had faint-heartedly failed in the attempt, because it could not bring itself to do the one thing necessary to make the reform genuine and effectual, namely, break up the control of small groups of bankers. It had been oblivious, or indifferent, to the fact that the farmers, upon whom the country depends for its food and in the last analysis for its prosperity, were without standing in the matter of commercial credit, without the protection of standards in their market transactions, and without systematic knowledge of the markets themselves; that the laborers of the country, the great army of men who man the industries it was professing to father and promote, carried their labor as a mere commodity to market, were subject to restraint by novel and drastic process in the courts, were without assurance of compensation for industrial accidents, without federal assistance in accommodating labor disputes, and without national aid or advice in finding the places and the industries in which their labor was most needed. The country had no national system of road construction and development. Little intelligent attention was paid to the army, and not enough to the navy. The other republics of America distrusted us, because they found that we thought first of the profits of American investors and only as an afterthought of impartial justice and helpful friendship. Its policy was provincial in all things; its purposes were out of harmony with the temper and purpose of the people and the timely development of the nation's interests.

So things stood when the Democratic party came into power. How do they stand now? Alike in the domestic field and in the wide field of the commerce of the world, American business and life and industry have been set free to move as they never moved before.

The tariff has been revised, not on the principle of repelling foreign trade, but upon the principle of encouraging it, upon something like a footing of equality with our own in respect of the terms of competition, and a Tariff Board has been created whose function it will be to keep the relations of American with foreign business and industry under constant observation, for the guidance alike of our business men and of our Congress. American energies are now directed towards the markets of the world.

The laws against trusts have been clarified by definition, with a view to making it plain that they were not directed against big business but only against unfair business and the pretense of competition where there was none; and a Trade Commission has been created with powers of guidance and accommodation which have relieved business men of unfounded fears and set them upon the road of hopeful and confident enterprise.

By the Federal Reserve Act the supply of currency at the disposal of active business has been rendered elastic, taking its volume, not from a fixed body of investment securities, but from the liquid assets of daily trade; and these assets are assessed and accepted, not by distant groups of bankers in control of unavailable reserves, but by bankers at the many centers of local exchange who are in touch with local conditions everywhere.

Effective measures have been taken for the re-creation of an American merchant marine and the revival of the American carrying trade indispensable to our emancipation from the control which foreigners have so long exercised over the opportunities, the routes, and the methods of our commerce with other countries.

The Interstate Commerce Commission has been reorganized to enable it to perform its great and important functions more promptly and more efficiently. We have created, extended and improved the service of the parcels post.

So much we have done for business. What other party has understood the task so well or executed it so intelligently and energetically? What other party has attempted it at all? The Republican leaders, apparently, know of no means of assisting business but "protection." How to stimulate it and put it upon a new footing of energy and enterprise they have not suggested.

For the farmers of the country we have virtually created commercial credit, by means of the Federal Reserve Act and the Rural Credits Act. They now have the standing of other business men in the money market. We have successfully regulated speculation in "futures" and established standards in the marketing of grains. By an intelligent Warehouse Act we have assisted to make the standard crops available as never before both for systematic marketing and as a security for loans from the banks. We have greatly added to the work of neighborhood demonstration on the farm itself of improved methods of cultivation, and, through the intelligent extension of the functions of the Department of Agriculture, have made it possible for the farmer to learn systematically where his best markets are and how to get at them.

The workingmen of America have been given a veritable emancipation, by the legal recognition of a man's labor as part of his life, and not a mere marketable commodity; by exempting labor organizations from processes of the courts which treated their members like fractional parts of mobs and not like accessible and responsible individuals; by releasing our seamen from involuntary servitude; by making adequate provision for compensation for industrial accidents; by providing suitable machinery for mediation and conciliation in industrial disputes; and by putting the Federal Department of Labor at the disposal of the workingman when in search of work.

We have effected the emancipation of the children of the country by releasing them from hurtful labor. We have instituted a system of national aid in the building of highroads such as the country has been feeling after for a century. We have sought to equalize taxation by means of an equitable income tax. We have taken the steps that ought to have been taken at the outset to open up the resources of Alaska. We have provided for national defense upon a scale never before seriously proposed upon the responsibility of an entire political party. We have driven the tariff lobby from cover and obliged it to substitute solid argument for private influence.

This extraordinary recital must sound like a platform, a list of sanguine promises; but it is not. It is a record of promises made four years ago and now actually redeemed in constructive legislation.

These things must profoundly disturb the thoughts and confound the plans of those who have made themselves believe that the Democratic party neither understood nor was ready to assist the business of the country in the great enterprises which it is its evident and inevitable destiny to undertake and carry through. The breaking up of the lobby must especially disconcert them; for it was through the lobby that they sought and were sure they had found the heart of things. The game of privilege can be played successfully by no other means.

This record must equally astonish those who feared that

the Democratic party had not opened its heart to comprehend the demands of social justice. We have in four years come very near to carrying out the platform of the Progressive party as well as our own; for we also are progressives.

There is one circumstance connected with this program which ought to be very plainly stated. It was resisted at every step by the interests which the Republican party had catered to and fostered at the expense of the country, and these same interests are now earnestly praying for a reaction which will save their privileges—for the restoration of their sworn friends to power before it is too late to recover what they have lost. They fought with particular desperation and infinite resourcefulness the reform of the banking and currency system, knowing that to be the citadel of their control; and most anxiously are they hoping and planning for the amendment of the Federal Reserve Act by the concentration of control in a single bank which the old familiar group of bankers can keep under their eye and direction. But while the "big men" who used to write the tariffs and command the assistance of the Treasury have been hostile—all but a few with vision—the average business man knows that he has been delivered, and that the fear that was once every day in his heart that the men who controlled credit and directed enterprise from the committee rooms of Congress would crush him, is there no more, and will not return—unless the party that consulted only the "big men" should return to power—the party of masterly inactivity and cunning resourcefulness in standing pat to resist change.

The Republican party is just the party that *cannot* meet the new conditions of a new age. It does not know the way and it does not wish new conditions. It tried to break away from the old leaders and could not. They still select its candidates and dictate its policy, still resist change, still hanker after the old conditions, still know no methods of encouraging business but the old methods. When it changes its leaders and its purposes and brings its ideas up to date it will have the right to ask the American people to give it power again; but not until then. A new age, an age of revolutionary change, needs new purposes and new ideas. . . .

Woodrow Wilson, Speech at Pueblo, Colorado
September 25, 1919

[Republican opposition to the League of Nations in the summer of 1919 caused Wilson to go to the people, and on September 4 he embarked on his remarkable tour of the Far West, delivering thirty-seven major speeches in twenty-seven cities. His last speech was at Pueblo, Colorado, where he broke down from exhaustion. A week later he suffered a stroke which rendered him *hors de combat* for much of the time while the struggle over the Versailles Treaty was taking place in Congress.]

Do not think of this treaty of peace as merely a settlement with Germany. It is that. It is a very severe settlement with Germany, but there is not anything in it that she did not earn. Indeed, she earned more than she can ever be able to pay for, and the punishment exacted of her is not a punishment greater than she can bear, and it is absolutely necessary in order that no other nation may ever plot such a thing against humanity and civilization. But the treaty is so much more than that. It is not merely a settlement with Germany; it is a readjustment of those great injustices which underlie the whole structure of European and Asiatic society. This is only the first of several treaties. They are all constructed upon the same plan. The Austrian treaty follows the same lines. The treaty with Hungary follows the same lines. The treaty with Bulgaria follows the same lines. The treaty with Turkey, when it is formulated, will follow the same lines. What are those lines? They are based upon the purpose to see that every government dealt with in this great settlement is put in the hands of the people and taken out of the hands of coteries and of sovereigns who had no right to rule over the people. It is a people's treaty, that accomplishes by a great sweep of practical justice the liberation of men who never could have liberated themselves, and the power of the most powerful nations has been devoted not to their aggrandizement but to the liberation of people whom they could have put under their control if they had chosen to do so. Not one foot of territory is demanded by the conquerors, not one single item of submission to their authority is demanded by them. The men who sat around that table in Paris knew that the time had come when the people were no longer going to consent to live under masters, but were going to live the lives that they chose themselves, to live under such governments as they chose themselves to erect. That is the fundamental principle of this great settlement.

And we did not stop with that. We added a great international charter for the rights of labor. Reject this treaty, impair it, and this is the consequence to the laboring men of the world, that there is no international tribunal which can bring the moral judgments of the world to bear upon the great labor questions of the day. What we need to do with regard to the labor questions of the day, my fellow countrymen, is to lift them into the light, is to lift them out of the haze and distraction of passion, of hostility, not into the calm spaces where men look at things without passion. The more men you get into a great discussion the more you exclude passion. Just so soon as the calm judgment of the world is directed upon the question of justice to labor, labor is going to have a forum such as it never was supplied with before, and men everywhere are going to see that the problem of labor is nothing more nor less than the problem of the elevation of humanity. We must see that all the questions which have disturbed the world, all the questions which have eaten into the confidence of men toward their governments, all the questions which have disturbed the processes of industry, shall be brought out where men of all points of view, men of all attitudes of mind, men of all kinds of experience, may contribute their part to the settlement of the great questions which we must settle and cannot ignore.

At the front of this great treaty is put the Covenant of the League of Nations. It will also be at the front of the Austrian treaty and the Hungarian treaty and the Bulgarian treaty and the treaty with Turkey. Every one of them will contain the Covenant of the League of Nations, because you cannot work any of them without the Covenant of the League of Nations. Unless you get the united, concerted

purpose and power of the great Governments of the world
behind this settlement, it will fall down like a house of cards.
There is only one power to put behind the liberation of mankind, and that is the power of mankind. It is the power of
the united moral forces of the world, and in the Covenant
of the League of Nations the moral forces of the world are
mobilized. For what purpose? Reflect, my fellow citizens,
that the membership of this great League is going to include all the great fighting nations of the world, as well as
the weak ones. It is not for the present going to include
Germany, but for the time being Germany is not a great
fighting country. All the nations that have power that can
be mobilized are going to be members of this League, including the United States. And what do they unite for? They
enter into a solemn promise to one another that they will
never use their power against one another for aggression; that
they never will impair the territorial integrity of a neighbor;
that they never will interfere with the political independence of a neighbor; that they will abide by the principle
that great populations are entitled to determine their own
destiny and that they will not interfere with that destiny;
and that no matter what differences arise amongst them they
will never resort to war without first having done one or
other of two things—either submitted the matter of controversy to arbitration, in which case they agree to abide by
the result without question, or submitted it to the consideration of the council of the League of Nations, laying before
that council all the documents, all the facts, agreeing that
the council can publish the documents and the facts to the
whole world, agreeing that there shall be six months allowed
for the mature consideration of those facts by the council,
and agreeing that at the expiration of the six months, even
if they are not then ready to accept the advice of the council with regard to the settlement of the dispute, they will
still not go to war for another three months. In other words,
they consent, no matter what happens, to submit every matter of difference between them to the judgment of mankind,
and just so certainly as they do that, my fellow citizens, war
will be in the far background, war will be pushed out of
that foreground of terror in which it has kept the world for

generation after generation, and men will know that there will be a calm time of deliberate counsel. The most dangerous thing for a bad cause is to expose it to the opinion of the world. The most certain way that you can prove that a man is mistaken is by letting all his neighbors know what he thinks, by letting all his neighbors discuss what he thinks, and if he is in the wrong you will notice that he will stay at home, he will not walk on the street. He will be afraid of the eyes of his neighbors. He will be afraid of their judgment of his character. He will know that his cause is lost unless he can sustain it by the arguments of right and of justice. The same law that applies to individuals applies to nations. . . .

CHAPTER IX. THE 1920S:
PROSPERITY AND REACTION

America had experienced many periods of prosperity in her history, but none were comparable to the one that took place between 1922 and 1929. This particular boom was unusual not so much for the quantity of wealth produced, though that was considerable (production increased 25 per cent in six years), as for the quality. In effect, America underwent a second industrial revolution in the twenties—a consumer revolution. Until then the economy had been engaged primarily in accumulating capital, in creating such industries as iron and steel, transportation, and mining. But by the end of the 1920s private consumption had become the chief motive force of the economy, and most of the capital was being invested in the production of automobiles, homes, radios and electrical appliances of every description, in chemicals, in telephones, in mass entertainment, and so forth.

The consumer revolution opened up vast new possibilities for enrichment, and the country lost no time in taking advantage of them. The distance separating the 1920s from the progressive era could be measured by the new attitude toward business enterprise. The middle class repudiated the ideal of social reform and re-embraced the traditional verities of individualism, liberty and progress—only now more than ever individualism meant cupidity, liberty meant privilege, and progress meant the unfettered acquisition of private fortune. The old hostility to big business and Wall Street gave way to a joyous celebration of their works. Americans no longer seemed to care that, thanks to a complex system of holding companies, mergers, interlocking directorates and patent ownership, larger and more powerful combinations than ever before were being established (so that by 1929 some 200 corporations out of a national total of over 300,000 controlled half the industrial output); that the absence of competition kept prices and profits egregiously high; and that not since President Grant's time had there been so much collusion between high government officials, including cabinet members, and predatory special interests.

To workers and farmers, the main beneficiaries of the progressive era, it became especially clear that the country had said farewell to reform. To be sure, labor's standard of living rose perceptibly in the 1920s, but this was due to the upward swing of the economy, and not to the efforts of trade unions, that is, the workers themselves. In fact, unions were generally powerless before the combined might of big business and government. The strikes that broke out between 1919 and 1922 in major industries—steel, coal and railroads—invariably failed, thanks to intervention in behalf of the employers by the courts, local police and, on occasion, federal troops. Both in magnitude and intensity 1919 marked the high point of labor conflict. In all there were 3,630 strikes that year, involving over four million men. In the steel strike alone twenty men died in the course of a bloody three-month war between pickets and police.

By the end of the 1920s union strength had diminished in nearly every industry. The United Mine Workers shrank from 500,000 members in 1919 to a little more than 100,000 in 1929. In some industries, most notably steel, the unions disappeared altogether. Total union membership fell from five million at the start of the decade to just over three at the end, and all but a fraction of these belonged to craft unions and railroad brotherhoods. In short, industrial unionism, having been defeated in every important encounter, was moribund. Not since the 1893 Depression had the labor movement been so badly off as it was in the 1920s.

The farmers were even worse off. Cotton and wheat prices in particular fell disastrously in 1921 and remained low throughout the decade. Even in 1928, when there was a slight improvement, prices reached only half the 1920 level. The story must have been a familiar one to those farmers who remembered the terrible crises of the 1880s and early 1890s.

The international market, which had devoured everything American farmers could produce during and immediately after World War I, suddenly contracted. And as competition from abroad increased, prices fell still further. As usual, farmers were defenseless against competition; they lacked the strategies that manufacturers employed to regulate the market—the creation of international cartels, for example. Meanwhile, the price of all non-agricultural commodities rose, as did the value of credit. Once again farmers found themselves victimized by a cruel economic cycle: to pay their burgeoning debts they had to grow more, but in growing more they drove prices down even further, and so their debts increased. Once again mortgages were being foreclosed, and the rate of tenancy, along with the rate of concentration in agricultural property, which had been rising steadily since the nineteenth century, was sharply accelerated; by 1929 nearly half the farmers' income was going to only 11 per cent of the farmers.

Even though farmers controlled the whole bloc of Midwestern states and constituted an organized, disciplined interest group in the Republican party, they were able to accomplish little in their own behalf. Riven by class differences, they found it difficult to agree on remedial legislation. Moreover the conservative Republican administrations refused to intervene in their behalf. Twice President Coolidge vetoed the McNary-Haugen Bill because, he maintained, it sought to fix prices. The bill, which was designed to benefit the larger producers, would have ordered the government to buy agricultural goods at a price guaranteeing a profit and then to sell them abroad at the prevailing market price. In 1929 the government did come up with a plan, the Agricultural Marketing Act, that promised relief by providing loans to farmers' co-operatives which withdrew their crops from the market until such time as prices rose to a profitable level. The Depression, however, made the Act unworkable. Farmers withdrew their crops, but prices continued to fall. The government then bought the crops outright, with the result that the farmers, having found a customer, produced as much as they could. Finally, in 1931 the government gave up and dumped everything it had bought onto the open market, thus bringing prices to an all-time low and reducing farmers to hopeless desperation. It was obvious by then that the agricultural problem had proved too intractable for conservative government. Only the most radical measures, such as regulating production or pegging prices and buying up the surplus, could have lifted agriculture from its slough of despond.

Yet it would be a mistake to conclude that the administrations of Harding, Coolidge and Hoover were unsympathetic to workers and farmers. The three Republican Presidents merely reflected the dominant ethic of the 1920s in believing that what was good for business enterprise was good for the country as a whole. They faithfully subscribed to the Hamiltonian philosophy, according to which the chief function of government was to act as steward of the great corporations. They assumed that the destiny of the nation was secure so long as men of business initiative were free to practice their skills—free, that is, from the constraints imposed by reformers, demagogues and bureaucrats. Accordingly, they looked back on the period from McKinley's day to their own as a sad interregnum, a period when the American people had been led astray in the name of equal rights and progressivism. "America's present need," said Warren Harding in 1920, announcing the theme for the whole decade, "is not heroes but healing; not nostrums but normalcy; not revolution but restoration."

The Hamiltonianism of Harding, Coolidge and Hoover, however, was Hamiltonianism in new dress, decked out in the guise of states' rights and distrust of federal authority. While the underlying ideology of government support for business remained the same as ever, the procedures were reversed. To achieve Hamiltonian ends in the twentieth century it became necessary to advocate Jeffersonian means, Jeffersonianism in this case meaning the idealization of local government; local government was, of course, powerless against big business. For its part, the Democratic party had undergone a comparable reversal of form. Under the leadership of Bryan and Wilson, the traditional party of Jefferson had called for policies that were boldly federalist and interventionist—in a word, Hamiltonian.

Government solicitude for business did not actually settle

into a fixed policy or dogma until the election of Coolidge in 1924. Harding's administration was beset by one scandal after another, by a sharp recession, and by strong opposition in Congress from a still formidable alliance of insurgent Republicans and Democrats. By 1924, however, both parties had surrendered themselves to the mammon of prosperity. That year, the Democrats nominated, in John W. Davis, a prominent corporation lawyer, their most conservative presidential candidate since Grover Cleveland, and in their platform they said nothing about the larger social and economic issues of the day. Bryan and Wilson were the ghosts of time past; the leaders of the Democratic party, themselves industrialists and financiers, were content with the status quo.

With both parties in the conservative camp, liberals, socialists, disaffected farmers and organized labor combined forces in 1924 to support Robert LaFollette, then in his seventy-first year and more radical than ever, as the presidential candidate of the Progressive party. The platform of this hastily contrived party accurately represented the views of the disparate groups that made it up. The government was to nationalize railroads and water-power sites, actively help organized labor and small farmers, limit the Court's power of judicial review, and severely regulate "private" monopoly. Though LaFollette received more votes than any previous third-party candidate in American history—nearly five million against a little more than eight for Davis and more than sixteen for Coolidge—only a handful of Progressives were elected to Congress and the state legislatures. Also, there is good reason to believe that German and Scandinavian Americans, who voted heavily for LaFollette, favored him more for his opposition to the war than for his progressivism. At any rate, Coolidge's overwhelming victory cleared the way for the full restoration of normalcy by the masters of business enterprise.

The first imperative was to change the graduated income tax, which had first been imposed on a very modest scale in 1913 but had been raised considerably during the war. The business community and the leaders of the Republican party thought that high taxes in general, and on the rich in particular, was a dangerous practice because it deprived industry of investment capital. They assumed that untaxed wealth would be pumped back into the economy, creating jobs, high wages, and low-priced consumer goods. If the government left the rich alone the blessings of affluence would trickle down to all the people, or at least all who wanted to work.

The man most responsible for incorporating the "trickle-down" theory of economics into law was Andrew Mellon, Secretary of the Treasury under Harding, Coolidge and Hoover. Before turning to statesmanship Mellon had headed one of the largest banks in the country and had founded the Aluminum Company of America. The Revenue Act of 1926 was his crowning achievement as Secretary of the Treasury. This act sharply reduced income and inheritance taxes—excess profits taxes having already been eliminated—and also made it exceedingly difficult for the government to check on the veracity of the returns, so that, in effect, rich taxpayers were put on their honor. Mellon's prescription seemed to be the right one, for the economy gained rapid momentum with the passage of the Revenue Act, and in 1928 taxes were reduced still further. This time the country waited in vain for a fresh spurt of prosperity.

There were other legacies of the progressive era that the 1920s removed or emasculated in the name of business enterprise. Between 1914 and 1920 federal commissions had been set up to regulate interstate trade, railroads and electric power. While the architects of Republican policy could not eliminate these commissions, they could staff them with the right kind of men—men sympathetic to the needs of corporations. Business learned in the 1920s that commissions, by shielding rather than regulating industry, could become valuable allies in the struggle for high profits. Another Wilsonian legacy was the huge government-owned merchant fleet built during the war. This was a ripe plum waiting to be plucked. Accordingly, under the provisions of the Merchant Marine Act of 1928 the fleet was sold to private shippers at a small fraction of cost. Moreover, to ensure that the shipping industry suffered no subsequent loss, the Act provided generous loans and a subsidy in the form of mail cargo.

During the period of Republican restoration the Supreme

Court resumed its role as the arch defender of property rights. In the decade or so before America's entry into the war, the Court had permitted the states to restrict private contracts that were injurious to the public good. But this liberal hiatus ended abruptly with Harding's four appointments to the bench. They were: ex-President Taft, who had grown increasingly conservative since leaving office in 1913; George Sutherland, a railroad attorney and Senator known for his loyalty to the Republican machine; Pierce Butler, who was also a railroad attorney; and E. T. Sanford, a conservative federal judge. These four, when added to three other conservatives—James McReynolds, Willis VanDevanter and Joseph McKenna—provided a safe margin for the cause of unreconstructed property rights. On the juridical left sat the two great dissenters of the day, Oliver Wendell Holmes, Jr., then in his eighties but as alert and sharp-witted as ever, and Louis Brandeis. They were joined in 1925 by Harlan Fiske Stone.

To laymen uninitiated in the mysteries of constitutional interpretation, the Court's reasoning must have seemed arbitrary and inconsistent. Between 1921 and 1930 the majority, returning to the traditional practice of the late nineteenth century, indiscriminately invoked the due process of law clause of the Fourteenth Amendment to throw out well over a hundred state laws that curtailed individual liberty, a euphemism for property rights. The Court thus asserted to an extreme degree the supremacy of the national government over and against the states. But at the same time the Court upheld the states by striking down federal legislation that allegedly trespassed upon their prerogatives. Two important attempts at reform—the Child Labor Law of 1916 (Keating-Owen Act) and the Child Labor Law of 1919—were thus erased from the statute books for having violated the reserve clause of the Tenth Amendment. These decisions were curious, since the Court had sustained the Narcotics Act of 1914, which gave the federal government broad authority in state affairs. Beneath these apparent contradictions, however, the Court acted with fixed purpose to guarantee the sanctity of contracts, and it carried out this purpose by the twofold strategy of protecting the states from the federal government on the one hand and the individual from the states on the other.

This exercise of judicial sovereignty posed a dilemma to the Court's liberal critics. If it was wrong to defend property from legislative assaults, was it right to defend civil liberties from them? Juridically, the issue of civil liberties arose for the first time in the 1920s. Until then the Court had maintained that the Bill of Rights—on all matters except property—did not apply to the separate states; it set a limit on the federal government alone. But as a result of the hysteria provoked by the war and the Russian Revolution, the federal government along with the states passed laws investing police with extensive, in some cases limitless, powers to suppress rights of association, assembly and press. In 1919 the Court upheld the Espionage and Sedition acts, thereby enabling the Attorney General, A. Mitchell Palmer, to carry out his sweeping raids against putative subversives. But after the hysteria had died down the Court began to raise a wall of defense around the Bill of Rights. Accordingly, in 1925, in *Gitlow* v. *New York*, the Court struck down a state law, notorious even in that era for its scope and harshness, on the grounds that it violated the due process clause of the Fourteenth Amendment. In defending human rights as well as property rights against states and localities, the Court established a historic precedent, which it reaffirmed in a host of subsequent cases.

Jeffersonian liberals might applaud this tendency to nationalize the Bill of Rights. But then could they logically fault the Court for practicing judicial review in behalf of property? What was sauce for the goose should be sauce for the gander. This was the liberal dilemma, and it was to become increasingly acute down through the years.

No event in American history with the single exception of the Civil War so sharply defined the end of one era and the beginning of another as the Great Depression. When the economy went to smash in 1929, the hopes on which the 1920s had built its edifice of prosperity went to smash as well. Events had catastrophically refuted the policies of business and government. The maldistribution of wealth, the vast amount of money pumped into the stock market by reputable banks and corporations, the depressed state of the farmers, the unusually high rate of unemployment throughout the decade—all of these conspired to help bring on the collapse. The incredible decline in the stock market was no mere symptom, or harbinger, of the disaster. Between October 1929 and July 1932, seventy-five billion dollars worth of securities was wiped out. This staggering loss alone nullified any chance that the economy would recover by the natural processes of laissez faire.

The enormity of the Great Depression defies description. At its height over a third of the labor force—some sixteen million people—was unemployed. Millions of Americans lived like the beggars of Calcutta; they had no homes and survived on scraps of food and handouts. Farmers were banding together to prevent by force the foreclosure of their mortgages. The entire credit structure seemed to dissolve. Most of the banks and insurance companies went out of business or closed their doors indefinitely, thus depriving people of the savings that might have seen them through for a while at least. America's prodigious economic machine, which had worked miracles, ground to a dead halt, and the business men who had claimed credit for its achievements were now denounced for running it down. The ethic of American business civilization, recently praised as the salvation of mankind, was cursed and desecrated for having proved a false idol. The myth of rugged individualism lay in ruins.

President Hoover was the unhappy prisoner of that myth. Nothing in the past, certainly nothing in his own life, had provoked him to question it. His career as engineer, businessman and humanitarian had been one of the remarkable success stories of the age. He had an unshakable faith in the power of personal initiative and a corresponding aversion to collectivism of any kind. Government intervention was anathema to him. For that reason he resisted any suggestion that the federal government should put the unemployed to work. Instead he advanced a scheme of co-ordinating local work relief and private philanthropy, self-help being in his view the only answer to the Depression. Finally, when this scheme did not avail, Hoover consented to a modest federal program that anticipated, in a miniscule way, the projects later undertaken by the New Deal. He was compelled to approve other emergency measures that he would never have dreamed of sanctioning in 1929. But these were feeble palliatives as the nation sank deeper and deeper into despair, bewilderment and paralysis.

Abrams v. United States
1919

[In *Schenck* v. *United States* Justice Holmes, writing the majority opinion, had upheld the conviction of a radical under the Espionage Act of 1917 for having distributed antiwar pamphlets. The state, he had then asserted, could limit opinions that constituted "a clear and present danger" to the community. In the Abrams case, however, he dissented from the Court's decision upholding the conviction of a radical pamphleteer, this time under the provisions of the 1918 Sedition Act. But it should be noted that he does not, in the opinion below, take issue with the Sedition Act itself, only with the government's application of it.]

HOLMES, J., dissenting. This indictment is found wholly upon the publication of two leaflets which I shall describe in a moment. The first count charges a conspiracy pending the war with Germany to publish abusive language about the form of government of the United States, laying the preparation and publishing of the first leaflet as overt acts. The second count charges a conspiracy pending the war to publish language intended to bring the form of government into contempt, laying the preparation and publishing of the two leaflets as overt acts. The third count alleges a conspiracy to encourage resistance to the United States in the same war and to attempt to effectuate the purpose by publishing the same leaflets. The fourth count lays a conspiracy to incite curtailment of production of things necessary to the prosecution of the war and to attempt to accomplish it by publishing the second leaflet to which I have referred. . . .

No argument seems to me necessary to show that these

pronunciamentos in no way attack the form of government of the United States, or that they do not support either of the first two counts. What little I have to say about the third count may be postponed until I have considered the fourth. With regard to that it seems too plain to be denied that the suggestion to workers in the ammunition factories that they are producing bullets to murder their dearest, and the further advocacy of a general strike, both in the second leaflet, do urge curtailment of production of things necessary to the prosecution of the war within the meaning of the Act of May 16, 1918, c. 75, 40 Stat. 553, amending part 3 of the earlier Act of 1917. But to make the conduct criminal that statute requires that it should be "with intent by such curtailment to cripple or hinder the United States in the prosecution of the war." It seems to me that no such intent is proved.

I am aware of course that the word intent as vaguely used in ordinary legal discussion means no more than knowledge at the time of the act that the consequences said to be intended will ensue. Even less than that will satisfy the general principle of civil and criminal liability. A man may have to pay damages, may be sent to prison, at common law might be hanged, if at the time of his act he knew facts from which common experience showed that the consequences would follow, whether he individually could foresee them or not. But, when words are used exactly, a deed is not done with intent to produce a consequence unless that consequence is the aim of the deed. It may be obvious, and obvious to the actor, that the consequence will follow, and he may be liable for it even if he regrets it, but he does not do the act with intent to produce it unless the aim to produce it is the proximate motive of the specific act, although there may be some deeper motive behind. . . .

I do not see how anyone can find the intent required by the statute in any of the defendants' words. The second leaflet is the only one that affords even a foundation for the charge, and there, without invoking the hatred of German militarism expressed in the former one, it is evident from the beginning to the end that the only object of the paper is to help Russia and stop American intervention there against the popular government—not to impede the United States in the war that it was carrying on. . . .

In this case sentences of twenty years imprisonment have been imposed for the publishing of two leaflets that I believe the defendants had as much right to publish as the Government has to publish the Constitution of the United States now vainly invoked by them. Even if I am technically wrong and enough can be squeezed from these poor and puny anonymities to turn the color of legal litmus paper; I will add, even if what I think the necessary intent were shown; the most nominal punishment seems to me all that possibly could be inflicted, unless the defendants are to be made to suffer not for what the indictment alleges but for the creed that they avow—a creed that I believe to be the creed of ignorance and immaturity when honestly held, as I see no reason to doubt that it was held here, but which, although made the subject of examination at the trial, no one has a right even to consider in dealing with the charges before the Court.

Persecution for the expression of opinions seems to me perfectly logical. If you have no doubt of your premises or your power and want a certain result with all your heart you naturally express your wishes in law and sweep away all opposition. To allow opposition by speech seems to indicate that you think the speech impotent, as when a man says that he has squared the circle, or that you do not care wholeheartedly for the result, or that you doubt either your power or your premises. But when men have realized that time has upset many fighting faiths, they may come to believe even more than they believe the very foundations of their own conduct that the ultimate good desired is better reached by free trade in ideas—that the best test of truth is the power of the thought to get itself accepted in the competition of the market, and that truth is the only ground upon which their wishes safely can be carried out. That at any rate is the theory of our Constitution. It is an experiment, as all life is an experiment. Every year if not every day we have to wager our salvation upon some prophecy based upon imperfect knowledge. While that experiment is part of our system I think that we should be eternally vigilant against attempts to check the expression of opinions that we loathe and believe to be fraught with death, unless they so imminently threaten immediate interference with the lawful and pressing purposes of the law that an immediate check is required to save the country. I wholly disagree with the argument of the Government that the First Amendment left the common law as to seditious libel in force. History seems to me against the notion. I had conceived that the United States through many years had shown its repentance for the Sedition Act of 1798, by repaying fines that it imposed. Only the emergency that makes it immediately dangerous to leave the correction of evil counsels to time warrants making any exception to the sweeping command, "Congress shall make no law . . . abridging the freedom of speech." Of course I am speaking only of expressions of opinion and exhortations, which were all that were uttered here, but I regret that I cannot put into more impressive words my belief that in their conviction upon this indictment the defendants were deprived of their rights under the Constitution of the United States.

Mr. Justice Brandeis concurs with the foregoing opinion.

Warren Gamaliel Harding, "Business and Government"

1921

[Following are excerpts* from chapter II of Harding's book *Our Common Country*, published the year he became President.]

We are the great business nation of the world. We shall be able to save that business and prosper it by a fair measure of common sense, and we ought and must do it. We will preserve a willingness to listen to the will of the people, and will construe the desire for a common good fortune to mean the necessary good fortune of business, which is the life-blood of material existence.

American business is not big business. Wilful folly has been in those persons in distended power over our national affairs who have spoken of American business as if it were a large and selfish interest seeking special privileges, and who, on that basis, have put their bungling hands upon its throat and tried tinkering and experimenting with it, and abusing it and treating it with suspicion. Let us put an end to holding success to be a crime.

It will be the American people who will do this because American business is everybody's business. Nearly nine-tenths of those who depend for their living and the legitimate fruits of their labors in American manufacturing are the wage-earners. The blow directed at American business, the pulling and hauling of American business by weird economic and social theories, is less menacing, for instance, to the one-tenth who in manufacturing are business executives than it is to the nine-tenths who are our American laborers. . . .

We must face the new task. We have had a fever of high prices and excessive production out of the sacrificed billions of treasure and millions of lives, but the reconstruction must be sober business, founded on unchanging principle. We must summon the best abilities of America to put America back on the main road, and to remove the debris of the last eight years, and to keep our industries running, and to restore the proper ratio of prosperity to our American agriculture so that it can again bid for good American standard labor.

If our memory is directed again to 1914, we will recall that world war alone saved us from a disaster in peace. We were sharpening our wits in competition with the world, as the President then expressed it, but we dulled our capacity to buy, then war saved us psychologically and commercially; but to-day we are at peace, actual though not proclaimed, and our problems are the problems of peace.

We must always exact, from ourselves and our business, high, honorable and fair dealing by law, and by law's rigid enforcement when necessary, but we must repeal and wipe out a mass of executive orders and laws which, failing to serve effectively that purpose, serve only to leave American business in anxiety, uncertainty and darkness.

We must readjust our tariff, and this time with especial regard for the new economic menace to our American agriculture as well as manufacturing.

We must readjust our internal taxation, especially the excess profits tax, to remove the burdens it imposes upon the will to create and produce, whether that will is the will of the big corporation, of the small corporation, or of the individual.

We must uproot from our national government the yearning to undertake enterprises and experiments which were never intended as the work of our government, which have proved ineffective to a point which sickens us all, and which our government is incapable of performing without wreckage or chaos. Of necessity the machinery of government expands as we grow in numbers as a people, but before government expands in bureaucratic control of business its sponsors ought first to demonstrate a capacity to conduct the business of the government. When government itself has a budget of more than three billions a year, in times of peace, it has a business of its own to look after—and it needs looking after —without seeking new fields to conquer until it has proved capacity for the tasks it must perform.

We must, instead of such experiments, establish a closer understanding between American government and American business, so that one may serve the other, and the other obey and seek cooperation.

We must give government cooperation to business, we must protect American business at home, and we must aid and protect it abroad by the upbuilding of our merchant marine, and a restoration of our self-respecting measure of American protection to her citizens wherever they may go upon righteous errands.

We must build our economic life into new strength and we must do it so that our prosperity shall not be the prosperity of profiteers nor of special privilege.

We must do it so that abroad we are known not as a nation strutting under a plumage of fine words, but as one that knits friendly and peaceful relations by the shuttle of honorable deeds.

We must do it so that at home our economic life yields

opportunity to every man not to have that which he has not earned, whether he be the capitalist or the humblest laborer, but to have a share in prosperity based upon his own merit, capacity and worth—under the eternal spirit of "America First."

American business has suffered from staggering blows because of too much ineffective meddling by government, and it is equally true that good government has almost been allowed to die on our hands, because it has not utilized the first sound principles of American business. . . .

Let them who say that the American people are not awake to these matters take new counsel. The government is the people's business, and they will not see it broken down. The government is the concern of every American—of every man, woman and child. We are shareholders in it and we are looking forward with relief to an end of mismanagement.

This great federal machine has grown up in a century of haphazard expansion, until, as recently described, it resembles "an antiquated central building with a large number of surrounding sheds and cottages, overcrowded with overlapping officials and saturated with methods of organization and administration fully fifty years behind the times."

An eminent senator once said he could substitute his private business methods for government practises and save hundreds of millions. It was thought to be true when he said it, and we might treble the figures for the saving now.

Here in America we have developed the most proficient and most efficient types of business organization and administration in the world; they have shown the greatest capacity for administrative vision. We mean to call that administrative quality and fitness into the service of the government, and establish an advance in government business, not merely talk about government progress.

Conditions are calling, capabilities await, the needs are urging and we pledge a new order—a business government, with business efficiency, and a business concern for public approval.

Adkins v. *Children's Hospital*

1923

[In 1918 Congress empowered the District of Columbia Wage Board to set minimum wage standards for women and children. Five years later, in *Adkins* v. *Children's Hospital*, the Court forbade the Board to exercise such power. No decision revealed more blatantly than this just how conservative the Court was in the 1920s.]

SUTHERLAND, J. . . . The statute now under consideration is attacked upon the ground that it authorizes an unconstitutional interference with the freedom of contract included within the guaranties of the due process clause of the 5th Amendment. That the right to contract about one's affairs is a part of the liberty of the individual protected by this clause is settled by the decisions of this Court and is no longer open to question. Within this liberty are contracts of employment of labor. In making such contracts, generally speaking, the parties have an equal right to obtain from each other the best terms they can as the result of private bargaining. . . .

There is, of course, no such thing as absolute freedom of contract. It is subject to a great variety of restraints. But freedom of contract is, nevertheless, the general rule and restraint the exception; and the exercise of legislative authority to abridge it can be justified only by the existence of exceptional circumstances. Whether these circumstances exist in the present case constitutes the question to be answered. . . .

If now, in the light furnished by the foregoing exceptions to the general rule forbidding legislative interference with freedom of contract, we examine and analyze the statute in question, we shall see that it differs from them in every material respect. It is not a law dealing with any business charged with a public interest, or with public work, or to meet and tide over a temporary emergency. It has nothing to do with the character, methods or periods of wage payments.

It does not prescribe hours of labor or conditions under which labor is to be done. It is not for the protection of persons under legal disability or for the prevention of fraud. It is simply and exclusively a price-fixing law, confined to adult women (for we are not now considering the provisions relating to minors), who are legally as capable of contracting for themselves as men. It forbids two parties having lawful capacity—under penalties as to the employer—to freely contract with one another in respect of the price for which one shall render service to the other in a purely private employment where both are willing, perhaps anxious, to agree, even though the consequence may be to oblige one to surrender a desirable engagement and the other to dispense with the services of a desirable employee. The price fixed by the board need have no relation to the capacity or earning power of the employee, the number of hours which may happen to constitute the day's work, the character of the place where the work is to be done, or the circumstances or surroundings of the employment; and, while it has no other basis to support its validity than the assumed necessities of the employee, it takes no account of any independent resources she may have. It is based wholly on the opinions of the members of the board and their advisers—perhaps an average of their opinions, if they do not precisely agree—as to what will be necessary to provide a living for a woman, keep her in health and preserve her morals. It applies to any and every occupation in the District, without regard to its nature or the character of the work. . . .

The feature of this statute which perhaps more than any other, puts upon it the stamp of invalidity is that it exacts from the employer an arbitrary payment for a purpose and upon a basis having no causal connection with his business, or the contract or the work the employee engages to do. The declared basis as already pointed out, is not the value of the service rendered but the extraneous circumstances that the employee needs to get a prescribed sum of money to insure her subsistence, health and morals. The ethical right of every worker, man or woman, to a living wage, may be conceded. One of the declared and important purposes of trade organizations is to secure it. And with that principle and with every legitimate effort to realize it in fact, no one can quarrel; but the fallacy of the proposed method of attaining it is that it assumes that every employer is bound at all events to furnish it. . . .

Finally, it may be said that if, in the interest of the public welfare, the police power may be invoked to justify the fixing of a minimum wage, it may, when the public welfare is thought to require it, be invoked to justify a maximum wage. The power to fix high wages connotes, by like reasoning, the power to fix low wages. If, in the face of the guaranties of the 5th Amendment, this form of legislation shall be legally justified, the field for the operation of the police power will have been widened to a great and dangerous degree. If, for example, in the opinion of future lawmakers, wages in the building trades shall become so high as to preclude people of ordinary means from building and owning homes, an authority which sustains the minimum wage will be invoked to support a maximum wage for building laborers and artisans, and the same argument which has been here urged to strip the employer of his constitutional liberty of contract in one direction will be utilized to strip the employee of his constitutional liberty of contract in the opposite direction. A wrong decision does not end with itself; it is a precedent, and, with the swing of sentiment, its bad influence may run from one extremity of the arc to the other.

It has been said that legislation of the kind now under review is required in the interest of social justice, for whose ends freedom of contract may lawfully be subjected to restraint. The liberty of the individual to do as he pleases, even in innocent matters, is not absolute. It must frequently yield to the common good, and the line beyond which the power of interference may not be pressed is neither definite nor unalterable but may be made to move, within limits not well defined, with changing need and circumstance. Any attempt to fix a rigid boundary would be unwise and futile. But, nevertheless, there are limits to the power, and when these have been passed, it becomes the plain duty of the courts in the proper exercise of their authority to so declare. To sustain the individual freedom of action contemplated by the Constitution, is not to strike down the common good but to exalt it; for surely the good of society as a whole cannot be better served than by the preservation against arbitrary restraint of the liberties of its constituent members.

It follows from what has been said that the act in question passes the limit prescribed by the Constitution, and, accordingly, the decrees of the court below are

Affirmed.

HOLMES, J., dissenting: The question in this case is the broad one, whether Congress can establish minimum rates of wages for women in the District of Columbia, with due provision for special circumstances, or whether we must say that Congress has no power to meddle with the matter at all. To me, notwithstanding the deference due to the prevailing judgement of the court, the power of Congress seems absolutely free from doubt. The end—to remove conditions leading to ill health, immorality, and the deterioration of the race—no one would deny to be within the scope of constitutional legislation. The means are means that have the approval of Congress, of many states, and of those governments from which we have learned our greatest lessons. When so many intelligent persons who have studied the matter more than any of us can, have thought that the means are effective and are worth the price, it seems to me impossible to deny that the belief reasonably may be held by reasonable men. . . . But, in the present instance, the only objection that can be urged is founded in the vague contours of the 5th Amendment, prohibiting the depriving any person of liberty or of property without due process of law. To that I turn.

The earlier decisions upon the same words in the 14th Amendment began within our memory, and went no farther than an unpretentious assertion of the liberty to follow the ordinary callings. Later that innocuous generality was expanded into the dogma Liberty of Contract. Contract is not specially mentioned in the text that we have to construe. It is merely an example of doing what you want to do, embodied in the word "liberty". But pretty much all law, consists in forbidding men to do some things that they want to do, and contract is no more exempt from law than other acts. . . .

Calvin Coolidge, "Our Heritage from Hamilton"
January 11, 1922

[The following remarks* are taken from a speech by Coolidge before the Hamilton Club of Chicago. It was included in *The Price of Freedom*, a volume of his speeches published in 1924.]

. . . [Hamilton] did not make his appeal to the more ordinary and common motives of human action, which characterized the appeal of Jefferson. He did not trust so implicitly in the popular side of our institutions. He did not realize so thoroughly that whatever forms of government have been provided, whatever economic system has been adopted, that however great and necessary these contributions may have been, the liberty, good order, prosperity, and the moral and spiritual condition of the people depend upon themselves. His great contribution was in providing the means by which these results might be secured. The disposition to ignore or to adopt these means can only be determined by the people themselves. He had faith that they would make the right choice. That faith has been justified. When great tests have come, when supreme choices have been made, the American people have always stood with Washington, with Hamilton, and with Marshall.

The party now in power in this country, through its present declaration of principles, through the traditions which it inherited from its predecessors, the Federalists and the Whigs, through their achievements and through its own, is representative of those policies which were adopted under the lead of Alexander Hamilton. They are the parties which have kept steadily in view the Union, and the whole Union. They cherished it through the necessary compromises of Henry

* Reprinted with the permission of Charles Scribner's Sons from *The Price of Freedom*, pp. 108–10, 112–13, 114–15, by Calvin Coolidge. Copyright 1924 Charles Scribner's Sons; renewal copyright 1952 Grace Anna Coolidge.

Clay. They supported it through the wise and patient states-manship of Abraham Lincoln. Without their vision the Union would never have been formed. Without their sacrifice it would not have been preserved.

No one speaks of dissolving the Union now. Its neces-sary advantages, supplemented by that true spirit of loyalty, make such an appeal impossible. Yet such proposals have their counterpart in those who, while remaining in the Union, selfishly undertake to escape bearing their share of its burdens and rendering due allegiance to its laws. This sometimes ap-pears in the form of sectionalism, sometimes in an attempted class distinction. I do not object to sectionalism because through its action there might be worked an injury to that part of the country in which I live; I do not object to al-leged class distinctions because thereby that class to which I should be presumed to belong might suffer harm; I object to them because, by whatever section or class they may be exhibited, they are an injury and a menace to my country; they are narrowing and withering, undertaking to substitute a temporary advantage for the permanent welfare. They are bound to end in destruction. When a people begin to cherish plans for anything save the common welfare, the decay of that country has begun. No party can survive which does not minister to national integrity.

As the inheritors of those principles which saved the young republic from repudiation in its weakness and infancy, we saved it again in its strength and maturity from the attempt at repudiation through the issues of greenbacks in the 1870s, and from the delusions of free silver in the 1890s.

There are those who give great expression to their solici-tude for the welfare of the people. Their expressions are, no doubt, sincere, and they may entertain a candid desire to ac-complish such a purpose; but the great power of production which diversification of industry has brought about has cre-ated a condition of interdependence. There is no such thing as the general welfare of the people in a period of business depression. If those policies are adopted which do all that can be done to produce a business prosperity which follows, there is no power which can prevent such prosperity from being diffused among the people. It is the doctrine of the

Republican party to encourage business, not merely for its own sake but because that is the surest method of administering to the general welfare. Those who criticise will be justified in their criticism when they can point out a better way.

Amid the changing conditions of the present day, hampered by the uncertain fluctuations in foreign exchange, confused by those costs of production abroad, which cannot be estimated, nevertheless the party is undertaking to reestablish the ancient and always beneficial policy of protection. It is seeking to give it the quality of elasticity that it may be administered in accordance with duly ascertained facts. It will undertake to be a national tariff under which different groups will profit in accordance with duly ascertained facts. It will undertake to be a national tariff under which different groups will profit in accordance with what such action will contribute to the national welfare. It will undertake to be a tariff under which the individual will benefit whenever such benefit would accrue to the common good. While the manufacturer might appear to benefit most in the first instance because he comes into direct competition with foreign production, if the theory of Hamilton be sound the indirect benefit to agriculture will be as large, if not larger. The products of agriculture are consumed by the industrial population. They are the customers of the farmer. If they be prosperous, his markets will grow. On the other hand, the great outlet for manufactured products is on the farm. A prosperous state of agriculture is the foundation of all national prosperity. The manufacturer must look to the farmer not only for his supply of food but for the sale of his commodities. Not in trying to overreach each other, but in putting forth their effort to assist each other, each will find a common salvation.

The ancient power of leadership has not left the republic, the wisdom and statesmanship of those who contributed to its beginnings and supported its continuation are with us yet. . . .

But it is not merely through economic grandeur that the Republican party desires to see this nation serve itself and serve mankind. Unsupported by a moral grandeur all this glory fades away. Unless these resources can be so administered that they increase the material and spiritual welfare of the people, their accumulation has been in vain. All the elaborate functions of the government will be of no avail, unless there abide in the people the simple, homely virtues of industry and thrift, honesty and charity. Without these characteristics there can be no advance in the general effectiveness of the government or the general welfare of the people. All of our natural resources, all of our attempted industrial organization, all of our guarantees of freedom will avail nothing without the support of character. There can be no national greatness which does not rest upon the personal integrity of the people. . . .

Andrew Mellon, *Taxation the People's Business*
1924

[Mellon's book *Taxation the People's Business* admirably sets forth the philosophy that guided him in his eleven years as Secretary of the Treasury. The excerpts below* are from chapters one and five.]

I have never viewed taxation as a means of rewarding one class of taxpayers or punishing another. If such a point of view ever controls our public policy, the traditions of freedom, justice and equality of opportunity, which are the distinguishing characteristics of our American civilization, will have disappeared and in their place we shall have class legislation with all its attendant evils. The man who seeks to perpetuate prejudice and class hatred is doing America an ill service. In attempting to promote or to defeat legislation by arraying one class of taxpayers against another, he shows a complete misconception of those principles of equality on which the country was founded. Any man of energy and initiative in this country can get what he wants out of life. But when that initiative is crippled by legislation or by a tax system which denies him the right to receive a reasonable

* Reprinted with permission of the publisher from *Taxation the People's Business*, by Andrew Mellon. Copyright 1924 by The Macmillan Company. Renewed 1952 by Nora McMullen Mellon.

share of his earnings, then he will no longer exert himself and the country will be deprived of the energy on which its continued greatness depends.

This condition has already begun to make itself felt as a result of the present unsound basis of taxation. The existing tax system is an inheritance from the war. During that time the highest taxes ever levied by any country were borne uncomplainingly by the American people for the purpose of defraying the unusual and ever-increasing expenses incident to the successful conduct of a great war. Normal tax rates were increased, and a system of surtaxes was evolved in order to make the man of large income pay more proportionately than the smaller taxpayer. If he had twice as much income, he paid not twice, but three or four times as much tax. For a short time the surtaxes yielded a large revenue. But since the close of the war people have come to look upon them as a business expense and have treated them accordingly by avoiding payment as much as possible. The history of taxation shows that taxes which are inherently excessive are not paid. The high rates inevitably put pressure upon the taxpayer to withdraw his capital from productive business and invest it in tax-exempt securities or to find other lawful methods of avoiding the realization of taxable income. The result is that the sources of taxation are drying up; wealth is failing to carry its share of the tax burden; and capital is being diverted into channels which yield neither revenue to the Government nor profit to the people. . . .

Initiative has always been the most valuable American characteristic. It was this spirit in the early colonists which brought them to America, not to find an easier existence, but to enjoy religious and political freedom, as well as to better their material condition. They faced death by savages and starvation in order to build up a new country. It was the same spirit of adventure which peopled and developed the West. And it is this same spirit extended into business that has made America the great and prosperous nation she is today.

The United States is no mere happy accident. What we have has been achieved by courage and hard work. The spirit of business adventure has built up in this country a civilization which offers unprecedented rewards to any man who is willing to work. But where the Government takes away an unreasonable share of his earnings, the incentive to work is no longer there and a slackening of effort is the result. To share not at all in a man's losses and to take one-half of his gains, making him work three days out of six for the Government, is to impose odds too heavy to be borne. More and more the business adventure becomes too hazardous and the high spirit of initiative disappears in discouragement. An economic system which permits wealth in existence to escape its share in the expense of the Government, and wealth in creation to be penalized until the creative spirit is destroyed, cannot be the right system for America.

Henry Ford is one of the outstanding examples of what American initiative has accomplished in the last twenty years. Under the conditions which then obtained in this country, he has built up one of the great industrial establishments of the world, giving employment to thousands and adding to the comfort of millions of individuals by placing within their reach an automobile of moderate cost. In a recent interview he told why such an accomplishment would have been impossible under the present high surtaxes.

Starting out with a small capital, he put his profits back into the business and these in turn were used to buy better machinery, thus making it possible to reduce the price of his cars. If the present tax rates had been in force, most of these profits would have been paid to the Government and Mr. Ford doubts that it would have been possible ever to reach a point where he could have produced a car under $1500. Mr. Ford added:

> High taxes on the rich do not take burdens off the poor. They put burdens on the poor. As far as our company is concerned, we can go on about as we now are, whether the surtax be 25% or 50%. We can make some improvements, but we cannot do the great things we should do had we more money. We cannot make such progress in the next fifteen years as we have in the last fifteen, and all other forward-looking companies will be in exactly the same boat. . . .

Progressive Party Platform
July 4, 1924

[The scattered and disparate native radical groups had no place to go in the early 1920s, both major parties having succumbed to conservatism, and so they decided to form a new Progressive party for the 1924 election. Meeting in Cleveland on July 4, they chose Robert LaFollette to run for the presidency. He was supported by the Farmer-Labor party, by the Socialist party and by the American Federation of Labor, among others.]

The great issue before the American people today is the control of government and industry by private monopoly.

For a generation the people have struggled patiently, in the face of repeated betrayals by successive administrations, to free themselves from this intolerable power which has been undermining representative government.

Through control of government, monopoly has steadily extended its absolute dominion to every basic industry.

In violation of law, monopoly has crushed competition, stifled private initiative and independent enterprise, and without fear of punishment now exacts extortionate profits upon every necessity of life consumed by the public.

The equality of opportunity proclaimed by the Declaration of Independence and asserted and defended by Jefferson and Lincoln as the heritage of every American citizen has been displaced by special privilege for the few, wrested from the government of the many.

FUNDAMENTAL RIGHTS IN DANGER

That tyrannical power which the American people denied to a king, they will no longer endure from the monopoly system. The people know they cannot yield to any group the control of the economic life of the nation and preserve their political liberties. They know monopoly has its representatives in the halls of Congress, on the Federal bench, and in the executive departments; that these servile agents barter away the nation's natural resources, nullify acts of Congress by judicial veto and administrative favor, invade the people's rights by unlawful arrests and unconstitutional searches and seizures, direct our foreign policy in the interests of predatory wealth, and make wars and conscript the sons of the common people to fight them.

The usurpation in recent years by the federal courts of the power to nullify laws duly enacted by the legislative branch of the government is a plain violation of the Constitution. . . .

DISTRESS OF AMERICAN FARMERS

The present condition of American agriculture constitutes an emergency of the gravest character. The Department of Commerce report shows that during 1923 there was a steady and marked increase in dividends paid by the great industrial corporations. The same is true of the steam and electric railways and practically all other large corporations. On the other hand, the Secretary of Agriculture reports that in the fifteen principal wheat growing states more than 108,000 farmers since 1920 have lost their farms through foreclosure or bankruptcy; that more than 122,000 have surrendered their property without legal proceedings, and that nearly 375,000 have retained possession of their property only through the leniency of their creditors, making a total of more than 600,-000 or 26 percent of all farmers who have virtually been bankrupted since 1920 in these fifteen states alone.

Almost unlimited prosperity for the great corporations and ruin and bankruptcy for agriculture is the direct and logical result of the policies and legislation which deflated the farmer while extending almost unlimited credit to the great corporations; which protected with exorbitant tariffs the industrial magnates, but depressed the prices of the farmers' products by financial juggling while greatly increasing the cost of what he must buy; which guaranteed excessive freight rates to the railroads and put a premium on wasteful management while saddling an unwarranted burden on to the backs of the American farmer; which permitted gambling in the products of the farm by grain speculators to the great detriment of the farmer and to the great profit of the grain gambler.

A COVENANT WITH THE PEOPLE

Awakened by the dangers which menace their freedom and prosperity the American people still retain the right and courage to exercise their sovereign control over their government. In order to destroy the economic and political power of monopoly, which has come between the people and their government, we pledge ourselves to the following principles and policies:

THE HOUSE CLEANING

1. We pledge a complete housecleaning in the Department of Justice, the Department of the Interior, and the other executive departments. We demand that the power of the Federal Government be used to crush private monopoly, not to foster it.

NATURAL RESOURCES

2. We pledge recovery of the navy's oil reserves and all other parts of the public domain which have been fraudulently or illegally leased, or otherwise wrongfully transferred, to the control of private interests; vigorous prosecution of all public officials, private citizens and corporations that participated in these transactions; complete revision of the water-power act, the general leasing act, and all other legislation relating to the public domain. We favor public ownership of the nation's water power and the creation and development of a national super-water-power system, including Muscle Shoals, to supply at actual cost light and power for the people and nitrate for the farmers, and strict public control and permanent conservation of all the nation's resources, including coal, iron and other ores, oil and timber lands, in the interest of the people. . . .

TAX REDUCTION

4. We favor reduction of Federal taxes upon individual incomes and legitimate business, limiting tax exactions strictly to the requirements of the government administered with rigid economy, particularly by the curtailment of the eight hundred million dollars now annually expended for the army and navy in preparation for future wars; by the recovery of the hundreds of millions of dollars stolen from the Treasury through fraudulent war contracts and the corrupt leasing of the public resources; and by diligent action to collect the accumulated interest upon the eleven billion dollars owing us by foreign governments.

We denounce the Mellon tax plan as a device to relieve multi-millionaires at the expense of other tax payers, and favor a taxation policy providing for immediate reductions upon moderate incomes, large increases in the inheritance tax rates upon large estates to prevent the indefinite accumulation by inheritance of great fortunes in a few hands; taxes upon excess profits to penalize profiteering, and complete publicity, under proper safeguards, of all Federal tax returns.

THE COURTS

5. We favor submitting to the people, for their considerate judgment, a constitutional amendment providing that Congress may by enacting a statute make it effective over a judicial veto.

We favor such amendment to the constitution as may be necessary to provide for the election of all Federal Judges, without party designation, for fixed terms not exceeding ten years, by direct vote of the people.

THE FARMERS

6. We favor drastic reduction of the exorbitant duties on manufactures provided in the Fordney-McCumber tariff legislation, the prohibiting of gambling by speculators and profiteers in agricultural products; the reconstruction of the Fed-

eral Reserve and Federal Farm Loan Systems, so as to eliminate control by usurers, speculators and international financiers, and to make the credit of the nation available upon fair terms to all and without discrimination to business men, farmers, and home-builders. We advocate the calling of a special session of Congress to pass legislation for the relief of American agriculture. We favor such further legislation as may be needful or helpful in promoting and protecting co-operative enterprises. We demand that the Interstate Commerce Commission proceed forthwith to reduce by an approximation to pre-war levels the present freight rates on agricultural products, including live stock, and upon the materials required upon American farms for agricultural purposes.

LABOR

7. We favor abolition of the use of injunctions in labor disputes and declare for complete protection of the right of farmers and industrial workers to organize, bargain collectively through representatives of their own choosing, and conduct without hindrance co-operative enterprises.

We favor prompt ratification of the Child Labor Amendment, and subsequent enactment of a Federal law to protect children in industry. . . .

PEACE ON EARTH

12. We denounce the mercenary system of foreign policy under recent administrations in the interests of financial imperialists, oil monopolies and international bankers, which has at times degraded our State Department from its high service as a strong and kindly intermediary of defenseless governments to a trading outpost for those interests and concession-seekers engaged in the exploitations of weaker nations, as contrary to the will of the American people, destructive of domestic development and provocative of war. We favor an active foreign policy to bring about a revision of the Versailles treaty in accordance with the terms of the armistice, and to promote firm treaty agreements with all na-

tions to outlaw wars, abolish conscription, drastically reduce land, air and naval armaments, and guarantee public referendum on peace and war.

Gitlow v. People of New York
1925

[With the Gitlow decision the Supreme Court entered a new phase of its career: it began to recognize that civil liberties deserved as much protection from the states under the Fourteenth Amendment as property rights. The Court came to this conclusion even though the majority upheld the New York Criminal Anarchy Act of 1902, under which Benjamin Gitlow had been convicted.]

SANFORD, J.: Benjamin Gitlow was indicted in the supreme court of New York, with three others, for the statutory crime of criminal anarchy. . . .

The indictment was in two counts. The first charged that the defendants had advocated, advised, and taught the duty, necessity, and propriety of overthrowing and overturning organized government by force, violence, and unlawful means, by certain writings therein set forth, entitled, "The Left Wing Manifesto"; the second, that the defendants had printed, published, and knowingly circulated and distributed a certain paper called "The Revolutionary Age," containing the writings set forth in the first count, advocating, advising, and teaching the doctrine that organized government should be overthrown by force, violence, and unlawful means. . . .

There was no evidence of any effect resulting from the publication and circulation of the Manifesto.

No witnesses were offered in behalf of the defendant.

Extracts from the Manifesto are set forth in the margin. Coupled with a review of the rise of Socialism, it condemned the dominant "moderate Socialism" for its recognition of the necessity of the democratic parliamentary state; repudiated its policy of introducing Socialism by legislative measures; and advocated, in plain and unequivocal language, the necessity of accomplishing the "Communist Revolution" by a militant and "revolutionary Socialism," based on "the class struggle" and mobilizing the "power of the proletariat in action," through mass industrial revolts developing into mass political strikes and "revolutionary mass action," for the purpose of conquering and destroying the parliamentary state and establishing in its place, through a "revolutionary dictatorship of the proletariat," the system of Communist Socialism. The then recent strikes in Seattle and Winnipeg were cited as instances of a development already verging on revolutionary action and suggestive of proletarian dictatorship, in which the strike workers were "trying to usurp the functions of municipal government"; and Revolutionary Socialism, it was urged, must use these mass industrial revolts to broaden the strike, make it general and militant, and develop it into mass political strikes and revolutionary mass action for the annihilation of the parliamentary state. . . .

The precise question presented, and the only question which we can consider under this writ of error, then, is whether the statute, as construed and applied in this case by the state courts, deprived the defendant of his liberty of expression, in violation of the due process clause of the Fourteenth Amendment.

The statute does not penalize the utterance or publication of abstract "doctrine" or academic discussion having no quality of incitement to any concrete action. It is not aimed against mere historical or philosophical essays. It does not restrain the advocacy of changes in the form of government by constitutional and lawful means. What it prohibits is language advocating, advising, or teaching the overthrow of organized government by unlawful means. . . .

The Manifesto, plainly, is neither the statement of abstract doctrine nor, as suggested by counsel, mere prediction that industrial disturbances and revolutionary mass strikes will result spontaneously in an inevitable process of evolution in the economic system. It advocates and urges in fervent language mass action which shall progressively foment industrial disturbances, and, through political mass strikes and revolutionary mass action, overthrow and destroy organized parliamentary government. . . .

The means advocated for bringing about the destruction of organized parliamentary government, namely, mass industrial revolts usurping the functions of municipal government, political mass strikes directed against the parliamentary state, and revolutionary mass action for its final destruction, necessarily imply the use of force and violence, and in their essential nature are inherently unlawful in a constitutional government of law and order. That the jury was warranted in finding that the Manifesto advocated not merely the abstract doctrine of overwhelming organized government by force, violence, and unlawful means, but action to that end, is clear.

For the present purposes we may and do assume that freedom of speech and of the press—which are protected by the First Amendment from abridgment by Congress—are among the fundamental personal rights and "liberties" protected by the due process clause of the Fourteenth Amendment from impairment by the states. . . .

It is a fundamental principle, long established, that the freedom of speech and of the press which is secured by the Constitution does not confer an absolute right to speak or publish, without responsibility, whatever one may choose, or an unrestricted and unbridled license that gives immunity for every possible use of language, and prevents the punishment of those who abuse this freedom. . . .

And, for yet more imperative reasons, a State may punish utterances endangering the foundations of organized government and threatening its overthrow by unlawful means. These imperil its own existence as a constitutional state. Freedom of speech and press, said Story (supra), does not protect disturbances of the public peace or the attempt to subvert the government. It does not protect publications or teachings which tend to subvert or imperil the government, or to impede or hinder it in the performance of its governmental duties. It does not protect publications prompting the overthrow of government by force; the punishment of those who publish articles which tend to destroy organized society being essential to the security of freedom and the stability of the state. And a State may penalize utterances which openly advocate the overthrow of the representative and constitutional form of government of the United States and the several states, by violence or other unlawful means. In short, this freedom does not deprive a State of the primary and essential right of self-preservation, which, so long as human governments endure, they cannot be denied. . . .

. . . The state cannot reasonably be required to measure the danger from every such utterance in the nice balance of a jeweler's scale. A single revolutionary spark may kindle a fire that, smoldering for a time, may burst into a sweeping and destructive conflagration. It cannot be said that the state is acting arbitrarily or unreasonably when, in the exercise of its judgment as to the measures necessary to protect the public peace and safety, it seeks to extinguish the spark without waiting until it has enkindled the flame or blazed into the conflagration. It cannot reasonably be required to defer the adoption of measures for its own peace and safety until the revolutionary utterances lead to actual disturbances of the public peace or imminent and immediate danger of its own destruction; but it may, in the exercise of its judgment, suppress the threatened danger in its incipiency. . . .

We cannot hold that the present statute is an arbitrary or unreasonable exercise of the police power of the state, unwarrantably infringing the freedom of speech or press; and we must and do sustain its constitutionality. . . .

HOLMES, J., dissenting:

Mr. Justice Brandeis and I are of opinion that this judgment should be reversed. The general principle of free speech, it seems to me, must be taken to be included in the Fourteenth Amendment, in view of the scope that has been given to the word "liberty" as there used, although perhaps it may be accepted with a somewhat larger latitude of interpretation than is allowed to Congress by the sweeping language that governs, or ought to govern, the laws of the United States. If I am right, then I think that the criterion sanctioned by the full court in *Schenck* v. *United States*, 249 U. S. 47, 52, applies: "The question in every case is whether the words used are used in such circumstances and are of such a nature as to create a clear and present danger that they will bring about the substantive evils that [the state] has a right to prevent." . . . If what I think the correct test is applied, it is manifest that there was no present danger of an attempt to overthrow the government by force on the part of the admittedly small minority who shared the defendant's views. It is said that this Manifesto was more than a theory, that it was an incitement. Every idea is an incitement. It offers itself for belief, and, if believed, it is acted on unless some other belief outweighs it, or some failure of energy stifles the movement at its birth. The only difference between the expression of an opinion and an incitement in the narrower sense is the speaker's enthusiasm for the result. Eloquence may set fire to reason. But whatever may be thought of the redundant discourse before us, it had no chance of starting a present conflagration. If, in the long run, the beliefs expressed in proletarian dictatorship are destined to be accepted by the dominant forces of the community, the only meaning of free speech is that they should be given their chance and have their way.

If the publication of this document had been laid as an attempt to induce an uprising against government at once, and not at some indefinite time in the future, it would have presented a different question. The object would have been one with which the law might deal, subject to the doubt whether there was any danger that the publication could produce any result; or, in other words, whether it was not futile and too remote from possible consequences. But the indictment alleges the publication and nothing more.

Franklin D. Roosevelt, "Is There a Jefferson on the Horizon?" December 3, 1925

[While still in political retirement Roosevelt wrote a review of Claude Bowers's recently published *Jefferson and Hamilton*, for the New York *Evening World*.]

. . . A year ago I took occasion in a letter addressed to more than a thousand Democratic leaders throughout the country to refer in passing to the difference between the

Jeffersonian and Hamiltonian ideals for an American method of government, and to apply their fundamental differences to present-day policies of our two great parties. Immediately many editors, including even some of the metropolitan press, launched sneers at the mere suggestion that Jeffersonianism could, in any remote manner, bear upon the America of 1925. A materialistic press reflects a materialistic age, but I still boil inwardly when I think of these smug writers who, wish being father to the thought, deny that the forces hostile to control of government by the people which existed in the crisis of 1790–1800 could still be a threat in our day and land.

The other personal reason is that for some years I have been, frankly, fed up with the romantic cult which has, since the publication of an historical novel, surrounded the name of Alexander Hamilton; and I have longed to write this very book, which now so much more ably comes from the delightful pen and untiring research of Mr. Bowers.

What is more valuable, however, is that in this study of a period which was, in every way, as important to the preservation of the Union as was the Civil War itself, a spirit of fairness and calm judgment is shown which makes the book not merely convincing to the general reader but of permanent value to the advanced student.

For Hamilton emerges still a romantic and fascinating figure, albeit in his true character of aristocrat and convinced opponent of popular government. And in Jefferson we see not only the savior of the deeper ideals of the Revolution, but also the man with human failings, the consummate politician.

The history of the United States may be interesting to some for the mere fact of events or personalities, but it is of value to us as a whole because of the application we make of these facts to present problems. It is in this spirit in which the book must be read: if we obtain from its pages only the knowledge of the definite establishment of a democratic republic because of the leadership of Jefferson and his associates, we fail unless we in addition apply the basic ideals of those days to the later events in American history and to the often essentially similar problems that still lie unsolved before us. . . .

There were no political parties, yet the line of demarcation was drawn before ever Washington was inaugurated. It is the little things which germinate. The World War had its murder of Sarajevo; the birth of American party battles had rise in the problem of the titles by which the President, the Cabinet and the Congress should be addressed. Next the social climbers, the snobbery, the appointment of Hamilton and Jefferson to the Cabinet, the rise of Hamilton to a position of supremacy and with it the control of the infant Government by the moneyed class. All still in the stage of experiment, and who, even to-day, can say that immediate success did not lie in the establishment of the Republic's finances and commercial credit? Alexander Hamilton we honor because of his master stroke for sound money, his genius for finance. Yet we must take into account the scandal of the day, the unconscionable profiteering of his followers—even some in Congress—in that same moneyed class who made veritable fortunes from the stupidity or the need or the lack of inside information on the part of the thousands of veterans, tradesmen, farmers or frontier settlers away from the larger seaport towns.

Slowly the lines were being formed. Within the Cabinet itself Jefferson, a veritable Westerner of his day, mistrusting the fondness of Hamilton for his Chambers of Commerce and his contempt for the opinion of the masses; Hamilton, confident of his power, confident of the power of his leaders among merchants and aristocrats, wholly lacking in understanding or in fear of the rights of what he thought of as the rabble—the poor, the uneducated, the average human being who, even then, made up the mass of his countrymen.

The scene changes to Philadelphia, the next temporary capital. More display, greater snobbery, an increased assurance on the part of the men and women of wealth, of family, of commercial prestige; and, most important, a growth of the pro-British sentiment on the part of these, and an abhorrence for the successes and excesses of the onrushing French Revolution.

It is natural that in this environment the demarcation into parties grew apace. Jefferson, eclipsed in the Cabinet by Hamilton, the natural democrat against the natural aristocrat, began then the mobilization of the masses against the autocracy of the few. It was a colossal task. With Hamilton were the organized compact forces of wealth, of birth, of commerce, of the press. With him at heart was Washington, the President. Jefferson could count only on the scattered raw material of the working masses, difficult to reach, more difficult to organize. . . .

I have a breathless feeling as I lay down this book—a picture of escape after escape which this Nation passed through in those first ten years; a picture of what might have been if the Republic had been finally organized as Alexander Hamilton sought. But I have a breathless feeling, too, as I wonder if, a century and a quarter later, the same contending forces are not again mobilizing. Hamiltons we have to-day. Is a Jefferson on the horizon?

Owen D. Young, "What Is Right in Business?" March 1929

[Young, Chairman of the Board of General Electric, was considered one of the leading business statesmen of the age. His article, which appeared in the *Review of Reviews*, reflects the optimism, confidence and belief in the legitimacy of big business in the late 1920s.]

In 1905, my old friend David did not like motor cars. He had had his experience with them. He would have been glad to have shut them off the road altogether. But some years later I had the pleasure of taking him in a motor on what he described as the best ride of his life. Then he thought better of motor cars and finally he came to understand, as we all have, the great contribution which they have made to the health, wealth, and happiness of all people.

It was much the same with big business. Sometimes its drivers were reckless; sometimes they were highly careful and conscientious, but the old horses of business were not yet adjusted to the new device. Dire prophecies were indulged in as to what would happen if large business units were to be permitted. It was said the masses of the people would become their slaves.

The business machines have become better adjusted through a quarter of a century. The drivers of them have become more skilled. In a sense, they are people trained for the job like the motor-car drivers. And while we still have left with us some of the reckless and irresponsible ones who are a menace to the road, by and large we move motor cars by the millions with amazing skill and safety, and so we do our business. The horses remaining take no notice of them, and David today, were he living, could ride down the road in Van Hornesville with safety, without irritation, without bitterness or even envy, because the chances are, even if he kept his horse, he would have a motor in the barn standing beside it.

So our big business has not justified the fears of our people. Exploiters no longer own the big concerns. Bankers no longer own them. Their shares, like motor cars, are spread from one end of the country to the other in every city and village. And broadly speaking, the vast organizations are in skilled hands and the road is reasonably safe.

When we think of what is right or wrong in business, we must take account of the conditions under which such impressions are formed. Everything was wrong with business, or especially big business, in common opinion in 1905. Such prejudices as exist today are much more largely due to the recollections of the old days than to real complaints of this day. Just as the horse driver today is less considerate and less careful on the highway, so it is likely to be true that the smaller units of business, not the larger ones, are less considerate and less careful. . . .

During the last thirty years the moral standards of business have been advanced. A certain amount of astuteness and cleverness and sharpness of the earlier day has disappeared. They would not work very well in large business. A storekeeper may short-measure or short-weigh his customer and make a little by that method. He may even induce his clerk to short-weigh or short-measure. But he cannot organize a vast department store on that basis. Either his employees are honest people who would refuse to do it, or he would soon have as employees a vast organization of crooks who would beat each other and soon ruin the proprietor himself.

Big business does not lend itself readily to dishonesty and crookedness. Great organizations of human beings cannot be built on that theory. You cannot teach an organization to steal from your customer and object very much if your cashier takes money out of the till. Honesty and uprightness must exist in great business organizations on the simple grounds of expediency, if no other. And so as our business has grown larger, I think we can say that moral standards have improved. It is safe for you to buy today, under great trademarks, almost anything you wish without previously examining the package. You will find quantity, quality, and price right. It may be no moral tribute to the managers of business. It may be only the result of their intelligence, for they know that any other practice spells ruin. . . .

Just what is right in all cases we cannot foresee even with the greatest effort. We make mistakes. We learn from our mistakes. We try to correct them in the future. Turbines will blow up occasionally, notwithstanding the multiplication table, when the engineers misapply the rules. Capital will get too much or labor too little, or the public not enough occasionally, when the management misjudges the application of the golden rule to the complicated problems which we have. But by and large, looking over the quarter of a century with which I have been familiar, I am pleased with the rapid progress which we are making toward the right in business.

We are not perfect and never shall be, but we are now training young men with a sense of these great responsibilities and we are providing them experience from our own mistakes. It is our one consolation for making them. As time goes on, I feel that the right in business will more and more prevail. The larger business becomes, the more scrupulously careful the administrators of it will be.

We have had much difficulty with questions of technical competence and moral responsibility in the offices of aldermen, but we have had practically none in the great office of President of the United States. Somehow, as responsibility increases, men are found big enough to meet adequately the great questions of right and wrong which come to them. So I welcome big business and big responsibility, not in the fear that it will make business wrong, but in the hope and belief that it will make business right.

Herbert Hoover, "Dangers from Centralization and Bureaucracy" February 12, 1931

[When the Great Depression had been on for more than a year, President Hoover continued to preach self-reliance, individual initiative and freedom from government controls—as he did in this radio address to the American people.]

. . . In Lincoln's day the dominant problem in our form of government turned upon the issue of states rights. Though less pregnant with disaster, the dominant problem today in our form of government turns in large degree upon the issue of the relationship of Federal, state, and local government responsibilities. We are faced with unceasing agitation that the Federal Government shall assume new financial burdens, that it shall undertake increased burdens in regulation of abuses and in the prosecution of crime.

It is true that since Lincoln's time many forces have swept across state borders and have become more potent than the state or local community can deal with alone either financially or by jurisdiction. Our concept of Federal, state, and local responsibilities is possible of no unchangeable definitions and it must shift with the moving forces in the Nation, but the time has come when we must have more national consideration and decision of the part which each shall assume in these responsibilities.

The Federal Government has assumed many new responsibilities since Lincoln's time, and will probably assume more in the future when the states and local communities can not alone cure abuse or bear the entire cost of national programs, but there is an essential principle that should be maintained in these matters. I am convinced that where Federal action is essential then in most cases it should limit its responsibilities to supplement the states and local communities, and that it should not assume the major rôle or the entire responsibility, in replacement of the states or local government. To do otherwise threatens the whole foundations of local government, which is the very basis of self-government.

The moment responsibilities of any community, particularly in economic and social questions, are shifted from any part of the Nation to Washington, then that community has subjected itself to a remote bureaucracy with its minimum of understanding and of sympathy. It has lost a large part of its voice and its control of its own destiny. Under Federal control the varied conditions of life in our country are forced into standard molds, with all their limitations upon life, either of the individual or the community. Where people divest themselves of local government responsibilities they at once lay the foundation for the destruction of their liberties.

And buried in this problem lies something even deeper. The whole of our governmental machinery was devised for the purpose that through ordered liberty we give incentive and equality of opportunity to every individual to rise to that highest achievement of which he is capable. At once when government is centralized there arises a limitation upon the liberty of the individual and a restriction of individual opportunity. The true growth of the Nation is the growth of character in its citizens. The spread of government destroys initiative and thus destroys character. Character is made in the community as well as in the individual by assuming responsibilities, not by escape from them. Carried to its logical extreme, all this shouldering of individual and community responsibility upon the Government can lead but to the superstate where every man becomes the servant of the State and real liberty is lost. Such was not the government that Lincoln sought to build.

There is an entirely different avenue by which we may both resist this drift to centralized government and at the same time meet a multitude of problems. That is to strengthen in the Nation a sense and an organization of self-help and coöperation to solve as many problems as possible outside of government. We are today passing through a critical test in such a problem arising from the economic depression.

Due to lack of caution in business and to the impact of forces from an outside world, one-half of which is involved in social and political revolution, the march of our prosperity has been retarded. We are projected into temporary unemployment, losses, and hardships. In a Nation rich in resources, many people were faced with hunger and cold through no fault of their own. Our national resources are not only material supplies and material wealth but a spiritual and moral wealth in kindliness, in compassion, in a sense of obligation of neighbor to neighbor and a realization of responsibility by industry, by business, and the community for its social security and its social welfare.

The evidence of our ability to solve great problems outside of Government action and the degree of moral strength with which we emerge from this period will be determined by whether the individuals and the local communities continue to meet their responsibilities.

Throughout this depression I have insisted upon organization of these forces through industry, through local government and through charity, that they should meet this crisis by their own initiative, by the assumption of their own responsibilities. The Federal Government has sought to do its part by example in the expansion of employment, by affording credit to drought sufferers for rehabilitation, and by coöperation with the community, and thus to avoid the opiates of Government charity and the stifling of our national spirit of mutual self-help.

We can take courage and pride in the effective work of thousands of voluntary organizations for provision of employment, for relief of distress, that have sprung up over the entire Nation. Industry and business have recognized a social obligation to their employees as never before. The State and local governments are being helpful. The people are themselves succeeding in this task. Never before in a great depression has there been so systematic a protection against distress; never before has there been so little social disorder;

never before has there been such an outpouring of the spirit of self-sacrifice and of service.

The ever-growing complexity of modern life, with its train of evermore perplexing and difficult problems, is a challenge to our individual characters and to our devotion to our ideals. The resourcefulness of America when challenged has never failed. Success is not gained by leaning upon government to solve all the problems before us. That way leads to enervation of will and destruction of character. Victory over this depression and over our other difficulties will be won by the resolution of our people to fight their own battles in their own communities, by stimulating their ingenuity to solve their own problems, by taking new courage to be masters of their own destiny in the struggle of life. This is not the easy way, but it is the American way. And it was Lincoln's way.

The ultimate goal of the American social ideal is equality of opportunity and individual initiative. These are not born of bureaucracy. This ideal is the expression of the spirit of our people. This ideal obtained at the birth of the Republic. It was the ideal of Lincoln. It is the ideal upon which the Nation has risen to unparalleled greatness. . . .

Herbert Hoover, Veto of the Muscle Shoals Bill
March 3, 1931

[Following is President Hoover's veto of the bill to create government-run power and fertilizer plants at Muscle Shoals on the Tennessee River. One of Franklin Roosevelt's first acts as President was to sign an expanded version of this bill into law, thereby establishing the Tennessee Valley Authority.]

. . . I am firmly opposed to the Government entering into any business the major purpose of which is competition with our citizens. There are national emergencies which require that the Government should temporarily enter the field of business, but they must be emergency actions and in matters where the cost of the project is secondary to much higher considerations. There are many localities where the Federal Government is justified in the construction of great dams and reservoirs, where navigation, flood control, reclamation or stream regulation are of dominant importance, and where they are beyond the capacity or purpose of private or local government capital to construct. In these cases power is often a by-product and should be disposed of by contract or lease. But for the Federal Government deliberately to go out to build up and expand an occasion to the major purpose of a power and manufacturing business is to break down the initiative and enterprise of the American people; it is destruction of equality of opportunity of our people; it is the negation of the ideals upon which our civilization has been based.

This bill raises one of the important issues confronting our people. That is squarely the issue of Federal Government ownership and operation of power and manufacturing business not as a minor by-product but as a major purpose. Involved in this question is the agitation against the conduct of the power industry. The power problem is not to be solved by the project in this bill. The remedy for abuses in the conduct of that industry lies in regulation and not by the Federal Government entering upon the business itself. I have recommended to the Congress on various occasions that action should be taken to establish Federal regulation of interstate power in cooperation with State authorities. This bill would launch the Federal Government upon a policy of ownership and operation of power utilities upon a basis of competition instead of by the proper Government function of regulation for the protection of all the people. I hesitate to contemplate the future of our institutions, of our country if the preoccupation of its officials is to be no longer the promotion of justice and equal opportunity but is to be devoted to barter in the markets. That is not liberalism, it is degeneration.

This proposal can be effectively opposed upon other and perhaps narrower grounds. The establishment of a Federal-operated power business and fertilizer factory in the Tennessee Valley means Federal control from Washington with all the vicissitudes of national politics and the tyrannies of remote bureaucracy imposed upon the people of that valley without voice by them in their own resources, the overriding of State and local government, the undermining of State and local responsibility. The very history of this project over the past 10 years should be a complete demonstration of the ineptness of the Federal Government to administer such enterprise and of the penalties which the local community suffers under it.

This bill distinctly proposes to enter the field of powers reserved to the States. It would deprive the adjacent States of the right to control rates for this power and would deprive them of taxes on property within their borders and would invade and weaken the authority of local government. . . .

The real development of the resources and the industries of the Tennessee Valley can only be accomplished by the people in that valley themselves. Muscle Shoals can only be administered by the people upon the ground, responsible to their own communities, directing them solely for the benefit of their communities and not for purposes of pursuit of social theories or national politics. Any other course deprives them of liberty. . . .

CHAPTER X. THE NEW DEAL

When Franklin D. Roosevelt took office on March 4, 1933, the American people had little idea of what lay before them. Unlike Jefferson, Jackson, Lincoln and Wilson, Roosevelt professed no commitment to an ideology and led no grass roots reform movement. His campaign speeches and his post-election remarks gave little indication of what he intended to do. The Democratic platform of 1932 promised some reforms—notably the enactment of a law providing for state-controlled old age and unemployment insurance—but was otherwise vague or downright conservative, accusing Hoover of having spent more money than the country could afford. Roosevelt vowed that he would deal energetically with the emergency that confronted him, the most serious in American history since the Civil War, and he appealed to the beleaguered nation to follow him as it would a wartime commander, not as it would the head of a party.

He quickly proved himself a superb commander, inspiring confidence, calming fears, devising bold new strategies as conditions dictated. During the first hundred days of his administration he sent to Congress, and Congress promptly passed, sixteen major (and innumerable minor) pieces of legislation that affected every community, class and interest in America. There were laws providing large-scale relief to the unemployed (the Federal Emergency Relief Act and the Public Works Administration), establishing a government-run public power and regional planning corporation (the Tennessee Valley Authority), bringing banks and securities under federal control (the Emergency Banking Act, the Banking Act of 1933 and the Federal Securities Act), creating extensive work programs for youth (the Civilian Conservation Corps Act), granting easier credit to farmers (the Farm Credit Act) and homeowners (the Home Owners Loan Act) and, above all, regulating the prices and production of agricultural commodities (the Agricultural Adjustment Act) and industrial goods (the National Industrial Recovery Act). Roosevelt and his "brain trust" drew up these measures without any over-all plan to guide them. Radical experimentation was their only dogma. To restore the economy they were willing to try any method that worked, short of outright nationalization and dictatorship.

But by the summer of 1933 a coherent political pattern had begun to emerge from the chaos of legislation and executive orders. It had become apparent that the Roosevelt administration intended to bring the major economic groups in the country—business, labor and agriculture—into close partnership with one another. In its quest for social harmony the administration pursued a twofold strategy. In the first place, it sought to maintain a genuine parity among the interests. Chiefly, this meant strengthening organized labor so that it could meet organized capital as an equal. Section 7a of the NIRA gave workers the right to "organize and bargain collectively through representatives of their own choosing." And the government enforced this right by means of a special Labor Board, whose chairman was Senator Robert Wagner of New York, a staunch friend of unions.

In the second place, the administration sought to do away with competition as the governing ethic of American economic life. Under the provisions of the NIRA the corporations of each industry, led by the giants, were to join with the government in framing codes regulating prices, profits, wages, output, etc. Roosevelt and his brain trust assumed that overproduction had brought about the collapse of the economy. It followed that if production could be limited through industry-wide planning, prices would inevitably rise and business would begin to move again. Co-operation and controlled scarcity also underlay the thinking behind the Agricultural Adjustment Act. The government paid farmers generous subsidies for reducing crop acreage, with the result that farm income rose as production diminished. In general, the architects of the early New Deal foresaw a moderately planned society in which the major interest groups, acting in concert, would resolve their historic antagonisms and bring order and equity to the market place.

Not all the New Dealers were pleased with the neo-Hamiltonian policies of the administration. The more liberal among them thought that too much solicitude was being shown to large corporations. To be sure, workers and farmers received special concessions under the legislation passed during the first hundred days. Yet, these dissatisfied New Dealers argued, the old problems arising from the maldistribution of wealth would reassert themselves unless radical reforms of banking and industry were instituted. Roosevelt himself might have subscribed to these views. He had always considered himself a Jeffersonian democrat. As a Wilsonian progressive he had always distrusted the moneyed aristocracy. And as a two-term governor of New York he had carried forward the liberal reforms begun by his predecessor, Al Smith. But the national emergency forced Roosevelt to cast aside his sentiments, at least for the moment, in the interest of unity and recovery. For the time being he was concerned only that the federal government should set down rational guidelines for every organized group in society. In its main features the early New Deal harked back to the "New Nationalism" of Theodore Roosevelt and the Bull Moose party.

But the unity established in 1933 began to break down the following year. As economic conditions improved, the partners in the New Deal's grand coalition fell out, each accusing the administration of favoring the other. Big business complained that the National Recovery Administration was partial to labor and meddled too much in prescribing industrial codes. Bankers and conservative Democrats protested against the administration's monetary and fiscal policies, charging that the abandonment of the gold standard, the devaluation of the dollar, the billions spent purchasing silver —all designed to "reflate" the economy and mollify the silver and easy money bloc in Congress—amounted to criminal anarchy. Wall Street investors and the banking community were particularly angry at the Securities and Exchange Act because it imposed rigorous controls over investment procedures. And the wealthy classes in general denounced Roosevelt for blithely incurring huge deficits to finance his boondoggling relief projects. Having learned nothing and forgotten nothing, the bankers, the "gold Democrats," and the industrialists urged Roosevelt to cut the budget, release supererogatory bureaucrats and restore the fiscal responsibility that had obtained in the 1920s.

In the meantime, opposition to the New Deal consensus rose up from the left. Labor unions, protected now by federal law, struck more often and more violently in 1934 than they had at any time since 1919. The unemployed, whose ranks had not appreciably diminished despite the various relief measures, insisted that the government act at once to provide jobs. By the hundreds of thousands they joined Huey Long's "Share Our Wealth" clubs. Long, the Louisiana autocrat, proposed a tax on the rich sufficient to guarantee each family a "homestead" of its own: an annual income of $5000. Equally extravagant in its promises, and even more popular, was Francis E. Townsend's Old Age Revolving Pension scheme, according to which the government was to pay each person over sixty a $200-a-month pension. The Western agrarians demanded that the government nationalize the large federal banks, issue cheap credit, and buy still greater amounts of silver at still higher prices. Small businessmen and small farmers complained of the government's indifference, even hostility, to their needs. For it had become a notorious fact that the New Deal programs mostly benefited the big producers.

The ideal of unity was completely shattered by 1935, forcing Roosevelt to choose between conservative and liberal courses, between advancing the New Deal under pressure from below or abandoning reform in the name of retrenchment and stability. In his annual message on January 4, 1935, he announced the course he would follow. The government, he said, was going to start up a huge public works program for the jobless, clear slums and build houses for low-income families, and establish a comprehensive social security system covering old age, sickness and unemployment. Accordingly, in April Congress passed its most significant law in nearly two years, the Emergency Relief Appropriation Act. The government was given billions of dollars to be spent by the Works Progress Administration in constructing highways, parks, bridges and public buildings of every description and in subsidizing scholarship and the arts. The President was also given sweeping powers under the Act to deal with other aspects of poverty: to resettle the urban and rural poor, lend money to sharecroppers and tenant farmers, help local communities build and manage their own power facilities (through the Rural Electrification Administration), and (under the National Youth Administration) create jobs or provide assistance for hundreds of thousands of youths between the ages of sixteen and twenty-five.

The Supreme Court's invalidation of the NIRA in late May 1935 hastened Roosevelt's movement to the left. The ruling destroyed the foundation of his recovery program, and he had to act quickly to stave off the insurgent movement, led by Long and Townsend, that issued forth from the cities. And so, between June and August 1935, in the "Second Hundred Days" of the New Deal, Congress enacted five momentous laws which transformed the existing property and class relations of American life. First, the government threw its weight behind the cause of organized labor with the passage of the Wagner Act. The new National Labor Relations Board prevented employers from obstructing the workers' right to join unions, prohibited unfair labor practices and ensured that both sides bargained collectively over contracts. The Wagner Act ended once and for all the fiction that the individual worker met the corporation as an equal on the free market, where he exchanged his labor for wages, under the best terms possible for both parties.

Then, in rapid succession, Congress passed the following laws: the Social Security Act, which set up the rudiments of an old age and unemployment insurance scheme, the premiums to be paid equally by workers and employers; the Banking Act of 1935, which brought the Federal Reserve System, and therefore the country's credit facilities, under government supervision; the Public Utilities Act, which gave federal regulatory agencies authority over the utilities, and more especially over the holding companies that ran them; and the Wealth Tax Act, sometimes referred to as the "Soak the Rich Act," which attempted to reduce the great concentration of wealth at the top stratum of American society by imposing a sharply graduated tax on income, inheritance, excess profits and corporations. These far-reaching reforms silenced the thunder on the left. Organized labor, the unemployed, the elderly, the small entrepreneurs and farmers remained within the Democratic fold, loyal to the President who had made good his promises to them.

The 1936 election crystallized political differences between the administration and its enemies. Roosevelt had thrown off the Hamiltonian aspect of the early New Deal and affirmed a philosophy of neo-Jeffersonianism. The ideal of equal rights, if it was to apply to the twentieth century, required the intervention of big government on the side of the powerless, who constituted the majority, and opposition to the privileged few. Roosevelt conceived Jeffersonianism to mean economic as well as political democracy; thanks to his New Deal, the welfare state became an inseparable part of the country's Jeffersonian inheritance.

But the New Deal's opponents also called themselves Jeffersonians. The debates of 1935–36 were reminiscent of those that had taken place in the late 1890s, when Northern Republicans and Southern Democrats had laid claim to the same set of principles. Like the Northern Republicans, the New Dealers sought in the name of equal rights to strengthen the national government and so bring about a new balance of social power, a new set of legal and political norms. The Jeffersonianism of the anti-New Dealers, like that of the ante-bellum Democrats, was narrow and fundamentalist; it valued states' rights and the sanctity of property, regarded the national government as despotic, and opposed any change of policy that threatened the status quo. This was the Jeffersonianism repeatedly espoused by ex-President Hoover and by Roosevelt's onetime friend and mentor, Al Smith, now the spokesman of the ultraconservative Liberty League. "It is all right with me," Smith said in 1936, in one of his attacks on the New Deal before a typical Liberty League audience of bankers, corporation lawyers and industrialists, "it is all right with me if they want to disguise themselves as Norman Thomas or Karl Marx or Lenin or any of the rest of that bunch, but what I won't stand for is allowing them to march under the banner of Jefferson, Jackson and Cleveland."

The 1936 election results were astonishing, not so much

because Alf Landon, the Republican candidate, received only eight electoral votes to Roosevelt's 523 and only 16,600,000 popular votes to Roosevelt's 27,700,000, but because the third parties lost so badly. William Lemke, the choice of the Long-Townsend-Coughlin forces, won only 900,000 votes; Norman Thomas, the Socialist candidate, won a mere 187,000, a fifth of his 1932 total; and the Communist candidate received 80,000 votes, compared to more than 100,000 four years before. In short, Roosevelt had neutralized the left and the right, and in the process had forged a powerful urban coalition consisting of labor, the major ethnic groups and Negroes.

This coalition had actually begun to form before the Great Depression: it was in the 1920s that the children of Eastern and Southern European immigrants came of age; by 1928 the big cities had gone Democratic by a slight margin for the first time since the Civil War. In 1932 the urban vote for Roosevelt was enormous; in 1936 it was spectacular. The shift in the Negro vote was especially dramatic. In 1932 a majority of Negroes still voted Republican, just as they had done in every national election since the Civil War. It was in 1936 that they first voted Democratic. But Negroes supported Roosevelt less for racial than for economic reasons; Roosevelt scrupulously avoided civil rights issues because he was unwilling to antagonize the Southerners who ran most of the Congressional committees. He did appoint numerous Negroes to federal jobs, however, and New Deal social reforms benefited both urban and rural Negroes, nearly all of whom were desperately poor. "My friends," said a Negro leader in 1932, "go turn Lincoln's picture to the wall. The debt has been paid in full."

Roosevelt's fortunes took a turn for the worse precisely at the moment of his triumph. The 1936 election reduced the Republican party to a corporal's guard. When the Seventy-fifth Congress opened in 1937 it contained only 16 Republican Senators (out of 96) and 89 Representatives (out of 435). There was nothing, it appeared, that Roosevelt could not do. In his inaugural address he strongly implied that he would carry the New Deal forward and propose further reforms. Something had to be done, he insisted, to help the "tens of millions" of Americans who were "denied the greater part of what the very lowest standards of today call the necessities of life." American democracy, he feared, would not long endure if "one third of a nation" remained "ill-housed, ill-clad, ill-nourished."

But one obstacle still stood in the government's way: the Supreme Court. Exercising its power of judicial review to the extreme, the Court had singlehandedly abolished the early New Deal, declaring unconstitutional the NIRA and the AAA as well as the Farm Bankruptcy Act, the Railroad Retirement Act, the Guffey-Snyder Bituminous Coal Conservation Act, and other measures. Roosevelt, like Jefferson, Jackson and Lincoln before him, felt that the Court, not the President or Congress, was violating the Constitution by imposing its will, often the will of five men, upon the country. Accordingly, as his first order of business in the new congressional term, he presented a bill that would have reorganized the whole court system. Its central provision gave the President authority to appoint up to six new Supreme Court justices—one for each incumbent justice who failed to retire at seventy. Passage of the bill would have enabled Roosevelt to staff the Court with his own men and so ensure the success of his program.

Here was the issue that the New Deal's opponents were waiting for. They accused Roosevelt of trying to "pack" the Court, of usurping its prerogatives, of following the dictators of Europe in seeking to destroy the independence of the judiciary (although in fact Roosevelt's reorganization bill was modest, given the problems that confronted him and the mandate he had just received, and it did not threaten the judiciary's independence). Most defenders of the Court, moreover, were less than disinterested, since they were about to break with the administration anyway. Democrats from the Far West and Midwest, representing silver and easy money interests and the more prosperous farmers, were opposed to the "socialistic" direction that the New Deal was taking. Defending the Court too were the "Bourbon" Democrats of the South, who resented federal help to sharecroppers and tenant farmers. In short, a viable anti-New Deal coalition had been gestating for some time; the "Court-packing" issue only served as the midwife to its birth.

Roosevelt lost his fight over the reorganization bill (though Congress did pass a law giving federal judges over seventy the option of retiring with a pension), but he won the battle over the Court. While the bill was being considered in committee, the Court, by one-vote margins, validated the major reforms of 1935, namely the Wagner Act, the Social Security Act and the Farm Mortgage Moratorium Act (which saved thousands of farms about to go under). And in the midst of the fight, one of the implacable foes of the New Deal, Justice Willis VanDevanter, retired. During the next four years six more justices, including three extreme conservatives, left the Bench, allowing Roosevelt to "pack" the Court just as he had wanted to do in the first place.

By the end of the decade the Court had come fully to accept the constitutionality of social reform. Interpretation of the commerce and general welfare clauses of the Constitution was sufficiently broadened to permit Congress to deal with the economy as it saw fit. The Court now interpreted the due process clauses of the First and Fourteenth Amendments to mean simple conformity to constitutional procedure; they were no longer seen as furnishing unqualified protection for property rights. At the same time, however, the Court extended its protection to civil liberties and began to strike down state laws interfering with freedom of speech, press, assembly, petition and religion. The Court was clearly moving toward the nationalization of the Bill of Rights; it was establishing a new hierarchy of legal values, with political and personal freedom occupying the summit and economic freedom the base. And some justices, led by Hugo Black (Roosevelt's first appointee) were later to affirm that the First Amendment laid down absolute guarantees to the individual, guarantees that neither the federal government nor the states could infringe in the slightest. On the other hand, some justices were to argue that no absolute rule, no alleged hierarchy of freedoms should restrict the public's right to experiment and act according to pragmatic need, and that consequently the legislatures could limit the political rights of citizens just as they could the economic. These two liberal schools were to dominate legal debate in the decades following World War II.

Differences between pro- and anti-New Dealers intensified after the Court conflict had died down. Conservatives were alarmed by the sit-down strikes that took place in the large automobile, steel, rubber and electrical plants, and by the organization of immense industrial unions, whose rise could, in part, be attributed to the Wagner Act. What was more, Roosevelt conspicuously failed to defend employer property in refusing to send troops to drive out the strikers. Southern politicians were dismayed by the Farm Tenants Act of 1937, which contained truly radical features in behalf of poor farmers. And the banking and real estate interests were displeased by the National Housing Act, which provided loans to communities for slum clearance and public housing developments; it was the beginning of a permanent federal involvement in low-cost housing.

Between 1935 and 1937 the economy improved steadily, and Roosevelt was able to cut the WPA rolls in the hope of attaining a balanced budget. But then there was a sudden and spectacular drop in production. Between Labor Day and Christmas of 1937 two million men lost their jobs (on top of the eight million or so who had never gone back to work), and by the following spring the number of recent unemployed had risen to four million. Roosevelt was persuaded that the great corporations, by maintaining artificially high prices, were responsible for the new setback. His attitude toward big business changed. He now felt that only a policy of competition, preferably between small producers, could save the economy from inevitable destruction. Roosevelt had come around to the Wilson-Brandeis position.

Accordingly, he embarked on a trust-busting campaign in 1938. The Justice Department's anti-trust division, armed with a battery of militant young lawyers, was placed under the command of Thurman Arnold, who, paradoxically, had written books decrying the American "myth" of free competition. But while Arnold did bring a large number of suits against industries engaged in restraint of trade, in general very little came of the trust-busting campaign, for Roosevelt asked for no drastic—it would have amounted to revolutionary

—legislation to break up the trusts. Instead a joint executive-legislative committee (the Temporary National Economic Committee) was established in 1938 to examine monopoly practices. The TNEC, which held hearings for a little more than two years, issued a series of enlightening, though not very profound, reports on the concentration of industry and wealth, and made some moderate recommendations. These gave big business no cause for alarm.

Long before the creation of the TNEC it was obvious that the coalition of Southern Democrats and Northern Republicans had grown strong enough to stand off the New Deal. The extra session of Congress that Roosevelt called in November 1937 to take up important new legislation produced nothing of consequence. The following year, after much pulling and hauling, Congress passed one major reform, the Fair Labor Standards Act, which prescribed minimum wages and hours for workers engaged in interstate commerce and outlawed the employment of children under sixteen. It excluded, however, precisely the people who needed help most, those *not* engaged in interstate commerce—i.e., laundry workers, agricultural workers, restaurant and hotel workers. Moreover, before conceding to pass the Fair Labor Standards Act, Congress demonstrated just how conservative it had become when it severely reduced the taxes on wealthy corporations and individuals.

Roosevelt felt that he and the American people were being betrayed. After all, hadn't the people given him an incontestable mandate to carry out his program, and under his leadership hadn't the Democratic party won an unprecedented series of victories? Yet party conservatives, mainly the Southerners who ran the congressional committees, were sabotaging his program and therefore the will of the majority. Concluding that such men should join a party that reflected their political philosophies, Roosevelt publicly opposed a number of conservative Democrats in the 1938 primary. In doing so he was in effect calling for the transformation of the American party system; he was asking that it be centralized under presidential leadership and made to conform to ideological differences. The primary results demonstrated that most Americans were not prepared for such a transformation. With one exception, all the politicians Roosevelt opposed were returned to office. And in the congressional elections that took place several months later the Republicans scored heavily, winning eighty seats in the House—most of them from liberal Northern constituencies—and seven in the Senate. The election resolved all doubts: as the agent of domestic reform the New Deal was dead.

Though future generations would ponder the larger meaning of the New Deal, its accomplishments and failures were already evident at the time of its passing. When Roosevelt took office, few people could have confidently asserted that America would not succumb to "the wave of the future"—to some form of totalitarianism. Yet America in 1939 was as democratic as she had ever been. In fact, she was more democratic, for the New Deal helped to redress the tremendous imbalance of social power that had been a feature of American life since the Civil War. By 1939 collective bargaining was an established procedure in the major industries, enabling labor for the first time to confront capital on an equal basis. To the rights of the workingman were added the rights of the aged under social security, and also the rights of farmers, who, thanks to price supports, now enjoyed protection from the vagaries of the market. The New Deal created the rudiments of a welfare state for people otherwise powerless in an advanced technological society.

The New Deal's public works programs left a rich legacy for future generations. In ten years, the PWA and the WPA had built two thirds of the country's school buildings, city halls, courthouses, playgrounds and sewage plants, and nearly half its hospitals and clinics, museums, libraries, dock facilities and airports, not to mention numerous bridges and tunnels. The country owed a great debt to the National Youth Administration, which, in the course of its eight-year existence, helped millions of students attend high school or college, or learn skilled trades; and also to the CCC, which cleared hundreds of streams and reservoirs, built thousands of wildlife shelters, planted hundreds of millions of trees and stocked over a billion fish. And among the New Deal's most impressive accomplishments was the cheap electric power it brought to poor people in rural communities and small towns.

These facts only make it clear that the New Deal "revolution" was no revolution at all. Actually, by reforming the system the New Deal preserved it. American capitalism came out of its ordeal stronger than before, though few capitalists then realized it or were willing to acknowledge it. The creation of powerful industrial unions and the practice of collective bargaining reduced the number of strikes and, from management's point of view, radically increased labor efficiency. Management also discovered that social security taxes constituted no intolerable burden: they could easily be passed on to consumers.

In other respects the rich had little to complain about and much to be grateful for, considering the distemper of American life in the 1930s. The Roosevelt administration nationalized no industry and confiscated no one's private property. And despite all its reforms the New Deal brought about no significant redistribution of wealth. Income differences between various strata were roughly the same in 1939 as they had been in 1929. To be sure, the New Deal enabled millions of American workers to obtain property of their own—if one assumes that social security is a property right. But that right was not acquired at the expense of the rich. Furthermore, even the better-paid workers, who derived the most under the system, received only barely enough to subsist on if they were lacking other sources of income. The American welfare state was, and has continued to be, at once regressive in its taxation and niggardly in its benefits.

It took World War II to settle the most difficult problem that beset the New Deal. As late as 1939, between a fourth and a third of the labor force was still unemployed and dependent on government relief. Thanks to the conflict in Europe, more especially to Nazi Germany's spectacular victories, the administration began to spend billions for defense. This was just the stimulus that the economy needed, and by 1940 the rate of gross national production had finally attained its 1929 level. The subsequent development of a full-scale war economy abolished unemployment.

The war launched the New Deal on another phase of its career, as Roosevelt attempted to fulfill the promise that Woodrow Wilson had made during World War I. Wilson had sought and failed to impart the gift of American freedom to mankind, to establish the principles of Jeffersonian democracy as the basis of international relations. The American people were much more receptive to Wilsonian ideals in 1945 than they had been in 1919. Roosevelt did not have to inspire them with high-minded rhetoric nor lead a crusade to prove that *this* war certainly was a war for democracy, that its outcome would determine whether the world would be free or slave. For who could doubt that the triumph of Fascism would lead to the enslavement of mankind? With near unanimity Americans supported Roosevelt's program of a just peace, based on the maintenance of international law, opposition to colonialism, and a more equitable distribution of the world's wealth, as defined in general terms in the Four Freedoms, the Atlantic Charter and the United Nations Charter. No longer was there an isolationist movement capable of challenging, much less vitiating, such a program. The Republican party was not about to repeat the mistake of 1919.

Franklin D. Roosevelt, The Commonwealth Club Speech September 23, 1932

[Roosevelt's speech before the Commonwealth Club of San Francisco, the most important of his presidential campaign, defined the character of the early New Deal.]

. . . When we look about us, we are likely to forget how hard people have worked to win the privilege of government. The growth of the national governments of Europe was a struggle for the development of a centralized force in the nation, strong enough to impose peace upon ruling barons. In many instances the victory of the central government, the creation of a strong central government, was a haven of refuge to the individual. The people preferred the master far away to the exploitation and cruelty of the smaller master near at hand.

But the creators of national government were perforce

ruthless men. They were often cruel in their methods, but they did strive steadily toward something that society needed and very much wanted, a strong central state, able to keep the peace, to stamp out civil war, to put the unruly nobleman in his place, and to permit the bulk of individuals to live safely. The man of ruthless force had his place in developing a pioneer country, just as he did in fixing the power of the central government in the development of nations. Society paid him well for his services and its development. When the development among the nations of Europe, however, had been completed, ambition and ruthlessness, having served its term, tended to overstep its mark.

There came a growing feeling that government was conducted for the benefit of a few who thrived unduly at the expense of all. The people sought a balancing—a limiting force. There came gradually, through town councils, trade guilds, national parliaments, by constitution and by popular participation and control, limitations on arbitrary power.

Another factor that tended to limit the power of those who ruled, was the rise of the ethical conception that a ruler bore a responsibility for the welfare of his subjects.

The American colonies were born in this struggle. The American Revolution was a turning point in it. After the revolution the struggle continued and shaped itself in the public life of the country. There were those who because they had seen the confusion which attended the years of war for American independence surrendered to the belief that popular government was essentially dangerous and essentially unworkable. They were honest people, my friends, and we cannot deny that their experience had warranted some measure of fear. The most brilliant, honest and able exponent of this point of view was Hamilton. He was too impatient of slow-moving methods. Fundamentally he believed that the safety of the republic lay in the autocratic strength of its government, that the destiny of individuals was to serve that government, and that fundamentally a great and strong group of central institutions, guided by a small group of able and public spirited citizens could best direct all government.

But Mr. Jefferson, in the summer of 1776, after drafting the Declaration of Independence turned his mind to the same problem and took a different view. He did not deceive himself with outward forms. Government to him was a means to an end, not an end in itself; it might be either a refuge and a help or a threat and a danger, depending on the circumstances. We find him carefully analyzing the society for which he was to organize a government. "We have no paupers. The great mass of our population is of laborers, our rich who cannot live without labor, either manual or professional, being few and of moderate wealth. Most of the laboring class possess property, cultivate their own lands, have families and from the demand for their labor, are enabled to exact from the rich and the competent such prices as enable them to feed abundantly, clothe above mere decency, to labor moderately and raise their families."

These people, he considered, had two sets of rights, those of "personal competency" and those involved in acquiring and possessing property. By "personal competency" he meant the right of free thinking, freedom of forming and expressing opinions, and freedom of personal living each man according to his own lights. To insure the first set of rights, a government must so order its functions as not to interfere with the individual. But even Jefferson realized that the exercise of the property rights might so interfere with the rights of the individual that the government, without whose assistance the property rights could not exist, must intervene, not to destroy individualism but to protect it.

You are familiar with the great political duel which followed; and how Hamilton, and his friends, building towards a dominant centralized power were at length defeated in the great election of 1800, by Mr. Jefferson's party. Out of that duel came the two parties, Republican and Democratic, as we know them today.

So began, in American political life, the new day, the day of the individual against the system, the day in which individualism was made the great watchword of American life. The happiest of economic conditions made that day long and splendid. On the Western frontier, land was substantially free. No one, who did not shirk the task of earning a living, was entirely without opportunity to do so. Depressions could, and did, come and go; but they could not alter the fundamental fact that most of the people lived partly by selling their labor and partly by extracting their livelihood from the soil, so that starvation and dislocation were practically impossible. At the very worst there was always the possibility of climbing into a covered wagon and moving west where the untilled prairies afforded a haven for men to whom the East did not provide a place. So great were our natural resources that we could offer this relief not only to our own people, but to the distressed of all the world; we could invite immigration from Europe, and welcome it with open arms. Traditionally, when a depression came a new section of land was opened in the West; and even our temporary misfortune served our manifest destiny.

It was in the middle of the 19th century that a new force was released and a new dream created. The force was what is called the industrial revolution, the advance of steam and machinery and the rise of the forerunners of the modern industrial plant. The dream was the dream of an economic machine, able to raise the standard of living for everyone; to bring luxury within the reach of the humblest; to annihilate distance by steam power and later by electricity, and to release everyone from the drudgery of the heaviest manual toil. It was to be expected that this would necessarily affect government. Heretofore, government had merely been called upon to produce conditions within which people could live happily, labor peacefully, and rest secure. Now it was called upon to aid in the consummation of this new dream. There was, however, a shadow over the dream. To be made real, it required use of the talents of men of tremendous will, and tremendous ambition, since by no other force could the problems of financing and engineering and new developments be brought to a consummation.

So manifest were the advantages of the machine age, however, that the United States fearlessly, cheerfully, and, I think, rightly, accepted the bitter with the sweet. It was thought that no price was too high to pay for the advantages which we could draw from a finished industrial system. The history of the last half century is accordingly in large measure a history of a group of financial Titans, whose methods were not scrutinized with too much care, and who were honored in proportion as they produced the results, irrespective of the means they used. The financiers who pushed the railroads to the Pacific were always ruthless, often wasteful, and frequently corrupt; but they did build railroads, and we have them today. It has been estimated that the American investor paid for the American railway system more than three times over in the process; but despite this fact the net advantage was to the United States. As long as we had free land; as long as population was growing by leaps and bounds; as long as our industrial plants were insufficient to supply our own needs, society chose to give the ambitious man free play and unlimited reward provided only that he produced the economic plant so much desired.

During this period of expansion, there was equal opportunity for all and the business of government was not to interfere but to assist in the development of industry. This was done at the request of business men themselves. The tariff was originally imposed for the purpose of "fostering our infant industry", a phrase I think the older among you will remember as a political issue not so long ago. The railroads were subsidized, sometimes by grants of money, oftener by grants of land; some of the most valuable oil lands in the United States were granted to assist the financing of the railroad which pushed through the Southwest. A nascent merchant marine was assisted by grants of money, or by mail subsidies, so that our steam shipping might ply the seven seas. Some of my friends tell me that they do not want the Government in business. With this I agree; but I wonder whether they realize the implications of the past. For while it has been American doctrine that the government must not go into business in competition with private enterprises, still it has been traditional particularly in Republican administrations for business urgently to ask the government to put at private disposal all kinds of government assistance. The same man who tells you that he does not want to see the government interfere in business—and he means it, and has plenty of good reasons for saying so—is the first to go to Washington and ask the government for a prohibitory tariff on his product. When things get just bad enough—as they did two years ago —he will go with equal speed to the United States government and ask for a loan; and the Reconstruction Finance Corporation is the outcome of it. Each group has sought protection from the government for its own special interests, without realizing that the function of government must be to favor no small group at the expense of its duty to protect the rights of personal freedom and of private property of all its citizens.

In retrospect we can now see that the turn of the tide came with the turn of the century. We were reaching our last frontier; there was no more free land and our industrial combinations had become great uncontrolled and irresponsible units of power within the state. Clear-sighted men saw with fear the danger that opportunity would no longer be equal; that the growing corporation, like the feudal baron of old, might threaten the economic freedom of individuals to earn a living. In that hour, our antitrust laws were born. The cry was raised against the great corporations. Theodore Roosevelt, the first great Republican progressive, fought a Presidential campaign on the issue of "trust busting" and talked freely about malefactors of great wealth. If the government had a policy it was rather to turn the clock back, to destroy the large combinations and to return to the time when every man owned his individual small business.

This was impossible; Theodore Roosevelt, abandoning the idea of "trust busting", was forced to work out a difference between "good" trusts and "bad" trusts. The Supreme Court set forth the famous "rule of reason" by which it seems to have meant that a concentration of industrial power was permissible if the method by which it got its power, and the use it made of that power, was reasonable.

Woodrow Wilson, elected in 1912, saw the situation more clearly. Where Jefferson had feared the encroachment of political power on the lives of individuals, Wilson knew that the new power was financial. He saw, in the highly centralized economic system, the despot of the twentieth century, on whom great masses of individuals relied for their safety and their livelihood, and whose irresponsibility and greed (if it were not controlled) would reduce them to starvation and penury. The concentration of financial power had not proceeded so far in 1912 as it has today; but it had grown far enough for Mr. Wilson to realize fully its implications. . . .

A glance at the situation today only too clearly indicates that equality of opportunity as we have known it no longer exists. Our industrial plant is built; the problem just now is whether under existing conditions it is not overbuilt. Our last frontier has long since been reached, and there is practically no more free land. More than half of our people do not live on the farms or on lands and cannot derive a living by cultivating their own property. There is no safety valve in the form of a Western prairie to which those thrown out of work by the Eastern economic machines can go for a new start. We are not able to invite the immigration from Europe to share our endless plenty. We are now providing a drab living for our own people.

Our system of constantly rising tariffs has at last reacted against us to the point of closing our Canadian frontier on the north, our European markets on the east, many of our Latin American markets to the south, and a goodly proportion of our Pacific markets on the west, through the retaliatory tariffs of those countries. It has forced many of our great industrial institutions who exported their surplus production to such countries, to establish plants in such countries, within the tariff walls. This has resulted in the reduction of the operation of their American plants, and opportunity for employment.

Just as freedom to farm has ceased, so also the opportunity in business has narrowed. It still is true that men can start small enterprises, trusting to native shrewdness and ability to keep abreast of competitors; but area after area has been preempted altogether by the great corporations, and even in the fields which still have no great concerns, the small man starts under a handicap. The unfeeling statistics of the past three decades show that the independent business man is running a losing race. Perhaps he is forced to the wall; perhaps he cannot command credit; perhaps he is "squeezed out", in Mr. Wilson's words, by highly organized corporate competitors, as your corner grocery man can tell you. Recently a careful study was made of the concentration of business in the United States. It showed that our economic life was dominated by some six hundred odd corporations who controlled two-thirds

of American industry. Ten million small business men divided the other third. More striking still, it appeared that if
the process of concentration goes on at the same rate, at the
end of another century we shall have all American industry
controlled by a dozen corporations, and run by perhaps a
hundred men. Put plainly, we are steering a steady course
toward economic oligarchy, if we are not there already.

Clearly, all this calls for a re-appraisal of values. A mere
builder of more industrial plants, a creator of more railroad
systems, an organizer of more corporations, is as likely to be a
danger as a help. The day of the great promoter or the financial Titan, to whom we granted anything if only he would
build, or develop, is over. Our task now is not discovery or
exploitation of natural resources, or necessarily producing
more goods. It is the soberer, less dramatic business of administering resources and plants already in hand, of seeking
to reestablish foreign markets for our surplus production, of
meeting the problem of underconsumption, of adjusting production to consumption, of distributing wealth and products
more equitably, of adapting existing economic organizations to the service of the people. The day of enlightened
administration has come.

Just as in older times the central government was first a
haven of refuge, and then a threat, so now in a closer economic system the central and ambitious financial unit is no
longer a servant of national desire, but a danger. I would
draw the parallel one step farther. We did not think because
national government had become a threat in the 18th century that therefore we should abandon the principle of national government. Nor today should we abandon the principle of strong economic units called corporations, merely
because their power is susceptible of easy abuse. In other
times we dealt with the problem of an unduly ambitious
central government by modifying it gradually into a constitutional democratic government. So today we are modifying
and controlling our economic units. . . .

Every man has a right to life; and this means that he has
also a right to make a comfortable living. He may by sloth or
crime decline to exercise that right; but it may not be denied
him. We have no actual famine or dearth; our industrial

and agricultural mechanism can produce enough and to spare. Our government formal and informal, political and economic, owes to every one an avenue to possess himself of a portion of that plenty sufficient for his needs, through his own work.

Every man has a right to his own property; which means a right to be assured, to the fullest extent attainable, in the safety of his savings. By no other means can men carry the burdens of those parts of life which, in the nature of things, afford no chance of labor; childhood, sickness, old age. In all thought of property, this right is paramount; all other property rights must yield to it. If, in accord with this principle, we must restrict the operations of the speculator, the manipulator, even the financier, I believe we must accept the restriction as needful, not to hamper individualism but to protect it.

These two requirements must be satisfied, in the main, by the individuals who claim and hold control of the great industrial and financial combinations which dominate so large a part of our industrial life. They have undertaken to be, not business men, but princes—princes of property. I am not prepared to say that the system which produces them is wrong. I am very clear that they must fearlessly and competently assume the responsibility which goes with the power. So many enlightened business men know this that the statement would be little more than a platitude, were it not for an added implication.

This implication is, briefly, that the responsible heads of finance and industry instead of acting each for himself, must work together to achieve the common end. They must, where necessary, sacrifice this or that private advantage; and in reciprocal self-denial must seek a general advantage. It is here that formal government—political government, if you choose, comes in. Whenever in the pursuit of this objective the lone wolf, the unethical competitor, the reckless promoter, the Ishmael or Insull whose hand is against every man's, declines to join in achieving an end recognized as being for the public welfare, and threatens to drag the industry back to a state of anarchy, the government may properly be asked to apply restraint. Likewise, should the group ever use its collective power contrary to the public welfare, the government must be swift to enter and protect the public interest.

The government should assume the function of economic regulation only as a last resort, to be tried only when private initiative, inspired by high responsibility, with such assistance and balance as government can give, has finally failed. As yet there has been no final failure, because there has been no attempt; and I decline to assume that this nation is unable to meet the situation.

The final term of the high contract was for liberty and the pursuit of happiness. We have learnt a great deal of both in the past century. We know that individual liberty and individual happiness mean nothing unless both are ordered in the sense that one man's meat is not another man's poison. We know that the old "rights of personal competency"—the right to read, to think, to speak, to choose and live a mode of life, must be respected at all hazards. We know that liberty to do anything which deprives others of those elemental rights is outside the protection of any compact; and that government in this regard is the maintenance of a balance, within which every individual may have a place if he will take it; in which every individual may find safety if he wishes it; in which every individual may attain such power as his ability permits, consistent with his assuming the accompanying responsibility. . . .

Faith in America, faith in our tradition of personal responsibility, faith in our institutions, faith in ourselves demands that we recognize the new terms of the old social contact. We shall fulfill them, as we fulfilled the obligation of the apparent Utopia which Jefferson imagined for us in 1776, and which Jefferson, Roosevelt and Wilson sought to bring to realization. We must do so, lest a rising tide of misery engendered by our common failure, engulf us all. But failure is not an American habit; and in the strength of great hope we must all shoulder our common load.

Franklin D. Roosevelt, First
"Fireside Chat" of 1934
June 28, 1934

[Roosevelt was a master of the relatively new medium of radio, and in his "fireside chats" he used his talents to particularly good effect. In this one he summarizes the achievements of the New Deal to date.]

It has been several months since I have talked with you concerning the problems of Government. Since January, those of us in whom you have vested responsibility have been engaged in the fulfillment of plans and policies which had been widely discussed in previous months. It seemed to us our duty not only to make the right path clear, but also to tread that path.

As we review the achievements of this session of the Seventy-third Congress, it is made increasingly clear that its task was essentially that of completing and fortifying the work it had begun in March, 1933. That was no easy task, but the Congress was equal to it. It has been well said that while there were a few exceptions, this Congress displayed a greater freedom from mere partisanship than any other peace-time Congress since the Administration of President Washington himself. The session was distinguished by the extent and variety of legislation enacted and by the intelligence and good-will of debate upon these measures.

I mention only a few of the major enactments. It provided for the readjustment of the debt burden through the corporate and municipal bankruptcy acts and the Farm Relief Act. It lent a hand to industry by encouraging loans to solvent industries unable to secure adequate help from banking institutions. It strengthened the integrity of finance through the regulation of securities exchanges. It provided a rational method of increasing our volume of foreign trade through reciprocal trading agreements. It strengthened our naval forces to conform with the intentions and permission of existing treaty rights. It made further advances toward peace in industry through the Labor Adjustment Act. It supplemented our agricultural policy through measures widely demanded by farmers themselves and intended to avert price-destroying surpluses. It strengthened the hand of the Federal Government in its attempts to suppress gangster crime. It took definite steps toward a national housing program through an act which I signed today designed to encourage private capital in the rebuilding of the homes of the Nation. It created a permanent Federal body for the just regulation of all forms of communication, including the telephone, the telegraph and the radio. Finally, and I believe most important, it reorganized, simplified and made more fair and just our monetary system, setting up standards and policies adequate to meet the necessities of modern economic life, doing justice to both gold and silver as the metal bases behind the currency of the United States.

In the consistent development of our previous efforts toward the saving and safeguarding of our national life, I have continued to recognize three related steps. The first was relief, because the primary concern of any Government dominated by the humane ideals of democracy is the simple principle that in a land of vast resources no one should be permitted to starve. Relief was and continues to be our first consideration. It calls for large expenditures and will continue in modified form to do so for a long time to come. We may as well recognize that fact. It comes from the paralysis that arose as the after-effect of that unfortunate decade characterized by a mad chase for unearned riches, and an unwillingness of leaders in almost every walk of life to look beyond their own schemes and speculations. In our administration of relief we follow two principles: first, that direct giving shall, wherever possible, be supplemented by provision for useful and remunerative work and, second, that where families in their existing surroundings will in all human probability never find an opportunity for full self-maintenance, happiness and enjoyment, we shall try to give them a new chance in new surroundings.

The second step was recovery, and it is sufficient for me to ask each and every one of you to compare the situation in agriculture and in industry today with what it was fifteen months ago.

At the same time we have recognized the necessity of reform and reconstruction—reform because much of our trouble today and in the past few years has been due to a lack of understanding of the elementary principles of justice and fairness by those in whom leadership in business and finance was placed—reconstruction because new conditions in our economic life as well as old but neglected conditions had to be corrected.

Substantial gains well known to all of you have justified our course. I could cite statistics to you as unanswerable measures of our national progress—statistics to show the gain in the average weekly pay envelope of workers in the great majority of industries—statistics to show hundreds of thousands reemployed in private industries, and other hundreds of thousands given new employment through the expansion of direct and indirect Government assistance of many kinds, although, of course, there are those exceptions in professional pursuits whose economic improvement, of necessity, will be delayed. I also could cite statistics to show the great rise in the value of farm products—statistics to prove the demand for consumers' goods, ranging all the way from food and clothing to automobiles, and of late to prove the rise in the demand for durable goods—statistics to cover the great increase in bank deposits, and to show the scores of thousands of homes and of farms which have been saved from foreclosure.

But the simplest way for each of you to judge recovery lies in the plain facts of your own individual situation. Are you better off than you were last year? Are your debts less burdensome? Is your bank account more secure? Are your working conditions better? Is your faith in your own individual future more firmly grounded?

Also, let me put to you another simple question: Have you as an individual paid too high a price for these gains? Plausible self-seekers and theoretical die-hards will tell you of the loss of individual liberty. Answer this question also out of the facts of your own life. Have you lost any of your rights or liberty or constitutional freedom of action and choice? Turn to the Bill of Rights of the Constitution, which I have solemnly sworn to maintain and under which your freedom rests secure. Read each provision of that Bill of Rights and ask yourself whether you personally have suffered the impairment of a single jot of these great assurances. I have no question in my mind as to what your answer will be. The record is written in the experiences of your own personal lives.

In other words, it is not the overwhelming majority of the farmers or manufacturers or workers who deny the substantial gains of the past year. The most vociferous of the Doubting Thomases may be divided roughly into two groups: First, those who seek special political privilege and, second, those who seek special financial privilege. About a year ago I used as an illustration the 90 percent of the cotton manufacturers of the United States who wanted to do the right thing by their employees and by the public but were prevented from doing so by the 10 percent who undercut them by unfair practices and un-American standards. It is well for us to remember that humanity is a long way from being perfect and that a selfish minority in every walk of life—farming, business, finance and even Government service itself—will always continue to think of themselves first and their fellow beings second. . . .

The program of the past year is definitely in operation and that operation month by month is being made to fit into the web of old and new conditions. This process of evolution is well illustrated by the constant changes in detailed organization and method going on in the National Recovery Administration. With every passing month we are making strides in the orderly handling of the relationship between employees and employers. Conditions differ, of course, in almost every part of the country and in almost every industry. Temporary methods of adjustment are being replaced by more permanent machinery and, I am glad to say, by a growing recognition on the part of employers and employees of the desirability of maintaining fair relationships all around.

So also, while almost everybody has recognized the tremendous strides in the elimination of child labor, in the payment of not less than fair minimum wages and in the shortening of hours, we are still feeling our way in solving problems which relate to self-government in industry, especially where such self-government tends to eliminate the fair operation of competition.

In this same process of evolution we are keeping before us the objectives of protecting, on the one hand, industry against chiselers within its own ranks, and, on the other hand, the consumer through the maintenance of reasonable competition for the prevention of the unfair sky-rocketing of retail prices.

But, in addition to this our immediate task, we must still look to the larger future. I have pointed out to the Congress that we are seeking to find the way once more to well-known, long-established but to some degree forgotten ideals and values. We seek the security of the men, women and children of the Nation.

That security involves added means of providing better homes for the people of the Nation. That is the first principle of our future program.

The second is to plan the use of land and water resources of this country to the end that the means of livelihood of our citizens may be more adequate to meet their daily needs.

And, finally, the third principle is to use the agencies of government to assist in the establishment of means to provide sound and adequate protection against the vicissitudes of modern life—in other words, social insurance.

Later in the year I hope to talk with you more fully about these plans.

A few timid people, who fear progress, will try to give you new and strange names for what we are doing. Sometimes they will call it "Fascism," sometimes "Communism," sometimes "Regimentation," sometimes "Socialism." But, in so doing, they are trying to make very complex and theoretical something that is really very simple and very practical.

I believe in practical explanations and in practical policies. I believe that what we are doing today is a necessary fulfillment of what Americans have always been doing—a fulfillment of old and tested American ideals.

Let me give you a simple illustration:

While I am away from Washington this summer, a long-needed renovation of and addition to our White House office building is to be started. The architects have planned a few new rooms built into the present all too small one-story structure. We are going to include in this addition and in this renovation modern electric wiring and modern plumbing and modern means of keeping the offices cool in the hot Washington summers. But the structural lines of the old Executive office building will remain. The artistic lines of the White House buildings were the creation of master builders when our Republic was young. The simplicity and the strength of the structure remain in the face of every modern test. But within this magnificent pattern, the necessities of modern government business require constant reorganization and rebuilding.

If I were to listen to the arguments of some prophets of calamity who are talking these days, I should hesitate to make these alterations. I should fear that while I am away for a few weeks the architects might build some strange new Gothic tower or a factory building or perhaps a replica of the Kremlin or of the Potsdam Palace. But I have no such fears. The architects and builders are men of common sense and of artistic American tastes. They know that the principles of harmony and of necessity itself require that the building of the new structure shall blend with the essential lines of the old. It is this combination of the old and the new that marks orderly peaceful progress, not only in building buildings but in building government itself.

Our new structure is a part of and a fulfillment of the old.

All that we do seeks to fulfill the historic traditions of the American people. Other Nations may sacrifice democracy for the transitory stimulation of old and discredited autocracies. We are restoring confidence and well being under the rule of the people themselves. We remain, as John Marshall said a century ago, "emphatically and truly, a government of the people." Our Government "in form and in substance . . . emanates from them. Its powers are granted by them, and are to be exercised directly on them, and for their benefits." . . .

Huey Long, Speech on the "Share Our Wealth" Program
March 7, 1935

[By 1935 Senator Long had become the virtual dictator of Louisiana on the strength of his popularity among the poor. Meanwhile, he had broken with Roosevelt, whom he accused of having capitulated to Wall Street and refusing to distribute the country's wealth. Long then formed his own national "Share Our Wealth" Society with the intention of challenging Roosevelt, possibly as a third-party candidate, in 1936. But he was assassinated on the steps of the Louisiana State Capitol Building on September 10, 1935.]

Ladies and Gentlemen:

It has been publicly announced that the White House orders of the Roosevelt administration have declared a war. . . .

What is the trouble with this administration of Mr. Roosevelt and of Mr. Johnson, Mr. Farley, Mr. Astor and all their spoilers and spellbinders?

They think that Huey Long is the cause of all their worry. They go gunning for me, but am I the cause of their misery? Well, they are like old David Crockett, who went out to hunt a possum. He saw there in the gleam of the moonlight a possum in the top of the tree, going from limb to limb, so he shot, but he missed. He looked again and he saw the possum. He fired a second time and missed again. Soon he discovered that it was not a possum that he saw at all in the top of that tree; it was a louse in his eyebrow.

I do not make this illustration to do discredit to any of these distinguished gentlemen; I make it to show how often some of us imagine that we see great trouble being done to us by someone at a distance, when in reality all it may be is a fault in our own make-up. And so is the case of Mr. Roosevelt or Mr. Farley or Mr. Johnson and of others undertaking to derange the situation today.

The trouble with the Roosevelt administration is that when their schemes and issues have failed, these things I told them not to do, and voted not to do, that they think it will help them to light out on those of us who warned them in the beginning that the tangled messes and experiments would not work.

The Roosevelt administration has had its way for two years. They have been allowed to set up or knock down anything and everybody. There was one difference between Roosevelt and Hoover. Hoover could not get the Congress to carry out the schemes he wanted to try, because we managed to lick him on a roll call in the United States Senate time after time when we had both the Democratic leaders and the Republican leaders trying to put them over.

But it is different with Mr. Roosevelt. He got his plans through Congress, but on cold analysis they were found to be the same things Hoover tried to pass and failed the year before. . . .

The whole thing of Mr. Roosevelt as run under General Johnson became such a national scandal that Roosevelt had to let Johnson slide out as a scapegoat. I am told that the day the general had to go, when they waited just as long as they would wait on him, he wanted to issue a blistering statement against Mr. Roosevelt, but they finally saddled him off because they didn't know but what Wall Street might want to lend him to some other President in the future, so he left without.

It was under this NRA and the other funny alphabetical combinations that followed it that we ran the whole country into a mare's nest. The Farleys and Johnsons combed the land with agents, inspectors, supervisors, detectives, secretaries, assistants, and so forth, all of them armed with the power to arrest anybody and send them to jail if they found them not living up to some one of the rules in these 900 catalogues they had out.

Now it is with the PWA, the WRA, GINS and every other flimsy combination that the country finds its affairs in business where no one can recognize it. More men are out of work than ever. The debt of the United States has gone up ten billion more dollars. There is starvation; there is homelessness; there is misery on every hand and corner. But, mind you, in the meantime Mr. Roosevelt has had his way. He is one man that can't blame any of his troubles on Huey Long. He has had his way.

Down in my part of the country, if any man has the measles he blames that on me; but there is one man that can't blame anything on anybody but himself, and that is Mr. Franklin De-La-No Roose-Velt.

And now on top of that they ordered a war on me because nearly four years ago I told Hoover's crowd it won't do, and because three years ago I told Roosevelt and his crowd it won't do. In other words, they are in a rage at Huey Long because I have had to say, "I told you so."

I was not overstating the conditions now prevailing in this country. In the own words of these gentlemen, they have confessed all that I now say or ever have said. Mr. Roosevelt, and Mrs. Roosevelt too, have lately bewailed the fact that food, clothes and shelter have not been provided for the people. Even this General Hugh H. Johnson has said in his speech of this last Monday night that there are 80,000 babies in America who are badly hurt or wrecked by this depression. He, of course, includes us all in that classification of babies.

Mr. Harry Hopkins, who runs the relief work, says the dole roll has risen now to 22,375,000 people, the highest it has ever been. And now what is there for the Roosevelt crowd to do but to admit the facts, and admit further that they are now in their third year making matters worse instead of better.

No one is to blame except them for what is going on when they have had their way, and they couldn't change the thing in two years. It is now worse than ever, and if they haven't been able to do any good in the way they have been going for two years, how can anyone expect any good of them for the next two years to come? God save us two more years of the disaster we have had under that gang. . . .

So now, my friends, I come to the point where I must in a few sentences describe to you just what was the cause of our trouble which became so serious in 1929 and which has been worse ever since.

The wealth in the United States was three times as much

in 1910 as it was in 1890, and yet the masses of our people owned less in 1910 than they did in 1890. In the year 1916 the condition had become so bad that a committee provided for by the Congress of the United States reported that 2 percent of the people of the United States owned 60 percent of the wealth in the country, and that 65 percent of the people owned less than 5 percent of the wealth. This report showed, however, that there was a middle class, some 33 percent of the people who owned 35 percent of the wealth.

This report went on to say that the trouble with the American people at that time was that too much of the wealth was in the hands of too few of the people, and recommended that something be done to correct the evil condition then existing. . . .

But what did we do to correct that condition? Instead of moving to take these big fortunes from the top and spreading them among the suffering people at the bottom, financial masses of America moved in to take complete charge of the government for fear that our lawmakers might do something along that line.

And as a result, 14 years after the report of 1916, the Federal Trade Commission made a study to see how the wealth of this land was distributed. And did they find it still as bad as it was in 1916? They found it worse. They found that 1 percent of the people owned 59 percent of the wealth, which was almost twice as bad as was said to be an intolerable condition in 1916, when 2 percent of the people owned 60 percent of the wealth.

And as a result of the foreclosures of mortgages and bankruptcies, which began to happen during the last years, it is the estimate of the conservative statisticians that 75 percent of the people in the United States don't own anything today, that is, not even enough to pay their debts, and that 4 percent of the people, or maybe less than 4 percent of the people, own from 85 to 95 percent of all the wealth in the United States.

Remember, in 1916 there was a middle class, 33 percent of the people who owned 35 percent of the wealth. That middle class is practically gone today; it no longer exists. They have dropped into the ranks of the poor. The thriving man of independent business standing is fast fading. The corner grocery store is becoming a thing of the past. Concentrated chain and merchandise stores and chain banking systems have laid waste to all middle-men opportunity.

. . . Those suffering on the bottom and the few lords at the top are all that is left. There is no middle class. Lords at the top; masses at the bottom.

It became apparent that the billionaires and multi-millionaires began to squeeze out the common, ordinary millionaire. In other words, the whales began to eat up the goggle-eyes after they had taken all the minnows in the catch, closing and taking their properties and wrecking their business.

And so we arrived, and we are still there at the place in abundant America where we have every thing for which a human heart can pray. The hundreds of millions, or, as General Johnson says, the eighty millions of our people, are crying in misery for want of the things which they need for life, notwithstanding the fact that the country has had, and can have, more than the entire race can consume.

One hundred and twenty-five million people of America have seated themselves at the barbecue table to eat the products which have been given to them by their Lord and Creator. There is provided by the Almighty what it takes for all of them to eat. Yea, more.

There has been provided for the people of America who have been called to this barbecue table more than is needed for all to eat, but the financial masses of America have taken off of the barbecue table 90 percent of the food placed thereon by the Lord, even before the feast began. And there is left on that table for 125,000,000 people about what is needed for the 10,000,000. In other words, there is not enough to feed one out of twelve.

What has become of the balance of those victuals placed on the table by the Lord for the use of us all? They are in the hands of the Morgans, the Rockefellers, the Mellons, the Baruchs, the Bakers, the Astors, the Vanderbilts, 600 families at the most, either possessing or controlling the entire 90 percent of all that is in America.

These big men cannot eat all the food, they cannot wear all the clothes, so they destroy it. They rot it up, they plow it up, they pour it in the river. They bring destruction to the acts of mankind to let humanity suffer, to let humanity go naked, to let humanity go homeless, so that nothing may occur that will do harm to their vanity and to their greed. Like the dog in the manger they command a wagon load of hay which the dog will not allow the cow to eat, though he could not eat it himself.

So now, ladies and gentlemen, I introduce again, for fear that there are some who have just tuned in and do not know who is talking. This is Huey P. Long, United States Senator from Louisiana, talking over a National Broadcasting Company hookup, from Washington, D.C.

We come to that plan of mine now for which I have been so recently and roundly condemned and denounced by the Roosevelt administration and by such men as Mr. Farley and Mr. Robinson and General Hugh S. Johnson, and other spellers and speakers and spoilers.

It is for the redistribution of wealth and for guaranteeing comfort and convenience to all humanity out of this abundance in our country. I hope none will be horror-stricken when they hear me say that we must limit the size of the big men's fortunes in order to guarantee a minimum of fortune, life and comfort to the little man, but if you are horror-stricken at my mention of that fact, think first that such is the declaration on which Mr. Roosevelt rode into nomination and election to President of the United States. . . .

Now I come to give you again that plan, taken from these leaders of all times and from the Bible, for the sponsoring of which I have been labeled by American men as a madman and pied piper and demagogue, so I give you that plan of our Share Our Wealth Society.

I propose, first, that every big fortune will be cut down immediately. We will cut that down by a capital levy tax to where no one will own more than a few millions of dollars. As a matter of fact, no one can own a fortune in excess of three or four millions of dollars, just between you and me, and I think that is too much. But we figure we can allow that size of a fortune and give prosperity to all of the people, even though it is done.

I propose that the surplus of all the big fortunes above a few millions to any one person, at the most, go into the United States ownership. Now, how would we get these surplus fortunes into the United States Treasury, Mr. Johnson wants to know. Well, now, if he will listen he won't have any trouble finding out. It is not hard to do. We would not do it by making everyone sell what he owned. No. We would send everyone a questionnaire, just like they did during the war, when they were taking us over there to make the world safe for democracy so that they might come back here and make America safe for autocracy.

On that questionnaire the man to whom it was sent would list the properties he owned, lands, the houses, stocks and bonds, factories and patents; every man would place an appraisal on his property which the government would review and maybe change. On that appraisal the big fortune holder would say out of what property he would retain the few millions allowed to him, the balance to go to the United States.

Let's say that Mr. Henry Ford should show that he owned all the stock of the Ford Motor Company, and that it was worth $2,000,000,000, we will say. He would claim, say $4,000,000 of the Ford stock, but $1,996,000,000 would go to the United States.

Say the Rockefeller Foundation was listed at $10,000,-000,000 in oil stocks, bank stocks, money and storehouses. Each Rockefeller could say whether he wanted his limit in the money, oil or bank stock, but about $9,900,000,000 would be left and that would go to the United States Government.

And so in this way this Government of the United States would come into the possession of about two-fifths of the wealth which on normal values would be worth from $165,-000,000,000 to $175,000,000,000.

Then we would turn to the inventories of the 25,000,000 families of America and all those showing properties and moneys clear of debt that were above $5,000 and up to the limit of a few millions. We wouldn't draw down a fortune that wasn't bigger than a few millions, and if a man had over $5,000 then he would have his guaranteed minimum. But those showing less than $5,000 for the family, free of debt, would be added to; so that every family would start life again with homestead possession of at least a home and the comforts needed for a home, including such things as a radio and an automobile.

Those things would go to every family as a homestead, not to be sold for debts or for taxes or even by consent of the owner, except the government would allow it, and then only on condition that the court hold it, that is, hold the money that was received for it, to be spent for the purpose of buying another home and the comforts thereof. . . .

Next we propose, second: That after homes and comforts of homes have been set up for the families of the country, that we will turn our attention to the children and the youth of the land, providing first for their education and training.

We would not have to worry about the problem of child labor, because the very first thing which we would place in front of every child would be not only a comfortable home during his early years, but the opportunity for education and training, not only through the grammar school and the high school, but through college, and to include vocational and professional training for every child.

If necessary, that would include the living cost of that child while he attended a college, if there wasn't a college close enough to live at home and conveniently attend it, and that would be the case with many of those living in rural areas, and we would have to pay their living cost while they went away to college. . . .

Won't you write me tonight? Won't you write me tomorrow? Won't you organize a "share our wealth" society? If you want a copy of my speech write to me. Organize a "share our wealth" society in your community; write to me, Huey P. Long, United States Senate, Washington, D.C.

I will send you the credentials, I will send you the material, but get out and organize your friends; let's make the fight, let's make the politicians keep their promises or vote somebody into the office that will keep the promise that in this land of abundance none shall have too much, none shall have too little; in the land of too much to eat and too much to wear and too many homes to live in and too many automobiles to ride in, that we will see the blessings of this land, given to us by God and by mankind, shall be reasonably shared by our people.

I thank you!

Schechter Poultry Corp. v. United States
1935

[The Court's decision in the Schechter case not only nullified the National Industrial Recovery Act; it served notice that no New Deal law was safe. In fact, the Court's conception of the commerce clause threatened to render the federal government impotent. The decision, written by Chief Justice Hughes, was unanimous.]

HUGHES, C. J.: Petitioners were convicted in the District Court of the United States for the Eastern District of New York on eighteen counts of an indictment charging violations of what is known as the "Live Poultry Code," and on an additional count for conspiracy to commit such violations. By demurrer to the indictment and appropriate motions on the trial, the defendants contended (1) that the Code had been adopted pursuant to an unconstitutional delegation by Congress of legislative power; (2) that it attempted to regulate intrastate transactions which lay outside the authority of Congress; and (3) that in certain provisions it was repugnant to the due process clause of the Fifth Amendment. . . .

The "Live Poultry Code" was promulgated under section 3 of the National Industrial Recovery Act. That section authorizes the President to approve "codes of fair competition." Such a code may be approved for a trade or industry, upon application by one or more trade or industrial associations or groups, if the President finds (1) that such associations or groups "impose no inequitable restrictions on admission to membership therein and are truly representative," and (2) that such codes are not designed "to promote monopolies or to eliminate or oppress small enterprises and will not operate to discriminate against them, and will tend to effectuate the policy" of Title I of the act. Such codes "shall not permit monopolies or monopolistic practices." As a condition of his approval, the President may "impose such conditions (including requirements for the making of reports and the keeping of accounts) for the protection of consumers, competitors, employees, and others, and in furtherance of the public interest, and may provide such exceptions to and exemptions from the provisions of such code as the President in his discretion deems necessary to effectuate the policy herein declared." Where such a code has not been approved, the President may prescribe one, either on his own motion or on complaint. Violation of any provision of a code (so approved or prescribed) "in any transaction in or affecting interstate or foreign commerce" is made a misdemeanor punishable by a fine of not more than $500 for each offense, and each day the violation continues is to be deemed a separate offense. . . .

Of the eighteen counts of the indictment upon which the defendants were convicted, aside from the count for conspiracy, two counts charged violation of the minimum wage and maximum hour provisions of the Code, and ten counts were for violation of the requirement (found in the "trade practice provisions") of "straight killing." The charges in the ten counts, respectively, were that the defendants in selling to retail dealers and butchers had permitted "selections of individual chickens taken from particular coops and half coops."

Of the other six counts, one charged the sale to a butcher of an unfit chicken; two counts charged the making of sales without having the poultry inspected or approved in accordance with regulations or ordinances of the City of New York; two counts charged the making of false reports or the failure to make reports relating to the range of daily prices and volume of sales for certain periods; and the remaining count was for sales to slaughterers or dealers who were without licenses required by the ordinances and regulations of the City of New York.

First. Two preliminary points are stressed by the Government with respect to the appropriate approach to the important questions presented. We are told that the provision of the statute authorizing the adoption of codes must be viewed in the light of the grave national crisis with which Congress was confronted. Undoubtedly, the conditions to which power is addressed are always to be considered when the exercise of power is challenged. Extraordinary conditions may call for extraordinary remedies. But the argument necessarily stops short of an attempt to justify action which lies outside the sphere of constitutional authority. Extraordinary conditions do not create or enlarge constitutional power. The Constitution established a national government with powers deemed to be adequate, as they have proved to be both in war and peace, but these powers of the national government are limited by the constitutional grants. Those who act under these grants are not at liberty to transcend the imposed limits because they believe that more or different power is necessary. Such assertions of extra-constitutional authority were anticipated and precluded by the explicit terms of the Tenth Amendment,—"The powers not delegated to the United States by the Constitution, nor prohibited by it to the States, are reserved to the States respectively, or to the people."

The further point is urged that the national crisis demanded a broad and intensive cooperative effort by those engaged in trade and industry, and that this necessary cooperation was sought to be fostered by permitting them to initiate the adoption of codes. But the statutory plan is not simply one for voluntary effort. It does not seek merely to endow voluntary trade or industrial associations or groups with privileges or immunities. It involves the coercive exercise of the law-making power. The codes of fair competition, which the statute attempts to authorize, are codes of laws. If valid, they place all persons within their reach under the obligation of positive law, binding equally those who assent and those who do not assent. Violations of the provisions of the codes are punishable as crimes.

Second. The question of the delegation of legislative power. For a statement of the authorized objectives and content of the "codes of fair competition" we are referred repeatedly to the "Declaration of Policy" in section one of Title I of the Recovery Act. Thus, the approval of a code by the President is conditioned on his finding that it "will tend to effectuate the policy of this title." Sec. 3 (a). The President is authorized to impose such conditions "for the protection of consumers, competitors, employees, and others, and in furtherance of the public interest, and may provide such exceptions to and exemptions from the provisions of such code as the President in his discretion deems necessary to effectuate the policy herein declared." . . .

Such a sweeping delegation of legislative power finds no support in the decisions upon which the Government especially relies.

To summarize and conclude upon this point: Section 3 of the Recovery Act is without precedent. It supplies no standards for any trade, industry or activity. It does not undertake to prescribe rules of conduct to be applied to particular states of fact determined by appropriate administrative procedure. Instead of prescribing rules of conduct, it authorizes the making of codes to prescribe them. For that legislative undertaking, section 3 sets up no standards, aside from the statement of the general aims of rehabilitation, correction and expansion described in section one. In view of the scope of that broad declaration, and of the nature of the few restrictions that are imposed, the discretion of the President in approving or prescribing codes, and thus enacting laws for the government of trade and industry throughout the country, is virtually unfettered. We think that the code-making authority thus conferred is an unconstitutional delegation of legislative power.

Second. The question of the application of the provisions of the Live Poultry Code to intrastate transactions. This aspect of the case presents the question whether the particular provisions of the Live Poultry Code, which the defendants were convicted for violating and for having conspired to violate, were within the regulating power of Congress.

These provisions relate to the hours and wages of those employed by defendants in their slaughterhouses in Brooklyn and to the sales there made to retail dealers and butchers.

(1) Were these transactions *"in"* interstate commerce? Much is made of the fact that almost all the poultry coming to New York is sent there from other States. But the code provisions, as here applied, do not concern the transportation of the poultry from other States to New York, or the

transactions of the commission men or others to whom it is consigned, or the sales made by such consignees to defendants. When defendants had made their purchases, whether at the West Washington Market in New York City or at the railroad terminals serving the City, or elsewhere, the poultry was trucked to their slaughterhouses in Brooklyn for local disposition. The interstate transactions in relation to that poultry then ended. Defendants held the poultry at their slaughterhouse markets for slaughter and local sale to retail dealers and butchers who in turn sold directly to consumers. Neither the slaughtering nor the sales by defendants were transactions in interstate commerce.

The undisputed facts thus afford no warrant for the argument that the poultry handled by defendants at their slaughterhouse markets was in a *"current"* or *"flow"* of interstate commerce and was thus subject to congressional regulation. The mere fact that there may be a constant flow of commodities into a State does not mean that the flow continues after the property has arrived and has become commingled with the mass of property within the State and is there held solely for local disposition and use. So far as the poultry here in question is concerned, the flow in interstate commerce had ceased. The poultry had come to a permanent rest within the State. It was not held, used, or sold by defendants in relation to any further transactions in interstate commerce and was not destined for transportation to other states. Hence, decisions which deal with a stream of interstate commerce—where goods come to rest within a State temporarily and are later to go forward in interstate commerce—and with the regulations of transactions involved in that practical continuity of movement, are not applicable here.

(2) Did the defendants' transactions directly *"affect"* interstate commerce so as to be subject to federal regulation? The power of Congress extends not only to the regulation of transactions which are part of interstate commerce, but to the protection of that commerce from injury.

In determining how far the federal government may go in controlling intrastate transactions upon the ground that they "affect" interstate commerce, there is a necessary and well-established distinction between direct and indirect effects. The precise line can be drawn only as individual cases arise, but the distinction is clear in principle. Direct effects are illustrated by the railroad cases we have cited, as *e. g.*, the effect of failure to use prescribed safety appliances on railroads which are the highways of both interstate and intrastate commerce, injury to an employee engaged in interstate transportation by the negligence of an employee engaged in an intrastate movement, the fixing of rates for intrastate transportation which unjustly discriminate against interstate commerce. But where the effect of intrastate transactions upon interstate commerce is merely indirect, such transactions remain within the domain of State power. If the commerce clause were construed to reach all enterprises and transactions which could be said to have an indirect effect upon interstate commerce, the federal authority would embrace practically all the activities of the people and the authority of the State over its domestic concerns would exist only by sufferance of the federal government. Indeed, on such a theory, even the development of the State's commercial facilities would be subject to federal control. . . .

The Government also makes the point that efforts to enact state legislation establishing high labor standards have been impeded by the belief that unless similar action is taken generally, commerce will be diverted from the States adopting such standards, and that this fear of diversion has led to demands for federal legislation on the subject of wages and hours. The apparent implication is that the federal authority under the commerce clause should be deemed to extend to the establishment of rules to govern wages and hours in intrastate trade and industry generally throughout the country, thus overriding the authority of the States to deal with domestic problems arising from labor conditions in their internal commerce.

It is not the province of the Court to consider the economic advantages or disadvantages of such a centralized system. It is sufficient to say that the Federal Constitution does not provide for it. Our growth and development have called for wide use of the commerce power of the federal government in its control over the expanded activities of interstate commerce, and in protecting that commerce from burdens, interferences, and conspiracies to restrain and monopolize it. But the authority of the federal government may not be pushed to such an extreme as to destroy the distinction, which the commerce clause itself establishes, between commerce "among the several States" and the internal concerns of a State. The same answer must be made to the contention that is based upon the serious economic situation which led to the passage of the Recovery Act,—the fall in prices, the decline in wages and employment, and the curtailment of the market for commodities. Stress is laid upon the great importance of maintaining wage distributions which would provide the necessary stimulus in starting "the cumulative forces making for expanding commercial activity." Without in any way disparaging this motive, it is enough to say that the recuperative efforts of the federal government must be made in a manner consistent with the authority granted by the Constitution.

We are of the opinion that the attempt through the provisions of the Code to fix the hours and wages of employees of defendants in their intrastate business was not a valid exercise of federal power.

On both the grounds we have discussed, the attempted delegation of legislative power, and the attempted regulation of intrastate transactions which affect interstate commerce only indirectly, we hold the code provisions here in question to be invalid and that the judgment of conviction must be reversed.

Franklin D. Roosevelt, Third Annual Message
January 3, 1936

[1936 would be a year of respite for the New Deal while Roosevelt concentrated his efforts on the election. Here he underlines the Jeffersonian theme of the coming campaign: it would be the people, represented by the government, against the selfish interests.]

. . . The evidence before us clearly proves that autocracy in world affairs endangers peace and that such threats do not spring from those nations devoted to the democratic ideal. If this be true in world affairs, it should have the greatest weight in the determination of domestic policies.

Within democratic nations the chief concern of the people is to prevent the continuation or the rise of autocratic institutions that beget slavery at home and aggression abroad. Within our borders, as in the world at large, popular opinion is at war with a power-seeking minority.

This is no new thing. It was fought out in the Constitutional Convention of 1787. From time to time since then the battle has been continued, under Thomas Jefferson, Andrew Jackson, Theodore Roosevelt and Woodrow Wilson.

In these latter years we have witnessed the domination of government by financial and industrial groups, numerically small but politically dominant in the twelve years that succeeded the World War. The present group of which I speak is indeed numerically small and, while it exercises a large influence and has much to say in the world of business, it does not, I am confident, speak the true sentiments of the less articulate, but more important elements that constitute real American business.

In March, 1933, I appealed to the Congress and to the people . . . in a new effort to restore power to those to whom it rightfully belonged. The response to that appeal resulted in the writing of a new chapter in the history of popular government. You, the members of the legislative branch, and I, the Executive, contended for an established new relationship between government and people.

What were the terms of that new relationship? They were an appeal from the clamor of many private and selfish interests, yes, an appeal from the clamor of partisan interest, to the ideal of public interest. Government became the representative and the trustee of the public interest. Our aim was to build upon essentially democratic institution, seeking all the while the adjustment of burdens, the help of the needy, the protection of the weak, the liberation of the exploited and the genuine protection of the people's property.

It goes without saying that to create such an economic

constitutional order more than a single legislative enactment was called for. We had to build, you in the Congress and I, as the Executive, upon a broad base. Now, after thirty-four months of work, we contemplate a fairly rounded whole. We have returned the control of the Federal Government to the city of Washington.

To be sure, in so doing, we have invited battle. We have earned the hatred of entrenched greed. The very nature of the problem that we faced made it necessary to drive some people from power and strictly to regulate others. I made that plain when I took the oath of office in March, 1933. I spoke of the practices of the unscrupulous money-changers who stood indicted in the court of public opinion. I spoke of the rulers of the exchanges of mankind's goods, who failed through their own stubbornness and their own incompetence. I said that they had admitted their failure and had abdicated.

Abdicated? Yes, in 1933, but now with the passing of danger they forget their damaging admissions and withdraw their abdication.

They seek the restoration of their selfish power. They offer to lead us back round the same old corner into the same old dreary street.

Yes, there are still determined groups that are intent upon that very thing. Rigorously held up to popular examination, their true character reveals itself. They steal the livery of great national constitutional ideals to serve discredited special interests. As guardians and trustees for great groups of individual stockholders, they wrongfully seek to carry the property and the interest entrusted to them into the arena of partisan politics. They seek—this minority in business and industry—to control and often do control and use for their own purposes legitimate and highly honored business associations; they engage in vast propaganda to spread fear and discord among the people—they would 'gang up' against the people's liberties.

The principle that they would instill into government if they succeed in seizing power is well shown by the principles which many of them have instilled into their own affairs: Autocracy toward labor, toward stockholders, toward consumers, toward public sentiment. Autocrats in smaller things, they seek autocracy in bigger things. 'By their fruits ye shall know them.'

If these gentlemen believe, as they say they believe, that the measures adopted by this Congress and its predecessor, and carried out by this administration, have hindered rather than promoted recovery, let them be consistent. Let them propose to this Congress the complete repeal of these measures. The way is open to such a proposal.

Let action be positive and not negative. The way is open in the Congress of the United States for an expression of opinion by yeas and nays. Shall we say that values are restored and that the Congress will, therefore, repeal the laws under which we have been bringing them back? Shall we say that because national income has grown with rising prosperity, we shall repeal existing taxes and thereby put off the day of approaching a balanced budget and of starting to reduce the national debt? Shall we abandon the reasonable support and regulation of banking? Shall we restore the dollar to its former gold content?

Shall we say to the farmer—'The prices for your products are in part restored, now go and hoe your own row'?

Shall we say to the home owners—'We have reduced your rates of interest. We have no further concern with how you keep your home or what you pay for your money. That is your affair'?

Shall we say to the several millions of unemployed citizens who face the very problem of existence—yes, of getting enough to eat—'We will withdraw from giving you work, we will turn you back to the charity of your communities and to those men of selfish power who tell you that perhaps they will employ you if the government leaves them strictly alone'?

Shall we say to the needy unemployed—'Your problem is a local one except that perhaps the Federal Government, as an act of mere generosity, will be willing to pay to your city or to your county a few grudging dollars to help maintain your soup kitchens'? . . .

We have been specific in our affirmative action. Let them be specific in their negative attack.

But the challenge faced by this Congress is more menacing than merely a return to the past—bad as that would be. Our resplendent economic autocracy does not want to return to that individualism of which they prate, even though the advantages under that system went to the ruthless and the strong. They realize that in thirty-four months we have built up new instruments of public power. In the hands of a people's government this power is wholesome and proper. But in the hands of political puppets of an economic autocracy such power would provide shackles for the liberties of the people. Give them their way and they will take the course of every autocracy of the past—power for themselves, enslavement for the public.

Their weapon is the weapon of fear. I have said—'The only thing we have to fear is fear itself,' and that is as true today as it was in 1933. But such fear as they instill today is not natural fear, a normal fear; it is a synthetic, manufactured, poisonous fear that is being spread subtly, expensively and cleverly by the same people who cried in those other days—'Save us, save us, else we perish.' . . .

Franklin D. Roosevelt, Second Term
Acceptance Speech
June 27, 1936

[In the 1936 campaign Roosevelt gave the New Deal a distinctly Populist-Progressive cast, as he inveighed against the "economic royalists" in a way that was reminiscent of Bryan and LaFollette. Following are portions of the speech he delivered before the Democratic national convention in Philadelphia.]

. . . Philadelphia is a good city in which to write American history. This is fitting ground on which to reaffirm the faith of our fathers; to pledge ourselves to restore to the people a wider freedom—to give to 1936 as the founders gave to 1776—an American way of life.

That very word freedom, in itself and of necessity, suggests freedom from some restraining power. In 1776 we sought freedom from the tyranny of a political autocracy—from the eighteenth century royalists who held special privileges from the crown. It was to perpetuate their privilege that they governed without the consent of the governed; that they denied the right of free assembly and free speech; that they restricted the worship of God; that they put the average man's property and the average man's life in pawn to the mercenaries of dynastic power—that they regimented the people.

And so it was to win freedom from the tyranny of political autocracy that the American Revolution was fought. That victory gave the business of governing into the hands of the average man, who won the right with his neighbors to make and order his own destiny through his own Government. Political tyranny was wiped out at Philadelphia on July 4, 1776.

But, since that struggle, man's inventive genius released new forces in our land which re-ordered the lives of our people. The age of machinery, of railroads, of steam and electricity; the telegraph and the radio; mass production, mass distribution—all of these combined to bring forward a new civilization and with it a problem for those who sought to remain free.

For out of this modern civilization economic royalists carved new dynasties. New Kingdoms were built upon concentration of control over material things. Through new uses of corporations, banks and securities, new machinery of industry and agriculture, of labor and capital—all undreamed of by the fathers—the whole structure of modern life was impressed into this royal service.

There was no place among this royalty for our many thousands of small business men and merchants who sought to make a worthy use of the American system of initiative and profit. They were no more free than the worker or the farmer. Even honest and progressive-minded men of wealth, aware of their obligation to their generation, could never know just where they fitted into this dynastic scheme of things.

And so it was natural and perfectly human that the privileged princes of these new economic dynasties, thirsting for power, reached out for control over government itself. They created a new despotism and wrapped it in the robes of legal sanction. In its service new mercenaries sought to regiment the people, their labor, their property. And as a result the average man once more confronts the problem that faced the Minute Man of seventy-six.

The hours men and women worked, the wages they received, the conditions of their labor—these had passed beyond the control of the people, and were imposed by this new industrial dictatorship. The savings of the average family, the capital of the small business man, the investments set aside for old age—other people's money—these were tools which the new economic royalty used to dig itself in.

Those who tilled the soil no longer reaped the rewards which were their right. The small measure of their gains was decreed by men in distant cities.

Throughout the Nation, opportunity was limited by monopoly. Individual initiative was crushed in the cogs of a great machine. The field open for free business was more and more restricted. Private enterprise, indeed, became too private. It became privileged enterprise, not free enterprise.

An old English judge said once upon a time: "Necessitous men are not free men." Liberty requires opportunity to make a living—a living decent according to the standard of the time, a living which gives man not only enough to live by, but something to live for.

For too many of us the political equality we once had won was meaningless in the face of economic inequality. A small group had concentrated into their own hands an almost complete control over other people's property, other people's money, other people's labor—other people's lives. For too many of us life was no longer free; liberty no longer real; men could no longer follow the pursuit of happiness.

Against economic tyranny such as this, the American citizen could only appeal to the organized power of government. We will remember that the collapse of 1929 showed up the despotism for what it was. The election of 1932 was the people's mandate to end it. Under that mandate it is being ended.

The royalists I have spoken of—the royalists of the economic order have conceded that political freedom was the business of the government, but they have maintained that economic slavery was nobody's business. They granted that the government could protect the citizen in his right to vote but they denied that the government could do anything to protect the citizen in his right to work and his right to live.

Today we stand committed to the proposition that freedom is no half and half affair. If the average citizen is guaranteed equal opportunity in the polling place, he must have equal opportunity in the market place.

These economic royalists complain that we seek to overthrow the institutions of America. What they really complain of is that we seek to take away their power. Our allegiance to American institutions requires the overthrow of this kind of power. In vain they seek to hide behind the Flag and the Constitution. In their blindness they forget what the Flag and the Constitution stand for. Now, as always, for over a century and a half, the Flag, the Constitution, stand against a dictatorship by mob rule and the over-privileged alike, and the Flag and the Constitution stand for democracy, not tyranny; for freedom, but not subjection. . . .

Governments can err—Presidents do make mistakes, but the immortal Dante tells us that divine justice weighs the sins of the cold-blooded and the sins of the warm-hearted in different scales.

Better the occasional faults of a government that lives in a spirit of charity than the consistent omissions of a government frozen in the ice of its own indifference.

There is a mysterious cycle in human events. To some generations much is given. Of other generations much is expected. This generation of Americans has a rendezvous with destiny.

In this world of ours in other lands, there are some people, who, in times past, have lived and fought for freedom, and seem to have grown too weary to carry on the fight. They have sold their heritage of freedom for the illusion of a living. They have yielded their democracy.

I believe in my heart that only our success can stir their ancient hope. They begin to know that here in America we are waging a great and successful war. It is not alone a war against want and destitution and economic demoralization.

It is more than that, it is a war for the survival of democracy. We are fighting, fighting to save a great and precious form of government for ourselves and for the world.

And so I accept the commission you have tendered me. I join with you. I am enlisted for the duration of the war.

Herbert Hoover, "This Challenge to Liberty" October 30, 1936

[One of the New Deal's incessant critics was ex-President Hoover. He spoke frequently about the dangers of collectivism and government controls, just as he had before 1933. He delivered the following speech* in Denver; it later appeared in his book *Addresses upon the American Road*.]

. . . Freedom does not die from frontal attack. It dies because men in power no longer believe in a system based upon Liberty.

Mr. Roosevelt on this eve of election has started using the phrases of freedom. He talks sweetly of personal liberty, of individualism, of the American system, of the profit system. He says now that he thinks well of capitalism, and individual enterprise. His devotion to private property seems to be increasing. He has suddenly found some good economic royalists. And he is a staunch supporter of the Constitution. Two days ago he rededicated the Statue of Liberty in New York. She has been the forgotten woman.

Four years ago we also heard many phrases which turned out not to mean what they were thought to have meant. In order that we may be sure this time will Mr. Roosevelt reply in plain words:

Does he propose to revive the nine acts which the Supreme Court has rejected as invasions of the safeguards of free men?

Has he abandoned his implied determination to change the

* Reprinted with the permission of Charles Scribner's Sons from *Addresses upon the American Road*, pp. 218–20, 226, by Herbert Hoover. Copyright 1938 Edgar Rickard.

Constitution? Why not tell the American people before election what change he proposes? Does he intend to stuff the Court itself? Why does the New Deal not really lay its cards on the table?

But their illegal invasions of the Constitution are but the minor artillery with which this New Deal philosophy of government is being forced upon us. They are now using a more subtle and far more effective method of substituting personal power and centralized government for the institutions of free men. It is not by violation of the Constitution that they are making headway today. It is through taking vast sums of the people's money and then manipulating its spending to build up personal power. By this route relief has been centralized in their hands. By this route government has entered into business in competition with the citizen. In his way a score of new instruments of public power have been created. By this route the ordinary functions of government have been uselessly expanded with a double bookkeeping to conceal it. Public funds are used right and left to subsidize special groups of our citizens and special regions of the country. At public expense there is a steady drip of propaganda to poison the public mind.

Through this spending there grows a huge number of citizens with a selfish vested interest in continuing this centralization of power. It has also made millions of citizens dependent upon the government.

Thus also have been built huge political bureaucracies hungry for more power. This use of money has enabled the independence of members of Congress to be sapped by the pork barrel. It has subtly undermined the rights and the responsibility of States and local governments. Out of all this we see government daily by executive orders instead of by open laws openly arrived at.

The New Deal taxes are in forms which stifle the growth of small business and discourage new enterprise. By stifling private enterprise the field is tilled for further extension of government enterprise. Intricate taxes are interpreted by political bureaucrats who coerce and threaten our business men. By politically managed currency the President has seized the power to alter all wages, all prices, all debts, all savings at will. But that is not the worst. They are creating personal power over votes. That crushes the first safeguard of liberty. . . .

We want recovery. Not alone economic recovery. We must have moral recovery. And there are many elements in this.

We must re-establish truth and morals in public life. No people will long remain a moral people under a government that repudiates its obligations, that uses public funds to corrupt the people, that conceals its actions by double bookkeeping.

We must have government that builds stamina into communities and men. That makes men instead of mendicants. We must stop this softening of thrift, self-reliance and self-respect through dependence on government. We must stop telling youth that the country is going to the devil and they haven't a chance. We must stop this dissipating the initiative and aspirations of our people. We must revive the courage of men and women and their faith in American liberty. We must recover these spiritual heritages of America.

All this clatter of class and class hate should end. Thieves will get into high places as well as low places and they should both be given economic security—in jail. But they are not a class. This is a classless country. If we hold to our unique American ideal of equal opportunity there can never be classes or masses in our country. To preach these class ideas from the White House is new in American life. There is no employing class, no working class, no farming class. You may pigeonhole a man or woman as a farmer or a worker or a professional man or an employer or even a banker. But the son of the farmer will be a doctor or a worker or even a banker, and his daughter a teacher. The son of a worker will be an employer —or maybe President. And certainly the sons of even economic royalists have a bad time holding the title of nobility. . . .

Franklin D. Roosevelt, Speech on Court Reform
March 9, 1937

[Roosevelt surprised the country, and even his party, when on February 5 he sent his court reorganization plan to Congress. A storm of opposition rose up against it. Roosevelt presented his views at length in a radio "report to the people."]

. . . The American people have learned from the depression. For in the last three national elections an overwhelming majority of them voted a mandate that the Congress and the President begin the task of providing that protection—not after long years of debate, but now.

The courts, however, have cast doubts on the ability of the elected Congress to protect us against catastrophe by meeting squarely our modern social and economic conditions.

We are at a crisis in our ability to proceed with that protection. It is a quiet crisis. There are no lines of depositors outside closed banks. But to the far-sighted it is far-reaching in its possibilities of injury to America.

I want to talk with you very simply about the need for present action in this crisis—the need to meet the unanswered challenge of one-third of a nation ill-nourished, ill-clad, ill-housed.

Last Thursday I described the American form of government as a three-horse team provided by the Constitution to the American people so that their field might be plowed. The three horses are, of course, the three branches of government —the Congress, the executive, and the courts. Two of the horses are pulling in unison today; the third is not. Those who have intimated that the President of the United States is trying to drive that team overlook the simple fact that the President, as Chief Executive, is himself one of the three horses.

It is the American people themselves who are in the driver's seat.

It is the American people themselves who want the furrow plowed.

It is the American people themselves who expect the third horse to pull in unison with the other two.

I hope that you have reread the Constitution of the United States. Like the Bible, it ought to be read again and again.

It is an easy document to understand when you remember that it was called into being because the Articles of Confederation under which the Original Thirteen States tried to operate after the Revolution showed the need of a National Government with power enough to handle national problems. In its preamble the Constitution states that it was intended to form a more perfect Union and promote the general welfare; and the powers given to the Congress to carry out those purposes can be best described by saying that they were all the powers needed to meet each and every problem which then had a national character and which could not be met by merely local action.

But the framers went further. Having in mind that in succeeding generations many other problems then undreamed of would become national problems, they gave to the Congress the ample broad powers "to levy taxes . . . and provide for the common defense and general welfare of the United States."

That, my friends, is what I honestly believe to have been the clear and underlying purpose of the patriots who wrote a Federal Constitution to create a National Government with national power, intended as they said, "to form a more perfect union . . . for ourselves and our posterity." . . .

But since the rise of the modern movement for social and economic progress through legislation, the Court has more and more often and more and more boldly asserted a power to veto laws passed by the Congress and State legislatures in complete disregard of this original limitation.

In the last 4 years the sound rule of giving statutes the benefit of all reasonable doubt has been cast aside. The Court has been acting not as a judicial body, but as a policy-making body.

When the Congress has sought to stabilize national agriculture, to improve the conditions of labor, to safeguard business against unfair competition, to protect our national resources, and in many other ways to serve our clearly national needs, the majority of the Court has been assuming the power to pass on the wisdom of these acts of the Congress —and to approve or disapprove the public policy written into these laws.

That is not only my accusation. It is the accusation of most distinguished Justices of the present Supreme Court. I have not the time to quote to you all the language used by dissenting Justices in many of these cases. But in the case holding the Railroad Retirement Act unconstitutional, for instance, Chief Justice Hughes said in a dissenting opinion that the majority opinion was "a departure from sound principles," and placed "an unwarranted limitation upon the commerce clause." And three other Justices agreed with him.

In the case holding the A. A. A. unconstitutional, Justice Stone said of the majority opinion that it was a "tortured construction of the Constitution." And two other Justices agreed with him.

In the case holding the New York Minimum Wage Law unconstitutional, Justice Stone said that the majority were actually reading into the Constitution their own "personal economic predilections," and that if the legislative power is not left free to choose the methods of solving the problems of poverty, subsistence, and health of large numbers in the community, then "government is to be rendered impotent." And two other Justices agreed with him.

In the face of these dissenting opinions, there is no basis for the claim made by some members of the Court that something in the Constitution has compelled them regretfully to thwart the will of the people.

In the face of such dissenting opinions, it is perfectly clear that as Chief Justice Hughes has said, "We are under a Constitution, but the Constitution is what the judges say it is."

The Court in addition to the proper use of its judicial functions has improperly set itself up as a third House of the Congress—a super-legislature, as one of the Justices has called it—reading into the Constitution words and implications which are not there, and which were never intended to be there.

We have, therefore, reached the point as a Nation where we must take action to save the Constitution from the Court and the Court from itself. We must find a way to take an appeal from the Supreme Court to the Constitution itself. We want a Supreme Court which will do justice under the Constitution—not over it. In our courts we want a government of laws and not of men.

I want—as all Americans want—an independent judiciary as proposed by the framers of the Constitution. That means a Supreme Court that will enforce the Constitution as written —that will refuse to amend the Constitution by the arbitrary exercise of judicial power—amendment by judicial say-so. It does not mean a judiciary so independent that it can deny the existence of facts universally recognized.

How, then, could we proceed to perform the mandate given us? It was said in last year's Democratic platform, "If these problems cannot be effectively solved within the Constitution, we shall seek such clarifying amendment as will assure the power to enact those laws, adequately to regulate commerce, protect public health and safety, and safeguard economic security." In other words, we said we would seek an amendment only if every other possible means by legislation were to fail.

When I commenced to review the situation with the problem squarely before me, I came by a process of elimination to the conclusion that short of amendments the only method which was clearly constitutional, and would at the same time carry out other much-needed reforms, was to infuse new blood into all our courts. We must have men worthy and equipped to carry out impartial justice. But at the same time we must have judges who will bring to the courts a present-day sense of the Constitution—judges who will retain in the courts the judicial functions of a court and reject the legislative powers which the courts have today assumed.

In 45 out of 48 States of the Union, judges are chosen not for life but for a period of years. In many States judges must retire at the age of 70. Congress has provided financial security by offering life pensions at full pay for Federal judges on all courts who are willing to retire at 70. In the case of Supreme Court Justices, that pension is $20,000 a year. But all Federal judges, once appointed, can, if they choose, hold office for life no matter how old they may get to be.

What is my proposal? It is simply this: Whenever a judge or justice of any Federal court has reached the age of 70 and does not avail himself of the opportunity to retire on a pension, a new member shall be appointed by the President then in office, with the approval, as required by the Constitution, of the Senate of the United States.

That plan has two chief purposes: By bringing into the judicial system a steady and continuing stream of new and younger blood, I hope, first, to make the administration of all Federal justice speedier and therefore less costly; secondly, to bring to the decision of social and economic problems younger men who have had personal experience and contact with modern facts and circumstances under which average men have to live and work. This plan will save our National Constitution from hardening of the judicial arteries.

The number of judges to be appointed would depend wholly on the decision of present judges now over 70 or those who would subsequently reach the age of 70.

If, for instance, any one of the six Justices of the Supreme Court now over the age of 70 should retire as provided under the plan, no additional place would be created. Consequently, although there never can be more than 15, there may be only 14, or 13, or 12, and there may be only 9.

There is nothing novel or radical about this idea. It seeks to maintain the Federal bench in full vigor. It has been discussed and approved by many persons of high authority ever since a similar proposal passed the House of Representatives in 1869.

Why was the age fixed at 70? Because the laws of many States, the practice of the civil service, the regulations of the Army and Navy, and the rules of many of our universities and of almost every great private business enterprise commonly fix the retirement age at 70 years or less.

The statute would apply to all the courts in the Federal system. There is general approval so far as the lower Federal courts are concerned. The plan has met opposition only so far as the Supreme Court of the United States itself is concerned. If such a plan is good for the lower courts, it certainly ought to be equally good for the highest court, from which there is no appeal.

Those opposing this plan have sought to arouse prejudice and fear by crying that I am seeking to "pack" the Supreme Court and that a baneful precedent will be established.

What do they mean by the words "packing the Court"?

Let me answer this question with a bluntness that will end all honest misunderstanding of my purposes.

If by that phrase "packing the Court" it is charged that I wish to place on the bench spineless puppets who would disregard the law and would decide specific cases as I wished them to be decided, I make this answer: That no President fit for his office would appoint, and no Senate of honorable men fit for their office would confirm, that kind of appointees to the Supreme Court.

But if by that phrase the charge is made that I would appoint and the Senate would confirm Justices worthy to sit beside present members of the Court who understand those modern conditions; that I will appoint Justices who will not undertake to override the judgment of the Congress on legislative policy; that I will appoint Justices who will act as Justices and not as legislators—if the appointment of such Justices can be called "packing the Courts"—then I say that I, and with me the vast majority of the American people, favor doing just that thing—now.

Is it a dangerous precedent for the Congress to change the number of the Justices? The Congress has always had, and will have, that power. The number of Justices has been changed several times before—in the administrations of John Adams and Thomas Jefferson, both signers of the Declaration of Independence, Andrew Jackson, Abraham Lincoln, and Ulysses S. Grant.

I suggest only the addition of Justices to the bench in accordance with a clearly defined principle relating to a clearly defined age limit. Fundamentally, if in the future America cannot trust the Congress it elects to refrain from abuse of our constitutional usages, democracy will have failed far beyond the importance to it of any kind of precedent concerning the judiciary. . . .

I am in favor of action through legislation—

First, because I believe that it can be passed at this session of the Congress.

Second, because it will provide a reinvigorated, liberal-minded judiciary necessary to furnish quicker and cheaper justice from bottom to top.

Third, because it will provide a series of Federal courts willing to enforce the Constitution as written, and unwilling to assert legislative powers by writing into it their own political and economic policies.

During the past half century the balance of power between the three great branches of the Federal Government has been tipped out of balance by the courts in direct contradiction of the high purposes of the framers of the Constitution. It is my purpose to restore that balance. You who know me will accept my solemn assurance that in a world in which democracy is under attack I seek to make American democracy succeed.

NLRB v. Jones and Laughlin Steel Corporation
1937

[The Fifth District U. S. Circuit Court of Appeals had declared the National Labor Relations Act unconstitutional, and the federal government appealed to the Supreme Court. Reversing its own decision in the Schechter case, the Court by a five-to-four majority now found that the federal government did in fact have broad authority to regulate the "stream of commerce."]

Hughes, C. J.: In a proceeding under the National Labor Relations Act of 1935, the National Labor Relations Board found that the petitioner, Jones & Laughlin Steel Corporation, had violated the Act by engaging in unfair labor practices affecting commerce. The proceeding was instituted by the Beaver Valley Lodge No. 200, affiliated with the Amalgamated Association of Iron, Steel and Tin Workers of America, a labor organization. The unfair labor practices charged were that the corporation was discriminating against mem-

bers of the union with regard to hire and tenure of employment, and was coercing and intimidating its employees in
order to interfere with their self-organization. The discriminatory and coercive action alleged was the discharge of certain
employees.

The National Labor Relations Board, sustaining the
charge, ordered the corporation to cease and desist from such
discrimination and coercion, to offer reinstatement to ten of
the employees named, to make good their losses in pay, and
to post for thirty days notices that the corporation would not
discharge or discriminate against members, or those desiring
to become members, of the labor union. As the corporation
failed to comply, the Board petitioned the Circuit Court of
Appeals to enforce the order. The court denied the petition, holding that the order lay beyond the range of federal
power. 83 F. (2d) 998. We granted certiorari. . . .

While respondent criticises the evidence and the attitude
of the Board, which is described as being hostile toward employers and particularly toward those who insisted upon their
constitutional rights, respondent did not take advantage of
its opportunity to present evidence to refute that which was
offered to show discrimination and coercion. In this situation, the record presents no ground for setting aside the order
of the Board so far as the facts pertaining to the circumstances and purpose of the discharge of the employees are
concerned. Upon that point it is sufficient to say that the
evidence supports the findings of the Board that respondent
discharged these men "because of their union activity and
for the purpose of discouraging membership in the union."
We turn to the questions of law which respondent urges in
contesting the validity and application of the Act.

First. The Scope of the Act.—The Act is challenged in its
entirety as an attempt to regulate all industry, thus invading
the reserved powers of the States over their local concerns.
It is asserted that the references in the Act to interstate and
foreign commerce are colorable at best; that the Act is not a
true regulation of such commerce or of matters which directly
affect it but on the contrary has the fundamental object of
placing under the compulsory supervision of the federal gov-

ernment all industrial labor relations within the nation. The argument seeks support in the broad words of the preamble and in the sweep of the provisions of the Act, and it is further insisted that its legislative history shows an essential universal purpose in the light of which its scope cannot be limited by either construction or by the application of the separability clause.

If this conception of terms, intent and consequent inseparability were sound, the Act would necessarily fall by reason of the limitation upon the federal power which inheres in the constitutional grant, as well as because of the explicit reservation of the Tenth Amendment. *Schechter Corporation v. United States,* 295 U. S. 495, 549, 550, 554. The authority of the federal government may not be pushed to such an extreme as to destroy the distinction, which the commerce clause itself establishes, between commerce "among the several States" and the internal concerns of a State. That distinction between what is national and what is local in the activities of commerce is vital to the maintenance of our federal system.

But we are not at liberty to deny effect to specific provisions, which Congress has constitutional power to enact, by superimposing upon them inferences from general legislative declarations of an ambiguous character, even if found in the same statute. The cardinal principle of statutory construction is to save and not to destroy. We have repeatedly held that as between two possible interpretations of a statute, by one of which it would be unconstitutional and by the other valid, our plain duty is to adopt that which will save the act. Even to avoid a serious doubt the rule is the same.

We think it clear that the National Labor Relations Act may be construed so as to operate within the sphere of constitutional authority. . . .

Section 8, subdivision (1), refers to Section 7, which is as follows:

SEC. 7. Employees shall have the right to self-organization, to form, join, or assist labor organizations, to bargain collectively through representatives of their own choosing, and to engage in concerted activities, for the purpose of collective bargaining or other mutual aid or protection.

Thus, in its present application, the statute goes no further than to safeguard the right of employees to self-organization and to select representatives of their own choosing for collective bargaining or other mutual protection without restraint or coercion by their employer.

That is a fundamental right. Employees have as clear a right to organize and select their representatives for lawful purposes as the respondent has to organize its business and select its own officers and agents. Discrimination and coercion to prevent the free exercise of the right of employees to self-organization and representation is a proper subject for condemnation by competent legislative authority. Long ago we stated the reason for labor organizations. We said that they were organized out of the necessities of the situation; that a single employee was helpless in dealing with an employer; that he was dependent ordinarily on his daily wage for the maintenance of himself and family; that if the employer refused to pay him the wages that he thought fair, he was nevertheless unable to leave the employ and resist arbitrary and unfair treatment; that union was essential to give laborers opportunity to deal on an equality with their employer.

Third. The application of the Act to employees engaged in production.—The principle involved.—Respondent says that whatever may be said of employees engaged in interstate commerce, the industrial relations and activities in the manufacturing department of respondent's enterprise are not subject to federal regulation. The argument rests upon the proposition that manufacturing in itself is not commerce. . . . The congressional authority to protect interstate commerce from burdens and obstructions is not limited to transactions which can be deemed to be an essential part of a "flow" of interstate or foreign commerce. Burdens and obstructions may be due to injurious action springing from other sources. The fundamental principle is that the power to regulate commerce is the power to enact "all appropriate legislation" for "its protection and advancement"; to adopt measures "to promote its growth and insure its safety"; "to

punishable by imprisonment for not less than one year nor more than ten years, or by a fine of not more than $1,000, or by both.

We are concerned with but one of the described offenses and with the validity of the statute in this particular application. The charge is that appellant assisted in the conduct of a meeting which was called under the auspices of the Communist party, an organization advocating criminal syndicalism. The defense was that the meeting was public and orderly and was held for a lawful purpose; that while it was held under the auspices of the Communist party, neither criminal syndicalism nor any unlawful conduct was taught or advocated at the meeting either by appellant or by others.

Appellant moved for a direction of acquittal, contending that the statute as applied to him, for merely assisting at a meeting called by the Communist party at which nothing unlawful was done or advocated, violated the due process clause of the Fourteenth Amendment of the Constitution of the United States.

This contention was overruled. Appellant was found guilty as charged and was sentenced to imprisonment for seven years. The judgment was affirmed by the Supreme Court of the State, which considered the constitutional question and sustained the statute as thus applied. 152 Ore. 315. The case comes here on appeal. . . .

The stipulation, after setting forth the charging part of the indictment, recites in substance the following:

That on July 27, 1934, there was held in Portland a meeting which had been advertised by hand-bills issued by the Portland section of the Communist party; that the number of persons in attendance was variously estimated at from 150 to 300; that some of those present, who were members of the Communist party, estimated that not to exceed 10 to 15 per cent of those in attendance were such members; that the meeting was open to the public without charge and no questions were asked of those entering with respect to their relation to the Communist party; that the notice of the meeting advertised it as a protest against illegal raids on workers' halls and homes and against the shooting of striking longshoremen by Portland police; that the chairman stated that it was a meeting held by the Communist party; that the first speaker dwelt on the activities of the Young Communist League.

That the defendant De Jonge, the second speaker, was a member of the Communist party and went to the meeting to speak in its name; that in his talk he protested against conditions in the county jail, the action of city police in relation to the maritime strike then in progress in Portland and numerous other matters; that he discussed the reason for the raids on the Communist headquarters and workers' halls and offices; that he told the workers that these attacks were due to efforts on the part of the steamship companies and stevedoring companies to break the maritime longshoremen's and seamen's strike; that they hoped to break the strike by pitting the longshoremen and seamen against the Communist movement; that there was also testimony to the effect that defendant asked those present to do more work in obtaining members for the Communist party and requested all to be at the meeting of the party to be held in Portland on the following evening and to bring their friends to show their defiance to local police authority and to assist them in their revolutionary tactics.

That there was also testimony that defendant urged the purchase of certain Communist literature which was sold at the meeting; that while the meeting was still in progress it was raided by the police; that the meeting was conducted in an orderly manner; that defendant and several others who were actively conducting the meeting were arrested by the police and that on searching the hall the police found a quantity of Communist literature.

The stipulation then set forth various extracts from the literature of the Communist party to show its advocacy of criminal syndicalism. The stipulation does not disclose any activity by the defendant as a basis for his prosecution other than his participation in the meeting in question. Nor does the stipulation show that the Communist literature distributed at the meeting contained any advocacy of criminal syndicalism or of any unlawful conduct.

It was admitted by the Attorney General of the State in his argument at the bar of this court that the literature distributed in the meeting was not of that sort and that the extracts contained in the stipulation were taken from Communist literature found elsewhere. Its introduction in evidence was for the purpose of showing that the Communist party as such did advocate the doctrine of criminal syndicalism, a fact which is not disputed on this appeal.

On the theory that this was a charge that criminal syndicalism and sabotage were advocated at the meeting in question, defendant moved for acquittal insisting that the evidence was insufficient to warrant his conviction. The trial court denied his motion and error in this respect was assigned on appeal.

The Supreme Court of the State put aside that contention by ruling that the indictment did not charge that criminal syndicalism or sabotage was advocated at the meeting described in the evidence, either by defendant or by any one else. . . .

The broad reach of the statute as thus applied is plain. While defendant was a member of the Communist party, that membership was not necessary to conviction on such a charge. A like fate might have attended any speaker, although not a member who "assisted in the conduct" of the meeting. However innocuous the object of the meeting, however lawful the subjects and tenor of the addresses, however reasonable and timely the discussion, all those assisting in the conduct of the meeting would be subject to imprisonment as felons if the meeting were held by the Communist party.

This manifest result was brought out sharply at this bar by the concessions which the Attorney General made, and could not avoid, in the light of the decision of the State court. Thus if the Communist party had called a public meeting in Portland to discuss the tariff, or the foreign policy of the government, or taxation, or relief, or candidacies for the offices of President, members of Congress, Governor or State legislators, every speaker who assisted in the conduct of the meeting would be equally guilty with the defendant in this case, upon the charge as here defined and sustained. . . .

While the States are entitled to protect themselves from the abuse of the privileges of our institutions through an attempted substitution of force and violence in the place of peaceful political action in order to effect revolutionary changes in government, none of our decisions go to the length of sustaining such a curtailment of the right of free speech and assembly as the Oregon statute demands in its present application.

Freedom of speech and of the press are fundamental rights which are safeguarded by the due process clause of the Fourteenth Amendment of the Federal Constitution. The right of peaceable assembly is a right cognate to those of free speech and free press and is equally fundamental. . . .

The First Amendment of the Federal Constitution expressly guarantees that right against abridgment by Congress. But explicit mention there does not argue exclusion elsewhere. For the right is one that cannot be denied without violating those fundamental principles of liberty and justice which lie at the base of all civil and political institutions, principles which the Fourteenth Amendment embodies in the general terms of its due process clause.

These rights may be abused by using speech or press or assembly in order to incite to violence and crime. The people, through their Legislatures, may protect themselves against that abuse. But the legislative intervention can find constitutional justification only by dealing with the abuse. The rights themselves must not be curtailed.

The greater the importance of safeguarding the community from incitements to the overthrow of our institutions by force and violence, the more imperative is the need to preserve inviolate the constitutional rights of free speech, free press and free assembly in order to maintain the opportunity for free political discussion, to the end that government may be responsive to the will of the people and that changes, if desired, may be obtained by peaceful means. Therein lies the security of the republic, the very foundation of constitutional government.

It follows from these considerations that, consistently with the Federal Constitution, peaceable assembly for lawful discussion cannot be made a crime. The holding of meetings for peaceable political action cannot be proscribed. Those who assist in the conduct of such meetings cannot be branded as criminals on that score. The question, if the rights of free speech and peaceable assembly are to be preserved, is not as to the auspices under which the meeting is held, but as to its purpose; not as to the relations of the speakers, but whether their utterances transcend the bounds of the freedom of speech which the Constitution protects.

If the persons assemblying have committed crimes elsewhere, if they have formed or are engaged in a conspiracy against the public peace and order, they may be prosecuted for their conspiracy or other violation of valid laws.

But it is a different matter when the State, instead of prosecuting them for such offenses, seizes upon mere participation in a peaceable assembly and a lawful public discussion as the basis for a criminal charge.

We are not called upon to review the findings of the State court as to the objectives of the Communist party. Notwithstanding those objectives, the defendant still enjoyed his personal right of free speech and to take part in a peaceable assembly having a lawful purpose, although called by that party. The defendant was none the less entitled to discuss the public issues of the day and thus in a lawful manner, without incitement to violence or crime, to seek redress of alleged grievances. That was of the essence of his guaranteed personal liberty.

We hold that the Oregon statute as applied to the particular charge as defined by the State court is repugnant to the due process clause of the Fourteenth Amendment. The judgment of conviction is reversed and the cause is remanded for further proceedings not inconsistent with this opinion. It is so ordered.

Franklin D. Roosevelt, Speech on Liberalizing
the Democratic Party
August 11, 1938

[Roosevelt delivered this remarkable speech at Barnesville, Georgia, the site of an administration rural electrification project. He used the occasion to call on the Georgia voters to defeat Senator Walter George, an inveterate foe of the New Deal, in the coming primary. It happened that Senator George was sitting next to Roosevelt on the platform. He went on to win the primary and the election.]

Fourteen years ago a democratic Yankee, a comparatively young man, came to a neighboring county in the State of Georgia, in search of a pool of warm water wherein he might swim his way back to health; and he found it. The place—Warm Springs—was at that time a rather dilapidated small summer resort. His new neighbors there extended to him the hand of genuine hospitality, welcomed him to their firesides and made him feel so much at home that he built himself a house, bought himself a farm, and has been coming back ever since. And he proposes to keep to that good custom. I intend coming back very often.

There was only one discordant note in that first stay of mine at Warm Springs. When the first of the month bill came in for electric light for my little cottage, I found that the charge was eighteen cents per kilowatt hour—about four times as much as I was paying in another community, Hyde Park, New York. That light bill started my long study of proper public utility charges for electric current, started in my mind the whole subject of getting electricity into farm homes throughout the United States.

So, my friends, it can be said with a good deal of truth that a little cottage at Warm Springs, Georgia, was the birthplace of the Rural Electrification Administration. Six years ago, in 1932, there was much talk about the more widespread and cheaper use of electricity; but it is only since

March 4, 1933, that your Government has reduced that talk to practical results. Electricity is a modern necessity of life, not a luxury. That necessity ought to be found in every village, in every home and on every farm in every part of the United States. The dedication of this Rural Electrification Administration project in Georgia today is a symbol of the progress we are making—and we are not going to stop.

As you know, when I want to go somewhere I generally try to choose the most direct route, but I slipped up this time. I wanted to come to Georgia, but I had to come via California, the Galapagos Islands, the Equator, the Panama Canal and Pensacola. But, before I left on that trip about a month ago, I invited a group of distinguished, broad-minded Southerners to meet in Washington to discuss the economic conditions and problems of the South. When they met, I said to them:

"My intimate interest in all that concerns the South is, I believe, known to all of you; but this interest is far more than a sentimental attachment born of a considerable residence in your section and of close personal friendship with so many of your people. It proceeds even more from my feeling of responsibility toward the whole Nation. It is my conviction that the South presents right now the Nation's No. 1 economic problem—the Nation's problem, not merely the South's. For we have an economic unbalance in the Nation as a whole, due to this very condition in the South itself.

"It is an unbalance that can and must be righted for the sake of the South and of the Nation."

The day before yesterday when I landed in Florida I received the report and the recommendations based on the advice of this distinguished commission. This report and the recommendations will be made public in the course of the next day or two; and I hope you will read it.

It is well said that this report "presents in only a small degree the manifold assets and advantages possessed by the South" because the report is concerned primarily not with boasting about what the South has, but in telling what the South needs. It is a short report divided into fifteen short sections; and it covers in a broad way subjects of vital importance, such as economic resources, soil, water, population, private and public income, education, health, housing, labor, ownership and use of land, credit, use of natural resources, industry and purchasing power.

I am listing those fifteen headings with a definite purpose in mind. The very fact that it is necessary to divide the economic needs of the South into fifteen important groups—each one a problem in itself—proves to you and to me that if you and I are to cover the ground effectively, there is no one single simple answer. It is true that many obvious needs ought to be attained quickly—such as the reduction of discriminatory freight rates, such as putting a definite floor under industrial wages, such as continuing to raise the purchasing power of the farm population. But no one of these things alone, no combination of a few of them, will meet the whole of the problem. Talking in fighting terms, we cannot capture one hill and claim to have won the battle, because the battlefront extends over thousands of miles and we must push forward along the whole front at the same time.

That is why the longer I live, the more am I convinced that there are two types of political leadership which are dangerous to the continuation of broad economic and social progress all along that long battlefront. The first type of political leadership which is dangerous to progress is represented by the man who harps on one or two remedies or proposals and claims that these one or two remedies will cure all our ills. The other type of dangerous leadership is represented by the man who says that he is in favor of progress but whose record shows that he hinders or hampers or tries to kill new measures of progress. He is that type of political leader who tells his friends that he does not like this or that or the other detail; and, at the same time, he utterly fails to offer a substitute that is practical or worthwhile.

The task of meeting the economic and social needs of the South, on the broad front that is absolutely necessary, calls for public servants whose hearts are sound, whose heads are sane—whose hands are strong, striving everlastingly to better the lot of their fellowmen.

The report to which I referred is a synopsis—a clear listing of the economic and social problems of the Southland.

It suggests the many steps that must be taken to solve the problems.

Some of these steps, it is true, can be taken by state governments, but you will readily realize that action by the states alone, even if such action on the part of many neighboring states could be simultaneous and immediate, would be wholly inadequate. The very good reason for that is that most of these problems involve interstate relationships, relationships not only among the states of this region but also between each and all of these states and the rest of the Nation.

It is not an attack on state sovereignty to point out that this national aspect of all these problems requires action by the Federal Government in Washington. I do not hesitate to say from long experience that during the past five years there has been a closer and more effective peacetime cooperation between the Governors of the forty-eight states and the President of the United States than at any other time in our whole national history.

You are familiar enough with the processes of Government to know that the Chief Executive cannot take action on national or regional problems, unless they have been first translated into Acts of Congress passed by the Senate and the House of Representatives of the United States.

Such action by the Congress, it is equally clear, must be vigorously supported by the Senators and Representatives whose constituents are directly concerned with Southern economics and Southern social needs. Senators and Congressmen who are not wholeheartedly in sympathy with these needs cannot be expected to give them vigorous support.

Translating that into more intimate terms, it means that if the people of the State of Georgia want definite action in the Congress of the United States, they must send to that Congress Senators and Representatives who are willing to stand up and fight night and day for Federal statutes drawn to meet actual needs—not something that serves merely to gloss over the evils of the moment for the time being—but laws with teeth in them which go to the root of the problems; which remove the inequities, raise the standards and, over a period of years, give constant improvement to the conditions of human life in this State.

You, the people of Georgia, in the coming Senatorial primary, for example, have a perfect right to choose any candidate you wish. I do not seek to impair that right, and I am not going to impair that right of the people of this State; but because Georgia has been good enough to call me her adopted son and because for many long years I have regarded Georgia as my "other state," I feel no hesitation in telling you what I would do if I could vote here next month. I am strengthened in that decision to give you my personal opinion of the coming Senatorial primary by the fact that during the past few weeks I have had many requests from distinguished citizens of Georgia—from people high and low—from the Chief Justice of the highest court of Georgia and many others.

Let me preface my statement by saying that I have personally known three of the candidates for the United States Senate for many years. All of them have had legislative or executive experience as Government servants. We may therefore justly consider their records and their public utterances —and we can justly, also, seek to determine for ourselves what is their inward point of view in relationship to present and future problems of government.

It has been pointed out by writers and speakers who do not analyze public questions very deeply that in passing through the State of Kentucky a month ago I gave as a reason for the reelection of Senator Barkley that he had had very long and successful service in the Congress of the United States and that his opponent did not have that experience. In Kentucky, there was no clear-cut issue between a liberal on the one side and a dyed-in-the-wool conservative on the other. Neither of the two principals on his record could be classified as a reactionary; therefore, the criterion of experience, especially that of the Majority Leadership of the Senate of the United States, weighed heavily, and properly, in favor of Senator Barkley.

Here in Georgia, however, my old friend, the senior Senator from this State, cannot possibly in my judgment be classified as belonging to the liberal school of thought—and, therefore, the argument that he has long served in the Senate falls by the wayside. Here in Georgia the issue is a different one from that in Kentucky.

I speak seriously and in the most friendly way in terms of liberal and conservative for the very simple fact that on my shoulders rests a responsibility to the people of the United States. In 1932 and again in 1936 I was chosen Chief Executive with the mandate to seek by definite action to correct many evils of the past and of the present; to work for a wider distribution of national income, to improve the conditions of life, especially among those who need it most and, above all, to use every honest effort to keep America in the van of social and economic progress.

To the Congress of the United States I make recommendations—that is all—in most cases recommendations relating to objectives, leaving it to the Congress to translate the recommendations into law. The majority of the Senate and House have agreed with those objectives, and have worked with me; and I have worked with them to translate those objectives into action. Some have given "lip service" to some of the objectives but have not raised their little fingers actively to attain the objectives themselves. Too often these few have listened to the dictatorship of a small minority of individuals and corporations who oppose the objectives themselves. That is a real dictatorship and one which we have been getting away from slowly but surely during the past five years. As long as I live, you will find me fighting against any kind of dictatorship—especially the kind of dictatorship which has enslaved many of our fellow citizens for more than half a century.

What I am about to say will be no news, to my old friend —and I say it with the utmost sincerity—Senator Walter George. It will be no surprise to him because I have recently had personal correspondence with him; and, as a result of it, he fully knows what my views are.

Let me make it clear that he is, and I hope always will be, my personal friend. He is beyond question, beyond any possible question, a gentleman and a scholar; but there are other gentlemen in the Senate and in the House for whom I have a real affectionate regard, but with whom I differ heartily and sincerely on the principles and policies of how the Government of the United States ought to be run.

For example, I have had an almost lifelong acquaintance and great personal friendship for people like Senator Hale from the State of Maine, for Representative James Wadsworth of New York and for the Minority Leader, Representative Snell. All of these lifelong conservative Republicans are gentlemen and scholars; but they and I learned long ago that our views on public questions were just as wide apart as the North Pole and the South.

Therefore, I repeat that I trust, and am confident, that Senator George and I shall always be good personal friends even though I am impelled to make it clear that on most public questions he and I do not speak the same language.

To carry out my responsibility as President, it is clear that if there is to be success in our Government there ought to be cooperation between members of my own party and myself—cooperation, in other words, within the majority party, between one branch of Government, the Legislative branch, and the head of the other branch, the Executive. That is one of the essentials of a party form of government. It has been going on in this country for nearly a century and a half. The test is not measured, in the case of an individual, by his every vote on every bill—of course not. The test lies rather in the answer to two questions: first, has the record of the candidate shown, while differing perhaps in details, a constant active fighting attitude in favor of the broad objectives of the party and of the Government as they are constituted today; and, secondly, does the candidate really, in his heart, deep down in his heart, believe in those objectives? I regret that in the case of my friend, Senator George, I cannot honestly answer either of these questions in the affirmative.

In the case of another candidate in the State of Georgia for the United States Senate—former Governor Talmadge—I have known him for many years. His attitude toward me and toward other members of the Government in 1935 and in 1936 concerns me not at all. But, in those years and in this year I have read so many of his proposals, so many of his promises, so many of his panaceas, that I am very certain in my own mind that his election would contribute very little to practical progress in government. That is all I can say about him. . . .

Franklin D. Roosevelt, Eighth Annual Message
January 6, 1941

[The United States had begun to prepare for the inevitable war with the Axis powers. In this message to Congress Roosevelt has proposed a lend-lease scheme to help Britain, now fighting alone against Germany and Italy, and he goes on to enunciate his famous Four Freedoms.]

. . . As men do not live by bread alone, they do not fight by armaments alone. Those who man our defenses, and those behind them who build our defenses, must have the stamina and the courage which come from unshakeable belief in the manner of life which they are defending. The mighty action that we are calling for cannot be based on a disregard of all the things worth fighting for.

The Nation takes great satisfaction and much strength from the things which have been done to make its people conscious of their individual stake in the preservation of democratic life in America. Those things have toughened the fibre of our people, have renewed their faith and strengthened their devotion to the institutions we make ready to protect.

Certainly this is no time for any of us to stop thinking about the social and economic problems which are the root cause of the social revolution which is today a supreme factor in the world.

For there is nothing mysterious about the foundations of a healthy and strong democracy. The basic things expected by our people of their political and economic systems are simple. They are:

Equality of opportunity for youth and for others.

Jobs for those who can work.

Security for those who need it.

The ending of special privilege for the few.

The preservation of civil liberties for all.

The enjoyment of the fruits of scientific progress in a wider and constantly rising standard of living.

These are the simple, basic things that must never be lost sight of in the turmoil and unbelievable complexity of our modern world. The inner and abiding strength of our economic and political systems is dependent upon the degree to which they fulfill these expectations.

Many subjects connected with our social economy call for immediate improvement.

As examples:

We should bring more citizens under the coverage of old-age pensions and unemployment insurance.

We should widen the opportunities for adequate medical care.

We should plan a better system by which persons deserving or needing gainful employment may obtain it.

I have called for personal sacrifice. And I am assured of the willingness of almost all Americans to respond to that call.

A part of the sacrifice means the payment of more money in taxes. In my Budget Message I will recommend that a greater portion of this great defense program be paid for from taxation than we are paying for today. No person should try, or be allowed, to get rich out of this program; and the principle of tax payments in accordance with ability to pay should be constantly before our eyes to guide our legislation.

If the Congress maintains these principles, the voters, putting patriotism ahead of pocketbooks, will give you their applause.

In the future days, which we seek to make secure, we look forward to a world founded upon four essential human freedoms.

The first is freedom of speech and expression—everywhere in the world.

The second is freedom of every person to worship God in his own way—everywhere in the world.

The third is freedom from want—which, translated into world terms, means economic understandings which will secure to every nation a healthy peacetime life for its inhabitants—everywhere in the world.

The fourth is freedom from fear—which, translated into world terms, means a world-wide reduction of armaments to such a point and in such a thorough fashion that no nation will be in a position to commit an act of physical aggression against any neighbor—anywhere in the world.

That is no vision of a distant millennium. It is a definite basis for a kind of world attainable in our own time and generation. That kind of world is the very antithesis of the so-called new order of tyranny which the dictators seek to create with the crash of a bomb.

To that new order we oppose the greater conception—the moral order. A good society is able to face schemes of world domination and foreign revolutions alike without fear.

Since the beginning of our American history, we have been engaged in change—in a perpetual peaceful revolution—a revolution which goes on steadily, quietly adjusting itself to changing conditions—without the concentration camp or the quick-lime in the ditch. The world order which we seek is the cooperation of free countries, working together in a friendly, civilized society.

This nation has placed its destiny in the hands and heads and hearts of its millions of free men and women; and its faith in freedom under the guidance of God. Freedom means the supremacy of human rights everywhere. Our support goes to those who struggle to gain those rights and keep them. Our strength is our unity of purpose.

To that high concept there can be no end save victory.

The Atlantic Charter
August 14, 1941

[Between August 9 and 14 President Roosevelt and Prime Minister Churchill secretly met aboard the American cruiser *Augusta* and the British battleship *Prince of Wales* off the coast of Newfoundland. Together they drew up the Atlantic

Charter, which announced their "hopes for a better future for the world."]

The President of the United States of America and the Prime Minister, Mr. Churchill, representing His Majesty's Government in the United Kingdom, being met together, deem it right to make known certain common principles in the national policies of their respective countries on which they base their hopes for a better future for the world.

First, their countries seek no aggrandizement, territorial or other;

Second, they desire to see no territorial changes that do not accord with the freely expressed wishes of the peoples concerned;

Third, they respect the right of all peoples to choose the form of government under which they will live; and they wish to see sovereign rights and self government restored to those who have been forcibly deprived of them;

Fourth, they will endeavor, with due respect for their existing obligations, to further the enjoyment by all States, great or small, victor or vanquished, of access, on equal terms, to the trade and to the raw materials of the world which are needed for their economic prosperity;

Fifth, they desire to bring about the fullest collaboration between all nations in the economic field with the object of securing, for all, improved labor standards, economic advancement and social security;

Sixth, after the final destruction of the Nazi tyranny, they hope to see established a peace which will afford to all nations the means of dwelling in safety within their own boundaries, and which will afford assurance that all the men in all the lands may live out their lives in freedom from fear and want;

Seventh, such a peace should enable all men to traverse the high seas and oceans without hindrance;

Eighth, they believe that all of the nations of the world, for realistic as well as spiritual reasons must come to the abandonment of the use of force. Since no future peace can be maintained if land, sea or air armaments continue to be employed by nations which threaten, or may threaten, aggression outside of their frontiers, they believe, pending the establishment of a wider and permanent system of general security, that the disarmament of such nations is essential. They will likewise aid and encourage all other practicable measures which will lighten for peace-loving peoples the crushing burden of armaments.

FRANKLIN D. ROOSEVELT
WINSTON S. CHURCHILL

Franklin D. Roosevelt, Eleventh Annual Message
January 11, 1944

[Here Roosevelt serves notice that after the war the New Deal would take up its unfinished business of providing economic security for all Americans.]

. . . It is our duty now to begin to lay the plans and determine the strategy for the winning of a lasting peace and the establishment of an American standard of living higher than ever before known. We cannot be content, no matter how high that general standard of living may be, if some fraction of our people—whether it be one-third or one-fifth or one-tenth—is ill-fed, ill clothed, ill housed, and insecure.

This Republic had its beginning, and grew to its present strength, under the protection of certain inalienable political rights—among them the right of free speech, free press, free worship, trial by jury, freedom from unreasonable searches and seizures. They were our rights to life and liberty.

As our nation has grown in size and stature, however—as our industrial economy expanded—these political rights proved inadequate to assure us equality in the pursuit of happiness.

We have come to a clear realization of the fact that true individual freedom cannot exist without economic security and independence. "Necessitous men are not free men." People who are hungry and out of a job are the stuff of which dictatorships are made.

In our day these economic truths have become accepted

as self-evident. We have accepted, so to speak, a second Bill of Rights under which a new basis of security and prosperity can be established for all—regardless of station, race or creed.

Among these are:

The right to a useful and remunerative job in the industries, or shops or farms or mines of the nation;

The right to earn enough to provide adequate food and clothing and recreation;

The right of every farmer to raise and sell his products at a return which will give him and his family a decent living;

The right of every business man, large and small, to trade in an atmosphere of freedom from unfair competition and domination by monopolies at home or abroad;

The right of every family to a decent home;

The right to adequate medical care and the opportunity to achieve and enjoy good health;

The right to adequate protection from the economic fears of old age, sickness, accident and unemployment;

The right to a good education.

All of these rights spell security. And after this war is won we must be prepared to move forward, in the implementation of these rights, to new goals of human happiness and well-being.

America's own rightful place in the world depends in large part upon how fully these and similar rights have been carried into practice for our citizens. For unless there is security here at home there cannot be lasting peace in the world.

One of the great American industrialists of our day—a man who has rendered yeoman service to his country in this crisis —recently emphasized the grave dangers of "rightist reaction" in this Nation. All clear-thinking business men share his concern. Indeed, if such reaction should develop—if history were to repeat itself and we were to return to the so-called "normalcy" of the 1920s—then it is certain that even though we shall have conquered our enemies on the battlefields abroad, we shall have yielded to the spirit of fascism here at home.

I ask the Congress to explore the means for implementing this economic bill of rights—for it is definitely the responsibility of the Congress so to do. Many of these problems are already before committees of the Congress in the form of proposed legislation. I shall from time to time communicate with the Congress with respect to these and further proposals. In the event that no adequate program of progress is evolved, I am certain that the Nation will be conscious of the fact.

Our fighting men abroad—and their families at home—expect such a program and have the right to insist upon it. It is to their demands that this Government should pay heed rather than to the whining demands of selfish pressure groups who seek to feather their nests while young Americans are dying. . . .

Franklin D. Roosevelt, Speech for Jefferson Day
April 13, 1945

[Roosevelt died the day before he was to deliver this speech honoring Jefferson's birthday.]

Americans are gathered together this evening in communities all over the country to pay tribute to the living memory of Thomas Jefferson—one of the greatest of all democrats; and I want to make it clear that I am spelling that word "democrats" with a small "d."

I wish I had the power, just for this evening, to be present at all these gatherings.

In this historic year, more than ever before, we do well to consider the character of Thomas Jefferson as an American citizen of the world.

As minister to France, then as our first Secretary of State and as our third President, Jefferson was instrumental in the establishment of the United States as a vital factor in international affairs.

It was he who first sent our Navy into far distant waters to defend our rights. And the promulgation of the Monroe Doctrine was the logical development of Jefferson's far-seeing foreign policy.

Today this Nation which Jefferson helped so greatly to build is playing a tremendous part in the battle for the rights of man all over the world.

Today we are part of the vast Allied force—a force composed of flesh and blood and steel and spirit—which is today destroying the makers of war, the breeders of hate, in Europe and in Asia.

In Jefferson's time our Navy consisted of only a handful of frigates—but that tiny Navy taught nations across the Atlantic that piracy in the Mediterranean—acts of aggression against peaceful commerce and the enslavement of their crews was one of those things which, among neighbors, simply was not done.

Today we have learned in the agony of war that great power involves great responsibility. Today we can no more escape the consequence of German and Japanese aggression than could we avoid the consequences of attacks by the Barbary corsairs a century and a half before.

We, as Americans, do not choose to deny our responsibility.

Nor do we intend to abandon our determination that, within the lives of our children and our children's children, there will not be a third World War.

We seek peace—enduring peace. More than an end to war, we want an end to the beginnings of all wars—yes, an end to this brutal, inhuman and thoroughly impractical method of settling the differences between governments.

The once powerful, malignant Nazi state is crumbling, the Japanese war lords are receiving, in their home land, the retribution for which they asked when they attacked Pearl Harbor.

But the mere conquest of our enemies is not enough.

We must go on to do all in our power to conquer the doubts and the fears, the ignorance and the greed, which made this horror possible.

Thomas Jefferson, himself a distinguished scientist, once spoke of the 'brotherly spirit of science, which unites into one family all its votaries of whatever grade, and however widely dispersed throughout the different quarters of the globe.'

Today, science has brought all the different quarters of the globe so close together that it is impossible to isolate them one from another.

Today we are faced with the pre-eminent fact that, if civilization is to survive, we must cultivate the science of human relationships—the ability of all peoples, of all kinds, to live together and work together in the same world, at peace.

Let me assure you that my hand is the steadier for the work that is to be done, that I move more firmly into the task, knowing that you—millions and millions of you—are joined with me in the resolve to make this work endure.

The work, my friends, is peace more than an end of this war—an end to the beginning of all wars, yes, an end, forever, to this impractical, unrealistic settlement of the differences between governments by the mass killing of peoples.

Today as we move against the terrible scourge of war—as we go forward toward the greatest contribution that any generation of human beings can make in this world—the contribution of lasting peace, I ask you to keep up your faith. I measure the sound, solid achievement that can be made at this time by the straight edge of your confidence and your resolve. And to you, and to all Americans who dedicate themselves with us to the making of an abiding peace, I say:

The only limit to our realization of tomorrow will be our doubts of today. Let us move forward with strong and active faith.

CHAPTER XI. THE POSTWAR ERA: THE NEW EQUILIBRIUM

Inspired by the ideals of the United Nations, the American people in 1945 looked forward to a world free at last of war, tyranny, poverty, disease and ignorance. Their optimism rested on the belief that, despite their ideological differences, the United States and Soviet Russia would co-operate in maintaining the peace, just as they had co-operated in defeating the Axis powers. This belief was written into the United Nations Charter, which required American and Russian agreement before any peace-keeping operations could be undertaken.

But as early as 1946 the two countries were finding it more and more difficult to agree on anything affecting their mutual interests. Feelings of distrust rapidly dissipated the glow of postwar optimism. The Communist countries of Eastern Europe, closing themselves off entirely from the West, grew increasingly strident in their attacks on the United States and increasingly Stalinist in their forms of government. To emphasize the point, Czechoslovakian Communists acting on orders from Moscow overthrew the democratic government in 1948 and dragged the country behind the "iron curtain." Before long, the United States and Soviet Russia were confronting each other as enemies. On several occasions—notably in Greece and Berlin—they were on the verge of open conflict. By 1949 they headed rival military alliances. It seemed like 1914 and 1939 all over again.

Throughout these early years of the Cold War the American people remained generally calm and temperate. Then, suddenly, there was a change of mood, set off by a succession of events. In September 1949 China came under Communist rule. Nothing in recent history wounded American pride so deeply as the "loss" of China. The people of the United

States had always regarded themselves as China's friend and protector, and for that very reason had fought Japan in the Second World War. Now, moreover, Communism dominated nearly the whole Eurasian land mass from the Elbe River to the China Sea. It was in September 1949, too, that the Soviet Union announced that she had exploded an atomic bomb, bringing about—or so Americans assumed—an alarming shift in the balance of power. Meanwhile, as a consequence of the Cold War, a series of sensational trials was taking place in the United States of men and women who had committed, or allegedly committed, espionage or who were advocating the forcible overthrow of the government. The trials of the eleven Communist leaders, of Alger Hiss, of Judith Coplon, of Julius and Ethel Rosenberg (who were executed for passing atomic secrets to the Russians) to mention only the most famous—all occurred between 1949 and 1951.

The event that aroused the American people most, of course, was the Korean War, which broke out in late June 1950, when the North attacked the South. It was an unpopular and inglorious war. At first the North Koreans drove the American-led United Nations forces to the southern tip of the peninsula. The UN, however, decisively defeated the North Koreans, and in a swift advance captured their capital of Pyongyang. With nearly all of the North taken, the war seemed to be over. But then a Chinese army crossed the Yalu River from Manchuria and routed the UN forces. Thereafter the war settled down to a stalemate at the 38th parallel, which separated the two Koreas. To many Americans, perhaps most, it seemed that the war had been fought in vain, since the enemy had not been defeated, but only checked. Truce talks dragged on interminably. In 1952 the impatient and exasperated public voted overwhelmingly for a change of administration, largely because the Republican presidential candidate, Dwight Eisenhower, had promised to visit Korea, presumably in search of a new formula to end the war. The Korean War did in fact end several months after Eisenhower took office, but the formula was the one worked out during the previous two years of negotiation.

The period between the Communist conquest of China and the end of the Korean War can be described as the

McCarthy era of American politics. Joseph R. McCarthy was an obscure Wisconsin Senator who first came to public notice in February 1950 when he declared that the State Department harbored hundreds of "card-carrying" Communists. He never revealed who they were, and in his succeeding speeches in the course of the year their number kept diminishing. Finally he came up with one name on which, as he said, his whole case rested—that of Professor Owen Lattimore, an authority on Asia who had occasionally acted as a consultant for the State Department. But again McCarthy offered no proof, and Lattimore was eventually exonerated. By then, however, the anxiety-ridden public was so convinced by him that it was no longer interested in proof. It was prepared to accept McCarthy's chief accusation—that China had gone Communist and America was losing the Cold War because of treason in the government and the Democratic party. McCarthy's power seemed awesome. Politicians who opposed him, including conservative Senator Millard Tydings of Maryland, who hitherto had been invulnerable, were voted out of office. After 1950 few politicians dared cross McCarthy.

It became a common practice for one or another Congressional committee to hold hearings for the sole purpose of destroying people's reputations or putting them in jail. Numerous institutions put out black lists of people who belonged to "leftist" organizations. Some of the best-known men in American public life were charged with selling out to Communism. No great cry of shame and horror rose up even when McCarthy and his friends denounced General George Marshall as a traitor. When the Republicans came into office in 1953 they promptly purged the State Department of anyone who had been tainted by accusations of guilt or who had fallen foul of the McCarthyites. The federal government also removed thousands of "security risks" by sweeping executive ukase, without a semblance of a fair hearing. The climate of fear was reflected in the anti-libertarian laws that Congress passed. Only the Alien and Sedition Acts of 1798 and the Espionage and Sedition acts of the World War I period compared with them in severity. Above all there was the Internal Security (or McCarran) Act of 1950, which ordered the registration of Communist and "Communist front" groups, and threatened to intern their members in camps during national emergencies; and there was the Communist Control Act of 1954, which amounted to a bill of attainder, arbitrarily denying the Communist party its rights and immunities and subjecting it to heavy penalties if it failed to register as a subversive organization.

The Supreme Court readily fell in with the repressive spirit of the age. In *Dennis* v. *United States*, its most important decision at the time (1951), the Court upheld the conviction of Communist party members under the provisions of the Smith Act, which forbade any person to advocate or teach the overthrow of the government by force or violence. Citing recent events in Czechoslovakia and elsewhere in the world, the majority—all of whom had been appointed by Roosevelt or Truman—argued that the government could justifiably protect itself from those who merely advocated overthrowing it by violence, even if there was no proof that a violent act was being planned. Concurring, Justice Frankfurter, while not necessarily approving of the Smith Act or the trials, felt that the Court should practice judicial restraint and avoid imposing its authority on Congress.

The great dissenters of the 1940s and '50s. Justices Hugo Black and William O. Douglas, asserted in rebuttal that the Smith Act blatantly violated the First Amendment, that the Communists had been convicted for teaching "Marxist-Leninist doctrine," not for committing, or conspiring to commit, an overt deed, and that the Court should return to Justice Holmes's rule of restricting civil liberties only when there was "a clear and present danger" to the community. But it was the majority's view, reflecting the prevailing fears of the community, that the advocacy of revolution did create a clear and present danger. Americans needed greater tolerance and self-confidence than they had in 1951 to see danger only in acts, not in radical speeches, pamphlets or associations.

The McCarthy era thus brought into clearer focus the contradictions *within* the two schools of twentieth-century Jeffersonianism. Some liberal Jeffersonians, like Black and Douglas, maintained that the government could regulate property rights almost without limit (provided it did so through due process of law), but had to be restrained, by the courts if necessary, from interfering with civil liberties. Others, like the Court majority in the Dennis case, or Senator Hubert Humphrey, the author of the Communist Control Act, denied the validity of such a distinction, both property rights and civil liberties being, in their view, equally subject to the will of the people. Conservatives were similarly divided. Most espoused Jeffersonian ideals of states' rights and laissez faire, but justified palpably anti-Jeffersonian restrictions on civil liberties. For example, Senator Robert Taft of Ohio, the avatar of conservatism in the 1940s and '50s, liked to regard himself as an apostle of John Stuart Mill and nineteenth-century liberalism; nevertheless, Taft supported the McCarran Act, among other anti-subversive measures, and cast a tolerant eye on McCarthy's assaults on innocent men—all of which interfered with the free market of ideas and associations. At the same time, however, a minority of conservatives, best represented by New England Republicans, such as Senators Ralph Flanders and George Aiken of Vermont and Margaret Chase Smith of Maine, were consistent in their defense of individual freedom, and objected to McCarthyism for the same reason that they objected to the New Deal. McCarthy himself found his nemesis among such conservatives as these.

Eisenhower's election to the presidency in 1952 marked the first significant break in the pattern of postwar politics. No American was more popular than Eisenhower, who during the war had led Allied armies in North Africa and France and between 1951 and 1952 had been the supreme commander of NATO forces in Europe. After Republican moderates had persuaded him to become their candidate, he defeated Senator Taft in a bitter struggle for the nomination and went on to win the election handily. Eisenhower was universally liked and respected, but few people knew his political views. Democratic corruption had been the dominant theme of his campaign, and he had vowed to lead a "crusade" for clean, non-partisan government. But his attitudes on the great questions raised during the last twenty years of Democratic rule—the radical right in his own party, the Cold War, the welfare state—were unknown.

The answers were soon forthcoming. Two months after Eisenhower's inauguration Stalin died; five months later the Korean truce agreement was signed, ending the one violent conflict between East and West. Slowly, the United States and the Soviet Union began to seek ways of unfreezing the Cold War, of learning to coexist peacefully. The two camps grew more amenable to compromise: in 1954 France left Indochina after a ten-year fight against Communist-led insurgents; in 1955 the "Big Four" agreed, finally, to grant Austria independence; and in the same year they met at Geneva in the first summit conference since World War II in the hope of finding ways to control armaments, especially nuclear weapons. While little came of this conference, and of the two more that Eisenhower subsequently attended, they did perceptibly reduce Cold War tensions. The iron curtain gradually opened up. The Communist countries admitted more and more foreign cultural groups, students and even tourists, and repudiated part of their Stalinist legacy. Following Yugoslavia's example, they began to liberalize their economies and to assert a larger degree of national autonomy. By the time Eisenhower left office it seemed that the worst period of the Cold War was over and that, barring unforseen incidents, relations between East and West would continue to improve.

Simultaneously, the Eisenhower years brought a measure of equanimity to American life. As the Cold War abated, Americans lost much of their obsessive fear of Communism. The heavy atmosphere of suspicion and terror began to clear, and people spoke out against McCarthyism in defense of men publicly accused and pilloried. The Eisenhower administration itself found that it could no longer appease McCarthy, who was repeatedly attacking the government for its tardiness in rooting out "subversives," its moderate policies toward Soviet Russia and its refusal to "unleash" Chiang Kai-shek against Communist China. By early 1954 the administration, concluding that a showdown with McCarthy was inevitable, accused him of attempting to intimidate the Army, which he had been investigating in his typical fashion, in order to secure privileges for one of his staff members who had recently been drafted. A Senate committee heard the charges and countercharges before the public, which viewed the proceedings on television day after day, week after week. Most Americans had never seen McCarthy in action, and what they saw of him obviously repelled them. He was hectoring and sinister, and he bullied the witnesses mercilessly, among them the Secretary of the Army and a number of distinguished generals. Later that year the Senate censured McCarthy for his contemptuous behavior toward one of its committees, which had been looking into alleged irregularities in his campaigns. After 1954 his popularity rapidly declined, the public no longer paid attention, nor politicians deference, to him, and by the time he died in 1957 he had returned to obscurity.

In general, Eisenhower fulfilled the promise of his administration. Regarding himself as a Federalist in the tradition of Washington and the framers of the Constitution, he sought primarily to compose differences, to reduce factional conflicts, to stand above partisanship and interest. The Democrats, in his view, had been divisive; Roosevelt and Truman had favored certain groups, especially labor unions, over others. But Eisenhower was unwilling to turn back the clock. He thought only that the President should take no new initiatives, that the status quo should prevail. The effect of this quiescent policy was to reconcile the Republican party once and for all to the social reforms of the 1930s, many of which it had never fully accepted while out of power. Eisenhower, in short, legitimated the radical changes of the past twenty years. In doing so he further alienated the far right, which vowed never again to compromise its beliefs and submit to the judgment of Eastern moderates.

Commanding Eisenhower's moderately conservative administration was a battery of high-level business executives—the ex-presidents, for example, of General Motors, the M. A. Hanna Company, Procter & Gamble, J. P. Stevens Company, and others. Along with these men Eisenhower felt that the federal government had acquired too much power over the states and the private sector of the economy, and in the early years of his administration he tried to turn over to private interests a number of public responsibilities, notably in housing, utilities and natural resources. But he met stubborn resistance from communities that stood to lose from the giveaway—e.g., those using public power in the TVA region —and he drew back or modified his position. He was more concerned to maintain national unity than to engage in conflict.

Consistent in his political philosophy, Eisenhower deplored big government in all its forms. He came to realize that the greatest concentration of federal power lay not in the administration of welfare—the bugbear of the extreme right— but in the organization of defense. Since the Korean War and the simultaneous build-up of NATO the government had been spending nearly half the annual budget and more than 10 per cent of the country's wealth in producing increasingly elaborate and costly weapons systems. Widespread and indissoluble ties developed between the military establishment and American industry, which employed millions of people in defense plants scattered throughout the country. A tremendous vested interest sprang up, as thousands of communities came to depend on defense orders for their prosperity. Furthermore, it was a rare general or admiral who on retirement failed to join a corporation engaged in the production of military goods.

For eight years Eisenhower had said nothing to indicate that he was disturbed by this new manifestation of concentrated wealth and power. Then, in his last speech as President, delivered three days before leaving office, he spoke out plainly, vigorously and with a touch of eloquence. He called attention to facts of which he felt Americans were unaware: that some three and a half million people worked for the defense establishment, that the government spent more on security than "the net income of all the United States corporations," and that the "influence" of this combination of an "immense military establishment and a large arms industry" was "felt in every city, every statehouse, every office of the federal government." This, he went on, was something new in the American experience, and the people should understand its grave implications. "In the councils of government," he said, "we must guard against the acquisition of unwarranted influence, whether sought or unsought, by the military-industrial complex. The potential for the disastrous rise of misplaced power exists and will persist." But Eisenhower was content merely to note the danger. He recommended no answer apart from vigilance by "an alert and knowledgeable citizenry." He thus accepted the fate to which America was condemned, for he knew that "the military-industrial complex" would continue to grow irresistibly so long as the Cold War continued.

During the Eisenhower era the Supreme Court began to remove the incubus of repression that affected American law at every level of government. Two Eisenhower appointees to the Court, Earl Warren and William Brennan, joined Black and Douglas to form a solid nucleus of civil libertarians who more and more often wrote the decisions for the majority. The Court thus served notice that it was no longer going to sanction outrages against the Bill of Rights. It struck down state laws which punished "subversion," imposed loyalty oaths, or granted legislatures broad and arbitrary powers of investigation. The Court went so far as to challenge, though still diffidently, the right of Congressional committees to indiscriminately question, expose and, in effect, convict recalcitrant witnesses. It also modified the Dennis decision of 1951, holding that the Justice Department, in prosecuting Communist party members, had interpreted the Smith Act too broadly. The new ruling made it exceedingly difficult for the government to win further convictions, although almost a hundred Communists had already been sent to jail for terms of up to five years.

The Warren Court gradually discarded the doctrine of self-imposed restraint dating from the late 1930s. It refused to accept the subordinate role of merely determining whether constitutional procedures were observed by the other two branches. Step by step, it adopted the philosophy of Black and Douglas, who believed that the judiciary branch must assert its independence. Specifically, the judiciary must invalidate laws or executive orders that transgress the Bill of Rights, since the Bill of Rights enjoyed a "preferred" place in the American hierarchy of values. The Court demonstrated the extent of its power in the case of *Brown* v. *Board of Education of Topeka*. This 1954 decision, the most far-reaching in modern times, outlawed segregation in public schools, thereby denying that the equal protection clause of the Fourteenth Amendment really meant "separate but equal," as the Court had held since 1896. Potentially, the new ruling applied to every aspect of American public life. The Court affirmed that racial equality, being the law of the land, represented an ideal that the nation must eventually put into practice, and it implicitly invited civil rights groups to test, through the courts and by means of direct action, all the local and state laws that conflicted with that ideal.

By declaring that the protection of civil rights was a national responsibility, the Court brought the federal government into direct and unavoidable conflict with the Southern states. According to the Brown ruling, the federal courts would determine when, where and how desegregation would be effected. It was inevitable that these local court orders would meet resistance, especially since militantly racist White Citizens' Councils were springing up throughout the South. The first showdown came in 1957 in Little Rock, Arkansas. The Arkansas governor, Orval Faubus, had moved the national guard into Little Rock to prevent the integration of students at a high school. When Faubus refused to obey a court injunction ordering him to remove the guardsmen, President Eisenhower sent in troops and federalized the guard, and the Negro children finally went to school. Eisenhower himself had never expressly approved of the Supreme Court's decision; he believed that integration should come about slowly and voluntarily. But circumstances compelled him to use force in upholding the Court and the Constitution. It was not to be the last time that the United States Army would be called upon to enforce an integration order.

By the time Eisenhower's administration drew to a close the political pendulum had swung left again; an increasingly large segment of the public had come to favor liberal reform. The reasons for this were clear. Since the end of the Korean War the country had been going through a series of minor recessions, each longer and more intense than the preceding one. Unemployment had been rising dangerously, while the rate of economic growth had been lagging further and further behind that of almost every other industrial nation, particularly the Soviet Union. The public showed its discontent in 1958 when liberal Democrats scored a spectacular victory in the Congressional elections, winning fifteen seats in the Senate and forty-eight in the House; this, on top of the majority that they already had, gave them overwhelming control of Congress. It was the Democratic upsurge of the late 1950s, especially in the industrial states, that carried John F. Kennedy into the presidency in 1960. He defeated Richard Nixon, Eisenhower's Vice-President, by a little more than a hundred thousand votes out of sixty-nine million cast, making it the closest presidential election in American history. Kennedy's margin would undoubtedly have been much greater had he not been a Catholic.

In his campaign Kennedy cited numerous statistics and surveys to prove that America was stagnating economically, was failing to maintain her military superiority, and was losing her prestige in the world—Soviet Russia having established a commanding lead in space exploration. Kennedy appealed to his own generation, born since World War I, to conquer the "new frontiers" of twentieth-century technology and power. To emphasize his point he staffed the higher echelons of the executive department with young academics, business managers and other professionals. Washington had not seen such an invasion of bright young men since the days of the early New Deal. As President, Kennedy launched programs calculated to make America "move": he significantly enlarged the size of the defense establishment; he provided tax benefits to industry to stimulate capital improvements; and he committed the nation to a space race, costing more than five billion dollars a year, for the purpose of landing an American on the moon by the end of the decade. The effects of this vast pump-priming program were soon felt. Prosperity returned and continued month after month, year after year, while national production rose at a rate double that of the Eisenhower years.

The domestic policies of the Kennedy administration proved especially advantageous to the large corporations that were part of "the military-industrial complex," and to the technocratic elite—scientists, engineers, managers, etc.—whose services commanded premium salaries on the open market.

Though the economy leaped ahead, setting new records every year, industrial unemployment remained high. Unskilled or semi-skilled workers found it more and more difficult to adjust to a complex technology, and they sank deeper and deeper into poverty and squalor. In the early 1960s it was estimated that between a fifth and a fourth of the country —some thirty-five to forty-five million people—lived at or below the poverty line. A permanent caste of poor people, largely Negroes, was filling up the slums of the great cities, sowing the dragons' teeth that would someday be reaped by the affluent middle and upper classes. Responding to these problems, Kennedy tried to introduce some modest social reforms, in particular a limited medical care system for the old under social security, and an anti-poverty program. But he was unable to crack the conservative-liberal stalemate in Congress that had prevailed since the late 1930s. Except for measures relieving depressed regions, none of his major welfare proposals passed during his administration.

Meanwhile, civil rights groups, impatient with the slow workings of the law, were taking en masse to the streets, employing tactics of civil disobedience to break down Jim Crow restrictions. They were joined by large numbers of whites, particularly students and clergymen, who were eager to participate in this latest Jeffersonian crusade for equality. The tide of protests issuing up from the South forced Kennedy to go beyond mere approval of the 1954 Court decision—itself an advance over the Eisenhower position of neutrality. With the conflict becoming more and more sharply drawn, Kennedy had to choose whether he would support or oppose an increasingly militant civil rights movement. The crisis point came in May 1963 as a result of events in Birmingham, Alabama. There, a group of Negroes led by Martin Luther King assembled to present a petition of grievances to the Birmingham mayor. They were met not by the mayor, but by truncheons, cattle prods and dogs. The country, which witnessed the cruel spectacle on television, was outraged. Soon after, large-scale riots broke out in the Negro working-class quarter of the city. Peace finally came when the city authorities reached an agreement with King. But it was obvious now that there would be many Birminghams in the

South unless the federal government acted soon to secure civil rights.

Several weeks after the Birmingham episode Kennedy delivered a notable speech declaring that Negroes had too long been denied their birthright as Americans and that their grievances should be redressed through legislation. Kennedy realized that the alternative to legislation was violence, perhaps race war. Accordingly, he framed a bill proposing to integrate many places of public accommodation—hotels, theaters, restaurants, etc.—as well as institutions regulated or protected by the government (e.g., labor unions). Though no President had ever spoken so sympathetically of Negro suffering in America, or had, since Reconstruction, recommended such radical civil rights legislation, Negro and church groups complained that the bill was not comprehensive enough and lacked adequate enforcement procedures. In September 1963, while the bill was pending, four Negro children were blown up in a Birmingham church, setting off a fresh wave of outrage. The bill was then enlarged to encompass just about every form of public accommodation. Kennedy's assassination in November ensured its passage. Few Northern Congressmen, however conservative, wished to oppose a cause that had become identified in the public mind with the martyred President.

It was left to Kennedy's successor, Lyndon B. Johnson, to oversee the implementation of the New Frontier program. Johnson, however, did more than implement it; he launched his own ambitious and astonishingly successful "Great Society" program. Not since the early New Deal was so much important national legislation passed as during the first two years of Johnson's presidency. In 1964 the Civil Rights Act became law and the vaunted "war on poverty" got under way. In 1965 Congress enacted a plethora of legislation, including another civil rights law, this one guaranteeing Negroes the opportunity to vote, a health insurance law (Medicare) for the old, and, most significant of all, a sweeping federal aid to education law, which promised to revolutionize educational practices in America by raising them to a more or less uniform national standard. The country had seen nothing like this burst of reform in thirty years. And it was not triggered by a national emergency like the Great Depression. In fact, the country as a whole had never been better off than in the years of Johnson's administration.

A paradox accounted for his extraordinary political success. In 1960 conservative Republicans, headed by Senator Barry Goldwater of Arizona, had decided to wrest control of the party once and for all from the "me-too" Eastern moderates and liberals. These conservatives reflected the views of small and medium-sized property owners throughout the country, especially in the West, who felt that America had become irremediably corrupt and iniquitous. They complained that while they bore the onerous cost of sustaining the welfare state, others received its benefits, that while they earned whatever they possessed by the sweat of their brows and by their exemplary personal initiative, the federal government gave extravagant handouts to the lazy, the incompetent, the improvident and the morally depraved. At the same time, more and more Southern whites were joining the conservative Republican movement in the belief that the Democratic party and its leaders were the instruments of Negro and other Northern minority groups, and therefore were bent on destroying Southern rights.

Goldwater, then, had no trouble securing the support of a majority of Republican committeemen in the South and West, and he went on with ease to win the party's presidential nomination in 1964. The convention was conservative, the platform was conservative, and the campaign that Goldwater conducted was conservative. He insisted that the party must present a real alternative to the welfare state by doing away with federal subsidies and supports, restoring the free enterprise system in its pristine form (though he said nothing critical against private monopolies and private restraints of trade), and pursuing an aggressive foreign policy, in effect a crusade, against Communism.

Predictably, Goldwater alienated Negro and other ethnic groups, the working class, professionals, most farmers and the moderates in his own party, including the managers and directors of the great banks and industrial corporations. He carried only four states of the deep South (Mississippi, Alabama, Louisiana and Georgia) and Arizona, while Johnson won more than sixty per cent of the popular votes—an unprecedented victory. But this was only part of the Republican debacle of 1964. The Democrats secured control of most of the traditionally Republican state legislatures, and enormously increased their already sizable Congressional majority. Moreover, practically all of the freshmen Congressmen were Northern liberals. The historic deadlock, made possible by the coalition of Republicans and Southern Democrats, was broken. The Eighty-ninth Congress, the most liberal in thirty years, was prepared to do what Johnson asked of it. And it was the militant conservatives who had made it all possible.

But the liberal upsurge was brief. The public reacted against Northern civil rights demonstrations for integrated housing, schools and jobs, against the burgeoning student movements, and against the government for instituting so many costly new programs. Also, the Vietnam War diverted the administration's energies and cut into funds that might otherwise have gone into Great Society projects. The Vietnam War was itself a remarkable piece of irony. In the 1964 campaign Johnson had accused Goldwater of "shooting from the hip" because Goldwater had proposed expanding the war, "defoliating" the jungles and bombing the North. But soon Johnson was carrying out these same proposals. Within a year after his inauguration several hundred thousand American troops had been sent to South Vietnam and full-scale bombing attacks on the North began. The war became the country's central preoccupation and divided public opinion as no war had in recent American history. At any rate the Great Society was over in 1966. In the Congressional election of that year the Republicans ousted the liberal Democrats who had won two years before. The old Congressional deadlock resumed.

The nature of the deadlock was changed, however. Few Republican politicians wanted to re-enact the 1964 tragedy. Because the majority of Americans had made it clear that they would not tolerate the destruction of the welfare state or move very far off center, it was inconceivable that the Republican party would again succumb to extreme conservatism. Indeed, the 1964 election proved that the traditional bulwark of the party, the large corporate and financial interests, had come to terms with twentieth-century realities. These interests now realized that the welfare state and strong unions were a small price to pay for stability and order. They further realized that big government was an indispensable aid to private enterprise, especially in the defense and space industries and in research. They certainly wanted no radical changes in the status quo. For these Republicans, who by and large controlled the party's wealth, the Hamiltonianism of the McKinley and Coolidge eras and the theories of classical economics were no longer relevant. The task, they held, was not to oppose big government but to turn it to their advantage.

The Democrats, for their part, hardly differed from these Republicans. The old Jeffersonian animus against the privileged interests, which had persisted through the Truman administration, lay moribund in the 1960s. The liberalism represented by Kennedy and Johnson assumed that the government should use its great power to maintain a proper equilibrium between all interests and classes, that technicians and experts were best equipped to handle the complex issues of the modern age. The new liberalism prided itself on its abandonment of ideology—its transcendence of both Hamiltonianism and Jeffersonianism.

But while the political parties were gravitating toward neutrality, the Supreme Court was becoming more and more political. By the mid-1960s the Court, once the most solid pillar of American conservatism and property rights, had emerged as the great proponent of Jeffersonian democracy. In a succession of landmark decisions it vastly enlarged the scope of individual freedom as it rigorously applied the Bill of Rights to the states. It granted protection to defendants against the arbitrary power of police officers, prosecutors and judges; to immigrants against arbitrary arrest and deportation; to the public at large against censors of books, magazines and movies, and against snoopers and other assorted invaders of privacy; to atheists and other minorities against coercion by religious groups; and, above all, to urban voters, who constituted the majority, against the rural communities that had run the state legislatures. Far more than Congress or the President, the Supreme Court upheld the American ideal of equal rights under law. But whether the people, and hence the country's political institutions, would sanction the Court's militant Jeffersonianism remained to be seen.

Majority Report of Committee Investigating Senator McCarthy's Charges
July 17, 1950

[After McCarthy had repeatedly accused members of the State Department of treason or of belonging to the Communist party, a Senate subcommittee, consisting of three Democrats and two Republicans, heard the charges. The majority report completely cleared the men named by McCarthy and, in turn, denounced him as a liar and a demagogue. Following are excerpts from it.]

FINDINGS AND CONCLUSIONS

Despite his denials on the Senate floor, publicly and before this subcommittee, that he made the statement, we find on the evidence that Senator Joseph R. McCarthy, on February 9, 1950, at Wheeling, W. Va., said:

"Ladies and Gentlemen: While I cannot take the time to name all the men in the State Department who have been named as active members of the Communist party and members of a spy ring, I have here in my hand a list of 205; a list of names that were made known to the Secretary of State as being members of the Communist party and who, nevertheless, are still working and shaping policy in the State Department."

Our investigation establishes that the foregoing allegations are false and, particularly, that Senator McCarthy had no such list as alleged and that there is not one member of the Communist party or of a "spy ring" employed in the State Department known to the Secretary of State or other responsible officials of that department.

We find that on Feb. 20, 1950, at Salt Lake City, Utah, Senator McCarthy said:

"Last night I discussed the Communists in the State Department. I stated that I had the names of fifty-seven card-carrying members of the Communist party."

Our investigation establishes that Senator McCarthy at no time has had the names of fifty-seven card-carrying members of the Communist party in the State Department, and that during the course of a four months' investigation he has been unable to produce competent evidence or to indicate where such evidence is obtainable concerning one member of the Communist party, card-carrying or otherwise, who is employed in the State Department.

We find that on the evening of Feb. 11, 1950, at Reno, Nev., Senator McCarthy again spoke on the question. As reported in the Nevada State Journal:

"Senator McCarthy, who had first typed a total of 205 employes of the State Department who could be considered disloyal to the United States and pro-Communists, scratched out that number and mentioned only 'fifty-seven card-carrying members' whom Secretary of State Dean Acheson should know as well as members of Congress."

We find that in making a speech on the Senate floor on Feb. 20, 1950, he read what purported to be the speech delivered by him at Wheeling, W. Va.; that the purported speech as read to the Senate was identical with the speech delivered at Wheeling, except that he withheld from the Senate the statement actually made, as set forth in Conclusion 1 above, and substituted in lieu thereof the following:

"I have in my hand fifty-seven cases of individuals who would appear to be either card-carrying members or certainly loyal to the Communist party, but who nevertheless are still helping to shape our foreign policy."

The substitution of the foregoing terminology constituted a misrepresentation of the true facts to the Senate.

We find that in making his speech on Feb. 20, 1950, which occasioned the passage of Senate Resolution 231, Senator McCarthy left the unmistakable inference that he had but recently obtained from unrevealed sources in the State Department the information which he was presenting to the Senate.

Our investigation establishes that the material presented in this speech was developed in 1947 by the Republican-controlled Eightieth Congress; and that representations indicating it had recently come from "loyal" State Department employes misled and deceived the Senate. . . .

We find that Senator McCarthy failed to cooperate with the subcommittee or to supply further information concerning the "eighty-one" individuals mentioned in his speech of Feb. 20, 1950, after having assured the Senate that he would "be willing, happy, and eager to go before any committee and give the names and all the information available."

Our investigation establishes that the only reason for the Senator's noncooperation and failure to supply further information was the fact that he had no information to supply. . . .

We feel that one of the most reprehensible aspects and unfortunate results of unwarranted charges of the type made in this matter is the actual injury done to the true fight against communism. Such charges, being unproved and not subject to proof, have the effect of dulling the awareness of our people to the menace of communism, unnecessarily embarrass and expose the methods and techniques of our intelligence agencies charged with protecting our security, interfere with and compromise their confidential investigations, destroy the effectiveness of confidential informants, and inevitably give basis for ridicule of those who fight communism with truth, the only weapon with which it can be destroyed.

At a time when American blood is being shed to preserve our dream of freedom, we are constrained fearlessly and frankly to call the charges and the methods employed to give them ostensible validity, what they truly are: A fraud and a hoax perpetrated on the Senate of the United States and the American people.

They represent perhaps the most nefarious campaign of halftruths and untruth in the history of this Republic. For the first time in our history we have seen the totalitarian technique of the "big lie" employed on a sustained basis.

The result has been to divide and confuse the American people, at a time when they should be strong in their unity, to a degree far beyond the hopes of the Communists themselves, whose stock in trade is confusion and division. In such a disillusioning setting, we appreciate as never before our Bill of Rights, a free press and the heritage of freedom that has made this nation great. . . .

Senator McCarthy's Reply to Majority Report
July 17, 1950

[Following is the whole text of McCarthy's reply.]

The Tydings-McMahon report is a green light to the Red fifth column in the United States.

It is a signal to the traitors, Communists, and fellow travelers in our Government that they need have no fear of exposure from this Administration. It is public notification that we will officially "turn our back" on traitors, Communists, and fellow travelers in our Government.

The most loyal stooges of the Kremlin could not have done a better job of giving a clean bill of health to Stalin's fifth column in this country. At a time when American blood is staining the Korean valleys, the Tydings-McMahon report gives unlimited aid and comfort to the very enemies responsible for tying the hands and shooting the faces off some of our soldiers.

In its dying gasp the Tydings-McMahon half of the committee is attempting to give birth to the most evil fraud that has ever besmirched and dishonored the good name of the United States Senate.

If allowed to succeed, this fraud will maintain in power those who will extend the trail of blood from the valleys of Korea, across the sands of Iran, to the streets of Berlin. It comes at a time when honest people were waiting and hoping for honest answers to the questions of why the terror of communism which has engulfed vast areas of the world has succeeded in spreading the filth of its fifth column into our way of life.

Instead the Tydings-McMahon half of the committee has degenerated to new lows of planned deception. The result of their work is a clever, evil thing to behold. It is gigantic in its fraud and deep in its deceit. It camouflages the facts and protects Communists and fellow travelers in our Government.

Harry S Truman, Veto of the McCarran Act
September 22, 1950

[The McCarran (or Internal Security) Act was the most sweeping federal attack on civil liberties since the Espionage and Sedition acts of World War I. The temper of Congress was evident in the fact that it overrode Truman's veto the day after he issued it.]

. . . This is an omnibus bill containing many different legislative proposals with only one thing in common: they are all represented to be "anti-Communist." But when the many complicated pieces of the bill are analyzed in detail, a startling result appears.

H. R. 9490 would not hurt the Communists. Instead, it would help them.

It has been claimed over and over again that this is an "anti-Communist" bill—a "Communist control" bill. But in actual operation the bill would have results exactly the opposite of those intended.

It would actually weaken our existing internal security measures and would seriously hamper the Federal Bureau of Investigation and our other security agencies. . . .

Sections 22 and 25 of this bill would make sweeping changes in our laws governing the admission of aliens to the United States and their naturalization as citizens.

The ostensible purpose of these provisions is to prevent persons who would be dangerous to our national security from entering the country or becoming citizens. In fact, present law already achieves that objective.

What these provisions would actually do is to prevent us from admitting to our country, or to citizenship, many people who could make real contributions to our national strength. The bill would deprive our Government and our intelligence agencies of the valuable services of aliens in security operations. It would require us to exclude and to deport the citizens of some friendly non-Communist countries. Furthermore, it would actually make it easier for subversive aliens to become United States citizens. Only the Communist movement would gain from such actions. . . .

In brief, when all the provisions of H. R. 9490 are considered together, it is evident that the great bulk of them are not directed toward the real and present dangers that exist from communism. Instead of striking blows at communism, they would strike blows at our own liberties and at our position in the forefront of those working for freedom in the world. At a time when our young men are fighting for freedom in Korea, it would be tragic to advance the objectives of communism in this country, as this bill would do.

Because I feel so strongly that this legislation would be a terrible mistake, I want to discuss more fully its worst features: sections 1 through 17 and sections 22 and 25. . . .

Unfortunately, these provisions are not merely ineffective and unworkable. They represent a clear and present danger to our institutions.

Insofar as the bill would require registration by the Communist Party itself, it does not endanger our traditional liberties. However, the application of the registration requirements to so-called Communist-front organizations can be the greatest danger to freedom of speech, press and assembly, since the alien and sedition laws of 1798. This danger arises out of the criteria or standards to be applied in determining whether an organization is a Communist-front organization.

There would be no serious problem if the bill required proof that an organization was controlled and financed by the Communist Party before it could be classified as a Communist-front organization. However, recognizing the difficulty of proving those matters, the bill would permit such a determination to be based solely upon "the extent to which the positions taken or advanced by it from time to time on matters of policy do not deviate from those" of the Communist movement.

This provision could easily be used to classify as a Communist-front organization any organization which is advocating a single policy or objective which is also being urged by the Communist Party or by a Communist foreign government. In fact, this may be the intended result, since the bill defines "organization" to include "a group of persons . . . permanently or temporarily associated together for joint action on any subject or subjects." Thus, an organization which advocates low-cost housing for sincere humanitarian reasons might be classified as a Communist-front organization because the Communists regularly exploit slum conditions as one of their fifth-column techniques.

It is not enough to say that this probably would not be done. The mere fact that it could be done shows clearly how the bill would open a Pandora's box of opportunities for official condemnation of organizations and individuals for perfectly honest opinions which happen to be stated also by Communists.

The basic error of these sections is that they move in the direction of suppressing opinion and belief. This would be a very dangerous course to take, not because we have any sympathy for Communist opinions, but because any governmental stifling of the free expression of opinion is a long step toward totalitarianism.

There is no more fundamental axiom of American freedom than the familiar statement: In a free country we punish men for the crimes they commit but never for the opinions they have. And the reason this is so fundamental to freedom is not, as many suppose, that it protects the few unorthodox from suppression by the majority. To permit freedom of expression is primarily for the benefit of the majority, because it protects criticism, and criticism leads to progress.

We can and we will prevent espionage, sabotage, or other actions endangering our national security. But we would betray our finest traditions if we attempted, as this bill would attempt, to curb the simple expression of opinion. This we should never do, no matter how distasteful the opinion may be to the vast majority of our people. The course proposed by this bill would delight the Communists, for it would make a mockery of the Bill of Rights and of our claims to stand for freedom in the world.

And what kind of effect would these provisions have on the normal expression of political views? Obviously, if this law were on the statute books, the part of prudence would be to avoid saying anything that might be construed by someone as not deviating sufficiently from the current Communist-propaganda line. And since no one could be sure in advance what views were safe to express, the inevitable tendency would be to express no views on controversial subjects.

The result could only be to reduce the vigor and strength of our political life—an outcome that the Communists would happily welcome, but that freemen should abhor.

We need not fear the expression of ideas—we do need to fear their suppression.

Our position in the vanguard of freedom rests largely on our demonstration that the free expression of opinion, coupled with government by popular consent, leads to national strength and human advancement. Let us not, in cowering and foolish fear, throw away the ideals which are the fundamental basis of our free society. . . .

Section 22 is so contrary to our national interests that it would actually put the Government into the business of thought control by requiring the deportation of any alien who distributes or publishes, or who is affiliated with an organization which distributes or publishes, any written or printed matter advocating (or merely expressing belief in) the economic and governmental doctrines of any form of totalitarianism. This provision does not require an evil intent or purpose on the part of the alien, as does a similar provision in the Smith Act. Thus, the Attorney General would be required to deport any alien operating or connected with a well-stocked bookshop containing books on economics or politics written by supporters of the present Governments of Spain, of Yugoslavia, or any one of a number of other countries. Section 25 would make the same aliens ineligible for citizenship. There should be no room in our laws for such hysterical provisions. The next logical step would be to "burn the books."

This illustrates the fundamental error of these immigration and naturalization provisions. It is easy to see that they are hasty and ill-considered. But far more significant—and far more dangerous—is their apparent underlying purpose. Instead of trying to encourage the free movement of people, subject only to the real requirements of national security, these provisions attempt to bar movement to anyone who is, or once was, associated with ideas we dislike and, in the process, they would succeed in barring many people whom it would be to our advantage to admit. . . .

I do not undertake lightly the responsibility of differing with the majority in both Houses of Congress who have voted for this bill. We are all Americans; we all wish to safeguard and preserve our constitutional liberties against internal and external enemies. But I cannot approve this legislation, which instead of accomplishing its avowed purpose would actually interfere with our liberties and help the Communists against whom the bill was aimed.

This is a time when we must marshal all our resources and all the moral strength of our free system in self-defense against the threat of Communist aggression. We will fail in this, and we will destroy all that we seek to preserve, if we sacrifice the liberties of our citizens in a misguided attempt to achieve national security.

There is no reason why we should fail. Our country has been through dangerous times before, without losing our liberties to external attack or internal hysteria. Each of us, in Government and out, has a share in guarding our liberties. Each of us must search his own conscience to find whether he is doing all that can be done to preserve and strengthen them.

No considerations of expediency can justify the enactment of such a bill as this, a bill which would so greatly weaken our liberties and give aid and comfort to those who would destroy us. I have, therefore, no alernative but to return this bill without my approval, and I earnestly request the Congress to reconsider its action.

Dennis v. *United States*
1951

[The Court's Dennis decision was written by Chief Justice Fred Vinson, Justice Robert Jackson concurring. Though Black and Douglas each wrote dissenting opinions, we have included only Black's.]

VINSON, C. J.: Petitioners were indicated in July, 1948, for violation of the conspiracy provisions of the Smith Act, § 11, during the period of April, 1945, to July, 1948. . . . A verdict of guilty as to all the petitioners was returned by the jury on October 14, 1949. The Court of Appeals affirmed the convictions. . . .

The indictment charged the petitioners with wilfully and knowingly conspiring (1) to organize as the Communist Party of the United States of America a society, group and assembly of persons who teach and advocate the overthrow and destruction of the Government of the United States by force and violence, and (2) knowingly and wilfully to advocate and teach the duty and necessity of overthrowing and destroying the Government of the United States by force and violence. The indictment further alleged that § 2 of the Smith Act proscribes these acts and that any conspiracy to take such action is a violation of § 3 of the Act. . . .

The obvious purpose of the statute is to protect existing Government, not from change by peaceable, lawful and constitutional means, but from change by violence, revolution and terrorism. That it is within the *power* of the Congress to protect the Government of the United States from armed rebellion is a proposition which requires little discussion. Whatever theoretical merit there may be to the argument that there is a "right" to rebellion against dictatorial governments is without force where the existing structure of the government provides for peaceful and orderly change. We reject any principle of governmental helplessness in the face of preparation for revolution, which principle, carried to its logical conclusion, must lead to anarchy. No one could conceive that it is not within the power of Congress to prohibit acts intended to overthrow the Government by force and violence. The question with which we are concerned here is not whether Congress has such *power*, but whether the *means* which it has employed conflict with the First and Fifth Amendments to the Constitution. . . .

The very language of the Smith Act negates the interpretation which petitioners would have us impose on that Act. It is directed at advocacy, not discussion. Thus, the trial judge properly charged the jury that they could not convict if they found that petitioners did "no more than pursue peaceful studies and discussions or teaching and advocacy in the realm of ideas." He further charged that it was not unlawful "to conduct in an American college and university a course explaining the philosophical theories set forth in the books which have been placed in evidence." Such a charge is in strict accord with the statutory language, and illustrates the meaning to be placed on those words. Congress did not intend to eradicate the free discussion of political theories, to destroy the traditional rights of Americans to discuss and evaluate ideas without fear of governmental sanction. Rather Congress was concerned with the very kind of activity in which the evidence showed these petitioners engaged.

But although the statute is not directed at the hypothetical cases which petitioners have conjured, its application in this case has resulted in convictions for the teaching and advocacy of the overthrow of the Government by force and violence, which, even though coupled with the intent to accomplish that overthrow, contains an element of speech. For this reason, we must pay special heed to the demands of the First Amendment marking out the boundaries of speech.

We pointed out in *Douds, supra,* that the basis of the First Amendment is the hypothesis that speech can rebut speech, propaganda will answer propaganda, free debate of ideas will result in the wisest governmental policies. It is for this reason that this Court has recognized the inherent value of free discourse. An analysis of the leading cases in this Court which have involved direct limitations on speech, however, will demonstrate that both the majority of the Court and the dissenters in particular cases have recognized that this is not an unlimited, unqualified right, but that the societal value of speech must, on occasion, be subordinated to other values and considerations. . . .

In this case we are squarely presented with the application of the "clear and present danger" test, and must decide what that phrase imports. . . .

Obviously, the words cannot mean that before the Government may act, it must wait until the *putsch* is about to be executed, the plans have been laid and the signal is awaited. If Government is aware that a group aiming at its overthrow is attempting to indoctrinate its members and to commit them to a course whereby they will strike when the leaders feel the circumstances permit, action by the Government is required. The argument that there is no need for Government to concern itself, for Government is strong, it possesses ample powers to put down a rebellion, it may defeat the revolution with ease needs no answer. For that is not the question. Certainly an attempt to overthrow the Government by force, even though doomed from the outset because of inadequate numbers or power of the revolutionists, is a sufficient evil for Congress to prevent. The damage which such attempts create both physically and politically to a nation makes it impossible to measure the validity in terms of the probability of success, or the immediacy of a successful attempt. In the instant case the trial judge charged the jury that they could not convict unless they found that petitioners intended to overthrow the Government "as speedily as circumstances would permit." This does not mean, and could not properly mean, that they would not strike until there was certainty of success. What was meant was that the revolutionists would strike when they thought the time was ripe. We must therefore reject the contention that success or probability of success is the criterion. . . .

The mere fact that from the period 1945 to 1948 petitioners' activities did not result in an attempt to overthrow the Government by force and violence is of course no answer to the fact that there was a group that was ready to make the attempt. The formation by petitioners of such a highly organized conspiracy, with rigidly disciplined members subject to call when the leaders, these petitioners, felt that the time had come for action, coupled with the inflammable nature of world conditions, similar uprisings in other countries, and the touch-and-go nature of our relations with countries with whom petitioners were in the very least ideologically attuned, convince us that their convictions were justified on this score. And this analysis disposes of the contention that a conspiracy to advocate, as distinguished from the advocacy itself, cannot be constitutionally restrained, because it comprises only the preparation. It is the existence of the conspiracy which creates the danger. . . .

We hold that § § 2 (a) (1), 2 (a) (3) and 3 of the Smith Act, do not inherently, or as construed or applied in the instant case, violate the First Amendment and other provisions of the Bill of Rights, or the First and Fifth Amendments because of indefiniteness. Petitioners intended to overthrow the Government of the United States as speedily as the circumstances would permit. Their conspiracy to organize the Communist Party and to teach and advocate the overthrow of the Government of the United States by force and violence created a "clear and present danger" of an attempt to overthrow the Government by force and violence. They were properly and constitutionally convicted for violation of the Smith Act. The judgments of conviction are

Affirmed.

JACKSON, V., concurring. This prosecution is the latest of never-ending, because never successful, quests for some legal formula that will secure an existing order against revolutionary radicalism. It requires us to reappraise, in the light of our own times and conditions, constitutional doctrines devised under other circumstances to strike a balance between authority and liberty.

Activity here charged to be criminal is conspiracy—that defendants conspired to teach and advocate, and to organize the Communist Party to teach and advocate, overthrow and destruction of the Government by force and violence. There is no charge of actual violence or attempt at overthrow.

The principal reliance of the defense in this Court is that the conviction cannot stand under the Constitution because the conspiracy of these defendants presents no "clear and present danger" of imminent or foreseeable overthrow. . . .

If we must decide that this Act and its application are constitutional only if we are convinced that petitioner's conduct creates a "clear and present danger" of violent overthrow, we must appraise imponderables, including international and national phenomena which baffle the best informed foreign offices and our most experienced politicians. We would have to foresee and predict the effectiveness of Communist propaganda, opportunities for infiltration; whether, and when, a time will come that they consider propitious for action, and whether and how fast our existing government will deteriorate. And we would have to speculate as to whether an approaching Communist *coup* would not be anticipated by a nationalistic fascist movement. No doctrine can be sound whose application requires us to make a prophecy of that sort in the guise of a legal decision. The judicial process simply is not adequate to a trial of such far-flung issues. The answers given would reflect our own political predilections and nothing more.

The authors of the clear and present danger test never applied it to a case like this, nor would I. If applied as it is proposed here, it means that the Communist plotting is protected during its period of incubation; its preliminary stages of organization and preparation are immune from the law; the Government can move only after imminent action is manifest, when it would, of course, be too late.

The highest degree of constitutional protection is due to the individual acting without conspiracy. But even an individual cannot claim that the Constitution protects him in advocating or teaching overthrow of government by force or violence. I should suppose no one would doubt that Congress has power to make such attempted overthrow a crime. But the contention is that one has the constitutional right to work up a public desire and will to do what it is a crime to attempt. I think direct incitement by speech or writing can be made a crime, and I think there can be a conviction without also proving that the odds favored its success by 99 to 1, or some other extremely high ratio.

The names of Mr. Justice Holmes and Mr. Justice Brandeis

cannot be associated with such a doctrine of governmental disability. After the *Schenck* case, in which they set forth the clear and present danger test, they joined in these words of Mr. Justice Holmes, spoken for a unanimous Court:

> ". . . [T]he First Amendment while prohibiting legislation against free speech as such cannot have been, and obviously was not, intended to give immunity for every possible use of language. *Robertson* v. *Baldwin*, 165 U. S. 275, 281. We venture to believe that neither Hamilton nor Madison, nor any other competent person then or later, ever supposed that to make criminal the counselling of a murder within the jurisdiction of Congress would be an unconstitutional interference with free speech." *Frohwerk* v. *United States*, 249 U. S. 204.

The same doctrine was earlier stated in *Fox* v. *Washington*, 236 U. S. 273, 277, and that case was recently and with approval cited in *Giboney* v. *Empire Storage & Ice Co.*, 336 U. S. 490, 502. . . .

BLACK, J., dissenting. . . .

At the outset I want to emphasize what the crime involved in this case is, and what it is not. These petitioners were not charged with an attempt to overthrow the Government. They were not charged with nonverbal acts of any kind designed to overthrow the Government. They were not even charged with saying anything or writing anything designed to overthrow the Government. The charge was that they agreed to assemble and to talk and publish certain ideas at a later date: The indictment is that they conspired to organize the Communist Party and to use speech or newspapers and other publications in the future to teach and advocate the forcible overthrow of the Government. No matter how it is worded, this is a virulent form of prior censorship of speech and press, which I believe the First Amendment forbids. I would hold § 3 of the Smith Act authorizing this prior restraint unconstitutional on its face and as applied.

But let us assume, contrary to all constitutional ideas of fair criminal procedure, that petitioners although not indicted for the crime of actual advocacy, may be punished for it. Even on this radical assumption, the only way to affirm these convictions, as the dissent of MR. JUSTICE DOUG-LAS shows, is to qualify drastically or wholly repudiate the established "clear and present danger" rule. This the Court does in a way which greatly restricts the protections afforded by the First Amendment. The opinions for affirmance show that the chief reason for jettisoning the rule is the expressed fear that advocacy of Communist doctrine endangers the safety of the Republic. Undoubtedly, a governmental policy of unfettered communication of ideas does entail dangers. To the Founders of this Nation, however, the benefits derived from free expression were worth the risk. They embodied this philosophy in the First Amendment's command that Congress "shall make no law abridging . . . the freedom of speech, or of the press . . . ." I have always believed that the First Amendment is the keystone of our Government, that the freedoms it guarantees provide the best insurance against destruction of all freedom. At least as to speech in the realm of public matters, I believe that the "clear and present danger" test does not "mark the furthermost constitutional boundaries of protected expression" but does "no more than recognize a minimum compulsion of the Bill of Rights." *Bridges* v. *California*, 314 U. S. 252, 263.

So long as this Court exercises the power of judicial review of legislation, I cannot agree that the First Amendment permits us to sustain laws suppressing freedom of speech and press on the basis of Congress' or our own notions of mere "reasonableness." Such a doctrine waters down the first Amendment so that it amounts to little more than an admonition to Congress. The Amendment as so construed is not likely to protect any but those "safe" or orthodox views which rarely need its protection. . . .

Public opinion being what it now is, few will protest the conviction of these Communist petitioners. There is hope, however, that in calmer times, when present pressures, passions and fears subside, this or some later Court will restore the First Amendment liberties to the high preferred place where they belong in a free society.

Dwight D. Eisenhower, Executive Order
on Security
April 27, 1953

[Executive Order 10450 introduced two decisive changes in the federal security system. It substituted "security risk"—a term redolent of the McCarthy era—for disloyalty as the basis for dismissal, and it placed the burden of proof on the accused.]

Whereas the interests of the national security require that all persons privileged to be employed in the departments and agencies of the Government shall be reliable, trustworthy, of good conduct and character, and of complete and unswerving loyalty to the United States . . . it is hereby ordered as follows:

Section 7. Any person whose employment is suspended or terminated under the authority granted to heads of departments and agencies by or in accordance with the said act of August 26, 1950, or pursuant to the said Executive Order No. 9835 or any other security or loyalty program relating to officers or employees of the Government, shall not be reinstated or restored to duty or reemployed in the same department or agency, and shall not be reemployed in any other department or agency, unless the head of the department or agency concerned finds that such reinstatement, restoration, or reemployment is clearly consistent with the interests of the national security, which finding shall be made a part of the records of such department or agency: *Provided,* that no person whose employment has been terminated under such authority thereafter may be employed by any other department or agency except after a determination by the Civil Service Commission that such person is eligible for such employment.

Section 8(a) The investigations conducted pursuant to this order shall be designed to develop information as to whether the employment or retention in employment in the Federal service of the person being investigated is clearly consistent with the interests of the national security. Such information shall relate, but shall not be limited, to the following:

(1) Depending on the relation of the Government employment to the national security:

(i) Any behavior, activities, or associations which tend to show that the individual is not reliable or trustworthy.

(ii) Any deliberate misrepresentations, falsifications, or omission of material facts.

(iii) Any criminal, infamous, dishonest, immoral, or notoriously disgraceful conduct, habitual use of intoxicants to excess, drug addiction, or sexual perversion.

(iv) An adjudication of insanity, or treatment for serious mental or neurological disorder without satisfactory evidence of cure.

(v) Any facts which furnish reason to believe that the individual may be subjected to coercion, influence, or pressure which may cause him to act contrary to the best interests of the national security.

(2) Commission of any act of sabotage, espionage, treason, or sedition, or attempts thereat or preparation therefor, or conspiring with, or aiding or abetting, another to commit or attempt to commit any act of sabotage, espionage, treason, or sedition.

(3) Establishing or continuing a sympathetic association with a saboteur, spy, traitor, seditionist, anarchist, or revolutionist, or with an espionage or other secret agent or representative of a foreign nation, or any representative of a foreign nation whose interests may be inimical to the interests of the United States, or with any person who advocates the use of force or violence to overthrow the government of the United States or the alteration of the form of government of the United States by unconstitutional means.

(4) Advocacy of use of force or violence to overthrow the government of the United States, or of the alteration of the form of government of the United States by unconstitutional means.

(5) Membership in, or affiliation or sympathetic association with, any foreign or domestic organization, association, movement, group, or combination of persons which is

totalitarian, Fascist, Communist, or subversive, or which has adopted, or shows, a policy of advocating or approving the commission of acts of force or violence to deny other persons their rights under the Constitution of the United States, or which seeks to alter the form of government of the United States by unconstitutional means.

(6) Intentional, unauthorized disclosure to any person of security information, or of other information disclosure of which is prohibited by law, or willful violation or disregard of security regulations.

(7) Performing or attempting to perform his duties, or otherwise acting, so as to serve the interests of another government in preference to the interests of the United States. . . .

The Senate Censure of Joseph McCarthy
December 2, 1954

[On July 30, 1954, Senator Flanders of Vermont introduced a resolution asking for McCarthy's censure for his insulting behavior toward the Senate. A special committee headed by Senator Watkins of Utah was formed to study the censure charges. It recommended censure, and the Senate as a whole accepted the recommendation by a vote of 67 to 22.]

Resolved, That the Senator from Wisconsin, Mr. McCarthy, failed to cooperate with the Subcommittee on Privileges and Elections of the Senate Committee on Rules and Administration in clearing up matters referred to that subcommittee which concerned his conduct as a Senator and affected the honor of the Senate and, instead, repeatedly abused the subcommittee and its members who were trying to carry out assigned duties, thereby obstructing the constitutional processes of the Senate, and that this conduct of the Senator from Wisconsin, Mr. McCarthy, is contrary to senatorial traditions and is hereby condemned.

SEC. 2. The Senator from Wisconsin, Mr. McCarthy, in writing to the chairman of the Select Committee to Study

Censure Charges (Mr. Watkins) after the Select Committee had issued its report and before the report was presented to the Senate charging three members of the Select Committee with "deliberate deception" and "fraud" for failure to disqualify themselves; in stating to the press on November 4, 1954, that the special Senate session that was to begin November 8, 1954, was a "lynch party"; in repeatedly describing this special Senate session as a "lynch bee" in a nationwide television and radio show on November 7, 1954; in stating to the public press on November 13, 1954, that the chairman of the Select Committee (Mr. Watkins) was guilty of "the most unusual, most cowardly thing I've heard of" and stating further: "I expected he would be afraid to answer the questions, but didn't think he'd be stupid enough to make a public statement"; and in characterizing the said committee as the "unwitting handmaiden," "involuntary agent" and "attorneys-in-fact" of the Communist Party and in charging that the said committee in writing its report "imitated Communist methods—that it distorted, misrepresented, and omitted in its effort to manufacture a plausible rationalization" in support of its recommendations to the Senate, which characterizations and charges were contained in a statement released to the press and inserted in the *Congressional Record* of November 10, 1954, acted contrary to senatorial ethics and tended to bring the Senate into dishonor and disrepute, to obstruct the constitutional processes of the Senate, and to impair its dignity; and such conduct is hereby condemned.

Brown v. Board of Education of Topeka
1954

[There were two reasons why the Court had to take up the question of segregation in public schools. First, because the moral sense of the country had changed since the *Plessy* v. *Ferguson* decision of 1896, and Americans no longer accepted the ideals of racism and colonialism. Second, because the "separate but equal" doctrine laid down in 1896 had grown legally unmanageable. Negroes were bringing more and more suits before the courts to prove that the education Negro children received in segregated schools was not equal to the education of white children. In short, the separate but equal doctrine did not and could not work. After long deliberation and after consulting with numerous social scientists who had studied the effects of segregation on children, the Court unanimously concluded that legal segregation in public schools violated the Constitution and must ultimately come to an end.]

WARREN, C. J.: These cases come to us from the States of Kansas, South Carolina, Virginia, and Delaware. They are premised on different facts and different local conditions, but a common legal question justifies their consideration together in this consolidated opinion.

In each of the cases, minors of the Negro race, through their legal representatives, seek the aid of the courts in obtaining admission to the public schools of their community on a nonsegregated basis. In each instance, they have been denied admission to schools attended by white children under laws requiring or permitting segregation according to race. This segregation was alleged to deprive the plaintiffs of the equal protection of the laws under the Fourteenth Amendment. In each of the cases other than the Delaware case, a three-judge federal district court denied relief to the plaintiffs on the so-called "separate but equal" doctrine announced by this Court in Plessy v. Ferguson, 163 U. S. 537. Under that doctrine, equality of treatment is accorded when the races are provided substantially equal facilities, even though these facilities be separate. In the Delaware case, the Supreme Court of Delaware adhered to that doctrine, but ordered that the plaintiffs be admitted to the white schools because of their superiority to the Negro schools.

The plaintiffs contend that segregated public schools are not "equal" and cannot be made "equal," and that hence they are deprived of the equal protection of the laws. Because of the obvious importance of the question presented, the Court took jurisdiction. Argument was heard in the 1952

Term, and reargument was heard this Term on certain questions propounded by the Court.

Reargument was largely devoted to the circumstances surrounding the adoption of the Fourteenth Amendment in 1868. It covered exhaustively consideration of the Amendment in Congress, ratification by the states, then existing practices in racial segregation, and the views of proponents and opponents of the Amendment. This discussion and our own investigation convince us that, although these sources cast some light, it is not enough to resolve the problem with which we are faced. At best, they are inconclusive. The most avid proponents of the post-War Amendments undoubtedly intended them to remove all legal distinctions among "all persons born or naturalized in the United States." Their opponents, just as certainly, were antagonistic to both the letter and the spirit of the Amendments and wished them to have the most limited effect. What others in Congress and the state legislatures had in mind cannot be determined with any degree of certainty.

An additional reason for the inconclusive nature of the Amendment's history, with respect to segregated schools, is the status of public education at that time. In the South, the movement toward free common schools, supported by general taxation, had not yet taken hold. Education of white children was largely in the hands of private groups. Education of Negroes was almost nonexistent, and practically all of the race were illiterate. In fact, any education of Negroes was forbidden by law in some states. Today, in contrast, many Negroes have achieved outstanding success in the arts and sciences as well as in the business and professional world. It is true that public education had already advanced further in the North, but the effect of the Amendment on Northern States was generally ignored in the congressional debates. Even in the North, the conditions of public education did not approximate those existing today. The curriculum was usually rudimentary; ungraded schools were common in rural areas; the school term was but three months a year in many states; and compulsory school attendance was virtually unknown. As a consequence, it is not surprising that there should be so little in the history of the Fourteenth Amendment relating to its intended effect on public education.

In the first cases in this Court construing the Fourteenth Amendment, decided shortly after its adoption, the Court interpreted it as proscribing all state-imposed discriminations against the Negro race. The doctrine of "separate but equal" did not make its appearance in this Court until 1896 in the case of Plessy v. Ferguson, supra, involving not education but transportation. American courts have since labored with the doctrine for over half a century. In this Court, there have been six cases involving the "separate but equal" doctrine in the field of public education. In Cumming v. Board of Education of Richmond County, 175 U. S. 528, and Gong Lum v. Rice, 275 U. S. 78, the validity of the doctrine itself was not challenged. In more recent cases, all on the graduate school level, inequality was found in that specific benefits enjoyed by white students were denied to Negro students of the same educational qualifications. State of Missouri ex rel. Gaines v. Canada, 305 U. S. 337; Sipuel v. Board of Regents of University of Oklahoma, 332 U. S. 631; Sweatt v. Painter, 339 U. S. 629; McLaurin v. Oklahoma State Regents, 339 U. S. 637. In none of these cases was it necessary to reexamine the doctrine to grant relief to the Negro plaintiff. And in Sweatt v. Painter, supra, the Court expressly reserved decision on the question whether Plessy v. Ferguson should be held inapplicable to public education.

In the instant cases, that question is directly presented. Here, unlike Sweatt v. Painter, there are findings below that the Negro and white schools involved have been equalized, or are being equalized, with respect to buildings, curricula, qualifications and salaries of teachers, and other "tangible" factors. Our decision, therefore, cannot turn on merely a comparison of these tangible factors in the Negro and white schools involved in each of the cases. We must look instead to the effect of segregation itself on public education.

In approaching this problem, we cannot turn the clock back to 1868 when the Amendment was adopted, or even to 1896 when Plessy v. Ferguson was written. We must consider public education in the light of its full development and its present place in American life throughout the Nation. Only in this way can it be determined if segregation in public schools deprives these plaintiffs of the equal protection of the laws.

Today, education is perhaps the most important function of state and local governments. Compulsory school attendance laws and the great expenditures for education both demonstrate our recognition of the importance of education to our democratic society. It is required in the performance of our most basic public responsibilities, even service in the armed forces. It is the very foundation of good citizenship. Today it is a principal instrument in awakening the child to cultural values, in preparing him for later professional training, and in helping him to adjust normally to his environment. In these days, it is doubtful that any child may reasonably be expected to succeed in life if he is denied the opportunity of an education. Such an opportunity, where the state has undertaken to provide it, is a right which must be made available to all on equal terms.

We come then to the question presented: Does segregation of children in public schools solely on the basis of race, even though the physical facilities and other "tangible" factors may be equal, deprive the children of the minority group of equal educational opportunities? We believe that it does.

In Sweatt v. Painter, supra [339 U. S. 629, 70 S.Ct. 850], in finding that a segregated law school for Negroes could not provide them equal educational opportunities, this Court relied in large part on "those qualities which are incapable of objective measurement but which make for greatness in a law school." In McLaurin v. Oklahoma State Regents, supra, the Court, in requiring that a Negro admitted to a white graduate school be treated like all other students, again resorted to intangible considerations: ". . . his ability to study, to engage in discussions and exchange views with other students, and, in general, to learn his profession." Such considerations apply with added force to children in grade and high schools. To separate them from others of similar age and qualifications solely because of their race generates a feeling of inferiority as to their status in the community that may affect their hearts and minds in a way unlikely ever to be undone. The effect of this separation on their educational opportunities was well stated by a finding in the Kansas case by a court which nevertheless felt compelled to rule against the Negro plaintiffs:

"Segregation of white and colored children in public schools has a detrimental effect upon the colored children. The impact is greater when it has the sanction of the law; for the policy of separating the races is usually interpreted as denoting the inferiority of the Negro group. A sense of inferiority affects the motivation of a child to learn. Segregation with the sanction of law, therefore, has a tendency to retard the educational and mental development of Negro children and to deprive them of some of the benefits they would receive in a racially integrated school system."

Whatever may have been the extent of psychological knowledge at the time of Plessy v. Ferguson, this finding is amply supported by modern authority. Any language in Plessy v. Ferguson contrary to this finding is rejected.

We conclude that in the field of public education the doctrine of "separate but equal" has no place. Separate educational facilities are inherently unequal. Therefore, we hold that the plaintiffs and others similarly situated for whom the actions have been brought are, by reason of the segregation complained of, deprived of the equal protection of the laws guaranteed by the Fourteenth Amendment. This disposition makes unnecessary any discussion whether such segregation also violates the Due Process Clause of the Fourteenth Amendment.

Because these are class actions, because of the wide applicability of this decision, and because of the great variety of local conditions, the formulation of decrees in these cases presents problems of considerable complexity. On reargument, the consideration of appropriate relief was necessarily subordinated to the primary question—the constitutionality of segregation in public education. We have now announced that such segregation is a denial of the equal protection of the laws. . . .

Dwight D. Eisenhower, Speech on
the Little Rock Crisis
September 24, 1957

[Following is President Eisenhower's explanation of his order sending federal troops to Little Rock.]

MY FELLOW CITIZENS . . . I must speak to you about the serious situation that has arisen in Little Rock. . . . In that city, under the leadership of demagogic extremists, disorderly mobs have deliberately prevented the carrying out of proper orders from a federal court. Local authorities have not eliminated that violent opposition and, under the law, I yesterday issued a proclamation calling upon the mob to disperse.

This morning the mob again gathered in front of the Central High School of Little Rock, obviously for the purpose of again preventing the carrying out of the court's order relating to the admission of Negro children to that school.

Whenever normal agencies prove inadequate to the task and it becomes necessary for the executive branch of the federal government to use its powers and authority to uphold federal courts, the President's responsibility is inescapable.

In accordance with that responsibility, I have today issued an Executive Order directing the use of troops under federal authority to aid in the execution of federal law at Little Rock, Arkansas. This became necessary when my Proclamation of yesterday was not observed, and the obstruction of justice still continues.

It is important that the reasons for my action be understood by all our citizens.

As you know, the Supreme Court of the United States has decided that separate public educational facilities for the races are inherently unequal and therefore compulsory school segregation laws are unconstitutional. . . .

In May of 1955, the Little Rock School Board approved a moderate plan for the gradual desegregation of the public schools in that city. It provided that a start toward integration would be made at the present term in the high school, and that the plan would be in full operation by 1963. . . . Now this Little Rock plan was challenged in the courts by some who believed that the period of time as proposed in the plan was too long.

The United States Court at Little Rock, which has supervisory responsibility under the law for the plan of desegregation in the public schools, dismissed the challenge, thus approving a gradual rather than an abrupt change from the existing system. The court found that the school board had acted in good faith in planning for a public school system free from racial discrimination.

Since that time, the court has on three separate occasions issued orders directing that the plan be carried out. All persons were instructed to refrain from interfering with the efforts of the school board to comply with the law.

Proper and sensible observance of the law then demanded the respectful obedience which the nation has a right to expect from all its people. This, unfortunately, has not been the case at Little Rock. Certain misguided persons, many of them imported into Little Rock by agitators, have insisted upon defying the law and have sought to bring it into disrepute. The orders of the court have thus been frustrated.

The very basis of our individual rights and freedoms rests upon the certainty that the President and the Executive Branch of Government will support and insure the carrying out of the decisions of the federal courts, even, when necessary with all the means at the President's command. . . .

A foundation of our American way of life is our national respect for law.

In the South, as elsewhere, citizens are keenly aware of the tremendous disservice that has been done to the people of Arkansas in the eyes of the nation, and that has been done to the nation in the eyes of the world.

At a time when we face grave situations abroad because of the hatred that communism bears toward a system of government based on human rights, it would be difficult to exaggerate the harm that is being done to the prestige and influence, and indeed to the safety, of our nation and the world.

Our enemies are gloating over this incident and using it everywhere to misrepresent our whole nation. We are portrayed as a violator of those standards of conduct which the peoples of the world united to proclaim in the Charter of the United Nations. There they affirmed "faith in fundamental human rights" and "in the dignity and worth of the human person" and they did so "without distinction as to race, sex, language or religion."

And so, with deep confidence, I call upon the citizens of the State of Arkansas to assist in bringing to an immediate end all interference with the law and its processes. If resistance to the federal court orders ceases at once, the further presence of federal troops will be unnecessary and the City of Little Rock will return to its normal habits of peace and order and a blot upon the fair name and high honor of our nation in the world will be removed.

Thus will be restored the image of America and of all its parts as one nation, indivisible, with liberty and justice for all.

Dwight D. Eisenhower, Farewell Address
January 17, 1961

[Following are Eisenhower's remarks on "the military-industrial complex," delivered three days before he was to leave office.]

. . . Throughout America's adventure in free government, our basic purposes have been to keep the peace; to foster progress in human achievement, and to enhance liberty, dignity and integrity among people and among nations. To strive for less would be unworthy of a free and religious people. Any failure traceable to arrogance, or our lack of comprehension or readiness to sacrifice would inflict upon us grievous hurt both at home and abroad.

Progress toward these noble goals is persistently threatened by the conflict now engulfing the world. It commands our whole attention, absorbs our very beings. We face a hostile ideology—global in scope, atheistic in character, ruthless in purpose, and insidious in method. Unhappily the danger it poses promises to be of indefinite duration. To meet it successfully, there is called for, not so much the emotional and transitory sacrifices of crisis, but rather those which enable us to carry forward steadily, surely, and without complaint the burdens of a prolonged and complex struggle—with liberty the stake. Only thus shall we remain, despite every provocation, on our charted course toward permanent peace and human betterment. . . .

A vital element in keeping the peace is our military establishment. Our arms must be mighty, ready for instant action, so that no potential aggressor may be tempted to risk his own destruction.

Our military organization today bears little relation to that known by any of my predecessors in peacetime, or indeed by the fighting men of World War II or Korea.

Until the latest of our world conflicts, the United States had no armaments industry. American makers of plowshares could, with time and as required, make swords as well. But now we can no longer risk emergency improvisation of national defense; we have been compelled to create a permanent armaments industry of vast proportions. Added to this, three and a half million men and women are directly engaged in the defense establishment. We annually spend on military security more than the net income of all United States corporations.

This conjunction of an immense military establishment and a large arms industry is new in the American experience. The total influence—economic, political, even spiritual—is felt in every city, every statehouse, every office of the federal government. We recognize the imperative need for this development. Yet we must not fail to comprehend its grave implications. Our toil, resources, and livelihood are all involved; so is the very structure of our society.

In the councils of government, we must guard against the acquisition of unwarranted influence, whether sought or unsought, by the military-industrial complex. The potential for the disastrous rise of misplaced power exists and will persist.

We must never let the weight of this combination endanger our liberties or democratic processes. We should take nothing for granted. Only an alert and knowledgeable citizenry can compel the proper meshing of the huge industrial and military machinery of defense with our peaceful methods and goals, so that security and liberty may prosper together.

Akin to, and largely responsible for the sweeping changes in our industrial-military posture, has been the technological revolution during recent decades.

In this revolution, research has become central; it also becomes more formalized, complex, and costly. A steadily increasing share is conducted for, by, or at the direction of, the federal government. . . .

The prospect of domination of the nation's scholars by federal employment, project allocations, and the power of money is ever present—and is gravely to be regarded.

Yet, in holding scientific research and discovery in respect, as we should, we must also be alert to the equal and opposite danger that public policy could itself become the captive of a scientific-technological elite.

It is the task of statesmanship to mold, to balance, and to integrate these and other forces, new and old, within the principles of our democratic system—ever aiming toward the supreme goals of our free society.

Another factor in maintaining balance involves the element of time. As we peer into society's future, we—you and I, and our government—must avoid the impulse to live only for today, plundering, for our own ease and convenience, the precious resources of tomorrow. We cannot mortgage the material assets of our grandchildren without risking the loss also of their political and spiritual heritage. We want democracy to survive for all generations to come, not to become the insolvent phantom of tomorrow.

Down the long lane of the history yet to be written America knows that this world of ours, ever growing smaller, must avoid becoming a community of dreadful fear and hate, and be, instead, a proud confederation of mutual trust and respect.

Such a confederation must be one of equals. The weakest

must come to the conference table with the same confidence as do we, protected as we are by our moral, economic, and military strength. That table, though scarred by many past frustrations, cannot be abandoned for the certain agony of the battlefield.

Disarmament, with mutual honor and confidence, is a continuing imperative. Together we must learn how to compose differences, not with arms, but with intellect and decent purpose. Because this need is so sharp and apparent I confess that I lay down my official responsibilities in this field with a definite sense of disappointment. As one who has witnessed the horror and the lingering sadness of war—as one who knows that another war could utterly destroy this civilization which has been so slowly and painfully built over thousands of years—I wish I could say tonight that a lasting peace is in sight. . . .

John F. Kennedy, Speech on Civil Rights
June 11, 1963

[A long series of civil rights demonstrations in the South, some of them meeting violent resistance from white extremists, led Kennedy to conclude that legislation was necessary to resolve the issue peaceably, through the courts. The occasion for this speech was Governor George Wallace's attempt to defy a federal court order requiring the University of Alabama to admit a Negro student. To enforce the order, President Kennedy on June 11 federalized the Alabama national guard, which then escorted the student past Wallace, who was left standing at the college entrance. That evening Kennedy went on the air to ask the country's help in ending racial inequality once and for all.]

This afternoon, following a series of threats and defiant statements, the presence of Alabama National Guardsmen was required at the University of Alabama to carry out the final and unequivocal order of the United States District Court of the Northern District of Alabama.

That order called for the admission of two clearly qualified young Alabama residents who happened to have been born Negro.

That they were admitted peacefully on the campus is due in a good measure to the conduct of the students of the University of Alabama who met their responsibilities in a constructive way.

I hope that every American, regardless of where he lives, will stop and examine his conscience about this and other related incidents.

This nation was founded by men of many nations and backgrounds. It was founded on the principle that all men are created equal, and that the rights of every man are diminished when the rights of one man are threatened.

Today we are committed to a worldwide struggle to promote and protect the rights of all who wish to be free. And when Americans are sent to Vietnam or West Berlin we do not ask for whites only.

It ought to be possible, therefore, for American students of any color to attend any public institution they select without having to be backed up by troops. It ought to be possible for American consumers of any color to receive equal service in places of public accommodation, such as hotels and restaurants, and theaters and retail stores without being forced to resort to demonstrations in the street.

And it ought to be possible for American citizens of any color to register and to vote in a free election without interference or fear of reprisal.

It ought to be possible, in short, for every American to enjoy the privileges of being American without regard to his race or his color.

In short, every American ought to have the right to be treated as he would wish to be treated, as one would wish his children to be treated. But this is not the case.

The Negro baby born in America today, regardless of the section or the state in which he is born, has about one-half as much chance of completing high school as a white baby, born in the same place, on the same day; one-third as much chance of completing college; one-third as much chance of becoming a professional man; twice as much chance of becoming unemployed; about one-seventh as much chance of earning $10,000 a year; a life expectancy which is seven years shorter and the prospects of earning only half as much.

This is not a sectional issue. Difficulties over segregation and discrimination exist in every city, in every state of the Union, producing in many cities a rising tide of discontent that threatens the public safety.

Nor is this a partisan issue. In a time of domestic crisis, men of good will and generosity should be able to unite regardless of party or politics.

This is not even a legal or legislative issue alone. It is better to settle these matters in the courts than on the streets, and new laws are needed at every level. But law alone cannot make men see right.

We are confronted primarily with a moral issue. It is as old as the Scriptures and is as clear as the American Constitution. The heart of the question is whether all Americans are to be afforded equal rights and equal opportunities; whether we are going to treat our fellow Americans as we want to be treated.

If an American, because his skin is dark, cannot eat lunch in a restaurant open to the public; if he cannot send his children to the best public school available; if he cannot vote for the public officials who represent him; if, in short, he cannot enjoy the full and free life which all of us want, then who among us would be content to have the color of his skin changed and stand in his place?

Who among us would then be content with the counsels of patience and delay? One hundred years of delay have passed since President Lincoln freed the slaves, yet their heirs, their grandsons, are not fully free. They are not yet freed from the bonds of injustice; they are not yet freed from social and economic oppression.

And this nation, for all its hopes and all its boasts, will not be fully free until all its citizens are free.

We preach freedom around the world, and we mean it. And we cherish our freedom here at home. But are we to say to the world—and much more importantly to each other—that this is the land of the free, except for the Negroes; that we have no second-class citizens, except Negroes; that we have no class or caste system, no ghettos, no master race, except with respect to Negroes.

Now the time has come for this nation to fulfill its promise. The events in Birmingham and elsewhere have so increased the cries for equality that no city or state or legislative body can prudently choose to ignore them.

The fires of frustration and discord are burning in every city, North and South. Where legal remedies are not at hand, redress is sought in the streets in demonstrations, parades and protests, which create tensions and threaten violence—and threaten lives.

We face, therefore, a moral crisis as a country and a people. It cannot be met by repressive police action. It cannot be left to increased demonstrations in the streets. It cannot be quieted by token moves or talk. It is time to act in the Congress, in your state and local legislative body, and above all, in all of our daily lives.

It is not enough to pin the blame on others, to say this is a problem of one section of the country or another, or deplore the facts that we face. A great change is at hand, and our task, our obligation is to make that revolution, that change peaceful and constructive for all.

Those who do nothing are inviting shame as well as violence. Those who act boldly are recognizing right as well as reality.

Next week I shall ask the Congress of the United States to act, to make a commitment it has not fully made in this century to the proposition that race has no place in American life or law.

The Federal Judiciary has upheld that proposition in a series of forthright cases. The Executive Branch has adopted that proposition in the conduct of its affairs, including the employment of Federal personnel, and the use of Federal facilities, and the sale of Federally financed housing.

But there are other necessary measures which only the Congress can provide, and they must be provided at this session.

The old code of equity law under which we live commands for every wrong a remedy. But in too many communities, in too many parts of the country wrongs are inflicted on Negro citizens and there are no remedies in law.

Unless the Congress acts their only remedy is the street.

I am, therefore, asking the Congress to enact legislation giving all Americans the right to be served in facilities which are open to the public—hotels, restaurants and theaters, retail stores and similar establishments. This seems to me to be an elementary right.

Its denial is an arbitrary indignity that no American in 1963 should have to endure, but many do.

I have recently met with scores of business leaders, urging them to take voluntary action to end this discrimination. And I've been encouraged by their response. And in the last two weeks over 75 cities have seen progress made in desegregating these kinds of facilities.

But many are unwilling to act alone. And for this reason nationwide legislation is needed, if we are to move this problem from the streets to the courts.

I'm also asking Congress to authorize the Federal Government to participate more fully in lawsuits designed to end segregation in public education. We have succeeded in persuading many districts to desegregate voluntarily. Dozens have admitted Negroes without violence.

Today a Negro is attending a state-supported institution in every one of our 50 states. But the pace is very slow.

Too many Negro children entering segregated grade schools at the time of the Supreme Court's decision nine years ago will enter segregated high schools this fall, having suffered a loss which can never be restored.

The lack of an adequate education denies the Negro a chance to get a decent job. The orderly implementation of the Supreme Court decision therefore, cannot be left solely to those who may not have the economic resources to carry their legal action or who may be subject to harassment.

Other features will also be requested, including greater protection for the right to vote.

But legislation, I repeat, cannot solve this problem alone. It must be solved in the homes of every American in every community across our country.

In this respect, I want to pay tribute to those citizens,

North and South, who've been working in their communities to make life better for all. They are acting not out of a sense of legal duty but out of a sense of human decency. Like our soldiers and sailors in all parts of the world, they are meeting freedom's challenge on the firing line and I salute them for their honor—their courage.

My fellow Americans, this is a problem which faces us all, in every city of the North as well as the South.

Today there are Negroes unemployed, two or three times as many compared to whites, inadequate in education, moving into the large cities, unable to find work, young people particularly out of work, without hope, denied equal rights, denied the opportunity to eat at a restaurant or a lunch counter, or go to a movie theater, denied the right to a decent education, denied the right to attend a state university even though qualified.

It seems to me that these are matters which concern us all—not merely Presidents, or Congressmen, or Governors, but every citizen of the United States.

This is one country. It has become one country because all of us and all the people who came here had an equal chance to develop their talents.

We cannot say to 10 percent of the population that "you can't have that right. Your children can't have the chance to develop whatever talents they have, that the only way that they're going to get their rights is to go in the street and demonstrate."

I think we owe them and we owe ourselves a better country than that.

Therefore, I'm asking for your help in making it easier for us to move ahead and provide the kind of equality of treatment which we would want ourselves—to give a chance for every child to be educated to the limit of his talent.

As I've said before, not every child has an equal talent or an equal ability or equal motivation. But they should have the equal right to develop their talent and their ability and their motivation to make something of themselves.

We have a right to expect that the Negro community will be responsible, will uphold the law. But they have a right to expect the law will be fair, that the Constitution will be color blind, as Justice Harlan said at the turn of the century.

This is what we're talking about. This is a matter which concerns this country and what it stands for, and in meeting it I ask the support of all our citizens.

Thank you very much.

Reynolds v. Sims
1964

[For decades the state legislatures, run by a dwindling rural minority, had been discriminating outrageously against urban voters. In 1962, in *Baker* v. *Carr*, the Supreme Court sought to end this practice by requiring that the states reapportion their legislatures in such a way as to guarantee equal voting rights to all their citizens. The Alabama legislature was one of the legislatures that subsequently had to reapportion itself in obedience to a federal court order; it did so through the Crawford-Webb Act. In 1964, on the complaint of some citizens, the act came before the Supreme Court as a test case. This was the background for the *Reynolds* v. *Sims* decision. In a sweeping opinion, Chief Justice Warren, in the course of invalidating the Crawford-Webb Act, demanded that the states strictly abide by the principle of one man, one vote implicit in the "equal protection" clause of the Fourteenth Amendment. The reapportionment of the state legislatures promised to change American politics root and branch by giving the cities and suburbs far greater representation than they ever had. But a movement quickly sprang up within Congress and the states to nullify the Reynolds decision through a constitutional amendment that would allow each state to have one house apportioned on a basis other than population. As this is being written, a proposal to call a convention for the purpose of taking up such an amendment needs the support of only two more state legislatures to be adopted.]

WARREN, C. J. . . . Legislators represent people, not trees or acres. Legislators are elected by voters, not farms or cities or economic interests. As long as ours is a representative form of government, and our legislatures are those instruments of government elected directly by and directly representative of the people, the right to elect legislators in a free and unimpaired fashion is a bedrock of our political system. It could hardly be gainsaid that a constitutional claim had been asserted by an allegation that certain otherwise qualified voters had been entirely prohibited from voting for members of their state legislature. And, if a State should provide that the votes of citizens in one part of the State should be given two times, or five times, or 10 times the weight of votes of citizens in another part of the State, it could hardly be contended that the right to vote of those residing in the disfavored areas had not been effectively diluted. It would appear extraordinary to suggest that a state could be constitutionally permitted to enact a law providing that certain of the state's voters could vote two, five, or 10 times for their legislative representatives, while voters living elsewhere could vote only once. And it is inconceivable that a state law to the effect that, in counting votes for legislators, the votes of citizens in one part of the State would be multiplied by two, five, or 10, while the votes of persons in another area would be counted only at face value, could be constitutionally sustainable. . . .

State legislatures are, historically, the fountainhead of representative government in this country. A number of them have their roots in colonial times, and substantially antedate the creation of our Nation and our Federal Government. In fact, the first formal stirrings of American political independence are to be found, in large part, in the views and actions of several of the colonial legislative bodies. With the birth of our National Government, and the adoption and ratification of the Federal Constitution, state legislatures retained a most important place in our Nation's governmental structure. But representative government is in essence self-government through the medium of elected representatives of the people, and each and every citizen has an inalienable right to full and effective participation in the political processes of his State's legislative bodies. Most citizens can achieve this participation only as qualified voters through the election of legislators to represent them. Full and effective participation by all citizens in state government requires, therefore, that each citizen has an equally effective voice in the election of members of his state legislature. Modern and viable state government needs, and the Constitution demands, no less.

Logically, in a society ostensibly grounded on representative government, it would seem reasonable that a majority of the people of a State could elect a majority of that State's legislators. To conclude differently, and to sanction minority control of state legislative bodies, would appear to deny majority rights in a way that far surpasses any possible denial of minority rights that might otherwise be thought to result. Since legislatures are responsible for enacting laws by which all citizens are to be governed, they should be bodies which are collectively responsive to the popular will. And the concept of equal protection has been traditionally viewed as requiring the uniform treatment of persons standing in the same relation to the governmental action questioned or challenged. With respect to the allocation of legislative representation, all voters, as citizens of a State, stand in the same relation regardless of where they live. Any suggested criteria for the differentiation of citizens are insufficient to justify any discrimination, as to the weight of their votes, unless relevant to the permissible purposes of legislative apportionment. Since the achieving of fair and effective representation for all citizens is concededly the basic aim of legislative apportionment, we conclude that the Equal Protection Clause guarantees the opportunity for equal participation by all voters in the election of state legislators. Diluting the weight of votes because of place of residence impairs basic constitutional rights under the Fourteenth Amendment just as much as invidious discriminations based upon factors such as race, . . . or economic status. . . . Our constitutional system amply provides for the protection of minorities by means other than giving them majority control of state legislatures. And the democratic ideals of equality and majority rule, which have served this Nation so well in the past, are hardly of any less significance for the present and the future.

We are told that the matter of apportioning representation in a state legislature is a complex and many-faceted one. We are advised that States can rationally consider factors other than population in apportioning legislative representation. We are admonished not to restrict the power of the States to impose differing views as to political philosophy on their citizens. We are cautioned about the dangers of entering into political thickets and mathematical quagmires. Our answer is this: a denial of constitutionally protected rights demands judicial protection; our oath and our office require no less of us. . . . To the extent that a citizen's right to vote is debased, he is that much less a citizen. The fact that an individual lives here or there is not a legitimate reason for overweighting or diluting the efficacy of his vote. The complexions of societies and civilizations change, often with amazing rapidity. A nation once primarily rural in character becomes predominantly urban. Representation schemes once fair and equitable become archaic and outdated. But the basic principle of representative government remains, and must remain, unchanged—the weight of a citizen's vote cannot be made to depend on where he lives. Population is, of necessity, the starting point for consideration and the controlling criterion for judgment in legislative apportionment controversies. A citizen, a qualified voter, is no more nor no less so because he lives in the city or on the farm. This is the clear and strong command of our Constitution's Equal Protection Clause. This is an essential part of the concept of a government of laws and not men. This is at the heart of Lincoln's vision of "government of the people, by the people, for the people." The Equal Protection Clause demands no less than substantially equal state legislative representation for all citizens, of all places as well as of all races.

We hold that, as a basic constitutional standard, the Equal Protection Clause requires that the seats in both houses of a bicameral state legislature must be apportioned on a population basis. Simply stated, an individual's right to vote for state legislators is unconstitutionally impaired when its weight is in a substantial fashion diluted when compared with votes of citizens living in other parts of the State. Since, under neither the existing apportionment provisions nor under either of the proposed plans was either of the houses of the Alabama Legislature apportioned on a population basis, the District Court correctly held that all three of these schemes were constitutionally invalid. Furthermore, the existing apportionment, and also to a lesser extent the apportionment under the Crawford-Webb Act, presented little more than crazy quilts, completely lacking in rationality, and could be found invalid on that basis alone. Although the District Court presumably found the apportionment of the Alabama House of Representatives under the 67-Senator Amendment to be acceptable, we conclude that the deviations from a strict population basis are too egregious to permit us to find that that body, under this proposed plan, was apportioned sufficiently on a population basis so as to permit the arrangement to be constitutionally sustained. Although about 43% of the State's total population would be required to comprise districts which could elect a majority in that body, only 39 of the 106 House seats were actually to be distributed on a population basis, as each of Alabama's 67 counties was given at least one representative, and population-variance ratios of close to 5-to-1 would have existed. While mathematical nicety is not a constitutional requisite, one could hardly conclude that the Alabama House, under the proposed constitutional amendment, had been apportioned sufficiently on a population basis to be sustainable under the requirements of the Equal Protection Clause. And none of the other apportionments of seats in either of the bodies of the Alabama Legislature under the three plans considered by the District Court, came nearly as close to approaching the required constitutional standard as did that of the House of Representatives under the 67-Senator Amendment.

Legislative apportionment in Alabama is signally illustrative and symptomatic of the seriousness of this problem in a number of the States. At the time this litigation was commenced, there had been no reapportionment of seats in the Alabama Legislature for over 60 years. Legislative inaction, coupled with the unavailabilty of any political or judicial remedy, had resulted, with the passage of years, in the perpetuated scheme becoming little more than an irrational anachronism. Consistent failure by the Alabama Legislature to comply with state applicability of the so-called federal analogy to state legislative apportionment arrangements. After considering the matter, the court below concluded that no conceivable analogy could be drawn between the federal scheme and the apportionment of seats in the Alabama Legislature under the proposed constitutional amendment. We agree with the District Court, and find the federal analogy inapposite and irrelevant to state legislative districting schemes. Attempted reliance on the federal analogy appears often to be little more than an after-the-fact rationalization offered in defense of maladjusted state apportionment arrangements. The original constitutions of 36 of our States provided that representation in both houses of the state legislatures would be based completely, or predominantly, on population. And the Founding Fathers clearly had no intention of establishing a pattern or model for the apportionment of seats in state legislatures when the system of representation in the Federal Congress was adopted. Demonstrative of this is the fact that the Northwest Ordinance, adopted in the same year, 1787, as the Federal Constitution, provided for the apportionment of seats in territorial legislatures solely on the basis of population.

The system of representation in the two Houses of the Federal Congress is one ingrained in our Constitution, as part of the law of the land. It is one conceived out of compromise and concession indispensable to the establishment of our federal republic. Arising from unique historical circumstances, it is based on the consideration that in establishing our type of federalism a group of formerly independent States bound themselves together under one national government. Admittedly, the original 13 States surrendered some of their sovereignty in agreeing to join together "to form a more perfect Union." But at the heart of our constitutional system remains the concept of separate and distinct governmental entities which have delegated some, but not all, of their formerly held powers to the single national government. The fact that almost three-fourths of our present States were never in fact independently sovereign does not detract from our view that the so-called federal analogy is inapplicable as a sustaining precedent for state legislative apportionments. The developing history and growth of our republic cannot cloud the fact that, at the time of the inception of the system of representation in the Federal Congress, a compromise between the larger and smaller States on this matter averted a deadlock in the constitutional convention which had threatened to abort the birth of our Nation. . . .

Political subdivisions of States—counties, cities, or whatever—never were and never have been considered as sovereign entities. Rather, they have been traditionally regarded as subordinate governmental instrumentalities created by the State to assist in the carrying out of state governmental functions. . . .

Thus, we conclude that the plan contained in the 67-Senator Amendment for apportioning seats in the Alabama Legislature cannot be sustained by recourse to the so-called federal analogy. Nor can any other inequitable state legislative apportionment scheme be justified on such an asserted basis. This does not necessarily mean that such a plan is irrational or involves something other than a "republican form of government." We conclude simply that such a plan is impermissible for the States under the Equal Protection Clause, since perforce resulting, in virtually every case, in submergence of the equal-population principle in at least one house of a state legislature. . . .

HARLAN, J., dissenting . . . The Court's elaboration of its new "constitutional" doctrine indicates how far—and how unwisely—it has strayed from the appropriate bounds of its authority. The consequence of today's decision is that in all but the handful of States which may already satisfy the new requirements the local District Court or, it may be, the state courts, are given blanket authority and the constitutional duty to supervise apportionment of the State Legislatures. It is difficult to imagine a more intolerable and inappropriate interference by the judiciary with the independent legislatures of the States. . . .

It should by now be obvious that these cases do not mark the end of reapportionment problems in the courts. Predictions once made that the courts would never have to face the problem of actually working out an apportionment have proved false. This Court, however, continues to avoid the consequences of its decisions, simply assuring us that the lower courts "can and . . . will work out more concrete and specific standards." Deeming it "expedient" not to spell out "precise constitutional tests," the Court contents itself with stating "only a few rather general considerations."

Generalities cannot obscure the cold truth that cases of this type are not amenable to the development of judicial standards. No set of standards can guide a court which has to decide how many legislative districts a State shall have, or what the shape of the districts shall be, or where to draw a particular district line. No judicially manageable standard can determine whether a State should have single-member districts or multimember districts or some combination of both. No such standard can control the balance between keeping up with population shifts and having stable districts. In all these respects, the courts will be called upon to make particular decisions with respect to which a principle of equally populated districts will be of no assistance whatsoever. Quite obviously, there are limitless possibilities for districting consistent with such a principle. Nor can these problems be avoided by judicial reliance on legislative judgments so far as possible. Reshaping or combining one or two districts, or modifying just a few district lines, is no less a matter of choosing among many possible solutions, with varying political consequences, than reapportionment broadside.

The Court ignores all this, saying only that "what is marginally permissible in one State may be unsatisfactory in another, depending on the particular circumstances of the case." It is well to remember that the product of today's decisions will not be readjustment of a few districts in a few States which most glaringly depart from the principle of equally populated districts. It will be a redetermination, extensive in many cases, of legislative districts in all but a few States.

Although the Court—necessarily, as I believe—provides only generalities in elaboration of its main thesis, its opinion nevertheless fully demonstrates how far removed these problems are from fields of judicial competence. Recognizing that "indiscriminate districting" is an invitation to "partisan gerrymandering," the Court nevertheless excludes virtually every basis for the formation of electoral districts other than "indiscriminate districting." In one or another of today's opinions, the Court declares it unconstitutional for a State to give effective consideration to any of the following in establishing legislative districts:

(1) history;

(2) "economic or other sorts of group interests";

(3) area;

(4) geographical considerations;

(5) a desire "to insure effective representation for sparsely settled areas";

(6) "availability of access of citizens to their representatives";

(7) theories of bicameralism (except those approved by the Court);

(8) occupation;

(9) "an attempt to balance urban and rural power";

(10) the preference of a majority of voters in the State.

So far as presently appears, the *only* factor which a State may consider, apart from numbers, is political subdivisions. But even "a clearly rational state policy" recognizing this factor is unconstitutional if "population is submerged as the controlling consideration. . . ."

I know of no principle of logic or practical or theoretical politics, still less any constitutional principle, which establishes all or any of these exclusions. Certain it is that the Court's opinion does not establish them. So far as the Court says anything at all on this score, it says only that "legislators represent people, not trees or acres"; that "citizens, not history or economic interests, cast votes"; that "people, not land or trees or pastures, vote." All this may be conceded. But it is surely equally obvious, and, in the context of elections, more meaningful to note that people are not ciphers and that legislators can represent their electors only by speaking for their interests—economic, social, political—many of which do reflect the place where the electors live. The Court does not establish, or indeed even attempt to make a case for the proposition that conflicting interests within a State can only be adjusted by disregarding them when voters are grouped for purposes of representation.

With these cases the Court approaches the end of the third round set in motion by the complaint filed in *Baker* v. *Carr*. What is done today deepens my conviction that judicial entry into this realm is profoundly ill-advised and constitutionally impermissible. As I have said before, *Wesberry* v. *Sanders*, I believe that the vitality of our political system, on which in the last analysis all else depends, is weakened by reliance on the judiciary for political reform; in time a complacent body politic may result.

These decisions also cut deeply into the fabric of our federalism. What must follow from them may eventually appear to be the product of State Legislatures. Nevertheless, no thinking person can fail to recognize that the aftermath of these cases, however desirable it may be thought in itself, will have been achieved at the cost of a radical alteration in the relationship between the States and the Federal Government, more particularly the Federal Judiciary. Only one who has an overbearing impatience with the federal system and its political processes will believe that that cost was not too high or was inevitable.

Finally, these decisions give support to a current mistaken view of the Constitution and the constitutional function of this Court. This view, in a nutshell, is that every major social ill in this country can find its cure in some constitutional "principle," and that this Court should "take the lead" in promoting reform when other branches of government fail to act. The Constitution is not a panacea for every blot upon the public welfare, nor should this Court, ordained as a judicial body, be thought of as a general haven for reform movements. The Constitution is an instrument of government, fundamental to which is the premise that in a diffusion of governmental authority lies the greatest promise that this Nation will realize liberty for all its citizens. This Court, limited in function in accordance with that premise, does not serve its high purpose when it exceeds its authority, even to satisfy justified impatience with the slow workings of the political process. For when, in the name of constitutional interpretation, the Court *adds* something to the Constitution that was deliberately excluded from it, the Court in reality substitutes its view of what should be so for the amending process.

I dissent in each of these cases, believing that in none of them have the plaintiffs stated a cause of action. To the extent that *Baker* v. *Carr*, expressly or by implication, went beyond a discussion of jurisdictional doctrines independent of the substantive issues involved here, it should be limited to what it in fact was: an experiment in venturesome constitutionalism. . . .

Barry Goldwater, Speech Accepting
Republican Nomination
July 16, 1964

[When the Republicans nominated Goldwater for the presidency in 1964 it marked the first time in the twentieth century that either of the major political parties had chosen an "extremist" candidate. Whether Goldwater in office would have been as conservative as he professed to be will never be known. But just before his nomination he voted against the Civil Rights Act of 1964, one of the very few Senators outside the South to do so; and he was one of only a handful of Senators to oppose the treaty banning nuclear tests in the atmosphere. What he thought of moderation could be discerned from his acceptance speech below.]

. . . In this world no person, no party, can guarantee anything, but what we can do and what we shall do is to deserve victory, and victory will be ours. The Good Lord raised this mighty Republican—Republic—to be a home for the brave and to flourish as the land of the free—not to stagger in the swampland of collectivism, nor to cringe before the bully of Communism.

Now, my fellow Americans, the tide has been running against freedom. Our people have followed false prophets.

We must, and we shall, return to proven ways, not because they are old, but because they are true.

We must, and we shall, set the tide running again in the cause of freedom. And this party, with its every action, every word, every breath and every heartbeat, has but a single resolve, and that is freedom.

Freedom made orderly for this nation by our Constitution. Freedom under a government limited by laws of nature and of nature's God. Freedom balanced so that order lacking liberty will not become the slavery of the prison cell; balanced so that liberty lacking order will not become the license of the mob and of the jungle.

Now, we Americans understand freedom; we have earned it; we have lived for it; and we have died for it. This nation and its people are freedom's models in a searching world. We can be freedom's missionaries in a doubting world.

But, ladies and gentlemen, first we must renew freedom's mission in our own hearts and in our own homes.

During four futile years, the Administration which we shall replace has distorted and lost that faith. It has talked and talked and talked and talked the words of freedom, but it has failed and failed and failed in the works of freedom.

Now failure cements the wall of shame in Berlin; failures blot the sands of shame at the Bay of Pigs; failures marked the slow death of freedom in Laos; failures infest the jungles of Vietnam; and failures haunt the houses of our once great alliances and undermine the greatest bulwark ever erected by free nations, the NATO community.

Failures proclaim lost leadership, obscure purpose, weakening wills and the risk of inciting our sworn enemies to new aggression and to new excesses.

And because of this Administration we are tonight a world divided. We are a nation becalmed. We have lost the brisk pace of diversity and the genius of individual creativity. We are plodding along at a pace set by centralized planning, red tape, rules without responsibility and regimentation without recourse.

Rather than useful jobs in our country, people have been offered bureaucratic makework; rather than moral leadership they have been given bread and circuses; they have been given spectacles, and, yes, they've even been given scandals.

Tonight there is violence in our streets, corruption in our highest offices, aimlessness among our youth, anxiety among our elderly, and there's a virtual despair among the many who look beyond material success toward the inner meaning of their lives. And where examples of morality should be set, the opposite is seen. Small men seeking great wealth or power have too often and too long turned even the highest levels of public service into mere personal opportunity.

Now, certainly simple honesty is not too much to demand of men in government. We find it in most. Republicans demand it from everyone. They demand it from everyone no matter how exalted or protected his position might be.

The growing menace in our country tonight, to personal safety, to life, to limb and property, in homes, in churches, on the playgrounds and places of business, particularly in our great cities, is the mounting concern, or should be, of every thoughtful citizen in the United States. Security from domestic violence, no less than from foreign aggression, is the most elementary and fundamental purpose of any government, and a government that cannot fulfill this purpose is one that cannot long command the loyalty of its citizens.

History shows us, demonstrates, that nothing, nothing, prepares the way for tyranny more than the failure of public officials to keep the streets safe from bullies and marauders.

Now we Republicans see this as more—much more—than the result of mere political differences, or mere political mistakes. We see this as the result of a fundamentally and absolutely wrong view of man, his nature and his destiny.

Those who seek to live your lives for you, to take your liberty in return for relieving you of yours; those who elevate the state and downgrade the citizen, must see ultimately a world in which earthly power can be substituted for Divine Will. And this nation was founded upon the rejection of that notion and upon the acceptance of God as the author of freedom. . . .

And I needn't remind you, but I will, that it's been during Democratic years that our strength to deter war has been stilled and even gone into a planned decline. It has been during Democratic years that we have weakly stumbled into conflicts, timidly refusing to draw our own lines against aggression, deceitfully refusing to tell even our own people of our full participation, and tragically letting our finest men die on battlefields unmarked by purpose, unmarked by pride or the prospect of victory.

Yesterday it was Korea; tonight it is Vietnam. Make no bones of this. Don't try to sweep this under the rug. We are at war in Vietnam. And yet the President, who is the Commander in Chief of our forces, refuses to say, refuses to say, mind you, whether or not the objective over there is victory, and his Secretary of Defense continues to mislead and misinform the American people, and enough of it has gone by.

And I needn't remind you, but I will, it has been during Democratic years that a billion persons were cast into Communist captivity and their fate cynically sealed.

Today, today in our beloved country, we have an Administration which seems eager to deal with Communism in every coin known—from gold to wheat, from consulates to confidence, and even human freedom itself.

Now the Republican cause demands that we brand Communism as the principal disturber of the peace in the world today. Indeed, we should brand it as the only significant disturber of the peace. And we must make clear that until its goals of conquest are absolutely renounced, and its relations with all nations tempered, Communism and the governments it now controls are enemies of every man on earth who is or wants to be free. . . .

We Republicans see in our constitutional form of government the great framework which assures the orderly but dynamic fulfillment of the whole man, and we see the whole man as the great reason for instituting orderly government in the first place.

We see in private property and in economy based upon and fostering private property the one way to make government a durable ally of the whole man rather than his determined enemy.

We see in the sanctity of private property the only durable foundation for constitutional government in a free society.

And beyond that we see and cherish diversity of ways, diversity of thoughts, of motives and accomplishments. We don't seek to live anyone's life for him. We only seek to secure his rights, guarantee him opportunity, guarantee him opportunity to strive, with government performing only those needed and constitutionally sanctioned tasks which cannot otherwise be performed.

We Republicans seek a government that attends to its inherent responsibilities of maintaining a stable monetary and fiscal climate, encouraging a free and competitive economy and enforcing law and order.

Thus do we seek inventiveness, diversity and creative difference within a stable order, for we Republicans define government's role where needed at many, many levels, preferably though, the one closest to the people involved: our towns and our cities, then our counties, then our states, then our regional contacts, and only then the national government. . . .

Anyone who joins with us in all sincerity we welcome. Those, those who do not care for our cause, we don't expect to enter our ranks in any case. And let our Republicanism so focused and so dedicated not be made fuzzy and futile by unthinking and stupid labels.

I would remind you that extremism in the defense of liberty is no vice!

And let me remind you also that moderation in the pursuit of justice is no virtue! . . .

Lyndon B. Johnson, Speech on Civil Rights
March 15, 1965

[On March 5, 1965, a group of Negroes and whites led by Martin Luther King assembled in the town of Selma, Alabama, for a march on Montgomery in behalf of voting rights. But before they could set off they were attacked by the state police, who used tear gas and truncheons to disperse them. The horrified nation witnessed the event on television. Several days later President Johnson spoke before a joint session of Congress to ask for a sweeping voting rights law. In the course of the speech he commended Negro demonstrators for advancing the cause of freedom—an astonishing thing for a President to say. The law passed later in the year, and since then Negro registration in the South has risen significantly. It is too soon to know what effect the new Negro vote will have on Southern politics.]

I speak tonight for the dignity of man and the destiny of democracy.

I urge every member of both parties, Americans of all religions and of all colors, from every section of this country, to join me in that cause.

At times history and fate meet at a single time in a single place to shape a turning point in man's unending search for freedom. So it was at Lexington and Concord. So it was a century ago at Appomattox. So it was last week in Selma, Alabama. There, long-suffering men and women peacefully protested the denial of their rights as Americans. Many were brutally assaulted. One good man, a man of God, was killed. There is no cause for pride in what has happened in Selma. There is no cause for self-satisfaction in the long denial of equal rights of millions of Americans. But there is cause for hope and for faith in our democracy in what is happening here tonight. For the cries of pain and the hymns and protests of oppressed people, have summoned into convocation all the majesty of this great government of the greatest nation on earth. . . .

Rarely in any time does an issue lay bare the secret heart of America itself. Rarely are we met with a challenge, not to our growth or abundance, or our welfare or our security, but rather to the values and the purposes and the meaning of our beloved nation.

The issue of equal rights for American Negroes is such an issue. And should we defeat every enemy, and should we double our wealth and conquer the stars and still be unequal to this issue, then we will have failed as a people and as a nation.

For with a country as with a person, "What is a man profited, if he shall gain the whole world, and lose his own soul?"

There is no Negro problem. There is no Southern problem. There is no Northern problem. There is only an American problem. And we are met here tonight as Americans, not as Democrats or Republicans, we are met here as Americans to solve that problem.

This was the first nation in the history of the world to be founded with a purpose. The great phrases of that purpose still sound in every American heart, North and South: "All men are created equal"—"government by consent of the governed"—"give me liberty or give me death." Those are not just clever words. Those are not just empty theories. In their name Americans have fought and died for two centuries, and tonight around the world they stand there as guardians of our liberty, risking their lives.

Those words are a promise to every citizen that he shall share in the dignity of man. This dignity cannot be found in a man's possessions. It cannot be found in his power or in his position. It really rests on his right to be treated as a man equal in opportunity to all others. It says that he shall share in freedom, he shall choose his leaders, educate his children, provide for his family according to his ability and his merits as a human being.

To apply any other test—to deny a man his hopes because of his color or race, or his religion, or the place of his birth—is not only to do injustice, it is to deny America and to dishonor the dead who gave their lives for American freedom.

Our fathers believed that if this noble view of the rights of man was to flourish, it must be rooted in democracy. The most basic right of all was the right to choose your own leaders. The history of this country in large measure is the history of expansion of that right to all of our people.

Many of the issues of civil rights are very complex and most difficult. But about this there can and should be no argument. Every American citizen must have an equal right to vote. There is no reason which can excuse the denial of that right. There is no duty which weighs more heavily on us than the duty we have to ensure that right.

Yet the harsh fact is that in many places in this country men and women are kept from voting simply because they are Negroes.

Every device of which human ingenuity is capable has been used to deny this right. The Negro citizen may go to register only to be told that the day is wrong, or the hour is late, or the official in charge is absent. And if he persists and if he manages to present himself to the registrar, he may be disqualified because he did not spell out his middle name or because he abbreviated a word on the application. And if he manages to fill out an application he is given a test. The registrar is the sole judge of whether he passes this test. He may be asked to recite the entire constitution, or explain the most complex provisions of state laws. And even a college degree cannot be used to prove that he can read and write.

For the fact is that the only way to pass these barriers is to show a white skin.

Experience has clearly shown that the existing process of law cannot overcome systematic and ingenious discrimination. No law that we now have on the books—and I have helped to put three of them there—can ensure the right to vote when local officials are determined to deny it.

In such a case our duty must be clear to all of us. The Constitution says that no person shall be kept from voting because of his race or his color. We have all sworn on oath before God to support and to defend that Constitution. We must now act in obedience to that oath.

Wednesday I will send to Congress a law designed to eliminate illegal barriers to the right to vote. . . .

This bill will strike down restrictions to voting in all elections—Federal, State, and local—which have been used to deny Negroes the right to vote. This bill will establish a simple, uniform standard which cannot be used, however ingenious the effort, to flout our Constitution. It will provide for citizens to be registered by officials of the United States government if the State officials refuse to register them. It will eliminate tedious, unnecessary lawsuits which delay the right to vote. Finally, this legislation will ensure that properly registered individuals are not prohibited from voting. . . .

To those who seek to avoid action by their national government in their own communities, who want to and who seek to maintain purely local control over elections, the answer is simple.

Open your polling places to all your people.

Allow men and women to register and vote whatever the color of their skin.

Extend the rights of citizenship to every citizen of this land.

There is no constitutional issue here. The command of the Constitution is plain.

There is no moral issue. It is wrong to deny any of your fellow Americans the right to vote in this country.

There is no issue of states rights or national rights. There is only the struggle for human rights.

I have not the slightest doubt what will be your answer.

But the last time a President sent a civil rights bill to the Congress it contained a provision to protect voting rights in Federal elections. That civil rights bill was passed after eight long months of debate. And when that bill came to my desk from the Congress for my signature, the heart of the voting provision had been eliminated.

This time, on this issue, there must be no delay, or no hesitation or no compromise with our purpose.

We cannot, we must not refuse to protect the right of every American to vote in every election that he may desire to participate in. And we ought not, we must not wait another eight months before we get a bill. We have already waited a hundred years and more and the time for waiting is gone. . . .

Even if we pass this bill, the battle will not be over. What happened in Selma is part of a far larger movement which reaches into every section and state of America. It is the effort of American Negroes to secure for themselves the full blessings of American life.

Their cause must be our cause too. Because it is not just Negroes, but really it is all of us, who must overcome the

crippling legacy of bigotry and injustice. And we shall overcome.

As a man whose roots go deeply into Southern soil I know
how agonizing racial feelings are. I know how difficult it is
to reshape the attitudes and the structure of our society.

But a century has passed, more than a hundred years,
since the Negro was freed. And he is not fully free tonight.

It was more than a hundred years ago that Abraham Lincoln, the great President of the Northern party, signed the
Emancipation Proclamation, but emancipation is a proclamation and not a fact.

A century has passed, more than a hundred years since
equality was promised. And yet the Negro is not equal.

A century has passed since the day of promise. And
the promise is unkept.

The time of justice has now come. I tell you that I believe
sincerely that no force can hold it back. It is right in the
eyes of man and God that it should come. And when it does,
I think that day will brighten the lives of every American.

For Negroes are not the only victims. How many white
children have gone uneducated, how many white families
have lived in stark poverty, how many white lives have been
scarred by fear because we wasted our energy and our substance to maintain the barriers of hatred and terror.

So I say to all of you here and to all in the nation tonight, that those who appeal to you to hold on to the past
do so at the cost of denying you your future.

This great, rich, restless country can offer opportunity
and education and hope to all—all black and white, all
North and South, sharecropper, and city dweller. These are
the enemies—poverty, ignorance, disease. They are enemies,
not our fellow man, not our neighbor, and these enemies too,
poverty, disease and ignorance, we shall overcome.

Now let none of us in any section look with prideful
righteousness on the troubles in another section or the
problems of our neighbors. There is really no part of
America where the promise of equality has been fully kept.
In Buffalo as well as in Birmingham, in Philadelphia as
well as in Selma, Americans are struggling for the fruits of
freedom.

This is one nation. What happens in Selma or in Cincinnati is a matter of legitimate concern to every American. But let each of us look within our own hearts and our own communities, and let each of us put our shoulder to the wheel to root out injustice wherever it exists.

The real hero of this struggle is the American Negro. His actions and protests, his courage to risk safety and even to risk his life, have awakened the conscience of this nation. His demonstrations have been designed to call attention to injustice, designed to provoke change, designed to stir reform. He has called upon us to make good the promise of America. And who among us can say that we would have made the same progress were it not for his persistent bravery, and his faith in American democracy.

BIBLIOGRAPHY

This bibliography is, of course, extremely selective. It includes only those books that might prove useful—or have proved useful to me—in detailing and clarifying the issues discussed above. For an exhaustive bibliography, through 1953, the reader should consult Oscar Handlin et al., *The Harvard Guide to American History* (New York, 1954).

Several studies evaluate the whole of American history in terms of sharply contending ideologies and social movements. By far the best of these, despite a tendency to oversimplify and ground all events in economic causes, remain Charles A. and Mary R. Beard, *The Rise of American Civilization* (New York, 1927) and Vernon Louis Parrington, *Main Currents in American Thought* (3 vols., New York, 1927–30). But two important books emphasize the absence of conflict in American history and the common assumptions that have underlain its liberal ethic: Richard Hofstadter, *The American Political Tradition* (New York, 1948) and Louis Hartz, *The Liberal Tradition in America* (New York, 1955). Worth noting, too, are a number of works that explore the role of political parties, both as institutions and as instruments of social conflict and change. Wilfred E. Binkley, *American Political Parties, Their Natural History* (3d ed., New York, 1958) is a reliable and entertaining survey of the subject down to the 1950s. The first volume of Moise Ostrogorskii, *Democracy and the Organization of Political Parties*, edited and abridged by Seymour Martin Lipset (2 vols., New York, 1964), written nearly seventy years ago, is magnificent in describing the rise of the party machine as an "extra-constitutional" organ of government. Leonard White's four-volume series, *The Federalists* (New York, 1948), *The Jeffersonians* (New York, 1951), *The Jacksonians* (New York, 1954) and *The Republican Era* (New York, 1958), though it contains much that will interest only the specialist, is invaluable for an understanding of the relations between parties and federal administration. A superior one-volume work on constitutional history is Carl Swisher, *American Constitutional Development* (2d ed., New York, 1954). And on economic history see Fred A. Shannon, *America's Economic Growth* (3d ed., New York, 1951).

John C. Miller, *The Federalist Era* (New York, 1960) is a good, straightforward account of Federalism in general. Hofstadter, *The American Political Tradition*, and volume one of Parrington, *Main Currents in American Thought*, both already cited, lucidly explain the ideology of the moderate Federalists who drew up the Constitution. The importance that Federalists attached to the judiciary is the theme of a study that has been neglected in recent years: Charles A. Beard, *The Supreme Court and the Constitution* (New York, 1914). Strangely, there is no first-rate biography of Hamilton. The best one available, Broadus Mitchell, *Alexander Hamilton* (2 vols., New York, 1957–62), is highly partisan and combative. Hamilton's fiscal and credit policies are admirably defined in Bray Hammond, *Banks and Politics in America from the Revolution to the Civil War* (Princeton, 1957). Joseph Charles, *The Origins of the American Party System* (Williamsburg, 1956) indicts Hamilton for provoking the controversies that rent the country in the 1790s. Manning Dauer, *The Adams Federalists* (Baltimore, 1953), distinguishes Adams's moderate Federalism from the extreme form espoused by Hamilton and his followers. Parrington (volume one) distinguishes them, too, in his trenchant essays on Hamilton and Adams.

The extent to which Jefferson was a product of his liberal milieu is made clear in the first volume of Dumas Malone's judicious biography, *Jefferson the Virginian* (Boston, 1948). Jefferson's social and political ideas are summarized in Adrienne Koch, *The Philosophy of Thomas Jefferson* (New York, 1943), Carl L. Becker, *The Declaration of Independence* (New York, 1922) and Charles A. Beard, *The Economic Origins of Jeffersonian Democracy* (New York, 1915). Noble E. Cunningham, Jr., has written two definitive volumes on the rise and triumph of the Jeffersonian Republican party: *The Jeffersonian Republicans* (Chapel Hill, 1957) and *The Jeffersonian Republicans in Power* (Chapel Hill, 1963). The conflict between the Republican dissidents, led by John Randolph, and the Jeffersonian nationalists is the subject of an interesting scholarly work: Norman K. Risjord, *The Old Republicans* (New York, 1965). Republican nationalism dominates Henry Adams's masterpiece, *History of the United States During the Administrations of Thomas Jefferson and James Madison* (9 vols., New York, 1889–91). Shaw Livermore, Jr., *The Twilight of Federalism* (Princeton, 1962), points out that after 1815 Federalists exerted considerable power on the local and state levels even as their party was disintegrating.

Frederick Jackson Turner, *The Rise of the New West* (New York, 1906), persuasively explains why democracy emerged in America in the early nineteenth century. The relationship between democracy and the party organization is adumbrated in White, *The Jacksonians*, already cited, and Arthur M. Schlesinger, Jr., *The Age of Jackson* (Boston, 1945). Marvin Meyer, *The Jacksonian Persuasion* (Stanford, 1957) is a masterful synthesis of the whole period. George Dangerfield, *The Era of Good Feelings* (New York, 1952) is a fine account of the last stage of Republican rule preparatory to the triumph of Jacksonianism. The best description of Jackson's achievements as President is found in Schlesinger, *The Age of Jackson*, already cited. But Hammond, *Banks and Politics in America from the Revolution to the Civil War*, already cited, discloses the complexities, contradictions and drawbacks of Jackson's war on the Bank of the United States. Alice F. Tyler, *Freedom's Ferment* (Minneapolis, 1944) is an excellent study of the numerous radical movements and societies that sprang up in America during the Jacksonian era.

Rollin G. Osterweis, *Romanticism and Nationalism in the Old South* (New Haven, 1948) argues that the South came to have a distinct and increasingly endogamous culture of its own. Clement Eaton, *Freedom of Thought in the Old South* (Durham, 1940) shows how freedom of thought disappeared in the South following the Nat Turner slave uprising in 1831. James C. N. Paul, *Rift in the Democracy* (Philadelphia, 1951) analyzes in detail the first signs of Democratic party disunity over the slavery issue. The reasons for the complete breakdown of the party, and therefore of the nation, in the 1850s is further analyzed—often unconvincingly, however—in Roy Nichols, *Disruption of American Democracy* (New York, 1948). A balanced discussion of the subject is contained in Allan Nevins's compendious history, *Ordeal of the Union* (2 vols., New York, 1947), and *The Emergence of Lincoln* (2 vols., New York, 1950). One of the serious lacunae in American historiography is a good biography of the central figure of the 1850s, Stephen Douglas. The best one is still Allen Johnson, *Stephen A. Douglas: A Study in American Politics* (New York, 1908).

Andrew W. Crandall, *The Early History of the Republican Party* (Boston, 1930) provides a detailed, though somewhat pedestrian, account of the party's rise between 1854 and 1856. For a discussion of Lincoln's, and the Republican party's, views in the 1850s, see two outstanding books: Don E. Fehrenbacher, *Prelude to Greatness, Lincoln in the 1850's* (Stanford, 1962) and, especially, Harry V. Jaffa, *Crisis of the House Divided* (Garden City, 1959). Fine one-volume biographies of Lincoln are: Lord Charnwood, *Abraham Lincoln* (New York, 1916) and Benjamin P. Thomas, *Abraham Lincoln; A Biography* (New York, 1952). James G. Randall, *Constitutional Problems under Lincoln* (rev. ed., Urbana, 1951) is indispensable for an understanding of the legal questions that Lincoln confronted as President. Allan Nevins, *The War for the Union* (2 vols., New York, 1956–60) presents a rich mosaic of events from Lincoln's inauguration to the Emancipation Proclamation. A comprehensive history of Reconstruction, written from an anti-Radical point of view, is James G. Randall and David Donald, *The Civil War and Reconstruction* (rev. ed., Boston, 1961). Similarly anti-Radical is Howard K. Beale's penetrating work *The Critical Year: A Study of Andrew Johnson and Reconstruction* (New York, 1930). But several recent books have cast a more sympathetic light on the motives and accomplishments of the Radicals: LaWanda Cox and John H. Cox, *Politics, Principles and Prejudices, 1865–1866* (New York, 1963), W. R. Brock, *An American Crisis: Congress and Reconstruction, 1865–1867* (New York, 1963) and, most important, Kenneth M. Stampp, *The Era of Reconstruction, 1865–1877* (New York, 1965).

By far the best history of the conservative era is Matthew Josephson, *The Politicos, 1865–1896* (New York, 1938). Ostrogorskii, *Democracy and the Organization of Political Parties* (volume two), already cited, is, despite his moral objurgations, particularly impressive in laying bare the nature of the spoils system. David J. Rothman, *Politics and Power: The United States Senate 1869–1901* (Cambridge, 1966) discusses the emergence of the Senate as the country's leading political institution. Robert J. McCloskey, *The Age of Conservatism* (Cambridge, 1951) is a valuable summary of the Hamiltonian philosophy that came to govern American life, in particular the federal judiciary, by the late nineteenth century. The first six chapters in Robert H. Wiebe, *The Search for Order, 1877–1920* (New York, 1967) are an intelligent study of the effects of industrialism on America. Horace Samuel Merrill, *Bourbon Leader: Grover Cleveland and the Democratic Party* (Boston, 1957) explains how the Democratic insurgents of the South and West wrested power from the Eastern conservatives. The ripening conflict of the 1890s is examined in a brief history: Paul W. Glad, *McKinley, Bryan and the People* (Philadelphia, 1964). The classic account of Populism, from its genesis to its demise, is John D. Hicks, *The Populist Revolt* (Minneapolis, 1931). Richard Hofstadter, *The Age of Reform* (New York, 1955) argues, however, that Populism was an unrealistic and wrongheaded response to industrialism. Three recent books, based on a careful study of the sources, take Hofstadter to task: Norman Pollack, *The Populist Response to Industrial America* (Cambridge, 1962), Walter T. R. Nugent, *The Tolerant Populists* (Chicago, 1963) and Michael Rogin, *Intellectuals and McCarthy* (Cambridge, 1967). A remarkable work, especially on the 1896 election, is Herbert Croly, *Marcus Alonzo Hanna* (New York, 1912).

For the Progressive era see Harold U. Faulkner's standard history, *The Quest for Social Justice* (New York, 1931). And still valuable for its assessment of the Progressive movement is William English Walling, *Progressivism—and After* (New York, 1914). LaFollette's struggle to become governor of

Wisconsin and his conflicts with the Senate oligarchy are best described in his own work, *LaFollette's Autobiography* (Madison, 1913). A surprisingly objective biography of him is the one by his wife and daughter: Belle and Fola La-Follette, *Robert LaFollette* (2 vols., New York, 1953). Louis Filler, *Crusaders for Liberalism* (New York, 1939), though it leaves much to be desired, is the standard work on the muckrakers. The uprising in the Republican West is well described in Kenneth Hechler, *Insurgency; Personalities and Politics of the Taft Era* (New York, 1940), Claude Bowers, *Beveridge and the Progressive Era* (New York, 1932) and Russel Nye, *Midwestern Progressive Politics* (East Lansing, 1951). John M. Blum, *The Republican Roosevelt* (Cambridge, 1954) is an incisive essay, but it makes T.R. more liberal than he in fact was. Highly commendable are two volumes in the New American Nation series: George Mowry, *The Era of Theodore Roosevelt and the Birth of Modern America* (New York, 1958) and Arthur S. Link, *Woodrow Wilson and the Progressive Era* (New York, 1954). Link's uncompleted biography, *Wilson* (5 vols., Princeton, 1947–66) is monumental but prolix. Two very critical books should be mentioned: John Chamberlain, *A Farewell to Reform* (New York, 1932), which regards Progressivism as a failure, and Gabriel Kolko, *The Triumph of Conservatism* (New York, 1963), which regards Progressivism as a sellout to big business.

There are a number of good books on the economy and business philosophy of the 1920s. See, for example: George Soule, *Prosperity Decade* (New York, 1947), Thomas Cochran, *The American Business System* (Cambridge, 1957), James Prothro, *Dollar Decade: Business Ideas in the 1920s* (Baton Rouge, 1954), Adolph A. Berle and Gardiner C. Means, *The Modern Corporation and Private Property* (New York, 1933) and, for the patient reader, *Recent Economic Changes in the United States* (2 vols., New York, 1929). John D. Hicks, *Republican Ascendancy, 1921–1933* (New York, 1960) is a good summary of the period. The first volume of Arthur Schlesinger, Jr.'s series on Franklin D. Roosevelt and the New Deal, *The Crisis of the Old Order* (Boston, 1957), offers a revealing portrait of the 1920s. Karl

Schriftgeisser, *This Was Normalcy* (Boston, 1948) is a devastating and not altogether fair critique of the Harding, Coolidge and Hoover administrations. Robert S. and Helen M. Lynd, *Middletown* (New York, 1929) is an unflattering sociological study of a "typical" American community (Muncie, Indiana) of the 1920s. The standard work on the campaign against civil liberties during and after the war is Zachariah Chafee, Jr., *Free Speech in the United States* (Cambridge, 1941). The Supreme Court's conservatism in the 1920s is chronicled in a definitive study: Louis Boudin, *Government by Judiciary* (2 vols., New York, 1932).

Perhaps the easiest guides through the thickets of New Deal legislation are Denis W. Brogan, *The Era of Franklin D. Roosevelt* (New Haven, 1950), Basil Rauch, *History of the New Deal, 1933–38* (New York, 1944) and William E. Leuchtenberg, *Roosevelt and the New Deal* (New York, 1963). Broadus Mitchell, *Depression Decade* (New York, 1947) is a good survey of the economy, as is Dixon Wector, *The Age of the Great Depression* (New York, 1948). Roosevelt has been fortunate in his biographers. The following works are recommended for their success in integrating Roosevelt's life and times: Robert E. Sherwood, *Roosevelt and Hopkins* (rev. ed., New York, 1950), James M. Burns, *Roosevelt, the Lion and the Fox* (New York, 1956) and the most recent volumes by Arthur Schlesinger, Jr., *The Coming of the New Deal* (Boston, 1958) and *The Politics of Upheaval* (Boston, 1960). On the Supreme Court's opposition to the New Deal, see Swisher, *American Constitutional Development*, already cited. A scholarly treatment of the "Court-packing" issue of 1937 is Edward S. Corwin, *Court Over Constitution* (New York, 1937). We still lack adequate studies of two important aspects of the New Deal era: Roosevelt's attempt in 1938 to "purge" the Democratic party, and his decision the year before to break up big business. Allan Nevins, *The New Deal and World Affairs* (New York, 1950) deals with the global ideology of the New Deal.

The development of the Cold War and the rise of McCarthyism form the background themes in Cabell Phillips, *The Truman Presidency* (New York, 1966). Eric F. Goldman, *The Crucial Decade and After* (New York, 1961) is a critical account of the Eisenhower years. The post-World War II disillusionment with radicalism is reflected in Leslie Fiedler, *An End to Innocence* (Boston, 1955). Richard H. Rovere, *Senator Joe McCarthy* (New York, 1960) describes McCarthy's spectacular rise and fall. Theodore H. White, *The Making of the President 1960* (New York, 1961) is a remarkable study of the Kennedy campaign and of American politics. The best history of the Kennedy administration is Arthur M. Schlesinger, Jr., *A Thousand Days* (Boston, 1965). But against Schlesinger's view of Kennedy as a pronounced liberal, Bernard Nossiter, *The Mythmakers: An Essay on Power and Wealth* (Boston, 1964) argues that Kennedy's economic reforms were designed to benefit the large corporations. This is confirmed in part in John Kenneth Galbraith's most recent book on the structure of the American economy, *The New Industrial State* (Boston, 1967). For an analysis of the 1964 election and of Goldwater Republicanism, see Richard H. Rovere, *The Goldwater Caper* (New York, 1965) and Theodore H. White, *The Making of the President 1964* (New York, 1965). Milton R. Konvitz, *Expanding Liberties* (New York, 1966) and Henry J. Abraham, *Freedom and the Court* (New York, 1967) are very thorough surveys of the progress that has been made in civil rights and civil liberties during Earl Warren's tenure as Chief Justice of the Supreme Court. America's role as world policeman is critically evaluated in two impressive recent books: Ronald Steel, *Pax Americana* (New York, 1967) and J. William Fulbright, *The Arrogance of Power* (New York, 1967).

INDEX